S0-BRV-314

Religion in America

Life, Letters and Travels

of

Father De Smet

Hiram Martin Chittenden
and
Alfred Talbot Richardson

VOLUME 1

ARNO PRESS & THE NEW YORK TIMES
New York 1969

Reprint edition 1969 by Arno Press, Inc.

*

Library of Congress Catalog Card No. 75-83418

*

Reprinted from a copy in the
Columbia University Libraries

*

Manufactured in the United States of America

Life, Letters and Travels of
Father De Smet among the
North American Indians.

FATHER DE SMET'S AUTOGRAPH MILEAGE RECORD FROM THE LINTON ALBUM.

LIFE, LETTERS AND TRAVELS

OF

FATHER PIERRE-JEAN DE SMET, S. J.

1801-1873

Missionary Labors and Adventures among the Wild Tribes of the
North American Indians, Embracing Minute Description of Their
Manners, Customs, Games, Modes of Warfare and Torture,
Legends, Tradition, etc., All from Personal Observations
Made during Many Thousand Miles of Travel,
with Sketches of the Country from St. Louis
to Puget Sound and the Altrabasca

*Edited from the original unpublished manuscript Journals
and Letter Books and from his Printed Works with
Historical, Geographical, Ethnological and other Notes;
Also a Life of Father De Smet*

MAP AND ILLUSTRATIONS

BY

HIRAM MARTIN CHITTENDEN

Major, Corps of Engineers, U. S. A.

AND

ALFRED TALBOT RICHARDSON

FOUR VOLUMES

VOL. I

NEW YORK

FRANCIS P. HARPER

1905

TO THE MEMORY

Of the Men

OF

WHATSOEVER CREED OR NATION WHO SPENT THEMSELVES

IN THE

Forming of the West

PREFACE.

The present work is an outgrowth of the interest which the editors have long taken in the pioneer history of the West. Explorers of this attractive field are constantly running across the trail of Father De Smet, which interlaces the whole Northwest from St. Louis to the Straits of Juan de Fuca. Wherever encountered, it is a tempting trail to follow, for it is marked in all its course by episodes romantic and interesting and frequently of weighty importance. A devout and zealous missionary, Father De Smet filled the Oregon country with religious establishments, some of which, in spite of the vast changes of later years, survive to the present day. He was acquainted with most of the native tribes of the Northwest and with many of them he was on terms of intimate friendship. Their trust in him was so complete and his influence over them so great that the government repeatedly besought his aid in paving the way for its negotiations with them. He assisted at the great Indian council of 1851 near Fort Laramie. In 1858 and 1859 he accompanied the Utah and Oregon expeditions under General Harney in the nominal capacity of Chaplain, but in the actual role of pacificator and intermediary between the military and the Indians. In 1864 he was sent by the government to pacify the Indians of the Upper Missouri, and again on a similar errand in 1867. In 1868, it was alone through his great influence that the hostile Sioux, who had declared war to the death with the white race and were spreading terror over the whole region of the Upper Missouri and Yellowstone valleys, were induced to meet commissioners of the government and enter into a treaty of peace.

[vii]

Father De Smet's travels were not confined to the western country. He visited many parts of the United States east of the Mississippi, crossed the Atlantic nineteen times and made one voyage around Cape Horn and two by way of Panama in the interest of his work. He was well known in both Europe and America, and on one occasion was made the bearer of dispatches from this government to several European courts. He took an active interest in public affairs and watched them with an eagerness which one would hardly expect from his exclusive order of life.

Wherever he went, whatever he did and much of what he saw were carefully recorded in letters to his superiors or to his personal friends. Many of these letters were published in his lifetime; many others were never published and are accessible only in the original letter-books. Altogether they constitute a rich fund of material upon the early history of the West, particularly during the critical period of our Indian wars. Unfortunately these writings are practically inaccessible to the general public. The unpublished letters are, of course, wholly so. The published works are nearly all out of print and some of them were published only in French. There has never been written a satisfactory biography of Father De Smet.

To supply these deficiencies and make the life-work of this great missionary and public man familiar to students of our country's history, the editors have prepared the present work—LIFE AND LETTERS OF FATHER DE SMET—comprising a complete biography, all his important letters both published and unpublished, illustrations characteristic of his missionary career, and a map showing the wide range of his travels west of the Mississippi.

The original arrangement in the published works has been discarded entirely and the letters have been reclassified according to periods and subjects. Even the English texts have not been literally followed, for they are nearly all translations, and the editors have felt at liberty to substitute their own rendering wherever they have thought it desirable. The English of the published texts is almost throughout a translation from Father De Smet's French letters, and none of it apparently is his own work. It is full of renderings of French phrases, and more particularly of geographical names, which show a lack of familiarity on the part of the translator with the subjects treated. No record has been kept of the pagination of the published letters for the reason that much of the matter was duplicated in different texts and in the present edition is extensively interspersed with new letters treating of the same subjects.

The narrative letters are classified under five chronological periods, each of which is prefaced with an itinerary of Father De Smet's travels during that period. Following the narrative portion are the letters containing observations upon Indian affairs, missionary work, public questions, etc.; personal letters to his friends in Europe and America which show the inner life and character of the man; and finally many of the letters received in the course of a long and active correspondence. The new matter in the present edition is about equal in volume·to all heretofore published, and contains everything which, in the opinion of the editors, would be of general interest. It omits several of the published letters relating solely to church matters.

The editors are under particular obligation to the Jesuit authorities of the St. Louis University for access to the old letter-books of Father De Smet, and for other valuable assistance. Thanks are also due the Reverend J. D'Aste, S. J., of St. Ignatius Mission, Montana; W. R. Logan, U. S. Indian Agent at Fort Belknap Agency, and James H. Monteath, U. S. Indian Agent at Blackfeet Agency, Montana, for information furnished. Among the published works consulted, Shea's *Catholic Missions in the United States, History of the St. Louis University,* by Father Walter H. Hill, S. J., and Palladino's *Indian and White in the Northwest,* are the most important.

CONTENTS OF VOLUME I.

CHAPTER III.

CHAPTER IV.

CHAPTER V.

CHAPTER VI.

CHAPTER VII.

CHAPTER VIII.

CHAPTER IX.

CHAPTER X.

CHAPTER XI.

LIST OF ILLUSTRATIONS.

[xv]

LIFE OF FATHER DE SMET.

CHAPTER I.

THE JESUITS IN AMERICA.

Birth of Society of Jesus — Wonderful growth and power — Down-
fall and restoration — Missionary work of Society in America — Early
Canadian missions — Insuperable obstacles — Novitiate at Whitemarsh
— Migration to St. Louis — Founding of the Florissant Novitiate —
The St. Louis University — Indian missions entrusted to Jesuits —
Field of labor in Far West.

FORTY-TWO years after the discovery of America there
arose in Europe a religious order destined to play a
leading part in the Christianization of those races which the
great achievement of Columbus made known to the world.
This was the Society of Jesus, founded by Ignatius Loyola
in 1534. The chief purposes of its creation were to stem
the swelling tide of Protestantism in Europe and to spread
the Catholic faith among infidel peoples in every quarter of
the globe. Its chosen motto, *Ad majorem Dei gloriam*[1]
(To the greater glory of God), was a fitting expression of
its exalted program for the spiritual regeneration of the race.

The career of the Society in Europe, for two hundred
years after its founding, forms one of the strangest and
most fascinating pages in the history of Christianity. Its
marvelous organization made it the most autocratic power
of its time, while the severity of the novitiate through which
its members had to pass insured a loyalty and obedience that
were superior to every test. The growth of the Society was
rapid, for it had come into existence at an opportune time,

[1] The monogrammatic form, A. M. D. G., is of universal use in
Jesuitic practices.

when the Church needed its powerful arm to extend her sway and defend her against her enemies. It became a mighty power, guiding the destinies of European nations and carrying its influence to the uttermost parts of the earth.

The proud place which the Society had acquired in the temporal affairs of the world it was destined not to hold, for the very greatness of its power excited the jealousy and hostility of European rulers, who one after another expelled it from their dominions. Finally, in 1773, the Church herself, yielding to the general outcry, decreed its total suppression, and it remained without recognized existence for forty-one years thereafter.

Our present inquiries relate solely to the missionary work of the Society in the western hemisphere, particularly in the western portion of the United States. The spread of the gospel among heathen peoples was a fundamental purpose of the Society. The discovery of America, with its vast but unknown population, offered a field of labor which from the first was one of great attractiveness. The Jesuits came early to America, and their missionary work on this continent has gone hand in hand with exploration and settlement, except in the English colonies. They went to Florida about the time of the founding of St. Augustine, but remained only a few years. They were in Mexico at a very early day, and in 1697 founded a mission at Loretto in Lower California which became the forerunner of the famous missions of Upper California, established at a later date by the Franciscans. The Jesuits themselves were not permitted to carry out their work in this inviting field. The growing hostility to the order in Europe led to their expulsion from the Spanish dominions in 1767, and on February 3, 1768, the Jesuits in California were all forcibly removed.

The principal work of the Jesuit missionaries in North America was done in Canada and the other possessions of France. Previous to 1629 there had been some progress in missionary work in Acadia and along the St. Lawrence; but in that year Quebec was captured by the English, and Catholic priests were forced to leave. The conquest was not a permanent one and it was restored to France in 1632. Missionary work was thereupon resumed and its prosecution soon fell into the hands of the Jesuits, who entered upon it with heroic zeal and devotion. The missions of New France became exceedingly popular in the parent country. Men of high-born connections entered the Society in the hope that they might be sent to Canada. Nuns and sisters of the Church offered themselves to the work, while the funds to carry it on were freely donated by all classes.

The missionary work of the Jesuits in New France extended from Maine to the Mississippi. The principal fields of labor were among the Abenakis in Maine; the Iroquois in New York; the Hurons in Ontario; the Illinois in the Mississippi valley, and other less important tribes scattered along the way. The zeal and devotion of the missionaries in all their undertakings, and the self-sacrifices they underwent for the sake of the faith, are the bright spots in a story which is one of uniform disaster. There was no faltering amid hardship, no yielding to discouragement, no flinching in the presence of danger; but a complete extinction of all personal considerations and a sublime devotion which looked forward to martyrdom as the most welcome reward of all their labors. Sebastian Rasles, Isaac Jogues, John de Brebeuf, Gabriel Lallemant and others are brilliant names in the Jesuit temple of fame.

In spite of the zeal and herculean toil of the Jesuits in New France, their work did not prosper. Causes beyond their control baffled all their efforts. The Iroquois destroyed the Hurons and the English gained control of the lands of the Iroquois and Abenakis. Traces of the work of the missionaries survived, and many proselytes remained true to their new faith; but the movement as a whole did not realize its expectations.

The same fate overtook the early missionary work farther

west. Following the discoveries of Marquette and Joliet and the enterprises of La Salle in the Mississippi valley, the zealous missionary penetrated these new fields, undeterred by the discouragements which he had already encountered. A good beginning was made and missions were planted along the way from the head of Lake Michigan to the Gulf of Mexico. Those in the valley of the Mississippi were governed from New Orleans and not from Canada. Although established with much promise of success, the same general causes which had proven fatal to the other missions soon began to operate here. The incompatibility of the Indian nature with the new order of life, the constant clashing of hostile tribes with one another, the irresistible progress of the English, which finally drove France from the soil of North America, were all against the success of the missions. To crown the difficulties with which they were contending, the Jesuits presently found themselves without an existence, cast out by the nations of Europe and deserted by the mother Church. Before their restoration a new nation had arisen on the soil where much of their toil had been expended, and had won a boundless expanse of territory beyond the Mississippi. It was in this newly-acquired empire that the Jesuits were to find their next important field of labor.

During the forty-one years of its suppression the members of the Society kept in touch with one another, working largely in the ranks of the secular clergy. Most of those who were living in 1773 died before the restoration, but nevertheless the elements of life were kept up, and, as old causes of enmity became forgotten and ancient prejudices were softened away, the Society won back the favor of European nations and was reinstated by the Pope in 1814.

At this time there were a few old Jesuit priests at Whitemarsh in Maryland who founded there the first novitiate of the Society in the United States. About 1820 the affairs of this establishment were in a precarious condition from lack of funds and an abandonment or removal seemed un-

avoidable; when, in 1823, at the suggestion of John C. Cal-
houn, Secretary of War, the Right Reverend Du Bourg,
Bishop of Louisiana, proposed to Father Van Quickenborne,
Master of Novices, that he would be given a tract of land
near St. Louis if he would establish a novitiate there.   The
offer was gladly accepted and steps were at once taken to
carry it into effect.

   In the company of twelve who set out on the long journey
from the Chesapeake to the Mississippi was a youth named
De Smet, the subject of the present sketch.   The date of departure, April 11, 1823, is a notable one in the history of the
Catholic Church in the United States, and the journey was
thoroughly characteristic of the pioneer times in which it was
made.   Two large wagons were hired to convey the heavier
articles from Baltimore to the Ohio river, and a light spring
wagon for the smaller articles.   As to the travelers themselves, they had no other transportation than that which
nature had provided them, and they made the entire distance "*pedibus apostolorum,* staff in hand," as Father De
Smet puts it.   The journey was full of interest in spite of
its genuine hardship at that season of the year.   The route
lay wholly through Protestant communities and most of the
people had doubtless never seen a priest before.   They
imagined the black-gowns to be a band of adventurers, seek-
ing their fortune, and they frequently besought them to remain.   The same petition with different motives came from
the few Catholics they met, who were longing for the services of a priest.

   At Wheeling on the Ohio the travelers purchased two
flatboats with the intention of making the descent of the
river by water.   The boats were lashed together into a
single craft, and in this manner the little party made its
way, borne by the current, between shores which were then
in their natural wildness and beauty.   At Louisville they
portaged their baggage around the Falls and sent the empty
boat over them in charge of a pilot.   They then continued
their voyage to Shawneetown, Illinois, where the old over-

land route from Louisville to St. Louis crossed the river. Here they debarked, disposed of their boats, sent most of their baggage by steamboat to St. Louis, and themselves started on foot across the country. It was still early in the spring, the ground was soaked with rain and in many places covered deep with water. Houses were few and far between, and in their absence barns and outhouses were their only shelter. It was a rough and trying journey and they were well-nigh exhausted when, on the last day of May, they found themselves on the east shore of the Mississippi opposite the city of St. Louis. Crossing the river they reached their destination in the future metropolis of the Mississippi valley. For the present, however, they were not to remain there, but to go on some fifteen miles farther to the little village of Florissant, in St. Ferdinand township, where they were to found the second novitiate of the Society of Jesus in the United States.

The new home of the young novices lay directly north of St. Louis not far from the Missouri river. It was a beautiful spot, typical of the attractive rural scenery in the environs of the city. It had formerly been the country seat of one of the Spanish governors of upper Louisiana. Here the little company from Whitemarsh fell to work in earnest, conscious that they were laying the foundation of a great institution in the religious and educational growth of their city and the surrounding country. It was truly an humble beginning for these young men, all of whom had given up homes of comfort and the promise of successful careers in their native land in order to devote their lives to the greater glory of God. " It is at such times," to quote Father De Smet on another occasion, " that one feels the full weight * * * of the sacrifice he makes in a good and holy cause." They must have felt this as they took up their abode in a rude log structure, in the low loft of which seven of their number were crowded together on pallets of straw in a single room. The lower room was divided by a curtain into two parts,

THE INDIAN SEMINARY NEAR FLORISSANT.

in one of which Father Van Quickenborne and a companion lived, the other being used for a chapel. Two small log cabins completed the list of buildings from which the now splendid St. Louis University took its rise. These buildings were enlarged as rapidly as possible, the manual labor being done by the novices themselves.

After a time schools were opened for Indian children, this being an important part of the missionary work of the Society. These schools, however, as has so often been the case, did not thrive as they had been expected to do. The wild nature of the Indian was ill adapted to that kind of life, and it is proof of the high sagacity of Father Van Quickenborne that he early recognized the wisdom of not building all his plans on so precarious a foundation. Although the good father and his companions had dedicated their lives to the spiritual and temporal welfare of the Indians, they soon became convinced "that no great or permanent results could ever be accomplished among the indolent, wandering and indocile aborigines of the woods and prairie which would at all compensate for sacrificing all their energies and resources in exclusive attention to the savages. They came to the conclusion, therefore, that more solid and lasting good might be done among the white population than with the well-nigh indomitable redmen."[2] Without abandoning any of their missionary purposes among the Indians, they resolved to found an institution of learning to meet the growing wants of a great center of population in which the proportion of Catholics was certain to be large. The conception rapidly developed into a concrete result. A suitable building was erected in the city of St. Louis and the reception of students began in the fall of 1829. Father P. J. Verhaegen, one of the seven novices from Whitemarsh but now an ordained priest, was made first president, and Father De Smet was a member of the faculty.

The Jesuits in St. Louis were now fairly well equipped

[2] *History of the St. Louis University*, p. 36.

for effective work except in the matter of numbers. These could be had only through the slow process of the novitiate or by recruits from Europe; but as the latter were generally themselves novices, the growth in numbers in early times was very slow.

In 1831 the Missouri Mission, which had heretofore been a dependency of the Province of Maryland, was made an independent mission. In 1833, October 27, the second Provincial Council of Baltimore petitioned that the Indian missions of the United States be confided to the Society of Jesus. The petition was favorably acted upon at Rome July 26, 1834, and the Society was now about to enter upon the last virgin field of its labors, the vast region, still almost unknown, which was then and is now known as the Far West.

This region, comprising more than half the area of the United States, was still the home of native tribes who were just beginning to be acquainted with the white man through intercourse with the traders. In some portions of the nearer territory, along the lower Missouri, were a few tribes, remnants of the great nations that had once held sway east of the Mississippi, but had been crowded from their homes by the resistless pressure of settlement; but for the most part the tribes were new to the missionary and he was entering an unbroken field. The more important of these tribes, beginning in the lower valley of the Missouri, were the Osages, the Kansas, the Omahas, the Pawnees, the Sioux nations, the Aricaras, the Mandans, the Grosventres of the Missouri, the Assiniboins, the Crows, the Blackfeet, including the Grosventres of the Prairies, the Shoshones with their manifold subdivisions, the Flatheads, Nez Percés, and other tribes of the upper Columbia valley, and finally the almost numberless and nameless tribes of the Pacific Coast. It was into this vast field that the Jesuits of St. Louis were about to enter, under the leadership of the greatest and most practical missionary who has ever labored among the Indian tribes of the United States.

CHAPTER II.

Ancestry and youth — Choice of missionary career — Leaves Belgium for America — Enters Whitemarsh Novitiate — Goes to St. Louis — Helps found Novitiate and University — Returns to Europe — Sends contributions to University — Returns to America — Goes to Council Bluffs — Work at the Potawatomi Mission — Visits the Sioux Country — Describes evils of liquor traffic among the Indians.

PIERRE-JEAN DE SMET was born in the village of Termonde, Belgium, at the very beginning of the 19th century.[1] His family, which has been traced back to the beginning of the 17th century, was one of the most respectable in Belgium, and the young De Smet came into the world in circumstances that assured him a satisfactory beginning in life. The parents, too, found in their offspring all the promise which they could well desire. He was a well-formed, healthy, and handsome child, and as

[1] Entry in the baptismal register of the Church of the Blessed Virgin Mary of Termonde, copied by C. L. Tede, the present dean or chief pastor, 1902.

" In the year 1801 on the 30th day of the month of January, I baptized Pierre-Jean, born this morning at about five o'clock, and Coleta Aldegunda, born at a quarter after five, twin children of Judocus De Smet of this parish and Joanna Maria Buydens, of this parish, his wife; the sponsors were John Baptiste Kollier of Smerrebe and Coleta De Saeger of Bottelière.

(Signed)   J. C. Ringoot, Pastor of B. V. M. of Termonde."

The father of Father De Smet was Josse-Arnaud De Smet, born April 28, 1738, and died February 15, 1827; was twice married — first to Jeanne-Marie Duerinck, by whom he had six children; and second, to Marie-Jeanne Buydens by whom he had nine children, Pierre-Jean being the fifth. Two of his brothers, Charles and Francis, grew to adult years, and both were men of character and distinction in their native land.

his mental and spiritual faculties began to develop, they
were in harmony with his physical qualities. His early
years were spent at his parents' home, but when he became
old enough to take up the more serious educational work
of youth, he was sent to the Seminary of Malines where
he remained until his twenty-first year.

In school, the young De Smet was a distinguished pupil,
and in particular exhibited those solid qualities of tact and
common sense which did him such great service in after
years. He was also noted for his great physical strength
and skill in youthful sports. So prominent was his superiority in these respects that his school-fellows gave him
the nick-name of Samson.

These qualities of body and mind were associated with
a fervent and sentimental nature, and the course of events
at this time was such as naturally to turn his mind to a religious career. The Church was strong in Flanders and
young De Smet's youth was spent in a religious atmosphere. The fiery ordeal of the French Revolution was past
and the natural reaction led men to look with renewed favor
upon the ancient church which had stood unscathed the
tempests of that fierce time. It was also about the time when
De Smet entered the seminary that the Jesuit Society was
restored. Whatever the particular influences, it is apparent that while yet at the seminary, De Smet had made up
his mind to follow a religious life, and probably to enter
the Society of Jesus. He had also formed a purpose of becoming a missionary and would naturally turn to the religious order whose principal purpose was that kind of work.

De Smet was near the close of his seminary career when
an event occurred that solved all doubts and settled the
young student definitely in his future career. Father
Charles Nerinckx, a native of Brabant, whom the events of
the French Revolution had driven across the sea, and
who had then become a zealous missionary, appeared in
Belgium at this time in quest of funds and recruits. His

vivid pictures of the untilled field in the New World and
his fervent appeal for workers roused the enthusiasm of
the young students at Malines and six of their number,
among them De Smet, volunteered to go.[2]

The deep meaning of a decision like this it is not easy
now to appreciate. It was not simply the giving up of
the natural pursuits and pleasures of life to follow a religious career, but it meant practical expatriation and a
literal exchange of the pleasures of civilization for a life
among barbarous people. It required an open and unselfish nature, and an abundant fund of spiritual faith to
take the step. It was literally following the injunction
of the divine Teacher — " Sell that thou hast and * * *
follow me."

Van Assche seems to have been the first of the young
men to decide to go to America. Imparting his plan to
his schoolmate Elet the latter also determined to go.
John B. Smedts was the next recruit and then followed
De Smet, Verreydt and Verhaegen. It was an exceptional
group of young men in more ways than one, and their
subsequent careers were in a high degree creditable to
themselves, their Society, and their native and adopted
countries. In nothing is their high character better
shown than in this early decision as to their life work.
In one case, at least, that of De Smet, and probably in
others, the step was contrary to parental counsel. The
young men were even compelled to pawn their personal
belongings to raise the necessary funds for the journey,
and the way in which they rendezvoused on the Island
of Texel before embarking does not indicate any joyous
Godspeed on the part of the friends behind.

The decision once made, preparations for carrying it
into effect swiftly followed. The little band presently
found themselves on board the brig *Columbus* at the Island

[2] Felix Verreydt, Judocus Van Assche, Pierre J. Verhaegen, Jean
Smedts, Jean Elet, and Pierre-Jean De Smet.

of Texel in July, 1821, en route for America. The voyage was a prosperous one, though slow, for steamboats had not yet crossed the ocean, and it took forty days to reach Philadelphia. Here, we are told, young De Smet was greatly surprised to find good buildings, as all his mental pictures of the America to which he was going were of an untamed wilderness, the home of wild Indians. But if he was astonished to find himself in a well-settled and highly-civilized country, the time was to come when he should find wilderness enough to satisfy him.

The young men visited Baltimore, Washington and Georgetown and finally entered the Jesuit novitiate at Whitemarsh to commence their long career as novices. We have related how a second novitiate came to be established at Florissant near St. Louis, and how, in something less than two years after their arrival in America, De Smet and his companions found themselves on the western shore of the Mississippi.

The years that followed before the end of De Smet's novitiate were naturally void of much interest, for the kind of life that the novices led offered little of excitement or unusual occurrence. The young student bore his full share in the work of the novitiate, helped erect the buildings, and was particularly relied upon in getting out the timber for the work. His great physical strength and restless energy won for him a fame which survives to this day and doubtless has assumed something of an apocryphal character. It was said that he accomplished three times as much work in a given time as any of his associates, and that he was always called upon when it was a question of cutting large trees, carrying heavy loads, etc. He was first at his task and last to leave, and in whatever of manual toil presented itself he did more than his full share.

In his studies likewise he made good progress, and he was one of the first teachers in the new university. He finished his novitiate and was ordained priest in 1827 and we shall henceforth give him the title by which he is universally known, Father De Smet.

At this time Father De Smet was a man of unusual attractiveness in his personal appearance. His face was full and frank in its expression, beaming with the natural buoyancy and good humor of his temperament. His stature was rather short for his otherwise heavy build and gave him an appearance of greater corpulency than he really possessed. In his full maturity his weight was above two hundred pounds. With advancing years the dignity of manhood's estate and the venerable figure of age became him well, and he was always noted for his commanding presence no less than for his mild and benevolent manner.[3]

In 1833 Father De Smet's health was in bad condition from some cause, and he was permitted to visit Europe. He was also charged with business for the Society, the particular purpose being to procure recruits for the work, and funds, instruments, books and other things for the new university. It has been stated that he contemplated never returning to the United States, but this is evidently not so. Besides his own recorded statement that he went abroad on business for the Society and for the benefit of his health, the fact that he took out his final naturalization papers and became a citizen of the United States[4] just before starting on his voyage, effectually negatives any such supposition.

Father De Smet reached Europe late in the year 1833 and went directly to his old home in Termonde. He remained in Belgium during the greater part of 1834 and succeeded in getting three recruits and an important outfit of instruments for the university. He then embarked at

[3] Passport, signed by William H. Seward, October 17, 1864, gives the following description: Age, sixty-four; stature, five feet seven; forehead, ordinary; eyes, blue; nose, ordinary; mouth, middle size; chin, round; hair, gray; complexion, natural; face, full.

[4] September 23, 1833.

Antwerp to return to America, but during the passage of the North Sea he was taken violently ill, and the physician advised him not to continue the voyage. He accordingly landed at Deal in England and returned to Termonde. He arranged to have the instruments sent on without him and they were received at the university March 7, 1835.[5]

Father De Smet now remained two years in Europe devoting his time to the procurement of funds and recruits for the missions and a further equipment for the university. During this period he sent to St. Louis several thousand volumes of books and a large number of fine church pictures. In 1837 he set out for America with three candidates for the priesthood and reached St. Louis after an absence of four years.

The time had now arrived when Father De Smet was to take up in earnest the great work of his life. In the spring of 1838 he was sent with Father Verreydt and two lay brothers to found a mission among the Potawatomies, a part of whom were then located about where the city of Council Bluffs, Iowa, now stands. There were also several other tribes or bands of Indians in the same vicin-

[5] " Whilst he was absent in Europe, and after his donations were received, the trustees of the university entered on their records the following honorable tribute to him as a benefactor :—

" ' Whereas the board and faculty of the St. Louis University are highly indebted to the liberality and exertions of the Rev. P. J. De Smet, for the splendid apparatus of physical and chymical instruments received at the university on the 7th of March, 1834;

" ' *Resolved,* that, besides the special thanks already tendered by the board and faculty of the St. Louis University to said Rev. P. J. De Smet on receipt of the above-mentioned apparatus of physical and chymical instruments, the register of the contributions to the Museum of St. Louis University be opened with a copy of this resolution, and his name be placed at the head of the list of contributors to the museum.

P. J. Verhaegen.

James Van de Velde, Secretary.

St. Louis University, Sept. 5, 1836.' "

(Historical sketch of St. Louis University, by Father Walter H. Hill, S. J., p. 58.)

ity, some of whom, like the Potawatomies, were remnants of eastern tribes transferred to new lands west of the Mississippi. It was considered an inviting and important field of labor.

Father De Smet left St. Louis by the steamboat *Howard* May 10, 1838, in company with the Father Superior, who wanted to visit the Kickapoo Indians near Fort Leavenworth. The rest of the party were to follow a few days later by another boat. After a brief delay at Leavenworth Father De Smet bade good-bye to the Father Superior and joined his companions on the *Wilmington*. They arrived at the site of the proposed mission on the 31st of May.

The outlook was discouraging. There were Indians enough, but instead of being eager for missionaries, as had been represented, they seemed wholly indifferent. Nevertheless the fathers set vigorously to work and in a short time began to arouse an interest among the Indians. They seem to have first occupied an abandoned fort turned over to them by Colonel S. W. Kearny; but Father De Smet says that they also erected a small house. The mission was named St. Joseph, although it has been more frequently referred to as St. Mary.[6] It was located within

[6] "*Nous érigeames une residence et une petite église en bois à l'honneur de St. Joseph.*" De Smet Letter, Book IV, p. 133. Shea (*Catholic Missions*, p. 462), says that the new church was built under the protection of the Blessed Virgin and St. Joseph. This last statement may account for the confusion as to the proper name of this mission.

St. Joseph's Mission at Council Bluffs seems to have been maintained for only three or four years. Father De Smet mentions it when he passed there in 1840, but not in 1842 nor in 1846. In 1838 Father De Smet founded another mission among a band of Potawatomies, recently arrived from east of the Mississippi. This mission was on Sugar Creek, a tributary of the Osage on the south, and seventeen miles west of the Kansas-Missouri line. In 1847 and 1848 the Potawatomies were moved to the banks of the Kansas river and a new mission was started there September 9, 1848. It became one of the most important and influential of the Indian missions and was frequently visited by Father De Smet, who took a deep interest in its welfare.

the present city limits of Council Bluffs, Iowa. Father De Smet, who put a cross on the roof of the church, wittily relates that when he " climbed the ladder to put it in place * * * Father Felix [Verreydt] beheld the devil clap his tail between his legs and take flight over the big hills."

In the year 1839 Father De Smet made an excursion to the Sioux post at the mouth of Vermillion river, a short distance above where Sioux City now stands. He left the mission April 29 by the American Fur Company steamboat *St. Peters*,[7] and returned about the middle of May by canoe. The purpose of Father De Smet's mission to the Sioux at this time was to bring about peace between them and the Potawatomies. It was the first of many similar excursions in which he went, comparatively alone and unprotected, among Indians whose friendship was doubtful.

The Potawatomi mission at Council Bluffs is of particular interest in this narrative, not so much for the results that it accomplished, as because it reveals at this early date the full character of Father De Smet as an Indian missionary. It was here that he began that famous series of letters which have made his name well known throughout the world. A few of those written at St. Joseph Mission have already been published; but the most interesting and important are now given out for the first time. They were probably not intended for publication, for they lack something of the clerical dignity in which the writer then doubtless thought that he ought to appear in public; but they are all the better for the omission and are equal, in force of expression, to anything he afterward produced. No more racy narrative is to be found in the pioneer literature of the period than the account of the voyage on the *Wilmington* from Fort Leavenworth to St. Joseph Mission in 1838; while the journal of 1839, copied in a letter written in December of that year,

[7] On the *St. Peters* was a Government exploring party under the celebrated geographer Jean N. Nicollet, whom Father De Smet knew well.

is of genuine historic value as a living picture of the state of things among the frontier tribes at that time. A single example will serve to show the fresh and vigorous manner in which the young missionary dealt with subjects that fell under his observation. Speaking of the liquor traffic, which never failed to arouse his indignation, he writes: "A war of extermination appears preparing around the poor Pota-watomies. Fifty large cannons have been landed ready charged with the most murderous grape shot, each contain-ing thirty gallons of whiskey, brandy, rum or alcohol. The boat was not as yet out of sight when the skirmishing com-menced. After the fourth, fifth and sixth rounds, the con-fusion became great and appalling. In all directions men, women and children were seen tottering and falling; the war-whoop, the merry Indian song, cries, savage roarings, formed a hideous medley. Quarrel succeeded quarrel; blow followed blow. The club, the tomahawk, spears, butcher knives, brandished together in the air. Strange! astonish-ing! only one man, in this dreadful affray, was lost — drowned in the Missouri. Another was severely stabbed and several noses were lost."

Father De Smet pictures what he saw in unvarnished colors. In particular he portrayed the evils of the abomi-nable liquor traffic in a more forcible light than had ever been done before. It is to be regretted that his trenchant and scathing denunciations of this crime were not made public at the time. His published letters were carefully pruned by his superiors of whatever savored too much of hostile criticism of the Government. He states that he wrote to the department on the subject, but the letter is not among his retained copies. If his accounts are true, and there is no reason to doubt it, these letters stand as a perpetual indict-ment against the Government for having permitted this hideous tragedy to be enacted within its territory.

The experience was a new one to Father De Smet, and it was his first real contact with the race to whose spiritual welfare he had dedicated his life work. It is plain to see

2

that his first impression was a dubious one. The revolting uncleanness, the lack of energy in work, the love of whiskey and debauchery, and the impenetrability of the Indian mind to the abstract notions of religion, all made the prospect seem anything but flattering. He saw in their full force the great obstacles that were always to be encountered in the attempt to improve the condition of the Indian, particularly where he had come into contact with the white man. The weakness of the Indian in the presence of temptation, and the greed of the white man, which was always placing temptation in his way, were everywhere in constant evidence. Nowhere in our Indian literature is there to be found a more graphic and faithful picture of the wrongs which the Indian suffered in the inevitable displacement of his race by the whites, than in these few fragmentary notes written at the St. Joseph mission of the Potawatomies.

CHAPTER III.

A ROMANCE OF AN INDIAN MISSION.

Nez Percé and Flathead Indians — The Iroquois among the Flatheads — Deputation of 1831 to St. Louis — Fact and fiction concerning
same — The mythical oration — Its far-reaching influence — The
Protestants send missionaries to Oregon — New deputation from the
Flatheads — The Jesuits decide to respond.

*T*HE Indian tribes in what is now western Montana,
northern Idaho, and eastern Washington were a peculiar people in the matter of their susceptibility to religious
influences. Especially true was this of the Flatheads and
Nez Percés (Pierced Noses),[1] the only Indians who, of their
own volition and without ever having seen a priest, have
sought the services of missionaries. They were naturally
of a turn of mind that was easily moved by religious teachings, and were relatively high in the scale of morality as
measured by the Indian standard.

As early as 1811 or 1812 the traders of the Northwest and
Pacific Fur Companies were among them, and their territory
remained a fruitful field in the fur trade until settlement
took possession of the country. The rank and file of the
trapping fraternity were made up of Canadian half-breeds
who, in spite of their lawless and irreligious lives, were
staunch Roman Catholics. With them, strange to say, were
many Iroquois, children of the tribe who had shut their
doors to the missionaries a hundred and fifty years before.
They were apparently descendants of the converts of a later
period; but whatever the origin of their religious belief, it
was now ardent and strong. It is a singular fact that the

---

[1] How those names came to be applied to these two tribes has always
been a mystery. There was nothing in the practices of either that
could suggest them.

tribe who cast out the missionaries with such relentless rigor should thus have been, through their children, a means of introducing them to other tribes of whose existence their fathers never heard. Irving gives in *Astoria* the names of the first two individuals of these classes that arrived on the Lower Columbia — Regis Brugière, a half-breed, and Ignace Shonowane, an Iroquois.[2]

The half-breeds and Iroquois circulated freely in quest of furs among the tribes of the Columbia Basin. They told these tribes of the priests of Canada — the famous black-gowns who taught the only true religion. Upon the suscept-ible minds of the Flatheads their accounts made a deep impression. They eagerly sought further knowledge and even learned such of the religious rites and customs of the Church as their ignorant preceptors could communicate. They became much concerned about their own spiritual state. If what was told them was true — that their religion was false and that they were all in danger of perdition and could be rescued therefrom only by embracing the new faith — was it not high time for them to learn what that faith was? These considerations crept into their minds slowly, not through any direct missionary preaching, but from the casual hints of the irreligious trappers who now and then talked with them on the subject, and perhaps even sought to work upon their feelings from mere motives of curiosity or amusement.

A dozen years or more of this intercourse had aroused a

[2] It is said that the Iroquois went to the Rocky Mountains in a company of about twenty-four. Whether the Ignace Shonowane of Irving was one of the number does not appear, but the name Ignace was a great one among the little band and shows from what past associations it must have sprung. The leader of these Iroquois was Ignace La Mousse, or Old Ignace, called the "Apostle of the Flatheads," who deserves to be canonized among the saints of the tribe. He early ac-quired a great influence over the Flatheads and it was largely upon his initiative that deputations were sent to St. Louis for the purpose of securing religious teachers.

deep desire to have instruction directly from the black-gowns themselves. Doubtless the Iroquois and the half-breeds also longed to see a priest again and resume the observance of their religious duties. The problem of securing one did not seem so very difficult to them. From two directions there was an established route of travel from the homes of the black-gowns to their country. There was the Canadian route from Montreal and Quebec; but it lay far to the north and the distance was very great. This was a natural route, however, considering the origin of the Iroquois and half-breeds, and it is not clear why they did not receive instruction from that direction. The other route was to St. Louis. It was much shorter, and every year the caravans of the traders came to the very borders of their country. It was a comparatively safe undertaking to send messengers to St. Louis with the traders. Furthermore, it was from that direction that the great explorers, Lewis and Clark, whom they held in sacred veneration, had come to their country. One of them still lived in St. Louis, and they well knew that his heart would be open to them if they could but see him and lay their petition before him.

The first deputation to make this journey, though whether Flathead or Nez Percé is not entirely clear, was in 1831 and consisted of four Indians. Whether these Indians accompanied the return caravan of the traders, which usually reached St. Louis in the beginning of October, does not appear, but it is probable that they did. The date of their arrival, which was about October 1, would confirm this view. In St. Louis the deputation called upon General Clark and visited the Catholic church. The complete change of life which residence in a city entailed was very hard on them, and they all fell ill, and two of their number died about a month after their arrival. They were attended by a priest and gave evidence of their knowledge of the Catholic faith by fervently seizing the crucifix when shown to them, and holding it with such tenacity that it was taken away only after death. The records of burial of these two Indians are in the books of the old Catholic Cathedral in St. Louis.[3]

And now an event took place which converted this simple yet inspiring episode into a thrilling romance that stirred the religious heart of the entire country. The Wyandot Indians were among the last of the tribes east of the Mississippi to take up homes to the westward of that stream. At this particular time the Government was trying to induce them to move, and they were investigating the question. They sent a party to explore the country, and among the number was one William Walker, an interpreter and himself a member of the nation. The party arrived in St. Louis about November 5, 1831, and before proceeding further Walker called upon General Clark. The General directed his attention to the presence of the Indian chiefs in the next room, all of whom were sick, one having died a few days previously. Mr. Walker went into the room to see them and he tells us how their personal appearance impressed him. When he came out General Clark explained to him the purpose of their visit.

A significant fact in Walker's description of his visit to these Indians is that he represents them as genuine *flatheads*, their heads exhibiting the well-known artificial deformity practiced by some of the Coast tribes, but never, according to all information, by the Flatheads themselves. This fact can be accounted for only on the supposition that the deputation was composed of Nez Percé Indians who

[3] Le trent et un d'Octobre mil huit cent trent et un, Je, sousigné ai inhumé dans le Cemetière de cette Paroisse le corps de Keepellelé ou Pipe Bard du Nez Percé de la tribu de Chopoweck Nation appellée Têtes Plates agé d'environ quarante quatre ans, administré du St. Baptême venant de la rivière Columbia au dela des Rocky Mountains.

Edm. Saulinier, Pr.

Le dix sept de Novembre mil huit cent trent et un, Je, sousigné, ai inhumé dans le Cemetière de cette Paroisse le corps de Paul sauvage de la Nation des Têtes Plattes venant de la rivière Columbia au dela des Rocky Mountains, administré du St. Baptême et de l'extrême onction.

Roux, Pr.

did, to some extent, follow the custom of flattening the head. There is indeed much evidence that this is the true fact in the case. They were neighbors of the Flatheads, and like them religiously inclined. The record of burial of one of the chiefs at St. Louis describes him as a Nez Percé of the Chopunnish tribe (another name for the Nez Percés), called the Flathead nation. A letter written by one H. Mc-Allister of St. Louis, April 17, 1833, in reference to this deputation, states that it was " from the Chopunnish tribe, residing on Lewis river, above and below the mouth of the Koos-koos-ka (Clearwater) river, and a small band of Flatheads that live with them." This information was apparently derived from General Clark. There are other authorities to the same end.

The question is therefore a doubtful one as to who these Indians really were, with the weight of evidence in favor of the Nez Percé identity instead of the Flatheads of Father De Smet. But whatever the truth, it does not affect the important fact that their visit produced a profound impression among all classes when it came to be generally known. It was given wide notoriety through the columns of the *Christian Advocate*. Under date of February 18, 1833, one G. P. Disoway of New York sent a letter to this journal, inclosing another from William Walker describing the circumstances of his call upon General Clark.[4] The publi-

[4] Walker's letter was dated Upper Sandusky, January 19, 1833. Both the Disoway and Walker letters were published March 1, 1833. In Mr. Disoway's letter the writer speaks of Mr. Walker as having made his expedition to St. Louis and the proposed Wyandot lands " in November last," which would clearly fix the date of the Flathead deputation in 1832 instead of 1831, and this is the date universally accepted by Protestant missionary writers upon the subject. Through these letters the author of this sketch was led into the same error in his *American Fur Trade of the Far West*, p. 643. See, among other authorities, records of Indian Superintendency at St. Louis now in possession of the Kansas Historical Society at Topeka; and a letter from Bishop Rosati of St. Louis dated December 31, 1831, published in the *Annals of the Propagation of the Faith,* and quoted by Palladino in his *Indian and White in the Northwest,* p. 11.

cation of Disoway's letter called forth a spirited editorial in
the issue of March 22, 1833, exhorting the Church to take
the matter up at once and respond to a call which appealed
so powerfully to the Christian conscience of the world. Additional correspondence appeared in the issue of May 10,
1833, and the whole subject had by this time become familiar
to Protestant churches throughout the United States.

There grew out of the event a curious myth, to the effect
that on the eve of the departure of the surviving Indians
for their home they were given a banquet, and that at this
banquet one of the Indians delivered a speech, in which he
declared that he and his companions had not found what
they came for and must therefore go home disappointed to
a disappointed people. The writer has never seen the
smallest evidence that this reported speech was genuine, nor
any as to who the real author was.[5] The speech itself, by
whomsoever prepared, holds a prominent place in the history of the Protestant Missions in the Columbia valley, and
is here given in full:

"I come to you over the trail of many moons from the
setting sun. You were the friends of my fathers, who have
all gone the long way. I came with an eye partly open
for my people, who sit in darkness. I go back with both
eyes closed. How can I go back blind, to my blind people?
I made my way to you with strong arms through many
enemies and strange lands that I might carry back much to
them. I go back with both arms broken and empty. Two
fathers came with us, they were the braves of many winters and wars. We leave them asleep here by your great
waters and wigwams. They were tired in many moons and
their moccasins wore out.

"My people sent me to get the 'White Man's Book of
Heaven.' You took me to where you allow your women

---

[5] It is said, upon the questionable authority of the Rev. H. H.
Spalding, who went to Oregon with Marcus Whitman, that a clerk
of the American Fur Company in St. Louis overheard the speech and
wrote it up and sent it to his friends in Pittsburg.

to dance as we do not ours, and the book was not there. You took me to where they worship the Great Spirit with candles and the book was not there. You showed me images of the good spirits and the pictures of the good land beyond, but the book was not among them to tell us the way. I am going back the long and sad trail to my people in the dark land. You make my feet heavy with gifts and my moccasins will grow old in carrying them, yet the book is not among them. When I tell my poor blind people after one more snow, in the big council, that I did not bring the book, no word will be spoken by our old men or by our young braves. One by one they will rise up and go out in silence. My people will die in darkness, and they will go a long path to other hunting grounds. No white man will go with them, and no White Man's Book to make the way plain. I have no more words."

The return of these Indians to their country is another matter about which there is great uncertainty. The orthodox version, as given by the latest writer on the subject,[6] is that they returned by the American Fur Company steamboat in the spring of 1832 as far as to the mouth of the Yellowstone whence they made their way home; that George Catlin, who was a passenger on the same boat, painted their pictures and that these are now numbers 207 and 208 in his well-known gallery of Indian paintings; and that the tribe at home agreed to go on their annual buffalo hunt to the Judith Basin on the Upper Missouri earlier than usual in the summer of 1832, in order to meet them. It can only be said of this version that it is extremely doubtful. No steamboat had ever yet ascended the Missouri anywhere near the mouth of the Yellowstone, and there had been no trading post built farther up than this point when the deputation left home in 1831. They could not, therefore, have expected a steamboat as far as the Yellowstone or any other craft beyond that point, and any pre-arranged plan to meet the Indians, based upon such a voyage, would

[6] By Mrs. Eva Emery Dye, in *The Conquest.*

have been wholly impossible. Moreover it would have been extremely hazardous for these Indians, alone as they would have been, to have traversed the territory of their enemies the Blackfeet. Finally, every consideration would have led them to return by the way they went, and while they may have traveled from St. Louis to Independence (near Kansas City) by boat, they probably joined the regular caravan at that point. The annual rendezvous of the Rocky Mountain Fur Company for 1832 was in Pierre's Hole, on the borders of their country, and here in fact a large band of both the Nez Percé and Flathead Indians were gathered. May they not have been looking for their absent brethren, and would not this have been the natural place to expect them?

As to the Catlin pictures the facts are even more uncertain. It is well known that, as an authority on historical or even descriptive matters, Catlin did not stand well, and his claim may be simply the embellished account of some commonplace incident. His general carelessness of statement is illustrated in his reference to the two men who died in St. Louis as " old and venerable men," whereas the record of their burial gives their age as about forty-one years. There were always Indians on the boats of the American Fur Company and generally in considerable numbers and of different tribes. The artist had no lack of subjects, and his subsequent identification of these particular two Indians as the ones who visited General Clark in the fall of 1831 cannot be accepted without question.

But again the manner of their journey home, or whether they ever reached there, like that of the mythical oration, is of comparatively little importance. The great fact is that they had sown seed in fertile ground. They had aroused the Christian spirit throughout the United States and the result was a prompt response to their call. In the year following that of the publications in the *Christian Advocate* the Methodists sent out two missionaries, Jason and Daniel Lee. These missionaries did not stop among the Flatheads or Nez Percés but went on to the Willamette Valley. In 1835 Marcus Whitman and Samuel Parker were sent out by the Presbyterians to investigate the field, and upon arriving at Green river were so favorably impressed that Doctor Whitman returned to report to the Board and recommend the forming of missions. While at home he married, and in the following year himself and bride, with Reverend H. H. Spalding and wife, started for their remote field of work. Doctor Whitman established himself among the Cayuses at Waiilatpu, near the Walla Walla river, while the Reverend Mr. Spalding commenced work among the Nez Percés at Lapwai.

Considered simply on the basis of evangelizing the Indian tribes, the Protestant missions in these parts were not a success. To the clear-sighted men who had founded them, it was apparent that they never could succeed. In one of his letters written from the mission Doctor Whitman said:

"I have no doubt our greatest work is to be to aid the white settlement of this country and help to found its religious institutions. Providence has its full share in all those events. Although the Indians have made, and are making, rapid advancement in religious knowledge and civilization, yet it cannot be hoped that time will be allowed to mature the work of Christianization or civilization before white settlers will demand the soil and the removal of both of the Indians and the missions.

"What Americans desire of this kind they always effect, and it is useless to oppose or desire it otherwise. To guide as far as can be done, and direct these tendencies for the best, is evidently the part of wisdom."

Such was likewise the feeling on the part of the Lees on the Willamette. So it resulted that these men became rather the forerunners of American civilization in Oregon than successful missionaries to the Indian tribes. Marcus Whitman in particular looked with a jealous eye upon his country's rights in that great region. In no other light can his famous journey back to the States in the winter of

1842–3 be explained, and however much his motives have been impugned, his name has become indelibly fixed in the national heart as one of its great heroes. The tragedy which awaited him upon his return, when he and his beloved Christian wife fell victims to savage cruelty, has made him a true martyr both to the cause which he nominally represented of Christianizing the Indians and to what he regarded the far greater cause of establishing American possession and civilization in the Columbia Valley.

The immediate result of the deputation of 1831 was therefore to start a Protestant missionary movement in Oregon. The Jesuits at St. Louis were still too weak in numbers to respond. They had had but very few recruits since the opening of the novitiate, and all these were needed in the new work incident to founding the university. It was impossible to spare any workers for this distant field.

In 1835 another deputation went to St. Louis. It appears that a Flathead chief, Insula by name, went to the Green river rendezvous in 1835 to meet the missionaries whom his people supposed to be Black-gowns, but who proved to be Protestant ministers. As they did not satisfy the description which the Indians had heard of the Catholic priests, Insula returned home and it was decided to send a deputation to St. Louis to ask for them. It was old Ignace who undertook the expedition and he took with him his two sons to have them baptized. He made the journey in the summer of 1835.[7] The little party reached St. Louis in safety; the

[7] Father Palladino, *Indian and White in the Northwest*, p. 19, says that "Ignace started with the intention of going to Canada, the place of his birth, where he thought he could more easily obtain missionaries for the Flatheads, which, as said, was the main object of his long, perilous journey. Learning, however, on his way that there were Jesuit Fathers at St. Louis, he turned his steps in that direction, and reached the place late in the fall, after frightful privations and sufferings." This, if true, is another indication that the 1831 deputation was not from the Flatheads, or they would have known of the presence of Jesuits in St. Louis, unless indeed none of the deputation succeeded in getting home.

sons were baptized December 2d with the Christian names Charles and Francis; and Ignace went to Bishop Rosati with his request for missionaries. In the following spring he returned home with his sons, where one of them, Francis, is still living.

In 1837 a third deputation started for St. Louis. It consisted of old Ignace, three Flatheads, and one Nez Percé. At Fort Laramie they fell in with a party of white men traveling in their direction, among them one of the Protestant ministers, W. H. Gray, returning from Oregon. At Ash Hollow on the North Platte, where the road started to cross over to the ford of the South Platte, the Indians were attacked by a band of Sioux. The whites were ordered to stand apart, as it was not intended to molest them. Ignace, being dressed as a white man, was mistaken for one and ordered apart with the rest, but heroically refused to abandon his companions. The five Indians were slain and this deputation never reached St. Louis.

A fourth, and this time successful, attempt was made in 1839. A deputation of two Indians, Pierre Gaucher and Young Ignace, set out with a party of trappers who were going to St. Louis. Their route was apparently by the Yellowstone and the Missouri rivers which they descended by canoe. In passing St. Joseph Mission, at Council Bluffs, they stopped to see the priests there, and it is an interesting coincidence that they should have found the very man who was to grant them their request in person and open a new era in the history of their nation. This is Father De Smet's account of their visit:

" On the 18th of last September two Catholic Iroquois came to visit us. They had been for twenty-three years among the nation called the Flatheads and Pierced Noses, about a thousand Flemish leagues from where we are. I have never seen any savages so fervent in religion. By their instructions and examples they have given all that nation a great desire to have themselves baptized. All that tribe strictly observe Sunday and assemble several times a week to pray and sing canticles. The sole object of these good Iroquois was to obtain a priest to come and finish what they had so happily commenced. We gave them letters of recommendation for our Reverend Father Superior at St. Louis. They thought nothing of adding three hundred leagues to the thousand they had already accomplished, in the hope that their request would be granted."

The two deputies arrived safely in St. Louis and presented themselves to Bishop Rosati, who gave them definite hope of a priest in the following spring. Thereupon one of them, Pierre Gaucher, set out for home, while Ignace remained to accompany the missionary who should be sent. The letter of Bishop Rosati to the Father General of the Society in Rome, detailing the circumstances and result of the visit, is dated October 20, 1839, and states that the Indian was to start the next day. If Pierre Gaucher made his journey home alone at that season of the year (it is said to have taken him all winter) it was a remarkable achievement. He arrived in the Bitter Root Valley, the home of the Flatheads, early in the spring of 1840 and announced to the tribe that a black-gown was surely coming.

CHAPTER IV.

THE FLATHEAD MISSION.

Father De Smet detailed for the Flathead Mission — Journey across
the plains — Meeting with Flathead envoys — The welcome at Pierre's
Hole — Flattering prospects — Joy of the Indians — Gratitude of
Father De Smet — Journey to Three Forks — John Baptiste de Velder
— Father De Smet starts home — Passage of the Crow country —
Interesting intercourse with the Crows — Dangerous journey to Fort
Union — Journey down the Missouri — Agreeable encounter with the
Sioux — Arrival in St. Louis — Disappointment in regard to funds —
Father De Smet seeks contributions — Signal success — Second journey
across the plains — Founding of St. Mary's Mission among the Flat-
heads — Difficulties and set-backs — Journey to Fort Colville and return — Work at the Mission — Visit to Fort Vancouver and the Willamette — Return to St. Mary's — Departure for St. Louis — Incidents
of the journey — Arrival in St. Louis.

WHEN it came to fulfilling the promise made to Ignace
and Pierre Gaucher, Father De Smet volunteered to
go and the task was assigned to him. It was at first expected
to send two priests but it was found impossible to raise
the necessary funds. Accordingly Father De Smet was
sent alone. He could at least survey the ground and report whether it would be worth while to carry the work
farther.

On the 27th of March, 1840, he set out on his long
journey. He traveled by steamboat to Westport (Kansas
City) and there joined the annual expedition of the American Fur Company to the mountains. It was under charge
of a trader, Andrew Drips, well-known in the early history of the west. The party left Westport on April 30,
following the general route of the Oregon Trail, and without any untoward event, reached the annual rendezvous
on Green river just two months later.

To Father De Smet, full of enthusiasm in his work and
with his active mind open to all around him, the long journey was a veritable pleasure tour except that he was un-
well much of the time. His letters are filled with interesting notes upon the country, and descriptions of his varied
experiences along the way. His buoyant and hopeful de-
meanor on this journey is a proof of his thoroughly optimis-
tic and cheerful temperament. He was suffering from chills
and fever and was at one time in such a state that he had to
be carried on a litter fixed up in a wagon. He was strongly
urged to turn back; but he felt that too much was at stake,
as he was the only person with the expedition that could
carry out the work, and his abandonment of it would be a
sore disappointment to the Indians. He therefore resolved
to keep on. The malaria did not finally leave him until on
his way home some three months afterward.

At Green river, to Father De Smet's joy and astonishment, he found a deputation of ten Flathead Indians who
had been sent on to meet him after the return of Pierre
Gaucher. There were also present other Indians, notably
of the Snake nation, and a motley crowd of trappers and
hunters,— making in all a curious assemblage such as only
a rendezvous of the fur trade in those early times could produce. Father De Smet enjoyed the novelty of it all, and
was especially delighted at the prospect of success which
the presence of the Flatheads assured. There was an instant bond of sympathy between him and his hosts which
made them from the first more brothers than strangers.
The Sunday following their arrival a formal mass was
celebrated on the prairie — the first ceremony of the kind
in the Rocky Mountains north of the Mexican possessions.

After four days delay at the Green river rendezvous,
Father De Smet and his Flatheads started to join the main
camp. Their route took them through the wonderful valley
of Jackson Hole and across the great Teton range into
the valley of Pierre's Hole, renowned for its beauty and

at one time a famous rendezvous in the fur trade. In Pierre's Hole was the camp of the Flatheads and Pend d'Oreilles, who had come thus far to the number of about 1,600 to welcome the long-expected black-gown. They had already set up his tent and when he arrived there was the most lively demonstration of joy. They led him to the lodge of the chief, who received him with a touching address of welcome, after which the Father at once began his instructions. With a marvelous eagerness the whole tribe set about learning their religious duties. A bell was presented to Father De Smet to call them to prayers and they were rigidly punctual at all the appointed exercises. The chief was the first up in the morning, and as he aroused his people, "Come, courage, my children," he cried, "open your eyes. Address your first thought and words to the Great Spirit. Tell him that you love him, and ask him to take pity on you. Courage, for the sun is about to appear, it is time you went to the river to wash yourselves. Be prompt at our Father's lodge, at the first sound of the bell; be quiet when you are there; open your ears to hear and your hearts to hold fast all the words that he says to you."

It was in truth a remarkable experience to find the wild tribes of the mountains absorbed in religious teaching with a fervor approaching that of the primitive Christians. To the earnest missionary who had come so far the full reward of his labors was already at hand. It was something far beyond his expectations, and tears of gratitude told of his emotion as the hope of spreading a knowledge of the faith among people ready and capable of receiving it seemed about to be realized. His narrative of these events, as given in his letters, can alone convey an adequate impression of this singular scene in the heart of the wilderness.

After sojourning a short time in Pierre's Hole the entire party took up their march in the direction of the Flathead country. They ascended Henry Fork of Snake river to its source in Henry Lake where they arrived on the 22nd

3

of July. This lake is close to the Continental Divide, and just across the ridge is Red Rock Lake, the ultimate source of the Missouri, 4,221 miles by water-course from the sea. Father De Smet climbed far up the side of a mountain where he could overlook this impressive scene, and then sat down, musing upon the works of God around him and the holy character of the service in which he was engaged. On a rock near him he inscribed a religious sentiment and the date July 27, 1840.

During the next month Father De Smet and his Flathead and Pend d'Oreille friends passed leisurely down the valley of the stream which flows from Red Rock Lake to join the Jefferson river, and down that stream to the Three Forks of the Missouri. His time was spent in instructing the Indians, in listening to their tales of war and peace, and in studying the prospects of missionary work among them. He became convinced that here was a field of genuine promise, and his proposition to establish a mission in their midst was received with the greatest enthusiasm. Father De Smet did not actually go into the Flathead country, which lay across the Divide in the Bitter Root Valley, as he thought it best not to take the time to go there on this occasion; but rather to hasten home, report the situation to his superiors, and get the necessary assistance for the commencement of a permanent mission. He imparted his plan to the Indians, and after giving them his word that he would return, he set out on his journey home.

He had as a companion a man whom he had picked up at the Green river rendezvous. Father De Smet thus describes him:

"A good Fleming of Ghent, John Baptiste de Velder, an old grenadier of Napoleon, who had left his native land at the age of thirty, and had spent the last fourteen years in the mountains in the capacity of beaver hunter, generously offered to serve and assist me in all my wanderings. He was resolved, he said, to pass the remainder of his days in the practice of his holy religion. He had almost forgotten the Flemish language, excepting his prayers and a song which he had learned on his mother's knee and which he repeated every day."

This man staid by Father De Smet in his long and perilous journey back to St. Louis and for a part of the way was his only companion. The Flatheads sent an escort of seventeen men as far as to Fort Alexander, on the Yellowstone. Amid the genuine sorrow of the Indians, tempered, however, by the Father's promise to return the following spring, the little cavalcade took up their route from the Three Forks very much along the modern line of the Northern Pacific Railroad. They crossed the Bozeman pass and reached the Yellowstone river at the Great Bend where Livingston now stands. With imminent danger from the hostile Blackfeet, they made their way down the right bank of the river until they reached a village of the Crow Indians in the Bighorn valley.

Here Father De Smet made new friends, as he always did whenever he met a band of Indians. He traveled with them two days and was forced to accept their burdensome hospitality during all this time. "Since I hide nothing from you," he says in one of his letters, "I hope you will not be scandalized at learning that in a single afternoon I took part in twenty different banquets." The religious teachings, which Father De Smet never failed to press upon his Indian hosts wherever he was, caused some surprise to the ruffian freebooters among whom he found himself. One of the chiefs exclaimed: "I think there are only two in all the Crow nation who will not go to the place you describe; * * * they are the only ones I know of who have never killed nor stolen nor been guilty of the excesses you speak of. I *may* be mistaken about them, and in that case we will all go to hell together." Still Father De Smet made a deep and lasting impression upon this wild tribe. He visited them on a subsequent occasion and was well received by them, and more than once they asked that he plant a mission in their country.

At Fort Alexander, which was the American Fur Company trading post for the Crows, Father De Smet's escort turned back at his request, and he was left with his Flemish friend to make the rest of the journey alone. This post was on the left bank of the Yellowstone opposite the mouth of the Rosebud river. The two travelers set out by land, keeping along the left bank of the river, and with great caution hastened their course to Fort Union on the Missouri, a little above the mouth of the Yellowstone. This journey was one of great risk and peril. They were liable at any moment to be slain by some wandering band of Indians and on one occasion escaped this catastrophe by the narrowest margin. Commenting upon their dangers, Father De Smet made the following beautiful reflection: "Such a solitude, with all its horrors and dangers, has notwithstanding one very real advantage; it is a place where one is constantly looking death in the face, and where it presents itself incessantly to the imagination in the most hideous forms. There one feels in a very special manner that he is wholly in God's hands. It is then easy to offer him the sacrifice of a life which belongs less to you than to the first savage who may see fit to take it; and to form the most generous resolutions a man is capable of. That was, in fact, the best 'retreat' that I have ever made in my life. My only consolation was the object for which I had undertaken the journey; my guide, my support, my refuge, was the fatherly providence of God."

But the great danger did not prevent the good priest from seeing the humorous side of things. On the second day of their journey they were in imminent peril of being discovered by a party of savages whose fresh trail they had come upon. They built no camp fire that night and cooked no supper. "I rolled myself in my blanket," says Father De Smet, "and stretched out on the sod, commending myself to the good God. My grenadier, braver than I, was soon snoring like a steam engine in full swing. Running through all the notes of the chromatic scale, he closed each move-

ment of his prelude with a deep sigh, by way of modulation.
As for me, I turned and rolled, but spent a sleepless night."

In due time they reached Fort Union. After a few days
of the hospitable entertainment which that fine trading post
always furnished to guests of merit, and after having baptized a good many half-breed children, the two travelers resumed their journey September 23d. They went by land
down the left bank of the Missouri to near the Mandan
village, where they crossed to the right bank. Here were
also the Aricaras and the Minnetarees, or Grosventres of
the Missouri, all of whom welcomed the black-gown and
did all in their power to entertain him. They stopped a
short time at Fort Clark, the trading post for these Indians,
and then, in company of a Canadian voyageur, set out down
the west, or right, bank of the river for Fort Pierre.

On this part of the journey they came near getting into
serious trouble. They had stopped for noon in a concealed
little nook on the brink of a clear spring, and were congratulating themselves on the security of their position, when
they were suddenly pounced upon by a band of Blackfeet-
Sioux who had been stealthily following them for some
time. The Indians were bedaubed with paint and otherwise decked out as if on the warpath. " I rose at once,"
says Father De Smet, " and presented my hand to him
whom I believed to be the chief of the band. He said
coldly, ' Why are you hiding in this ravine? ' I answered
him that we were hungry and that the spring had invited us
to take a moment's repose. He looked at me with wonder,
and addressing the Canadian, who could speak the Sioux
language a little better, said to him, ' I have never seen such
a man in my life. Who is he? ' My long black robe and
the missionary cross that I bore upon my breast especially
excited his curiosity. The Canadian answered (and under
the circumstances he was prodigal of his titles) : ' It is the
man who talks to the Great Spirit. It is a chief Black-
gown of the Frenchmen.' His fierce look changed at once ;
he ordered his warriors to put away their weapons and they

all shook hands with me. I made them a present of a big twist of tobacco and everybody sat down in a circle and smoked the pipe of peace and friendship."

Their further entertainment by these Indians was full of interest and it was an introduction to the Sioux nations which neither the Indians nor Father De Smet ever forgot. Although he never had the satisfaction of founding a mission in their midst he made many efforts to do so, and these Indians never ceased while he lived to send messages to him asking him to send them a teacher.

Thus the little party made their way onward amid danger and never-ending surprises. They stopped at Forts Pierre and Vermillion, and at the latter place took a canoe, under the guidance of an Iroquois half-breed. They reached St. Joseph Mission, at Council Bluffs, November 24th, and the river closed with ice the next day. The rest of the journey was made by land, and Father De Smet arrived among his brethren at the St. Louis University on the last day of the year.

Full of enthusiasm over the results of his journey and eager to commence preparations for the return, Father De Smet was not prepared for the deep disappointment that awaited him. "On my arrival at St. Louis," he writes, under date of May 1, 1841, "I gave an account to my superior of my journey and of the flattering prospects which a mission beyond the Rocky Mountains held out. You will easily believe me when I tell you that my heart sank within me on learning from him that the funds at his disposal for missionary purposes would not enable him to afford me scarcely half of what was necessary for the outfit and other expenses of an expedition. The thought that the undertaking would have to be given up, that I would not be able to redeem my promise to the poor Indians, pierced my very heart and filled me with the deepest sorrow. I would have desponded had I not already experienced the visible protection of the Almighty in the prosecution of this great work. My confidence in Him was unabated. Whilst in this state of mind one of my friends encouraged me to appeal to the zealous and learned coadjutor of Philadelphia and to his indefatigable clergy. I immediately acted upon the thought. I did appeal, and with what success the Catholic public already know."

Father De Smet practically took the matter of funds into his own hands, went to New Orleans, and in the course of a few months succeeded in raising the necessary amount from that city and several other sources. His great success on this occasion doubtless accounts for his being sent to Europe so often in after years on similar missions.

The funds being raised and the outfit made up, Father De Smet and his companions set out from St. Louis on the steamer *Oceana* April 30, 1841. The party consisted of two priests besides Father De Smet and three lay brothers. Father Nicholas Point, one of the number, was a most valuable acquisition and did a great work for the mission. He was a skilled draftsman, and left many sketches of the customs of the people among whom he was thrown.[1]

We shall not follow in detail this second long journey over the plains, though its interesting incidents fill many pages in Father De Smet's letters. The little party left Westport May 10th and reached Fort Hall on Snake river about the middle of August. Here they met the advance guard of the Flatheads. Resuming their journey August 19th, they traversed the plain of the Three Buttes to near the junction of Henry Fork with Snake river, and thence followed practically the modern line of the Oregon Short

[1] " To give them pleasure, the missionary (Point, winter of 1845–46) amused himself in his leisure time by sketching with the pen various historic incidents, taken from their own annals; such, namely, as were most to their taste, such as the moving of a camp, diverse occupations, the work of the chase, fine deeds of arms, amusing or tragic adventures, religious scenes, etc. It would be hard to depict the pleasure that this little collection gave them; but what is much more worth while, it contributed powerfully to increase the authority of the chiefs in the eyes of the young men, and to rouse in the latter a noble emulation for good."— *Indian and White in the Northwest. Palladino.*

Line Railroad to the Deer Lodge valley, where they arrived early in September. The main Flathead camp had joined them while passing through the ·Beaverhead valley. The party continued their route down the Deer Lodge and Hell Gate valleys to the modern site of Missoula, and then passed up the Bitter Root valley some thirty miles, where they chose the site of their first establishment and commenced work upon it September 24, 1841.

Notwithstanding all they had brought with them for the needs of the mission, it was at once seen that further provisions and tools would have to be procured, and as the nearest point where they could possibly be obtained was Fort Colville on the Columbia, it was decided that Father De Smet should make a journey thither before winter set in. He accordingly left St. Mary's Mission, the name of the new establishment, October 28th, and after a long and trying journey through dense forests and over a rough country he reached his destination in safety. He returned to St. Mary's early in December, having been absent but little over a month.

The missionaries now labored with unabating zeal, in which the Indians joined, to get their establishment into working order. Things were moving so prosperously that, as Father De Smet naively remarks, the jealousy of the demons of darkness was aroused, and they were treated to a few trifling set-backs; as for example the " sickness of the interpreter and sexton " when their assistance was most needed; a hurricane which came near demolishing in an instant all the fruits of their labors; and the church organ accidentally broken by one of the Indians. "All seemed to conspire against them; but the day of baptism arrives and every cloud disappears."

The fathers entered upon the religious portion of their work with determined zeal and devotion. They struck directly at the root of the evils of savage society as they understood them. One of their greatest difficulties was in regulating the subject of marriage. They adopted the principle that there could be but one legitimate marriage and that it must be solemnized according to the forms of the Church. It therefore became necessary for the Indians to choose, and then present themselves before a priest. The fathers had a good deal of trouble, as might naturally be expected, to convince the Indians of the necessity of this and other regulations of civilized society; and with a less well-disposed tribe they would not have succeeded.

Thus the winter of 1841-2 passed away. With the approach of spring Father De Smet decided to visit the lower Columbia for additional supplies, and to get in touch with the new Catholic missionary in that quarter and with the governor of the Hudson Bay Company who resided at Fort Vancouver. He left St. Mary's early in April and went first to Fort Colville. Thence he made his way down the Columbia by skiff, wherever navigation was possible. He had fortunately gone ashore to walk along the bank at the place called the Little Dalles on their second day out from Fort Colville, when the frail craft in which he usually rode was caught by the violent eddies, swamped, and five of the boatmen drowned. He arrived at Fort Vancouver June 8th, where to his great joy he found Father Blanchet and Father Demers, two Canadian priests who had been sent to that country two years before. He visited St. Paul's, the establishment of these priests on the Willamette, and conferred with them about what ought to be done to promote the general work in their respective territories. It was decided that, with the consent of his superiors, Father De Smet should go to Europe for recruits and funds.

Father De Smet also found that he had a most powerful and valuable ally in the venerable John McLoughlin, Governor for the Hudson Bay Company in these parts. This philanthropic and capable man was a power in the Columbia valley in these early years and his generous aid to settlers during the emigration to Oregon has won him a permanent place in the affections of the people of that region.[2]

[2] See pages 355 and 1553 to 1557 of the *Letters*.

Having accomplished the purpose of his journey, Father De Smet returned to St. Mary's.   Both on his way out and back he studied, as was always his wont, the spiritual condition of the tribes through which he passed and the prospects for establishing missions among them.   He found the feeling among the Cœur d'Alènes highly promising and he gave these Indians assurances that he would send them priests that very fall.   In fulfillment of this promise he directed Father Mengarini to open a mission and leave it in charge of Father Point and Brother Huet.

With all things arranged as far as his humble means would permit, and with assurances to his brethren and the Indians whom he was leaving that he would send them early succor from St. Louis and Europe, Father De Smet set out on his return eastward July 29th.   He spent two weeks in the plain of the Three Forks with the Flatheads who were there on a buffalo hunt, and then started for St. Louis by the route of the previous year.   He was escorted to the Crow country by twelve Flatheads and had as traveling companions an Iroquois by the name of Ignatius, and a Crow half-breed by the name of Gabriel.   His short stay among the Crows was full of interesting experiences, to some of which we shall refer later.   He left Fort Alexander with his two companions and also two American hunters and together they made the always perilous journey down the Yellowstone to Fort Union.   This is Father De Smet's description of their daily routine of travel: "At daybreak we saddled and set out and at about 10 A. M. we halted for an hour and a half, being careful to choose a place which, in case of attack, might offer some advantage for defense.   After this brief rest we resumed our course and kept up a trot until sunset.   After our evening meal we built a big fire and hastily constructed a hut from the branches of trees to make our enemies, who might be on the watch, think that we were encamped for the night.   *   *   *   Then we pursue our route until ten or eleven o'clock at night when, without fire or shelter, we dispose ourselves as best we can for repose. * * * Each one wraps himself in his buffalo robe, with his saddle for a pillow, and thanks to the fatigues of a forty-mile ride in a burning sun, falls to sleep the moment he lies down."

After a brief and enjoyable delay at Fort Union Father De Smet, with Ignatius and Gabriel, set out in a skiff for St. Louis. On their third day out they had the good fortune to meet a steamboat — the first one that had ever ascended the river so far at that season of the year — and they displayed no false modesty in accepting an invitation to ride in it the rest of the way to St. Louis. After returning with the boat to Fort Union all set out again down the river. The voyage was a tedious and dangerous one. " The waters were low;" says Father De Smet, " the sandbars and snags everywhere numerous; the boat consequently encountered many obstacles in her passage. We were frequently in great danger of perishing. Her keel was pierced with pointed rocks, her sides rent by the snags. Twenty times the wheels had been broken to pieces. The pilot-house had been carried away in the tempest; the whole cabin would have followed if it had not been made fast by a large cable. Our boat appeared to be little more than a mere wreck, and in this wreck, after forty-six days navigation from the Yellowstone, we arrived safely at St. Louis."

In deep gratitude for his preservation amid the manifold dangers that he had passed through, Father De Smet repaired at once to his church and offered up a grateful prayer of thanksgiving for the signal favors he had received.

CHAPTER V.

ATHER De SMET'S enthusiasm and faith in his new work were unbounded. He inspired his superiors with his own confidence and they gave him a free hand to work out his plans. Early in the year 1843 he went as far south as New Orleans and as far east as Boston soliciting funds for his work. He succeeded in getting together a goodly supply of articles needed for the missions and three recruits — Father Peter De Vos, who was made Vice-Superior of the Missions, Father Adrian Hoeken, and Brother J. B. McGean. Father De Smet accompanied the little party on their way as far as Westport, going by the steamer *John Auld*. Near Glasgow, May 1st, they saw the distinguished naturalist Audubon, who was on the American Fur Company boat *Omega* with a party of scientists making an exploration of the Missouri. During Father De Smet's absence three more recruits arrived from Europe, but as they were too late for the expedition they waited in St. Louis until the following year.

Immediately upon his return to St. Louis Father De Smet set out for Europe and after a voyage of twenty-one days landed in Ireland. While there he heard that great man, Daniel O'Connell, speak, and he records the following incident of the occasion, which impressed him deeply as an example of the intense feeling of the Irish people at the time: "An old woman had come many a mile to look at the Liberator. She had forced her way with difficulty through the immense crowd; she had even climbed on the platform from whence O'Connell spoke. I stood near him; she asked me, ' Is this the man?' At my answering yes, she pulled his coat exclaiming, ' Sir, let me look at you!' He turned with a smile and a bow. A gift of a thousand pounds could not have been more welcome to her. An old man had also reached the carriage. He took the hand of the Liberator and with tears in his eyes exclaimed — ' I have come far to see you, Sir, and to touch this hand; now I am happy and return home rejoiced.' As the man retired O'Connell whispered aloud — ' What a nation!' His broad chest heaved. No doubt his benevolent heart answered to his whispering — ' They must be free.' "

After leaving Ireland, Father De Smet traveled through the principal cities of England, France, Italy,[1] Holland and Belgium, and embarked at Antwerp, December 12th, with four fathers, a lay brother and six sisters, together with a large amount of supplies for the missions. They sailed in the *Infatigable* around Cape Horn for the Columbia. Whether the vessel was chartered for the purpose of the missions does not appear, but in any case she sailed

[1] " In Rome, when presented to His Holiness Gregory XVI by the Father-General of the Society of Jesus, the Pope rose from his throne and embraced him. But the cordial greetings were not long an unmixed pleasure for the soul of the humble missionary, who became much alarmed on the discovery that they had resolved to make him a bishop. With the help of the Father-General, however, he succeeded in throwing the burden on the shoulders of the Very Rev. F. N. Blanchet, who, besides being in every way qualified for the Episcopal dignity, was his senior both in years and as a missionary in the Rocky Mountains."— *Palladino.*

directly to Father De Smet's destination without other
than necessary outfitting delays at any place. They were
detained at Flushing near the mouth of the Scheld twenty-
eight days by contrary winds and did not finally get away
until January 9, 1844.

The story of this voyage of seven months, as told by
Father De Smet, is one of the most interesting on record.
It deals with all the incidents of the journey, the varying
moods of the weather, the crossing of the Equator with its
time-honored fun and frolic, the meeting of vessels on the
lonely ocean, the rise of the southern constellations into
view and their disappearance again, and a great variety of
other subjects which so long a voyage brings forth. To
a man of Father De Smet's temperament everything had
an interest and he was eminently qualified to derive the
utmost pleasure possible from such a journey.

Soon after passing the Horn they encountered a succession of terrific storms which almost drove them upon the
coast of Patagonia. It was a terrible time, but the danger
was met with consummate skill by the crew and with
calm resignation by the passengers. "A tempest is truly
a sublime spectacle," says Father De Smet in his account
of the storm, "but the description is infinitely more agreeable than the reality. If there had been less of the frightful about it, probably I should have enjoyed it more. Such
was the roaring of the winds and waves that the captain's
voice, even through the trumpet, could hardly be distinguished. The waves rose in pyramids around us, and
masses of water, torn off by the fury of the winds, were
hurled upon us in floods that filled the deck with foam.
Never in any of my voyages had I seen such evidence of
the might of wind and water, nor of the admirable manner
in which a vessel resists the fury of the elements."

The *Infatigable* stopped for a considerable time at both
Valparaiso in Chile and Callao in Peru, and Father De
Smet visited the capitals of these two countries. They were
full of interest to him and he devotes much interesting

space to his impressions of them.[2] These breaks in the long journey were most welcome to the weary passengers, who spent all the time on land. On the 27th of May, 1844, they sailed from the harbor of Callao and were not to land again until at the end of their voyage. For a while the winds were favorable and the vessel was soon back on the north side of the Equator. Then they fell into a zone of calms which continued until both passengers and crew were well-nigh exhausted. Father De Smet thus refers to these miserable experiences: "Then an expression of discouragement and melancholy appears on the captain's face and on those of all the crew. It seems as if one were condemned to perish here. A blackened sea all around, a somber sky above, and clouds on the horizon, like impenetrable obstacles, changing form every instant and calling to mind all kinds of phantoms; while the ship, like a weak toy upon a sea in torment, swelling and sinking unceasingly, rocks and rocks until the head and stomach both turn."

Presently they came to regions of better winds and the good ship resumed her speed. It was high time, for her supply of provisions was getting low. Finally, on the 28th of July, amid general exclamations of joy, the longed-for coast of Oregon came into view where the great "River of the West" pours its tribute into the sea. But scarcely had the first outburst of joy passed when the ominous sight of the rolling breakers at the mouth of the river changed all to gloomy foreboding. They were face to face with one of the greatest of maritime dangers, the bar of the Columbia. They had heard of its terrors— what sailor had not?— but it required actual observation to show them in their true light. Here they were at the end of their voyage. For nearly seven months they had been upon the sea and had survived its calms and tempests. A sail of two hours would place them within the mouth of

[2] See p. 420 *et seq.* of the *Letters.*

the river; but to get there they must brave the greatest peril of the entire voyage. It was a situation that caused the stoutest heart to sink.

We cannot follow the good ship through all of the experiences of the next three days, which Father De Smet has given in such graphic detail. Suffice it to say that the crew misunderstood warning signals from the shore, sent a boat to sound the channel, received a favorable report, set out to cross the bar, fell into the wrong channel, were practically aground several times, but by the most extraordinary good fortune escaped disaster and made the passage in safety. Little wonder that such a providential escape, coming upon the Feast Day (July 31st), of the great founder of the Society of Jesus, should have been ascribed by his devoted followers to his watchful guardianship.

On the 2d of August Father De Smet started by canoe for Fort Vancouver to announce his arrival to Bishop Blanchet and Dr. McLoughlin. The bishop happened to be absent at the time in the Willamette valley, but was immediately sent for. After the first greetings and the delays incident upon unloading their goods from the vessel, Father De Smet and his companions, with Father Blanchet, started for the Willamette valley, where, according to the plan agreed upon with the Father General in Rome, a central mission was to be established. After some difficulty in selecting a site the work was begun. During its progress an alarming epidemic prevailed and Father De Smet was for a time dangerously ill; but nevertheless kept his hand on the wheel and guided the rising establishment through its initial stages.

With an ardent longing to get back among his Indians in the mountains, whom he had not seen for two years, Father De Smet left the Willamette on October 3d for the upper country. He first came among the Kalispels of the Bay, whom he had promised to give a mission two years before. They were accompanied by Father Adrian Hoeken. They were overjoyed at Father De Smet's return and conducted him to their camp amid volleys of musketry and every demonstration of rejoicing. Then began a general interchange of news, the Indians relating what had happened in the past two years, and Father De Smet relating his wondrous journeys by sea and land, through great cities and nations and over vast oceans. To the simple Indians he must indeed have seemed like an envoy from the Great Spirit himself.

Father De Smet now turned his attention to planting an establishment among the Kalispels of the Bay, this last word being then applied to a great bend in Clark's Fork of the Columbia river some forty miles above its mouth. To this reduction the name St. Ignatius was given. It was Father De Smet's intention to visit the Flathead mission that fall and as the season was far advanced it was necessary for him to set out at once. He stopped for a time at the new mission, the Sacred Heart, among the Cœur d'Alènes, and then continued his journey. It was the 19th of November and winter in the mountains was already so far advanced that he could not get through. After several attempts, he was compelled to return and he passed the winter among the Kalispels of the Bay.

Early in February, 1845, while the snow was yet deep on the ground, Father De Smet started for St. Mary's, thinking he could make the journey and return before the spring melting should come. In this he was successful, and he got back to the Bay just as the snow-melting had well begun. After helping start the new buildings for this establishment, he went to Fort Vancouver and the Willamette for further supplies. With eleven horses laden with implements and provisions he soon started back to the upper country, and on his way established two new stations — one at Kettle Falls and the other at Lake de Boey.

When the 31st of July, the Feast of St. Ignatius, came, and Father De Smet reviewed the past year, he could not

4

but feel gratified at the progress that had been made. He
says in one of his letters: "Last year the Feast of St.
Ignatius proved for me a day of danger, trial and uneasiness. I love to recall it to my mind, for it terminated
joyfully, and so gloriously that I know my companions
can never forget it, and they will return lasting thanks
to the Almighty for the display of his mercy. Without a
chart or any knowledge of the mouth of the Columbia,
we traversed, as if borne on angels' wings, the bar of this
formidable river. This year I passed the Feast of St.
Ignatius amidst many occupations, but they were of such
a nature as to console the missionary's heart, and repay
him a hundred fold for the trifling privations, pains and
fatigues he endures."

The Blackfeet Indians, traditional enemies of the Flatheads and other tribes among which De Smet was operat-
ing, were at this time giving a great deal of trouble, and
even menacing the continued existence of St. Mary's Mission. It seemed a necessary step to bring about some
understanding with them. Father De Smet, in his capacity of spiritual envoy extraordinary, assumed, on more
than one occasion, the power to make treaties of peace.
With an admirable common sense he reasoned that peace
could never be objectionable and no exceptions could be
taken by the Government to his efforts to bring it about
wherever it did not exist. Accordingly he now resolved
to make a personal visit to the Blackfeet and endeavor to
put some check upon their warlike operations. He traveled by the Canadian route which took him far to the
north. It would have been much easier to reach the
Blackfeet by going from the Flatheads direct to the Missouri river, and the only reason which suggests itself for
his taking the course he did was to visit new tribes with
a view of spreading his work as widely as possible. His
mind was full of his vast design of building up in this
country a mighty spiritual empire and he stopped at no
hardships to carry out his scheme. He speaks of "taking

spiritual possession of this land, which was now for the first time trodden by a minister of the Most High." It was undoubtedly this purpose that led him to take the long and circuitous route that he did.

Father De Smet was now again in his element — exploring regions new to him; jotting down the experiences of each day in order that he might send them forth to the world where they would bring new workers to his vineyard. One of his observations at this time has become historical. He had already become convinced of the presence of gold and silver in these mountains; but knowing what its discovery by the whites would mean to the Indians, he had kept his knowledge to himself. He thus refers to the matter in a letter written on this journey: "Poor unfortunate Indians! They trample on treasures unconscious of their worth, and content themselves with the fishery and chase. When these resources fail, they subsist upon roots and herbs; whilst they eye, with tranquil surprise, the white man examining the shining pebbles of their territory. Ah! they would tremble indeed could they learn the history of those numerous and ill-fated tribes that have been swept from their land, to make place for Christians who have made the poor Indians the victims of their rapacity."

His route, which is given in detail in the published itinerary of his travels, was, in general terms, up the Kootenai river to the mouth of the Vermillion river; thence across the Divide to the sources of the Saskatchewan, and thence to the Rocky Mountain House, a Hudson Bay trading post on the north fork of that stream. The course of this journey had taken him momentarily across to the lakes at the source of the Columbia. Here occurred one of those interesting *rencontres* which were so frequent in his experience. He found there a Canadian family, named Morigeau, sole occupants of this empire of rugged grandeur. Morigeau had long been without a priest and in the meanwhile a numerous family had grown up. Upon hearing that Father De Smet was coming his way he hastened home to make ready for the baptism of his wife and children. When the priest arrived, " the august sacrifice of the mass was offered and Morigeau devoutly approached the holy table. At the foot of the humble altar he received the nuptial benediction; and the mother, surrounded by her children and six little Indians, was regenerated in the holy waters of baptism."

The presence of this Canadian family in such a place, cut off from all the world, appealed to the romantic side of Father De Smet's nature and he thus unburdened himself in their regard: " The Canadian! Into what part of the desert has he not penetrated? The monarch who rules at the source of the Columbia is an honest emigrant from St. Martin in the district of Montreal, who has resided for twenty-six years in this wilderness. The skins of the rein and moose deer are the materials of which his portable palace is composed; and to use his own expressions, he ' embarks ' on horseback with his wife and seven children, and ' lands ' wherever he pleases. Here no one disputes his right, and Polk and Peel, who are now contending for the possession of his dominions, are as unknown to him as the two greatest powers of the moon. His sceptre is a beaver trap, his law a carbine; and with the one on his back, the other on his arm, he reviews his numerous furry subjects — the beaver, otter, muskrat, marten, fox, bear, wolf, sheep and white goat of the mountains, * * * some of which respect his sceptre and others submit to his law. He exacts and receives from them the tribute of flesh and skins. Encircled by so much grandeur, undisturbed proprietor of all these skyward palaces and strongholds, the very last refuge which Nature has reared to preserve alive liberty on earth — solitary lord of these majestic mountains that elevate their icy summits to the clouds,— Morigeau (our Canadian) does not forget his duty as a Christian. Each day, morning and evening, he may be seen devoutly reciting his prayers in the midst of his little family."

From Rocky Mountain House Father De Smet made a long excursion to the south in search of the Blackfeet; but winter had come, the snow obliterated the trail of the Indians, and after intense suffering he returned to Rocky Mountain House and went thence to Fort Augustus in latitude 53° 30' north, where he arrived on the last day of the year 1845.

He spent the winter at Fort Augustus, making one trip to St. Anne Mission in that vicinity. As soon as the approach of spring held out a prospect of getting back across the mountains, he left for Fort Assiniboin on the Athabasca river, traveling on a sled drawn by four dogs. He left Fort Assiniboin on the 12th of March, 1846, and went a long step farther to Fort Jasper, traveling on the ice of the river. Here he remained until the 25th of April and then set out on the hazardous journey across the mountains. With numerous delays here and there, owing to the early season, the little party made their way across the pass to the point called Boat Encampment where the Canoe river enters the Columbia. This was undoubtedly the severest test of his physical powers to which Father De Smet was ever subjected. A large part of the way he had to wade the icy waters of the streams. He lost the nails of his toes and was so much affected otherwise that he declares he would surely have succumbed but for the aid of a small band of Indians whom they encountered. It had been the opinion of the people at Fort Augustus that Father De Smet's weight was too great to permit him to make the journey, much of which would have to be upon snowshoes. But with quick resolution he set out to reduce his flesh by a rigorous fast of thirty days and was measurably successful. After he started, the scant supply of provisions gave him no opportunity to regain his weight.

The long journey that remained was made in comparative ease. He was back at Fort Colville near the end of May and went thence to Fort Vancouver and the Willamette.

The large extent of the work now established made it necessary that additional aid be sought from the States or from Europe and it was unanimously the opinion of the missionaries that Father De Smet should go. Outfitting himself with supplies for the stations in the upper country, he set out from Fort Vancouver to visit them and then to go on to the States. He arrived at St. Mary's Mission about August 10th, and left there on the 16th. As his mission of the previous winter had miscarried, so far as making peace with the Blackfeet was concerned, he resolved to try to accomplish that desirable object on his way home.

It happened that a considerable body of the Flatheads with thirty lodges of Nez Percés and, strange to say, a few lodges of Blackfeet, were at this time in the Yellowstone valley on the borders of the Crow country. The Crows were at war with both the Blackfeet and Nez Percés, and perceiving their own strength to be greater than that of the united camp, were eager to attack it. At the urgent interposition of the Flatheads they deferred action for a time. Father De Smet, when he discovered that there were both Nez Percés and Blackfeet with the Flatheads, foresaw what would probably happen should they meet the Crows, and accordingly dispatched his interpreters, Gabriel and Charles, at their utmost speed to announce his approach. This had some effect, and the Crow chiefs made a strong effort to repress the turbulent spirit of their camp. But the strain was too great to be resisted and on the following day they attacked the allied camp with great impetuosity. Anticipating the attack, the allies had fortified themselves and were able to repulse it without loss. At the opportune moment, when their enemy was in disorder, they delivered a counter-charge which completely routed them. Fourteen of their warriors were slain while the allied camp lost but one man — a Nez Percé. The Crows fled entirely out of reach and Father De Smet was unable to communicate with them, though he ardently desired to do so and heal the unfortunate rupture that had taken place.

The valiant conduct of the Flatheads made a deep impression upon the Blackfeet and paved the way for the desired peace between the two tribes. " Shortly after my arrival," says Father De Smet, " the Blackfeet came in a body to my lodge, to express in a manner truly eloquent their admiration of the Flatheads, with whom in future they desired to live on terms of the closest friendship. ' To their prayers,' said they, ' must this extraordinary victory be attributed. While the battle lasted, we saw their old men, their women and children, on their knees imploring the aid of heaven. The Flatheads did not lose a single man; one only fell, a young Nez Percé, and another was mortally wounded. But the Nez Percés did not pray. We prayed morning and evening with the Flatheads, and heard the instructions of the chiefs.' Then they begged of me in their own affecting way to take pity on them and be charitable to them. They now determined to hear the words of the Great Manitou of the whites."

The allied camp then set out in a northwesterly direction to the buffalo country in the Judith Basin and thence to Fort Lewis which was later named Fort Benton. The incidents of this trip, the jealousies of the tribes, the constant exercise of diplomacy to meet their various whims, the growing admiration of the Blackfeet for the black-gown and his religion, and finally a peace between these Indians and the Flatheads, occupy many pages in Father De Smet's letters. His plan was successful and paved the way to founding a mission among this always dreaded tribe. With this result accomplished, it was decided that Father Point should remain with the tribe and himself go on to St. Louis.

Father De Smet left Fort Lewis September 28th, traveling by skiff on the long journey of 2,200 miles. Naturally it was full of interesting incident as they passed the various posts and Indian tribes along the way and these are recorded in great detail in the letters. We shall pass them by here and note only one of unusual character, the meeting with the Mormons at Council Bluffs. Father De Smet saw much of these people. He naturally shared the popular prejudice against what seemed a spurious religion, but he sympathized with them in the persecutions which had virtually exiled them from the United States. He became well acquainted with Young and it is possible that the information he gave him may have influenced that leader in choosing Salt Lake Valley as the future home of his people. The following reference from his letter will be of interest:

" In the fall of 1846, as I drew near to the frontier of the State of Missouri, I found the advance guard of the Mormons, numbering about 10,000, camped in the territory of the Omahas, not far from the old Council Bluffs. They had just been driven out for the second time from a state of the Union. They had resolved to winter on the threshold of the great desert, and then to move onward into it to put distance between themselves and their persecutors, without even knowing at that time the goal of their long wanderings, nor the spot where they should once more build for themselves permanent dwellings. They asked me a thousand questions about the regions I had explored and the spot which I have just described to you [the basin of Great Salt Lake] pleased them greatly from the account I gave them of it. Was that what determined them? I would not dare to assert it. They are there. In the last three years Utah has changed its aspect, and from a desert has become a flourishing territory which will soon become one of the states of the Union."

Father De Smet reached the University of St. Louis December 10, 1846, three years and six months after his departure in the opposite direction.

It is worth while to consider here what Father De Smet had accomplished in the past seven years. His prodigious labors, travels, hardships and perils must be placed in the very first rank of similar exploits. In these seven years he had traveled, by the slow methods of the time, a distance equal to more than twice the circumference of the earth. He had traveled in almost every clime and by every sort of conveyance. From the burning summer of the Equator he had passed to the frozen winters of 54° 30′ north. He had traveled by sailing vessel, by river barge and by canoe; by dog sled and snow shoe; on horseback and in wagon; and many a long mile on foot. He had endured hardships that seem to us almost impossible and which undoubtedly were the foundation of the ills he later suffered. It was to the period of 1844–6 that he referred in a letter to a fellow missionary who was complaining of the hardship of his lot: " I have been for years a wanderer in the desert. I was three years without receiving a letter from any quarter. I was two years in the mountains, without tasting bread, salt, coffee, tea, sugar. I was for years without a roof, without a bed. I have been six months without a shirt on my back, and often have I passed whole days and nights without a morsel of anything to eat."

The results of his labors, from a missionary point of view, were highly successful. The whole Columbia valley had been dotted with infant establishments, some of which had taken on the promise of permanent growth. He had indeed laid the foundation well for a spiritual empire throughout that region, and but for the approach of emigration his plans would have brought forth the full fruition that he expected.

But most important of all, from a public point of view, was the fact that he had become a great power among the Indian tribes. All now knew him, many personally, the rest by reputation. He was the one white man in whom they had implicit faith. The Government was beginning to look to him for assistance. The Mormon, the Forty-niner, the Oregon emigrant came to him for information and advice. His writings were already known on two continents and his name was a familiar one, at least in the religious world.

CHAPTER VI.

THE GREAT COUNCIL OF 1851.

Trials and discouragements — Restlessness of the Plains tribes — Government decides to hold council — De Smet asked to go — Voyage of the *St. Ange* — Cholera on board — Death of Father Hoeken — Arrival at Fort Union — Departure on overland journey to Fort Laramie — Fort Alexander — Lake De Smet — The Oregon trail — Arrival at the council ground — Proceedings of the council — Return to St. Louis.

IT is a fact not easily explained that Father De Smet never again returned to his great field of missionary work, nor ever revisited those regions except twice, and both times upon other business. And yet we have his repeated statements that it was the cherished desire of his heart to spend the remainder of his days among his dear Indians, and he undoubtedly sought, as much as he could consistently with his vows, to bring about such a result. " I am like a soldier," he wrote to a friend. " When I receive orders I march whither I am sent. Yet, like a soldier, I may have my preferences, and I need not tell you that these are decidedly for the Indian country." And again: " I regret very much the plains, the Indians and the wilderness with all their privations, miseries and dangers. They were treats indeed compared with the monotony with which I am surrounded." Again, in a very feeling letter to the Father General, he implores the privilege of being sent away to some obscure mission there to spend the remainder of his days.

The " monotony " which Father De Smet complains of undoubtedly relates to the character of the duties with which he was charged during the greater part of his life as an ordained priest. He occupied almost continuously the position of procurator of the Province, an office which related exclusively to the financial affairs of the Church. His great ability in securing contributions and in managing the always difficult task of their distribution made him admirably fitted for this work. But it was personally distasteful to him. " I hold the general purse," he once wrote, " and have to supply all needs; and this purse is never full; the greater part of the time it is flat; while I receive demands from all sides." In another letter to a distant friend he wrote: " Probably we shall never again see each other on this side of the grave. I hope we shall meet in heaven where all ciphering, quibbling and account-making are at an end."

But the principal reason why Father De Smet was not permitted personally to conduct his missions was a growing feeling in Rome that he was planning on too large a scale; that the ends would not justify the means. It had been reported to the Father General by other parties, that the field of work was not at all what had been represented, and that De Smet's descriptions were poetical flights of the imagination and not true pictures of the situation.[1] Father De Smet was deeply hurt at these accusations but promptly and vigorously defended himself, to the apparent satisfaction of the Father General; for soon after sending his reply to the charges against him he speaks with great satisfaction of the certain prospect before him of spending the rest of his life among the Indians.

[1] " When you were my Superior, you frequently corrected me for being too easily dejected when things were said against me, to which I must plead guilty. Something of the kind has occurred again, and from headquarters, which has brought me low indeed — the more so as I have the full conviction in my heart that the charges against me are untrue, false and unjust, and bring along great evil in their train — the neglect, in a great measure, of the Indians, for whom I would gladly have sacrificed the remainder of my days. I stand accused of the following: 1st. That my letters have done a great deal of harm in America; 2d. That they are only imagination and poetry, false and untrue; 3d. That I have lost the mission by over-liberality to the Indians, and by promises to them which the fathers have been unable to fulfill."
Letter to Bishop Van de Velde, Baltimore.

Immediately after his return to St. Louis in 1846, he
went to New Orleans, returning in January, 1847, and later
in the year made a journey to Europe returning to America
in midsummer, 1848. He was then sent on an expedition to
the Sioux country and returned to St. Louis late in December. The years 1849 and 1850 were spent in St. Louis
except for several journeys in the capacity of Socius with
the Father Provincial to Catholic institutions in various
parts of the country.

Here again we come upon an obscure spot in Father De
Smet's life. It is apparent that he now saw before him the
long-wished-for opportunity of spending the rest of his life
among the Indians. He repeatedly refers to this fact in his
letters, but always without explanation. Just before leaving
St. Louis on the expedition of 1851, which we shall next
relate, he wrote the words already quoted: "Probably we
shall never again see each other on this side of the grave."
In another letter written at the same time he says that he
expects never to return. Upon what he based these expectations or what brought about their prompt non-fulfillment,
we do not know, except that upon the very eve of departure
he received a letter from the Father General disapproving his
plan of going among the Indians. Preparations were, however, too far advanced to be countermanded, and his superiors in St. Louis decided that he should at least attend
the Indian council which the Government had decided to
hold that summer and at which Father De Smet had promised to assist.

The great rush of emigrants to Oregon which began in
the early Forties and kept on increasing year after year; and
the immeasurable tide that swept over the plains as a result
of the discovery of gold in California, wrought a profound
change of conditions in the western country. The Indian
saw his once undisputed domain slipping steadily from his
grasp. He became restless and discontented. It was apparent that trouble might arise at any time and it became
necessary to take some measures to avoid it. To that end

it was proposed, largely at the instance of D. D. Mitchell, Superintendent of Indian Affairs at St. Louis, to hold a general council of all the Western tribes east of the Rocky Mountains and come to some understanding in view of the changed conditions. This plan was approved by the Government and the year 1851 was fixed upon. Colonel Mitchell, to whom the actual work of the council was entrusted, earnestly besought the aid of Father De Smet, and his superiors consented that he should go. Thus began the long and valuable service which Father De Smet, in the capacity of pacificator, rendered the Government of the United States during the remaining years of his life.

It was in connection with this expedition that Father De Smet, in the letters quoted, speaks of never returning again. It was his plan, after attending the council, to go on to the missions and remain there the rest of his life. With him on this expedition was Father Christian Hoeken, one of the most efficient of the early missionaries. They left St. Louis June 7, 1851, on one of the finest boats ever on the river, the *St. Ange,* commanded by the distinguished pilot, Father De Smet's fast friend, Captain Joseph La Barge. Disaster attended the first part of the voyage. Cholera had been prevalent throughout the country for several years and was particularly bad this year. The spring floods of the Missouri had been high, the bottoms much overflowed, and malarial conditions were bad. Three days after leaving port the cholera broke out on board and raged with great fatality for the next ten days. In the meanwhile Father De Smet was seized with a malarial fever which itself came near proving fatal. He had besought Father Hoeken to hear his confession, when that priest was suddenly seized with the cholera. Father De Smet, barely able to drag himself to the bedside of his companion, administered the last sacraments and the good father passed away on the 19th of June. It was a great blow to Father De Smet, for Father Hoeken was one of his most cherished friends.

As soon as the boat had gotten above the flooded district and into a dryer atmosphere it was unloaded and thoroughly aired and the rest of the voyage passed off without further sickness.

As the boat threaded its way up the winding Missouri, amid scenes of rural beauty and the luxuriance of a fertile country, Father De Smet could not but ponder upon the changes which were on the eve of taking place. He was on his way even then to assist at a council which was to offer some temporary relief to an ever troublesome problem. In his narrative of this journey he writes: "Will not the President of the Republic, like some of his predecessors, pluck some plumes from the Indian eagle, once the emblem of their greatness and power, to place them among the trophies of his administration? In the limits which I trace he will find an extent of country vast enough to be represented by three or four stars more of the first magnitude, which will enhance the lustre of the galaxy in the flag of the Union. This great territory will hold an immense population, destined to form several great and flourishing States.

"But then, what will become of the Indians, who have already come from afar to abide in this land? What will become of the aborigines, who have possessed it from time immemorial? This is indeed a thorny question, awakening gloomy ideas in the observer's mind, if he has followed the encroaching policy of the United States in regard to the Indian. We may hope that the sad remnant of these numerous nations who once covered America, now reduced to earn their bread in the sweat of their brow (for they can no longer subsist by hunting), will find an asylum, a permanent abode, and will be incorporated, with the rights of citizens, into the Union."

The *St. Ange* arrived at Fort Union on the 14th of July, and preparations were begun for the journey overland to Fort Laramie, where the great council was to be held. It was a common experience in Father De Smet's career that important events in his work occurred on the 31st of July, the feast day of the founder of the Society. So now the considerable party of Indians and white men started on their long and important journey upon that day. There were representatives from the Assiniboins, Minnetarees and Crows and the party consisted in all of thirty-two men. Their route took them across the desolate waste west of the Yellowstone river in eastern Montana to Fort Alexander, which Father De Smet had visited twice or three times before. Thence they made their way southwardly, along the eastern base of the Bighorn mountains to the Platte river near the present town of Casper, Wyoming. At this point they came upon the Oregon Trail, which was then the route of the vast emigration that was on its way to California and Oregon. It was an impressive sight, even to white men, and as to the Indians, let Father De Smet tell of its effect upon them:

"Our Indian companions, who had never seen but the narrow hunting-paths, by which they transport themselves and their lodges, were filled with admiration on seeing this noble highway, which is as smooth as a barn-floor swept by the winds, and not a blade of grass can shoot up on it on account of the continual passing. They conceived a high idea of the countless White Nation, as they express it. They fancied that all had gone over that road, and that an immense void must exist in the land of the rising sun. Their countenances testified evident incredulity when I told them that their exit was in nowise perceived in the lands of the whites. They styled the route the great medicine road of the whites. * * * They visited and examined in detail all the forsaken camping-grounds on the way; they brought a great variety of objects to me to have their use and signification explained; they filled their pouches with knives, forks, spoons, basins, coffee-pots and other cooking articles, axes, hammers, etc. With the bits of earthenware which bore any figure or inscription, they fabricated some ornament for their necks and ears. How wonderful will be the accounts given of the great medicine road by our unsophisticated Indians when they go back to their villages and sit in the midst of an admiring circle of relatives."

This great California movement was a source of deep
interest to Father De Smet. When in St. Louis not a day
passed, he tells us, that some one did not come to ask his
advice about going thither. He generally discouraged them,
or at least advised extreme deliberation in undertaking such
a step. He had witnessed so much suffering and disappointment in these migrations that he could not see an intending
emigrant depart without wishing him to give it up. And
now along the great Trail he saw for himself the true meaning of such a journey, in the relics cast away by the emigrants, in the graves of those who had perished by the way,
and in many returning parties who had found their hopes of
fortune to be only barren dreams.

After striking the Oregon Trail the party marched eastward to Fort Laramie, where they found that the council
was to be held in the valley of Horse Creek still thirty miles
farther on. The next day this additional journey was made
and the whole party, with the several representatives of the
Government and some ten thousand Indians, were gathered
together in the plain. The council with its attendant incidents lasted from the 12th to the 23d of September, and
was terminated to the satisfaction of all concerned. Great
harmony prevailed. All features of the troublesome situation were discussed and earnest effort was made to reach
some good result. The principal men among the whites
were D. D. Mitchell, Robert Campbell, Thomas Fitzpatrick
and Father De Smet, although the latter had no official
powers. The treaties formed with the various tribes recognized the right of the whites to cross their lands with roads,
etc.; recompensed the Indians for losses sustained, and provided payments for losses in the future. On the 20th of
September an immense quantity of goods arrived for distribution as presents to the Indians and gave them great
satisfaction.

Father De Smet attended the council from beginning
to end. He used his great influence with the tribes to
promote a satisfactory understanding and he labored in-

cessantly for their spiritual and temporal welfare. His dignified and unselfish bearing won their hearts and his presence was a power among them.

The council broke up September 24th and the members of the commission started for the east. Father De Smet turned off from the main road on his way and visited the Mission of St. Mary's, in Kansas. He reached St. Louis on the 21st of October.

Upon his return home he found that his dear friend, Father Provincial Elet, had died. These two losses, Father Hoeken and Father Elet, were a great sorrow to him and, added to the failure of his plan of going among the Indians, made the year 1851 one of gloom to the good missionary. Only a year later we find him ready to return to his native land to remain there, for it doubtless seemed to him that his long-cherished hopes were doomed to disappointment. There seems to have been some plan on foot to this end emanating from his superiors. He thus refers to it: "In so far as this plan regards me, I will speak openly to you. I have nothing whatever to do with their choice, nor with the adoption of the plan. I affirm, nevertheless, that I am ready to execute in all things the will of my superiors. I will even admit to you, that in my secret soul, and after mature reflection and much prayer, I desire that the plan should be accomplished, and for the sole reason that I would be glad to be able to spend the few years that remain to me, should the Lord grant me any, in the strict observance and practice of all our holy rules and in perfect submission to the orders of my superiors. I feel the need of it, after having passed so many years in these remote American missions."

But this plan, like the other, was never realized and Father De Smet continued to labor in his accustomed field. The subsequent events of his life show that, whatever his own regrets or disappointments, his adopted country was the gainer by the action of his superiors.

CHAPTER VII.

THE UTAH AND OREGON EXPEDITIONS.

Visit to Europe in 1853 — Shipwreck of the *Humboldt*— Voyage to Europe in 1856 — The Mormon rebellion — Military expedition under Harney — De Smet accompanies as chaplain — Peace with the Mormons — Expedition interrupted — Yakima war in Oregon — Harney sent thither — De Smet goes with him — Voyage via Panama — Pacification of the Oregon Indians — Departure for home — Arrival at Fort Benton — Voyage by skiff to Omaha — Thence by steamer to St. Louis.

THE year 1852 was spent by Father De Smet in his regular duties as procurator of the Province. In the spring of 1853 he started on another trip to Europe accompanied by the Right Reverend Bishop Miege, Vicar Apostolic of the Indian Territory east of the Rocky Mountains. While passing through Washington they were presented to President Pierce by Colonel Thos. H. Benton and Father De Smet was made bearer of dispatches to several European powers. They sailed May 9th on the steamer *Fulton* and crossed in eleven days — a great contrast with the voyage of 1821, when it took forty days under sail to bring De Smet to America.

Father De Smet accompanied Bishop Miege only as far as Paris. While there an incident occurred that shows the humorous nature of the great missionary and also his fertility of resources in popularizing his work in America. He delivered an address upon his missions to the student fathers at the Sorbonne, and to make it more effective, decked out one of them in Indian paraphernalia that he had brought with him.

Father De Smet embarked on his return to America November 23d of the same year on the steamer *Humboldt*. The voyage was rough and slow and the steamer had to put into

Halifax for coal. Through the incompetence of the pilot the vessel was wrecked and lost but the crew and passengers were saved. After a short delay the passengers were taken on the steamer *Niagara* and carried to Boston. Father De Smet was back in St. Louis the day after Christmas.

The years 1854-5 and most of 1856 were spent in St. Louis, except for the journeys made as Socius with the Father Provincial to the various Catholic establishments in the Mississippi valley. In the year 1855 Father De Smet took the last important vows pertaining to membership of the Society of Jesus and one which is never permitted to members before they reach the age of forty-five. Father De Smet thus refers to this event: " On Assumption Day I took my last vows. Remember me in your holy sacrifices and prayers that I may remain faithful to my holy engagements."

In September, 1856, Father De Smet sailed again by the steamer *Fulton* for Europe, and after an extensive tour of the cities of Europe, re-embarked in April, 1857, on the *Leopold* for New York. This visit to Europe was a most unwelcome one to the much traveled priest. " The journey comes wonderfully hard on me on the present occasion," he writes. " I find consolation only that it is undertaken by obedience." Reluctant as he was to go, he was even more rejoiced to get back. " I embraced the floor of my room on entering it," he wrote, " and from my inmost heart thanked the Lord."

In December, 1857, Father Duerinck was drowned near Independence, Mo. He was descending the Missouri in an open boat with six men. The boat was wrecked on a snag. Duerinck was a close friend of Father De Smet, his aunt having been the first wife of De Smet's father. The occurrence completely prostrated Father De Smet.

Father De Smet had not at this time been to the Indian country for six years; but in 1858 a call came from quite an unexpected quarter. The Mormon Rebellion of

1857-8 was in progress. As is well known, the Mormons had migrated to the Salt Lake valley when that country was still a possession of Mexico. But the war with Mexico transferred it to the United States, and as it increased in population the responsibilities of territorial government followed. Brigham Young and his people opposed all Federal interference; indeed the Government was not at first disposed to trouble them; and to make such interference as was necessary as light as possible, Brigham Young was himself made first governor of the territory. The movement of people along the California trail had brought to the States the first real knowledge of the condition of things in Utah, and a feeling of prejudice against the Mormons gradually assumed formidable proportions. In 1857 the incoming administration at Washington appointed a new governor, Alfred Cummings, to succeed Young. The ex-governor and his people rebelled and decided that the change should not take place; and to make good their threat they prepared for active resistance.

It therefore became necessary to send a military force to protect the governor and other new officers in the discharge of their duties, and Albert Sidney Johnston was sent in command of the expedition. The Mormons at first got the better of the federal troops; destroyed large quantities of their supplies, and so crippled the usefulness of Fort Bridger as a base that the expedition was threatened with starvation when the winter of 1857-8 approached. Thereupon the Government assumed both a commanding and conciliatory tone. It organized a new military expedition, and it sent commissioners offering amnesty to such of the Mormons as ceased their resistance. These measures resulted in peace before the second military expedition reached the territory. General Johnston and Governor Cummings entered the Mormon capital in June and the authority of the governor was recognized by the people. The second military expedition was stopped at the ford of the South Platte river and turned back.

The commander of this second expedition was General William S. Harney. He asked to have Father De Smet accompany the expedition as chaplain and the Government approved his request. The Church authorities at St. Louis thought well of the project and so Father De Smet accepted the place at $1,200 per year and his expenses.[1] His letters inform us that he was contemplating a trip among the Missouri and Flathead Indians this year, and thought he could combine it with his official duties.

Father De Smet left St. Louis May 20, 1858, to join the command at Fort Leavenworth. It was seven years since he had crossed the plains and the progress which settlement had made in the meantime impressed him deeply. "No further back," he writes, "than 1851, at the time of my return from the great council held on the borders of the Platte, the plains of Kansas were almost entirely without inhabitants, containing only a few scattered villages of Indians, living for the most part by the chase, by fishing and on wild fruits and roots. But eight years have made an entire change: many towns and villages have sprung up, as it were, by enchantment; forges and mills of every kind are already numerous; extensive and beautiful farms have been established in all directions with extraordinary rapidity and industry."

Father De Smet records some interesting facts regarding the expedition. The magnitude of the supply trains excited his astonishment, as some of their idiosyncrasies provoked his laughter. "The most remarkable thing that I met * * * ," he says, "were the long wagon trains engaged in transporting to Utah provisions and stores of war. If the journals of the day may be believed, these cost the Government fifteen millions. Each train consisted of twenty-six wagons, each wagon drawn by six yoke of oxen, and containing near five thousand pounds.

[1] For a full statement of his account, see page 775.

The Quartermaster-General made the calculation and told me that the whole train would make a line of about fifty miles. We passed every day some wagons of this immense train. Each wagon is marked with a name, as in the case of ships, and these names serve to furnish amusement to the passer-by, the caprices of the captains in this respect having imposed upon the wagons such names as the *Constitution,* the *President,* the *Great Republic,* the *King of Bavaria, Lola Montes, Louis Napoleon, Dan O'Connell, Old Kentuck,* etc., etc. These names were daubed in great letters on each side of the carriage. On the plains, the wagoner assumes the style of ' captain,' being placed in command of his wagon and twelve oxen. The master-wagoner is admiral of this little land-fleet; he has control of twenty-six captains and 312 oxen. At a distance, the white awnings of the wagons have the effect of a fleet of vessels with all canvas spread."

The expedition made its way safely and prosperously as far as the ford of the South Platte, when its further progress was stopped by the events already related. Father De Smet returned to Leavenworth with General Harney and then went on to St. Louis with the intention of resigning his commission; but his plan was frustrated by other events occurring in the far distant Oregon which was the familiar field of his labors in years gone by. Following is his own account of the event that changed his plan: " Upon my arrival in St. Louis in the early part of September, 1858, I tendered to the Secretary of War my resignation of the post of Chaplain to the Army of Utah. It was not, however, accepted, because of fresh difficulties that had arisen with the Indian tribes west of the Rocky Mountains. The papers announced that a powerful coalition of Indians had been formed, and that Colonel Steptoe had been attacked, and two officers, a sergeant and several soldiers of his company killed in the first engagement. A general rising was feared of all the tribes in that section — the Palooses, Yakimas, Skoyelpi, Okinagans, Spokans,

Cœur d'Alénes, Kalispels, Kootenais and Flatheads. All these Indians, hitherto quiet and peaceable (especially the four tribes last named) had of late become more or less disturbed and irritated, chiefly through the incursions of white emigrants into the Indian lands on the southwest of the territories of Oregon and Washington, where, without the least ceremony and without any preliminary arrangement or agreement, they had taken possession of the most fertile lands and the most advantageous sites.

" The mountain Indians, especially, had become alarmed and had resolved to oppose the entry of the whites and their further advance into the land. The Indian force that was on foot consisted of 800 to 1,000 warriors. They had just won a victory: the hasty retreat of the brave Colonel Steptoe, who was hardly expecting an attack from the savages and had only 120 soldiers, appeared to them a flight. He had even abandoned to them all his train and provisions. Swollen with pride and presumption, the Indians thenceforth believed themselves invincible and capable of resisting and withstanding the whole United States Army. Accordingly they issued their defiance of the whites. The Government at any rate thought their opposition quite a serious matter, and decided to send out General Harney, who had covered himself with laurels on various occasions in Indian warfare in Florida, Texas, Mexico and the plains of the Missouri.

" I was once more invited by the Secretary of War, at General Harney's special request, to accompany him in his distant expedition. With the approval of my superiors, I consented to keep my post of army chaplain, with the hope especially that I might be able to be of some use to the mountain tribes of Indians, and be among my brethren in the difficulties which the war would bring upon them."[2]

---

[2] This outbreak is what is known in Oregon history as the Yakima War. It was induced, like nearly all our Indian wars, by the encroachment of white settlers on the Indian lands.

Father De Smet went to Oregon by way of Panama, sailing from New York September 20, 1858. He crossed the Isthmus on the 29th, stopped at San Francisco October 16th, and arrived at Vancouver October 28th. As in the case of the Utah expedition, the actual campaign was over before General Harney arrived on the ground. "The task, however, remained," says De Smet, "of removing the prejudices of the Indians, soothing their inquietude and alarm, and correcting, or rather refuting, the false rumors that are generally spread about after a war, and which otherwise might be the cause of its renewal."

For the accomplishment of a task like this, there was no other individual so well equipped as Father De Smet. It was decided that he should visit the upper tribes among whom his name was held in affectionate reverence, and use his efforts toward bringing about a general pacification. He left Fort Vancouver the next day after his arrival. He passed the winter at the Sacred Heart Mission among the Cœur d'Alènes and on the 18th of February, 1859, set out for the Flathead country. He visited the site of the abandoned mission in the Bitter Root valley, the scene of his first labors, and also the new mission of St. Ignatius in its beautiful and permanent home in Mission valley near the Great Flathead lake.

On the 16th of April, pursuant to orders from General Harney, he left St. Ignatius with the chiefs of the various mountain tribes, to take them to Fort Vancouver, where they could confer with the Government officers. They reached their destination on the 18th of May and the council took place on the following day. The result of the interview was all that had been desired. The Indians were then given about three weeks to visit the interesting points in the territory in the hope that an acquaintance with the number and power of the whites would be a wholesome restraint upon further outbreaks. This affair wound up in a manner so thoroughly characteristic of the Indian nature, that we give an account of it as told by Father De Smet:

"The visit which appeared the most to interest the chiefs was that which they made to the prison at Portland and its wretched inmates, whom they found chained within its cells. They were particularly interested in the causes, motives, and duration of their imprisonments. Chief Alexander kept it in his mind. Immediately on his return to his camp at St. Ignatius Mission, he assembled his people, and related to them all the wonders of the whites, and especially the history of the prison. 'We,' said he, 'have neither chains nor prisons; and for want of them, no doubt, a great number of us are wicked and have deaf ears. As chief, I am determined to do my duty; I shall take a whip to punish the wicked; let all those who have been guilty of any misdemeanor present themselves; I am ready.' The known guilty parties were called upon by name, many presented themselves of their own accord, and all received a proportionate correction. The whole affair terminated in a general rejoicing and feast."

Feeling that he could be of no further service on the expedition, the objects of which were now accomplished, Father De Smet asked permission to return to the States by way of the mountain missions and the Missouri river. The official correspondence which is given in the *Letters,* evinces the most affectionate esteem on the part of the military authorities for Father De Smet personally, and a high estimation of his official services. It is particularly noteworthy that Captain Alfred Pleasanton, who later won for himself such an eminent place in the history of his country, formed the most tender attachment for the venerable missionary and a profound admiration for his teaching.

Father De Smet left Fort Vancouver on the 15th of June, halted three days at the Sacred Heart Mission, and arrived at St. Ignatius on the 16th of July. He left this mission a week later by way of the Mullan road and reached Fort Benton on the Missouri on the 29th, visiting the Great Falls on the way. The last time he had been at Benton was in 1846, while the post still bore the name of Fort Lewis. It had been his intention on leaving General Harney to travel all the way to St. Louis on horseback, but his animals gave out and he decided to go on by skiff. After full conferences with the resident missionaries, he left the fort August 5th with a skiff and oarsman furnished him by the fur company. He made the trip in entire safety to Omaha, where he found a steamer, and in that way made the rest of the journey to St. Louis, arriving there September 23d.

It is not an easy thing in this day to appreciate what a journey like that meant — traveling day after day in a frail skiff on the waters of a turbulent and treacherous stream, amid scenes of utter wildness, without the sight of a white man's house except occasional trading posts, and all the way in a land of savage tribes. Father De Smet has left a record of this journey which is worth reading. He says of the manner in which they lived: " During this long trip on the river we passed the nights in the open air, or under a little tent, often on sandbars to avoid the troublesome mosquitoes, or on the skirts of a plain, or in an untrodden forest. We often heard the howlings of the wolves, and the grunting of the grizzly bear disturbed our sleep, but without alarming us. In the desert one perceives that God has implanted in the breast of these wild beasts the fear of man. In the desert also we are enabled in a particular way to admire and to thank the divine providence which watches with so much solicitude over his children. There is admirably verified the text of St. Matthew: ' Consider the birds of the air, they sow not, but your Heavenly Father feeds them; are ye not of much more value than they? '[3] During the whole route, our

[3] This and other scriptural quotations given by Father De Smet are not from the King James version.

wants were constantly supplied; yes, we lived in the midst of the greatest abundance. The rivers furnished us excellent fish, water-fowl, ducks, geese and swans; the forest and plains gave us fruits and roots. We never wanted for game; we found everywhere either immense herds of buffalo, of deer, antelope, mountain sheep and bighorn, or pheasants, wild turkeys and partridges."

Some idea of the strenuous zeal of the good missionary in carrying on the work of his calling may be inferred from the fact that on this journey he baptized about 900 Indian children. Along the Missouri he met many tribes, always stopping a day or two to give them religious instruction. They invariably showed him the greatest respect and affection and listened to his words with the utmost attention.

CHAPTER VIII.

JOURNEYINGS AT HOME AND ABROAD.
1860–1866.

Visits Europe in 1860 — Return, 1861 — Outbreak of the Rebellion — Business journeys to Washington — Voyage to Fort Benton in 1862 — The Sioux outbreak — Minnesota massacre — Campaigns of Sibley and Sully — Voyage to Fort Benton, 1863 — Stopped by low water at Milk River — Rest of journey by land — Danger of return by river — Decides to return via Panama — Incidents of journey — The situation in the Sioux country — Peace mission to Sioux in 1864 — Unsuccessful and why — Visits Europe — Voyage to Fort Benton in 1866.

FATHER DE SMET remained in St. Louis, except for some short side trips, until September, 1860, when he set out for Europe. He confined his travels on the continent to France, Belgium and Holland, and on the 2d of April, 1861, embarked for his return voyage. It was with many forebodings that he neared the shores of his adopted land, for it had become known to him before sailing that the " standard of rebellion had been raised by the South." He arrived in New York on April 15th only to find his worst fears confirmed. "A few hours before our arrival," he writes, " the great American metropolis had been thrown into the wildest excitement and consternation by the tidings that Fort Sumter in South Carolina had been taken by the Rebels, and that the Stars and Stripes, the far-and-wide honored flag of the great Republic, had been battered down by the enemies of the Union — once Union men themselves — reduced to mere shreds, a rag! Unpardonable outrage! — one which I fear will be avenged in a deluge of blood. On hearing the sad news of the insulting and arrogant deed, tears flowed freely from many an eye among the passengers of the *Fulton,* and were followed by loud imprecations and threats against the Secessionists. I am not a man for war and am averse to its horrors and bloodshed; but I was deeply moved at the scenes I witnessed on the day of my landing on the shores of my once happy and beloved adopted country. I prayed and prayed most earnestly, that the Lord in his mercy might allay and soften the rising passions, and that peace might again be restored in this now distracted land."

Father De Smet went directly to St. Louis and he notes that " on the long stretch of over a thousand miles nothing was heard but the clang of arms and the war cry repeated in every city, town, and hamlet; while from every house and spire, and on every mountain top and hill, and in every breeze, waved the insulted Stars and Stripes."

Father De Smet was a loyal citizen, a Union man; but he was not what he later calls a radical. His views were doubtless modified by the atmosphere of St. Louis, which was his home, and he saw more clearly the other side of the question than people of the North generally did. His prayers were for peace, but as between the North and South his sympathies were with the North. At one time he frankly doubted that the North would succeed, for he felt that so great a section of people of the Anglo-Saxon race could not be subdued. As the war progressed and the power of the North became more autocratic, he dissented from some of its extreme measures; but there was never a shadow of doubt of his unswerving loyalty to the Government.

A matter growing out of the war that gave the Jesuits considerable trouble was the draft, which made no exception in favor of the clerical profession. The Jesuits were few in number, and in addition to their priestly duties nearly all of them were teachers in institutions of learning. The Society was poor and had no funds to hire substitutes for their priests either in the field or in the schools. Besides this, they were on principle opposed to war, so that on the whole the situation was a trying one. Father De Smet went to Washington, saw President Lincoln and others, and obtained such a degree of exemption as it was possible to give under the rigid terms of the law. Later in the war two fathers were drafted and Father De Smet was compelled again to intercede. The authorities had no power to exempt them directly, but they were told to remain at their work and they would not be ordered to the front.

Father De Smet made a journey to Washington in the fall of 1861 and was there at the time of the disastrous battle of Bull Run. In the spring of 1862 he went again and made a third trip in the fall of that year. On this last journey he records that he " heard the roar of the cannon in the battle of Antietam."

In the *Letters* are some interesting notes upon the second of the above journeys, in which the modest priest is seen visiting the chief magistrate of the nation, dining with the ministers of foreign nations, and displaying a naive skill at diplomacy with the departments of the Government. They can best be told in his own words : " Towards the end of last February I had to go to Washington to arrange the accounts of our Indian Missions among the Potawatomies and Osages. Since the outbreak of the war and the great expenditures which it occasions, the Government is necessarily delayed in the payment of its contracts with the Indian tribes, the motto for to-day being ' the expenses of the war before everything else.' A sum of over eighteen thousand dollars was due the missions. I presented my request to the Superintendent of Indian Affairs, with the remark that a refusal or delay on the part of the Government of its debt and promise would singularly disarrange the ideas of our Indians, who have thus far been loyal and attached to the Union side; that if we were obliged by lack of means to send some 400 children back to their poor parents, they would conclude ' that their Great Father, President Lincoln, had taken the money that ought to have gone to the support of their children and used it for other purposes,' and that they might be led in consequence to lend a

favorable ear to the Secessionists. This all but *casus belli*
made the Superintendent smile and pleased him greatly,
and he promised to do his utmost to satisfy our good
savages."

In another letter he writes: " In Washington I had the
honor of being presented to our President, Lincoln, and I
talked with him for over an hour. Mr. Blondeel, the Belgian
Ambassador, showed me a great deal of attention; he is
very well disposed toward us. He obliged me to dine with
him, together with the ambassadors of France, Russia and
Spain. They all had their *grands cordons,* and I had a
frock-coat well worn and with two buttons gone. However,
it all went off very agreeably. I did the best I could among
these great personages; but I remain of the opinion that I
shall always be more at my ease sitting on the grass and
surrounded with savages, each one making his jokes and at
the same time eating with good appetite a bear rib, or roasting a piece of buffalo or fat dog."

In the summer of 1862 Father De Smet made the long
journey to Fort Benton and back. He traveled on the
American Fur Company steamer *Spread Eagle.* His purpose was to revisit the tribes, baptize their children, study
the prospects of new missions and carry supplies of various
kinds to the mountain missions. While at Fort Benton he
made one of a party to visit the Great Falls of the Missouri.
On his way back to St. Louis he left the boat at Fort Leavenworth and made a side trip to St. Mary's Mission, Kansas.

Father De Smet was deeply grieved and alarmed at the
state of things as he found it among the tribes of the Missouri, particularly the Sioux nations. He had never before
seen them so hostile and it was evident that they were on
the eve of an outbreak against the whites. In fact he had
scarcely returned to his home in St. Louis when the storm
burst. The historic Minnesota Massacre took place August
18-21, 1862, and a brief sketch of its rise and progress for
two or three years is necessary to a full understanding of
the subsequent course of events.

The massacre was an outburst of Indian rage and vengeance over the wrongs they had suffered at the hands of the whites and the evident fate that awaited them with the progress of settlement. The opportunity came with the American Civil War, which the Indians were led to believe had so crippled the Government that it could not make effective resistance. The Indians were unquestionably encouraged and abetted by British influence through the Canadian half-breeds who circulated freely south of the border. In the three days that the massacre lasted, nearly one thousand lives and two million dollars' worth of property were destroyed.

The Government instantly took the matter in hand and placed a military force in the field under General H. H. Sibley. The Indians were beaten in several battles in the fall of 1862, a large number of hostiles were captured, and thirty-eight of their number were hung, December 26, 1862.[1]

In 1863 a joint campaign under Generals Sibley and Sully was planned by General Pope, Commander of the Department. General Sibley was to proceed west to the Missouri, driving the Indians before him, and General Sully was to go up the Missouri and intercept them, forming a junction with Sibley. General Sibley defeated the Indians in three battles and reached the Missouri July 29th. Sully had failed to connect, but about a month later his own force met the Indians at Whitestone Hill and again defeated them. Still unsubdued the Indians kept up hostilities and in 1864 a very large force under General Sully was sent against them. The Indians were badly defeated in the battle of Kill Deer Mountain July 28th.

The severe chastisement which they had now received, and the final victory of the Government in the Civil War soon after, led to temporary peace with the Indians; but

[1] For Father De Smet's appeal to the Government in behalf of these Indians, see page 1510 of the *Letters*.

their hatred of the whites was not quenched and they remained hostile in spirit, if not in actual deed, until their final subjugation some twelve years later.

Such was the situation along the Missouri river from 1862 for several years. It greatly interfered with Father De Smet's plans. It was his intention to commence a mission among the Sioux in 1863, but he was compelled to abandon the attempt for the time, and content himself with a voyage to Fort Benton in the interest of the mountain missions. He left St. Louis May 9, 1863, with two Italian Brothers, on the American Fur Company steamer *Nellie Rogers*. The journey passed off without mishap of any kind until they reached the mouth of Milk river, where the water was found too low for the boat to proceed farther. The entire load of freight and all the passengers had to go ashore and await some means of getting to Fort Benton by land.

While encamped on the banks of the river for several weeks awaiting transportation from Fort Benton, Father De Smet worked assiduously among the Indians, principally the Crows and Grosventres of the Prairies. He had a large tent, given him by General Harney, which he used as a chapel, and in it he conducted religious exercises, just as he did on the boats on which he traveled. One day the camp was attacked by a war party of 600 Sioux and they were saved from what might have been a massacre by the courageous action of Father De Smet in going out alone to meet the Indians. They recognized him, received him in the utmost friendliness, and after an interview and some present-making withdrew without further hostile occurrence.

Before the *Nellie Rogers* turned back, a deplorable incident occurred, the details of which are very obscure. Father De Smet, who was certainly cognizant of the facts, makes no mention of it. It was the killing of Owen McKenzie by Malcom Clark. McKenzie, half-breed son of the distinguished trader, Kenneth McKenzie, was at this time in charge of Fort Galpin near by. Clark, a passenger on the

6

boat, was a noted character in the upper country and considered something of a desperado. He and McKenzie had
a standing grudge between them relating to some former
accounts. McKenzie was a great drinker and visited the
Nellie Rogers in an intoxicated condition. Accounts differ
as to what happened in detail, but the main fact is that Clark
shot McKenzie in the cabin, killing him instantly. Whether
he had sufficient provocation for his act, may never be
known, unless some surviving witness of the tragedy, if
there be any, shall tell the story; but tradition has handed
down the act as a cold-blooded murder.

The deed came near resulting in more serious consequences than the loss of the victim's life. McKenzie, besides being a half-breed, was married among the Indians
and was personally popular with them and with the white
population of that country. A band of Indians were encamped near by and when they heard of McKenzie's murder,
they were desperately wrought up over it and vowed summary vengeance. Father De Smet, it is said, interfered and
prevented trouble and Clark was promptly hustled out of
the way.[2]

After a time the ox trains came down from Fort Benton
to transport the cargo the rest of the way. It was a long
tedious journey of 350 miles, over parched plains, and in
the heat of summer; but it was accomplished in safety.
Father De Smet here met Father Imoda from St. Peter's on
Sun river and turned over to him the articles destined for
his mission, and the recruits whom he had brought with
him.

" I had thus far fulfilled the wishes of my superiors,"
writes Father De Smet. " I had brought the two Italian
Brothers to the first Rocky Mountain mission. My own
principal object was a missionary visit to the wandering
tribes of the plains. This I had accomplished only in part.

[2] There is a tradition that Father De Smet married Clark to his
second wife.

When I left St. Louis, I had intended to see a very large number of Indians during the summer and fall, but local conditions and the dangers of the cruel Sioux war had absolutely blocked my plan. The contagion of war had spread to the upper tribes of the Sioux, who had hitherto been at peace with the whites. The reports that reached us every day of robberies and massacres committed by the Indians of the plains, on the one hand, and on the Salt Lake route by marauders and murderers of another species, the off-scourings of civilization, living by robbery and assassination on the unhappy travelers whom they meet, caused me to take the resolution of returning to St. Louis by the Pacific Ocean."

Father De Smet might have added that no steamboat succeeded in reaching Benton that year and that he would have had to make all the way back in an open boat, which would have been practically equivalent to suicide. He left Fort Benton for St. Ignatius Mission on the 25th of August. This proved to be his last visit to the mountains. At St. Ignatius he found missionary affairs prospering, but he noted with great apprehension the vast changes then sweeping over the country as a result of the discovery of gold in Montana. He thus refers to this important matter: " It is impossible to overestimate the dangers which, just at this time, are threatening all the mountain tribes, through the approach of the whites, the ease with which liquor, so fatal to the Indians, can be obtained, and the accompaniment of all the vices and excesses of our modern civilization; especially as understood and practiced by our American pioneers. These things must be seen to be appreciated and believed."

But if Father De Smet saw much to fear for his Indians, he also saw much to hope in the new field opening up in this region. Where there used to be one savage he saw that there would soon be a hundred settlers, and the Church began at once to establish missions in the little mining towns, thus laying the real foundation of its present prosperous condition in Montana. With an affectionate pleasure, born of the memory of former years, Father De Smet found Father Ravalli, one of the noblest men that ever labored in the ranks of the Church in Montana, rebuilding the long neglected mission in St. Mary's valley.

Father De Smet left St. Ignatius on the 8th of September; reached the mission of the Sacred Heart on the 18th and Fort Vancouver on the 8th of October. After a brief delay here, he sailed from Portland, October 13th, stopped at Victoria, Vancouver Island, and reached San Francisco on the 21st. There were no incidents of especial importance on the rest of the journey. He left San Francisco on the 3d of November, crossed the Isthmus on the 18th and reached New York on Thanksgiving Day. He called at Washington on his way west and finally reached St. Louis on the 1st of December. " The day following," he writes, " I offered the holy sacrifice of the altar, as a thanksgiving service for all the benefits received from heaven in my long, painful and dangerous tour, upon rivers and seas and in diverse lands, through numerous bands of hostile Indians, in the mountainous portions of Idaho infested by white marauders and assassins of the lowest and vilest sort, and on the two great oceans, the Pacific and Atlantic, ranged at present by hostile ships of the American Confederacy." [3]

The terrible state of things in the Sioux country at this time gave the Government a good deal of uneasiness. It was unfortunate that just as the great strain of the Rebellion was taxing its energies to the utmost, it should find the most powerful confederacy of Indians on the continent in bitter hostility against it. When Father De Smet passed through Washington on his way home in December the Secretary of Interior and Commissioner of Indian Affairs besought him to try again to see the Sioux and induce them to come to terms. It was a difficult role which he was asked to fill. His mission had always been one of peace. On the banner

[3] In all these recent extensive travels and those yet remaining, it should be kept in mind that Father De Smet was getting to be an old man. He was now sixty-three years of age.

which he carried were only the mild emblems of Christianity. No weapons of slaughter ever accompanied him to the wigwams of the Indians. Now he was asked to accompany a military expedition to be sent against them. While it was the chief desire of his heart to stop the war, he felt that he would be compromising his entire influence among the Indians if he went to them in company with armed soldiers, or under the flag which they looked upon as the symbol of ruin to their people. His final decision in the matter is thus stated in his own words: " I have been requested, by the Commissioner of Indian Affairs in Washington, ' to undertake the journey and to bring about, if possible, a peace among the hostile Sioux, acting in concert with the commander of the troops and the appointed agents.' They offer to pay all my expenses, with a handsome remuneration for myself. Not being well as yet, I have not accepted their request. I fear I would lose all caste among the Indians. They have hitherto looked upon me as the bearer to them of the word of the Great Spirit and have universally been kind and attentive wherever I have met them. Should I present myself in their midst as the bearer of the word of the Big Chief of the Big Knives in Washington, no longer their Great Father but now their greatest enemy, it would place me in rather an awkward situation.[4] I have written to the Commissioner that if I can go, I will go on my own hook, without pay or remuneration; visit the friendly Sioux first, and in their company try to penetrate among their fighting brethren and do my utmost to preach peace and good will to them, and to make them come to a good understanding with the general in command and the agents of Government."

[4] In another letter Father De Smet wrote: " My reception would be very different if I presented myself in company with the General of the American army and the agents of the Government. Surely my black robe would then cease to be a passport for me into the Indian country. I tried to make the Commissioner of Indian Affairs see this."

In accordance with this resolution Father De Smet left St. Louis April 20th, going as far as Fort Berthold. He remained in that neighborhood nearly all summer, visiting several Sioux bands but spending most of his time among the Mandans, Aricaras and Minnetarees. At Fort Berthold he did a very brave and gallant thing. A large war party of Sioux appeared on the opposite bank. He crossed to meet them, contrary to the advice of every one in the post. He was well received and found that they had come there for the express purpose of seeing him. He remained with them for nearly three hours. The chiefs received with ready ear the message he brought from the Government and the conference was entirely satisfactory.

While at Berthold Father De Smet learned that the Santee Sioux, who were mainly instrumental in the Minnesota massacre, and who were then hovering on the British frontier, would like to see him and hear what the Government had to say to them. De Smet thought he ought to go, but before doing so felt that he must consult General Sully, who was coming up the river with a strong military force. He descended the river to meet him and told him what he proposed; but the General thought that it was his duty to deliver a blow to these Indians that they would remember, and that it was best to talk peace only after they had been punished for what they had done. " In consequence of the General's declaration and the circumstances of the case, my errand of peace, though sanctioned by the Government, became bootless and could only serve to place me in a false position — that of being face to face with the Indians without being able to do them the least service. So I took the resolution of returning to St. Louis." He arrived there in the latter part of August and a few days later set out for Washington to report the result of his labors.

A week after his return from Washington he left St. Louis for Europe and reached Liverpool late in October. He spent a little time in England, then crossed to Belgium and soon after went to Rome, where he was received with great consideration by Pope Gregory XVI. He returned to Belgium in December and spent the first part of the year 1865 in visiting the principal cities of that country and of Holland, England and Ireland. He sailed from Liverpool June 7th and was back in St. Louis on the last day of that month. He spent the rest of that year in St. Louis.[5] In the year 1866 Father De Smet made his last trip to Fort Benton. It was an interesting and profitable voyage and is told in great detail in the *Letters*. In particular, he prepared, at the request of a friend, descriptions of the Missouri river, the steamboats that plied it in his day, and the dangers and perils of its navigation, which are undoubtedly the most complete that have come down to us. Father De Smet left St. Louis April 9th. At Fort Sully he met many

[5] Soon after Father De Smet sailed from Europe on this occasion he was made Chevalier of the Order of Leopold by the Belgian king. Following is a record of the event in the official journal, *Le Moniteur Belge*, of June 24, 1865:

(1) Ministères de la Justice et des Affaires Etrangères.
Ordre de Léopold.— Nomination.

LEOPOLD, Roi des Belges,
A tous présents et à venir, SALUT.

Voulant donner au Révérend Père De Smet (P.-J.), missionnaire dans l'Amérique du Nord, un témoignage de Notre bienveillance;

Sur la proposition de Nos Ministres de la Justice et des Affaires Etrangères,

Nous avons arrêté et arrêtons:

Art. Ier. Le Révérend Père De Smet (P.-J.) est nommé chevalier de l'Ordre de Léopold.

Il portera la décoration civile.

Art. 2. Il prendra rang dans l'Ordre à dater de ce jour.

Art. 3. Notre Ministre des affaires étrangères, ayant l'administration de l'Ordre, est chargé de l'exécution du présent arrêté.

Donné à Laeken, le 18 juin 1865.
LEOPOLD.

Par le Roi.
Le Ministre de la Justice,
VICTOR TESCH.
Le Ministre des Affaires Etrangères.
Ch. ROGIER.

of the Sioux bands and they laid before him, as was their custom, all their wrongs and sufferings. They were still in a hostile mood and the boat had been thoroughly barricaded and put in fighting trim while passing through their country.

Father De Smet reached Fort Benton June 7, 1866, after a prosperous voyage in which he had satisfactory interviews with all the river tribes. There is little information covering the return trip. He was back in St. Louis by the middle of July and remained there the rest of the year.

CHAPTER IX.

PEACE COMMISSIONS OF 1867 AND 1868.

Critical situation in Indian country — Father De Smet, 1867, goes on peace mission to the Sioux — Incidents of the journey — Success of the mission — On way back meets Peace Commission — Invited to accompany them — Illness prevents — Mission of 1868 — Journey to Cheyenne — Father De Smet goes to Fort Rice — Starts in quest of hostile camp — Meeting envoys from same — Arrival at camp — Joyful welcome — The great council — Deputies sent to meet commissioners — Arrival at Fort Rice — Successful council — Father De Smet's great services.

*T*HE Indian affairs of the Government were at this time in critical shape and enlisted the constant efforts of the War and Interior Departments to prevent further outrages and to arrive at some peaceful solution of existing troubles. The years 1867 and 1868 were the most important in Father De Smet's life, because of the part which he took in this work of pacification. He had greater influence with the Indians than any other living white man, and the Government was glad to avail itself of his good offices. Early in 1867 the Secretary of the Interior requested him to go to the hostile tribes " to endeavor to bring them back to peace and submission and to prevent as far as possible the destruction of property and the murder of the whites." " I accepted the commission," Father De Smet writes, " there being nothing in it contrary to my duties as a missionary, and with the distinct understanding that I shall not accept any remuneration for my services. I prefer to be altogether independent in money matters, as my only object is to be of use to the whites and still more to the poor Indians."

In his account of his long journey this year Father De Smet gives an excellent summary of the wrongs which the Indians were suffering, and of the savage cruelties which

they were perpetrating upon the whites. His natural sympathies were with the Indians and they knew it, and this
may have been the secret of his wonderful influence over
them.

He left St. Louis April 12th by a different route from that
followed heretofore. He went by rail to Chicago and
thence started for Omaha on the Northwestern line, which
had just been opened through to the Missouri river. Unluckily there had been an extraordinary downpour of rain
for some days previously and the tracks and bridges were
badly washed out on the western end of the line. With
much delay he finally got as far as Dennison, whence he
was compelled to travel by wagon about a hundred miles to
Sioux City.

How constantly in service were Father De Smet's powers
of observation is well illustrated by the accurate description
he has given us of the rolling prairie country of Iowa — a
description which will at once appeal to any one who has
ever crossed that country: "All this region resembles an
agitated sea, suddenly become motionless. Day after day,
it is the same monotony. You go up and down an interminable succession of larger or smaller hills and valleys,
like terrestrial billows. A fringe of timber can be seen
along the streams and in some deep valleys and ravines in
the higher portions. In summer this region is an ocean of
verdure, adorned with flowers, always agreeable to the eye.
In autumn, fires run over it and cover the whole surface
with the sad black tint of mourning. Then comes winter
and spreads its shroud of white over all nature."

From Sioux City Father De Smet took the steamer *Gui-
don* and continued his route up the river. With him were
twenty-six Yankton Sioux and their chief Pananniapapi,
a Christian Indian, between whom and Father De Smet
there had long subsisted the most affectionate friendship.
The destination of the Indians was the Yankton Agency
near Fort Randall. Father De Smet stopped there a few
days until the *Bighorn,* which had his main outfit on board,

should arrive. He lodged at the house of the agent and there set up his altar and ministered to the spiritual welfare of the Indians while he was among them.

Upon the arrival of the *Bighorn* Father De Smet resumed his journey. All along the river from the Yankton Agency to Fort Buford at the mouth of the Yellowstone,— at Forts Thompson, Sully, Rice and Berthold — there were hundreds and thousands of Indians in waiting. Father De Smet's interviews with them were everywhere satisfactory and it seemed to him that peace was clearly in sight if the Indians could be assured of fair treatment on the part of the whites. " I am firmly convinced,." he writes, " that if the just claims of the Indians are attended to; if their annuities are paid them at the proper time and place; if the agents and other employees of the Government treat them with honesty and justice; if they are supplied with the necessary tools for carpentry and agriculture — the tribes of the Upper Missouri will maintain peace with the whites; and the warlike bands who to-day infest the plains of the Far West and the valley of the Platte, where there is so much destruction of property and loss of life, will promptly cease their depredations and would not be long in joining the stay-at-home tribes."

This was undoubtedly the case; but the conditions named by Father De Smet were impracticable. The onward rush of emigration could not be checked, and it was that that made the difficulty. It drew all the lesser evils in its train.

Father De Smet sent several embassies to the hostile Indians and succeeded in getting upward of a hundred chiefs and warriors to come to Fort Rice and meet Generals Sully and Parker; but owing to the delay of arrival of these two officers, the Indians were compelled to leave, on account of lack of provisions, without having seen them. They sent back word that they were very anxious to see them and that they were desirous of peace.

Father De Smet spent nearly four months on this mission, in which time he did a great deal to prepare the minds of the Indians for peace. On his way down the river he met, at Fort Leavenworth, the new Peace Commission appointed by the Government to take up the whole question of dealing with the Indians. It was composed of several of the leading officers of the Army. They invited Father De Smet to become one of their number and accompany them in all their visits to the tribes. He accepted, but his baggage having gone to St. Louis, he was obliged to go after it. While there he was taken seriously ill and his physicians would not consent to his going on the trip.[1]

As soon as Father De Smet's health would permit he took up with his accustomed energy the matter of reaching the hostile Indians the following year; for it was expected that he would accompany the new commission on their tour. His letters, both to the agents in the upper country and to his correspondents elsewhere, are full of the details of the important work. Briefly, his program was to penetrate the interior from Fort Rice or Fort Berthold and find the hostiles, and try to bring them to some point where the commissioners could meet them. It was a most dangerous undertaking, for it was not believed that any white man could approach them unprotected except at the cost of his life. It is saying a great deal that there was only one man in the United States who could do this, but we believe it to be the truth.[2]

On the 30th of March, 1868, Father De Smet left St. Louis on the most important mission of his whole career. He was in company with the members of the commission,

[1] The Secretary of the Interior wrote thus to Father De Smet concerning his work on this expedition: "You will please accept my thanks for the faithful and efficient manner in which you have discharged the duties entrusted to your care."

[2] "Father De Smet, alone of the entire white race, could penetrate to these cruel savages and return safe and sound. One of the chiefs, in speaking to him while he was in the hostile camp, said to him: 'If it had been any other man than you, Black-robe, this day would have been his last.'"— *General Stanley.*

including Generals Sherman, Sheridan, Harney, Terry and several others. They went to Omaha via Chicago and thence to Cheyenne, holding a council with some Sioux bands on the way. From Cheyenne they made a brief pleasure excursion to Sherman Pass across which the new Union Pacific railway had but recently been built. The commissioners then went to Fort Laramie while De Smet returned to Omaha to go from there to Fort Rice. He left Omaha on the steamer *Columbia*, but made slow progress owing to low water.

Father De Smet in his narrative of this voyage mentions some of the characteristic experiences which his long acquaintance with the Indian country had developed. If it was known that he was coming up the river there were always people at the landings to see him. "When the boat stopped to cut or load a supply of wood," he writes, "I often had occasion to exercise the holy ministry among the inhabitants of the region who came down to the woodyard or wharf, marrying couples who were awaiting the presence of a priest to receive the nuptial benediction, and regenerating in the holy waters of baptism a great number of children and numerous adults."

And this is the experience he usually passed through when he found himself among a boat-load of passengers: "When the priest appears in the midst of such a throng he is critically scrutinized. He is measured from head to foot. He is like a curious beast in a menagerie. He is regarded with surprise and people are slow to approach him. But once the ice is broken, he is overwhelmed with questions upon all points of religion. These questions are quite often sensible enough, but generally they are odd and sometimes even indelicate and gross, denoting a profound ignorance which inspires only pity and compassion."

The *Columbia* arrived at Fort Rice May 24th. Father De Smet passed a week in religious work among the Indians and Catholic soldiers, baptizing, marrying, and receiving

confessions.[3] He then spent two days in interviews with
the chiefs and in making preparations for departure.   His
plan seemed wildly audacious to both whites and Indians,
and they freely predicted a fatal termination; but he told
them that thousands of pure souls were praying for him
and that their prayers would be heard and he would return
in safety.   His answer inspired courage.   There were all
the volunteers that he needed.   Mr. Charles E. Galpin, an
old Indian trader of great experience, who had married
among the Sioux, accompanied him as interpreter.   There
were besides several of the principal chiefs and eighty warriors representing nearly all the Sioux bands.   They went
in the double capacity of protecting Father De Smet, if need
were, and of persuading their hostile brethren to listen to
him.

The first object of their journey was to find the camp of
the hostiles, made up of malcontents from the various
Sioux bands, who were uncompromising in their hatred
of the whites and who refused to enter into any treaties
with them.   It was these Indians, a very numerous and
powerful band, who were responsible for the depredations
and savage cruelties at that time so prevalent throughout
the West.   The start was made on the morning of the 3d
of June: " We were all assembled; " says Father De Smet,
" a large circle was formed, in which several officers from
the fort and some of the soldiers joined, besides a great
number of Indians from all these different tribes.   I then
offered a solemn prayer to the Great Spirit to put us in
his keeping, and made a short address to the numerous
friends who surrounded us, recommending us to their
pious recollection."

Father De Smet gives at considerable length the details

3 " In my quality of envoy extraordinary of the Government, I was
accorded the title of Major, singularly associated, it must be admitted,
with that of Jesuit. However, it had this advantage that it gave me
easier access to the soldiers, of whom a large number are Catholics.
I gave them, as priest, not as major, all my spare time."

of this remarkable expedition. The route lay directly west from Fort Rice, south of the modern line of the Northern Pacific Railroad, for upward of 350 miles to the place where the Powder river empties into the Yellowstone. It was a long and tedious march, involving a passage of the Bad Lands country; but everybody was in good cheer and the physical obstacles did no more than retard their progress. On the 9th of June, having seen no signs of the hostile band, some scouts were sent out to beat up the country. The line of march of the main column was agreed upon and the scouts were to rejoin it as soon as they should gain any definite information. They were given liberal presents of tobacco to present to the hostiles, if found, for the sending of tobacco "is the same thing as a formal invitation, or the announcement of the desire to meet and confer upon important matters. If the tobacco is accepted, it is a sure sign that you will be admitted among them; if, on the contrary, it is refused, you may understand that all communication is forbidden, and govern yourself accordingly."

On the 16th the scouts returned "at the head of a deputation of eighteen warriors, announcing their arrival by shouts and joyful songs. All came and shook hands with me with especial eagerness, and after we had smoked the pipe of peace together,— a first proof of their good will toward me — they announced in the name of the head chiefs of their camp, that 'my tobacco had been favorably received; that entry into their camp was open to the Black-robe alone; that no other white man would get out of it with his scalp; and that all the chiefs and warriors were awaiting me with impatience, wishing to hear me and learn the motives of my visit.' Afterwards we exchanged news. I learned that the big camp was three days' march away, in the Yellowstone valley, a few miles above the mouth of Powder river. The night was spent in feasts between the Indians of my escort and the newcomers, mingled with joyful songs and fraternal rounds of the calumet. There were uproarious reunions, *à la sauvage,* but harmony and cordiality prevailed."

Pursuing their march through a most difficult tract of country, they finally came, on the 19th, to the bluffs of Powder river, and beheld from their crest a beautiful panorama outspread before them. In a country where there is not moisture enough to sustain trees, and the eye is rarely refreshed by the sight of that beautiful object in nature, it is an exquisite joy to the weary traveler to come upon a large stream whose banks are lined with forests. Standing upon the lofty bluffs that define the courses of the Powder and Yellowstone valleys, our travelers beheld to the west the broad valley of the latter stream and to the south that of the Powder. Along each were lines of trees that marked the course of the streams as far as the eye could reach, while the glimmering water appeared here and there like quiet mirrors on the landscape.

But Father De Smet saw other sights on this occasion which gave him but little time to admire the beauties of nature. "Some four miles off in the Powder river bottoms," he writes, "we saw a strong force of horsemen composed of 400 to 500 warriors coming to meet me. I at once had my standard of peace hoisted, with the holy name of Jesus on one side and on the other the image of the Virgin Mary, surrounded with gilt stars. They took it at first sight for the hated flag of the United States. At this signal all the cavalcade halted and appeared to enter into consultation. Immediately afterward, the four head chiefs came toward us at full speed and seemed, as it were, to flit around the banner. They considered it, and upon preceiving its meaning and high importance, they came up and shook my hand and made signals to all their warriors to advance. They then formed into a single long line or phalanx; we did the same, and with the flag at our head we went to meet them. At the same time the air resounded with shouts and songs of joy on both sides. I

was touched even to tears at the sight of the reception
which these sons of the desert, still in paganism, had prepared for the poor Black-robe. It was the fairest spectacle in which I have ever had the happiness of taking
part."

There was much wild noise and commotion, but all in
good spirit, and when they reached the main body, Father
De Smet shook hands with all of them and won their
hearts at once by the benevolence of his manner and his
evident interest in their welfare. It now remained to
make the final march of some ten or twelve miles to the
main camp. Four head chiefs acted as a bodyguard to
Father De Smet to protect him against any treacherous
attack. After crossing Powder river close column was
formed and everything was conducted with military strict-
ness and precision. At the head of the column was Father
De Smet's banner. The Indians were decked out in the
ultra style of the wild warriors, to a degree, in fact, rarely
witnessed at that late day. It was an impressive and awe-
inspiring scene. "Nevertheless," says Father De Smet,
"my heart was as tranquil and my mind as calm as if I
had been in the midst of you."

They found the main camp to consist of some four or
five thousand Indians who received them with every demonstration of joy. A large lodge had been prepared for
Father De Smet by Sitting Bull, the leader of the hostiles.
The Father was weary with his long journey and after a
little luncheon lay down in his lodge and went to sleep.
When he awoke Sitting Bull was beside him, and with
him were three other leading chiefs. Sitting Bull at once
addressed Father De Smet: " Black-robe, I hardly sustain
myself beneath the weight of white men's blood that I have
shed. The whites provoked the war; their injustices, their
indignities to our families, the cruel, unheard-of and wholly
unprovoked massacre at Fort Lyon," (where Chivington
commanded) " of six or seven hundred women, children

7

and old men, shook all the veins which bind and support
me. I rose, tomahawk in hand, and I have done all the
hurt to the whites that I could. Today thou art amongst
us, and in thy presence my arms stretch to the ground as
if dead. I will listen to thy good words, and as bad as
I have been to the whites, just as good am I ready to become toward them."

The chiefs and Father De Smet then conferred about
the great council which it was proposed to hold on the
morrow to determine what should be done about going
to see the commissioners. The rest of the day until late
at night was spent in visits and conversations with the
leading men of the camp. Here occurred one of those
striking incidents with which Father De Smet's intercourse with the Indians was so full. We give it in the
Father's own words: "A venerable old man, of remarkable
stature, but bowed beneath the weight of age, supporting
himself on a staff tipped with an old bayonet, came to
offer me his hand and express his happiness at seeing me
again. He wore upon his breast a copper cross, old and
worn. This was the only religious token that I had observed in all the camp; it filled me with joy and emotion.
I questioned him eagerly and with interest, to know from
whom he had received it. After a moment's thought, and
counting on his fingers, he answered, ' It was you, Black-
robe, who gave me this cross. I have never laid it aside
for twenty-six snows. The cross has raised me to the
clouds among my people ' (meaning that it had made him
great and respectable). ' If I still walk on earth, it is to
the cross that I owe it, and the Great Spirit has blessed
my numerous family.'

"I begged him to explain further, and he continued:
' When I was younger, I loved whiskey to madness, and at
every chance I would get drunk and commit excesses. It
is now twenty-six snows since my last turbulent orgy. I
was stupid and sick from it; just then I had the good
fortune to meet you, and you made known to me that my

behavior was against the will of the Master of Life and offended him grievously. Since then I have often had opportunities; my friends have sometimes sought to induce me to join them in their illicit enjoyments, and often my old evil inclination would combat my good will which desired to resist the temptation. Every time the cross has come to my help. I would take it between my hands, imploring the Great Spirit to give me strength, and your words, Black-robe, would come to my mind. Ever since we first met, I have renounced drink, and have never tasted a drop.' "

Father De Smet was deeply touched by the incident and endeavored to instill into the mind of the Indian the deeper truths of the Christian life. The old man was so enraptured with the venerable apostle that when Father De Smet left the council he followed him over three hundred miles.

The 20th of June was the day set for the council and great preparations were made for it. A circular space of about 170 feet in diameter was inclosed by a high wall composed of large skin tepees of some twenty robes each, spread out flat and hung from pine posts set around the circumference of the circle. Father De Smet's banner was hoisted on the side of the circle opposite the entrance and a seat was prepared for him near it. When the Indians had taken their places, Father De Smet " was solemnly introduced into this *salon champêtre,* which was improvised for the occasion by the two head chiefs, Four Horns and Black Moon. I took my seat. The council was opened with songs and dances, noisy, joyful and very wild, in which the warriors alone took part. Then Four Horns lighted his calumet of peace; he presented it first solemnly to the Great Spirit, imploring his light and favor, and then offered it to the four cardinal points, to the sun and the earth, as witnesses to the action of the council. Then he himself passed the calumet from mouth to mouth. I was the first to receive it, with my interpreter, and every chief was placed according to the rank that he held in the tribe. Each one took a few puffs. When the ceremony of the calumet was finished, the head chief addressed me, saying, 'Speak, Black-robe, my ears are open to hear your words.' All this was done with the greatest gravity and amid a profound silence."

Father De Smet then arose and lifted his hands to heaven and offered a prayer to the Great Spirit, imploring his blessing upon this solemn occasion. Then for an hour he talked to them of his mission; the purely disinterested motives that had brought him there; the wish of the Great Father for peace; the atrocious crimes that had been committed on both sides; the readiness of the Great Father to aid them, and the uselessness of contending against his strength, so many times greater than their own. These points were all discussed at considerable length. Four chiefs spoke, but Father De Smet gives us only the speech of Black Moon, which, he says, was essentially the same as the others. With all the solemnity and stately form of Indian ceremony, " he rose, calumet in hand, and addressing his people, said: 'Lend an ear to my words.' Then he raised the calumet solemnly to heaven and lowered it to earth; thus invoking, by the Indian interpretation, heaven and earth as his witnesses. At his request I touched the calumet with my lips, putting my right hand on the stem. Then he said in a loud voice: 'The Black-robe has made a long journey to come to us; his presence among us makes me very glad, and with all my heart I wish him welcome to my country. I can understand all the words that the Black-robe has just said to us; they are good and filled with truth. I shall lay them up in my memory. Still, our hearts are sore; they have received deep wounds. These wounds have yet to be healed. A cruel war has desolated and impoverished our country; the desolating torch of war was not kindled by us; it was the Sioux east of us and the Cheyennes south of us who raised the war first, to revenge themselves for the white man's cruelties and injustice. We have been forced to take part, for we too have been victims of his rapacity and wrong-doing. To-day, when we ride over our plains, we find them spotted here and there with blood; and these are not the bloodstains of buffalo and deer killed in the chase, but those of our own comrades or of white men sacrificed to vengeance. The buffalo, the elk, the antelope, the bighorn and the deer have quitted our immense plains; we hardly find them any more, except at intervals, and always less numerous. May it not be the odor of human blood that puts them to flight?

" ' I will say further — against our will the whites are interlacing our country with their highways of transportation and emigration; they build forts at various points and mount thunders upon them. They kill our animals, and more than they need. They are cruel to our people, maltreat and massacre them without reason, or for the slightest cause, even when they are searching for food, for animals and roots, to nourish their wives and children. They cut down our forests in spite of us and without paying us their value. They are ruining our land. We are opposed to having these big roads which drive the buffalo away from our country. This soil is ours and we are determined not to yield an inch of it. Here our fathers were born and are buried. We desire, like them, to live here, and to be buried in this same soil. We have been forced to hate the whites; let them treat us like brothers and the war will cease. Let them stay at home; we will never go to trouble them. To see them come into our land and build their cabins revolts us, and we are determined to resist or die. Thou, Messenger of Peace, thou hast given us a glimpse of a better future. Very well; so be it; let us hope. Let us throw a veil over the past and let it be forgotten.

" ' I have only a word more to say. In the presence of all my people, I express to you here my thanks for the good news that you have announced and for all your good counsel and advice. We accept your tobacco. Some of our warriors will go with you to Fort Rice to hear the words and the propositions of the Great Father's commissioners. If their words are acceptable, peace shall be made.'"

Sitting Bull, Two Bears and Running Antelope followed Black Moon. After the council had lasted some four hours it was decided to send a deputation to meet the commissioners. The Indians begged Father De Smet to leave his banner with them as a memento of the occasion, and he acceded to their request. He then withdrew to his lodge, whither he was followed by many Indians and particularly by mothers with their children.

The return journey was begun on the morning of the 21st, and on the 30th of June they entered Fort Rice amid the enthusiastic greetings of all present. The council with the commissioners took place two days later, and a treaty of peace was signed by all the chiefs and principal warriors. Then, on the 3d and 4th of July, a general distribution of presents was made and the council closed to the joy and satisfaction of both parties.

Father De Smet's work on this occasion was now done and he at once set out for home. His achievement was one of the most remarkable in the history of our Indian wars. He was sixty-eight years old and suffering with bodily infirmities which in a few years were to end fatally. He made a journey of 350 miles through a rough and unknown country to a large force of Indians who had sworn death to any white man who might fall within their power. There was no other man who could approach them. Yet by virtue of his great reputation among all the tribes, their absolute faith in his word and their belief that he had their interests at heart, and, we may add, his devout trust in the Lord whom he served, he did this remarkable thing, and brought about a peace in the most hateful and difficult situation that our Government had been called upon to face in all its troubles with the Indians. The commissioners formally acknowledged that, but for Father De Smet, their work would have been a failure. "We are well aware," they wrote him, "that our thanks can be of little worth to you, and that you will find your true reward for your labors and for the dangers and privations which you have encountered in the consciousness that you have done much to promote peace on earth and good will to men."

Father De Smet stopped at Fort Sully on his way down the river to minister to the spiritual welfare of the Indians there, and then resumed his voyage. He next stopped at Fort Leavenworth and went to St. Mary's Mission, and finally arrived in St. Louis about August 20th.

CHAPTER X.

CHARACTER OF FATHER DE SMET.

Visit to Europe — Return in 1869 — Visit to the Sioux country in 1870 — Bodily ailments — Serious illness — Launching of the *De Smet* — Last sickness — Death and burial — Character sketch.

AFTER Father De Smet's return from the upper country he sailed for Europe, leaving St. Louis on the 21st of November, 1868. He arrived at Termonde, his native place, about the middle of December and remained there the rest of the year. In the spring he visited the principal cities of Belgium, Holland, France and England, and sailed for America on the 21st of June, reaching St. Louis July 4th. That fall he visited Omaha, St. Mary's Mission and Chicago.

On June 1, 1870, he left St. Louis on his last voyage to the Indian country, going as far as the Grand River Agency. The particular purpose of this trip was to arrange for the establishment of a mission among the Sioux — an object which had long been dear to him but which he was never able to carry out. He returned to St. Louis early in August.

Owing to bodily indispositions Father De Smet remained quietly in St. Louis, except for a brief visit to Chicago, until June 25, 1871, when he left for Europe. His time while abroad on this last visit to his native land was spent much as his other visits had been, in touring the principal cities from which he could expect aid to the Indian missions. He left Europe April 11, 1872, and crossed the Atlantic for the last time, being his nineteenth voyage in the past fifty years. He remained in St. Louis the rest of the year.

The frequent use of the word "last" in describing

Father De Smet's doings in later years suggests only too clearly that the end of his life was at hand. It was indeed so, but before recording this inevitable event in human life, it will be well to note some facts regarding the failing health of the good priest.

In spite of his longevity and great physical powers, Father De Smet was far from enjoying uninterrupted good health, and in the last twenty years of his life was never free from bodily ailments. This condition was undoubtedly due in large degree to the hardships of his missionary work and it began to develop soon after his return from Oregon in 1846. He was at this time and for several years afterward at the maximum of his physical weight, about 215 pounds. His corpulency did not please him, although he carried his flesh well, and was considered a remarkably fine looking man. "Pray hard for me," he wrote to a friend in 1851, "for my bones are getting too much covered. I begin to be uncomfortable, and daily must I hear 'How well you look!' 'You are improving!' 'What a fine country the Rocky Mountains must be!' Should I ever return to my old haunts, a great number of the lean gentry of St. Louis are determined to follow me and try their luck on buffalo, bear, badger and dog meat."

He was ailing a good deal in the years 1849-51, and in 1853 writes: "For two or three years back I find myself sensibly on the decline," his eyesight, in particular, failing rapidly. For the next few years he was very well, and in 1856 he records that "for years I have not been compelled to have recourse to a physician." But at the time of the Utah and Oregon expeditions he was suffering a good deal from an affection of his throat, and in 1861 he was very ill with some form of dyspepsia, and later in the same year with erysipelas. In the winter of 1863-4 he was dangerously ill with a combination of troubles, and he fully expected, at one time, that his end had come. He was ordered by his physician to let his beard grow for a

while, and with the natural mirthfulness of his temperament he had his picture taken in this condition and sent it
to his family in Europe.   In a letter home at this time he
refers to himself as "broken down with all sorts of infirmities."

A particular trouble which had afflicted him for many
years was deafness in one of his ears.   He frequently refers to his "good ear," and when, late in life, he seemed
liable to lose that also, he was naturally very much disturbed.   A strange result of the extraction of a large tooth
had filled his ear with such a constant ringing that he
could practically hear nothing.   He sought medical advice without any good result, and finally improved the
opportunity of a visit to Europe to see if he could get
relief.   Whether he ever experienced any material improvement in this respect his letters do not say.

The most serious of Father De Smet's physical ailments,
and the one which finally proved fatal, was a form of
Bright's disease which, in its later stages, was accompanied
by severe hemorrhages.   By 1867 this malady was already
giving him great trouble, and he notes in the fall of
that year, after a severe spell of sickness, that his weight
had fallen off to 167 pounds.   In Europe on his last
journey he experienced an almost fatal attack and after
his return to St. Louis in the spring of 1872 he did not
again leave that city.   He nevertheless kept very busy
with the duties of his office and carried on a great deal of
correspondence.   Some of his best work dates from that
period.   He began and made some progress in a history
of the Missouri Province which he hoped to see completed.
During most of this time he held from the Government
the privilege of nominating agents to be appointed for the
tribes where Catholic missions were located.

The last letter ever written by Father De Smet, or at
least the last one recorded, is dated May 12, 1873.   On
the next day Captain La Barge, who was perhaps at this
time Father De Smet's most intimate personal friend, was

St Stanislaus Novitiate, near Florissant, in 1847

BUILDINGS AT THE FLORISSANT GROUP.

going to launch a new steamboat which he had named *De Smet.* He besought Father De Smet to be present and bless the boat and at the same time visit his family. Though not at all well he did not feel like declining the request of his friend, particularly as the boat was named in his honor and was soon to visit those regions that he knew and loved so well.

Upon returning home in the evening he was taken quite ill and grew rapidly worse. His malady took a new form which necessitated an operation; and while it brought temporary relief, it made manifest the fact that death was not far away. On the 20th of May Father De Smet himself asked that the last sacraments be administered to him, and from that time on he lived only in prayer. The end came at a quarter after two on the morning of May 23, 1873.

The death of Father De Smet produced a deep grief in the city of St. Louis where he had made his home for almost exactly fifty years. His funeral was one of the most largely attended ever held in that city, and among the audience were many distinguished people. The funeral oration was pronounced by Monseigneur Ryan, Bishop Coadjutor of Monseigneur Kendrick, Archbishop of St. Louis, and was well worthy of its subject.[1] The press universally gave testimony of the high estimation in which the departed Jesuit was held.

Father De Smet was buried in the little cemetery of the Novitiate at Florissant, at the foot of the grave of Father Verhaegen, who had come to this place with him just fifty years before.

In the year 1878, on the fifth anniversary of Father De Smet's death, there was unveiled in Termonde, his native place, a fine statue of the great missionary. It is in bronze, designed by A. Frakin and executed by Charles Alker, director of the works at Haeren, Belgium. The

---

[1] See page 1592 of the *Letters.*

height of the statue is thirteen feet six inches, and the
weight of the bronze casting is 3,482 pounds.   The base
is carved from a single piece of blue limestone, with panels
and suitable inscriptions on its four faces.   The statue is
considered a very satisfactory work, the artist having succeeded well in his attempt to portray the spirit of a great
career.   The missionary is represented in his priestly robes
in the attitude of moving forward, with an eager expression
on the face, as if intent upon the great work before him.
In the right hand is a crucifix indicative of his calling as a
priest of God, and in the other an olive branch, symbolic
of his work as a peacemaker among the Indian tribes.
Termonde was proud of her distinguished offspring, and
Belgium, too, was proud of him; and he was fond of both.

In bidding farewell to this august character in our national history, it is well to review some of the traits of his
personality that marked it off from the average run of
men.   So far as it is in the power of man, in this network
of temptation which we call life, by the constant exercise
of religious faith and duty, to free his heart and conduct of
all sin, Father De Smet succeeded.   No one can read his
life, even the inner secrets of it as recorded in his personal
correspondence, without feeling that he is in the presence
of a good man.   There were narrow prejudices — prejudices that arose from his training and environment; but
he had practically mastered his personal cravings, and
looked with charity upon those who did him wrong.   He
has left us the remarkable statement that "no bitterness
toward any one whomsoever ever entered my heart;" a
statement, however, from which he would probably exclude certain political organizations which aroused all the
hatred that a heart like his was capable of.

He was of a genial and buoyant temperament, fond of
jest and merriment, and humorously disposed.   " I am
naturally inclined to laughter," he once said, and even the
staid formalities of the Indian councils so provoked his
mirth at times that he had hard work to keep a sober

countenance. He was as willing to tell a joke on himself as on any one else and evidently took a keen relish in depicting the awkward plights in which his varied experiences often placed him. Here is an example: "One day I found myself in a singular and critical position. In attempting to pass under a tree that inclined across the path, I perceived a small branch in form of a hook, which threatened me. The first impulse was to extend myself upon the neck of my horse. Unavailing precaution! It caught me by the collar of my surtout, the horse still continuing his pace. Behold me suspended in the air, struggling like a fish at the end of a hook. Several respectable pieces of my coat floated, in all probability, a long time in the forest, as a proof of my having paid toll in passing through it. A crushed and torn hat, an eye black and blue, two deep scratches on the cheek, would, in a civilized country, have given me the appearance of a bully issuing from the *Black Forest,* rather than of a missionary."

The distressing experience of sickness at sea always appealed to the funny side of his nature. He suffered as much in this respect as any of his fellow travelers, but he always made light of it (in more senses than one) and his letters abound in amusing descriptions of the manner in which Neptune collected the tax which he levied upon all who trespassed upon his domain.

Sometimes, in a quiet way to his close associates, he imparted his views upon the well-intentioned, yet often misdirected charity, to which he was subject as procurator of the missions. He once wrote to a friend in Paris:

* * * "Mademoiselle Therese de Coppens, in her little letter, announces that she has forwarded to me an alb and sundry other objects for the missions. I have known the excellent good demoiselle for many years past; there can be no doubt that she has the best intentions in the world. I will do as you advise about writing her a little note of thanks. * * * At the same time, I beg that you will

look into her shipment, or have somebody else do so, with my permission to take out anything that you may judge unsuitable or not worth the freight. Once, a few years ago, as I was leaving for Havre, Mademoiselle sent me a big package for America. I opened it up in Paris, and what do you think there was in it? Nothing but old rags, frightful images of saints, daubed with colors, exactly in the taste of the Blackfeet and Crows of the Rocky Mountains, and finally some German holy virgins and christs, which would really scare a man and make him laugh at the same time. I left the whole thing in Paris. In regard to these things, follow your own discretion, and do just as you think best."

He was very fond of good stories, and while he naturally did not indulge much in that line in his formal writings on missionary matters, a good many crept into his personal correspondence and some of them are given in the present edition of his writings.[2]

The cheerfulness and optimism of his temperament were united with the deepest sentiments of tenderness and affection. He was moved to tears as easily as a woman, and all his life long it was his natural manner to " rejoice with those that do rejoice and weep with those that weep."

He possessed in an eminent degree those qualities that go to the making of a home, and one cannot but feel that the world, in gaining a good priest, lost a better husband and father. He was passionately fond of his family in Belgium and his letters to his brothers, nephews and nieces breathe the tenderest affection. He was always impatient for letters from them. " Exilement, even when it is voluntary," he once wrote, " or when, rather, it is imposed by conscience or religion, cannot destroy in a man's heart the sweet sentiments there implanted by kinship or love of country. Hence the vacancy that I feel within me, at not having received for so long a time any of your letters, always so good and interesting, and so consoling to your American exile."

[2] See page 1416 of the *Letters*.

His priestly duties did not estrange him from the natural feelings that home and kindred inspire and he was ever alive to the pleasures and sorrows of his relatives across the sea. He thus wrote to one of his nieces upon the occasion of her marriage: " Since I now love my nephew, Mr. De Bare, as much as I love my niece Sylvie, you must be careful to give him a faithful description of your uncle, so that if I should happen in on him in your absence, he could recognize me without ever having seen me. Uncle Pierre, tell him, is a man of medium size, with gray hair, tending to white. The center of his wide face is occupied by a nose with which a Greek or a Roman would not find much fault. Its nearest neighbor is a mouth of ordinary size, which hardly ever opens save to laugh or to make others laugh; it makes people love the good Lord in that manner. The rest resembles a man of fifty years, who weighs 210 pounds. If ever you build a new house, give the door of my chamber six inches extra width, because I don't like to be bothered in getting into a room."

His friends at home likewise held him in the highest veneration and affection and a close and uninterrupted correspondence passed between them. On one of his visits to Europe, he officiated at the marriage of his nephew Paul with whom he had corresponded since he was a little boy. The church where the ceremony was performed was thronged with people eager to see the great missionary, and the scene is described as deeply touching and impressive.

These little glimpses of his inner life show how much of human nature he possessed, and how little it had been warped or withered by a calling which we are inclined to think sets men apart from the common run of humanity.

Father De Smet would have made a successful man of affairs and an ideal citizen in public life. The Society kept him constantly engaged in managing the business affairs of the Province; and his extensive travels at home and abroad gave him an acquaintance with men in all the walks of life which very few members of his order possessed. He was richly endowed by nature with what he calls "that most precious of social virtues, common sense." Although throughout his life he was thrown in contact with the world above the lot of the average priest, and in places where indiscretion would have cost him dear, he always bore himself in a way that won the respect and confidence of those who met him. He held rigidly aloof from politics even when his soul was aroused by the persecutions carried on against his religion. Referring, late in life, to his past career, he once wrote: " In my long missionary career of over thirty years I have made it a rule not to lend myself or interfere in any difference that may occur between parties. I try my best to attend solely to my spiritual ministry for the welfare of my white brethren and that of the well-disposed Indians."

A feature of Father De Smet's career which has strongly appealed to the author since he first became acquainted with the life-work of the great missionary is the absence of that longing for martyrdom which was so characteristic of the old Canadian missionaries. Apart from one's admiration of the wonderful fortitude that enabled Brebeuf and others to endure calmly the tortures of the savages, we cannot but feel that it was lost upon the barbarous nature of the savage and did not promote the cause of religion in any adequate degree. There is an involuntary feeling that these men would have better served their Master if they had made themselves soldiers of the cross, literally, and had met their savage assailants with sword and fire instead of meekly resigning themselves to a terrible and ineffectual fate. This, we are aware, is not the view of the Church, and it may be that, in the inscrutable wisdom of Providence, sacrifices like these bring about results which we are unable to trace.

Father De Smet was a different kind of man. He did not lack courage — he faced death too many times for that; but he believed that the life given him was given for a purpose, and that it should not be lightly thrown away. He always took the most careful precautions against disas-

ter. He could even practice the legitimate deceptions of war
when necessary to frustrate the plans of an enemy. While
he never himself carried arms — or at least we have no
record that he did — he aided his traveling companions in
their means of defense, and would undoubtedly have helped
them in battle if the necessity had arisen.

But when it came to situations where the sacrifice of his
life might promote the welfare of others, he did not hesitate.
Three times, at least, he went forth to meet hostile bands
when it was believed that a white man could not approach
them without certain death. And he informs us that he
did this in perfect calmness and with a sense of security
which could come only from his faith in the protecting care
of Providence. It is a singular fact that in all his experience in the Indian country, during the period of general
wars, he saw very little, if any, actual bloodshed. In 1846
he said, " I have never witnessed the shedding of one drop
of human blood " — and the same good fortune accompanied him during the remainder of his life.

It is entirely in harmony with a nature like that of Father
De Smet, that he should be an enthusiastic lover of the beauties of Nature. Whether on sea or land, among the mountains or on the prairie, he saw beauty and goodness in all
that God had made. His writings are full of his observations upon these subjects. He tells us, for instance, how on
one occasion, when nearing New York from Europe, a long
spell of rough weather was followed by a perfect day in
which everything combined to make Nature appear at her
best. There was a glorious sunset which drew from Father
De Smet the exquisite reflection that the setting of the sun
at sea is " among the great wonders of the Lord." He sat
up that night until two in the morning, drinking in this
natural elixir of life, and was up again in time to see the
rising of a May sun. This is the way it appeared to him:
" The sky was clear, the sea was tranquil, hardly a ripple
stirred the surface of its waters, and from its bosom rose the

8

majestic sun in all its lustre and glory, spreading and reflecting its dazzling beams, high and deep, above and below the horizon. Eastwardly the ocean appeared as in a blaze and resembled a boundless mass of molten gold. Truly, grand and sublime is the sight of the rising sun at sea."

He once wrote to a young student friend of poetic talent who was about to pass by Niagara Falls: "Take a peep at the great Niagara Falls; look well at them. No matter how much your mind may have been dried up by the holy fathers, by theology and philosophy, your poetic turn will there revive and feel a new inspiration."

Reference has already been made to the personal appearance of Father De Smet; but it is well to add here that there was that about his bearing and physiognomy, growing out of his religious life, which added vastly to the favorable impression produced by his well-developed physique. Father De Smet was particularly noted for the dignity and suavity of his manner, and the Christian character of his countenance. "His face was a benediction," once said a distinguished Montana pioneer who knew him well;[3] and another pioneer,[4] who had traveled with him part way across the continent, characterized him as "genial, of fine presence, and one of the saintliest men I have ever known, and I cannot wonder that the Indians were made to believe him divinely protected. He was a man of great kindness and great affability under all circumstances; nothing seemed to disturb his temper."

Having now noted the general traits of Father De Smet's character as a man and priest, we shall notice some of the more prominent phases of his life-work.

[3] Colonel W. F. Sanders of Helena, Mont.
[4] John Bidwell in *The Century* for November, 1890

CHAPTER XI.

THE INDIAN AND THE MISSIONARY.

A friend of the Indians — Their trust in him — Interesting intercourse with the tribes — The Indian Question — Missionary work — Comparison of Protestant and Catholic methods — Great obstacles to success — The destruction of the field by white settlement.

*T*HERE has never lived a more sincere, ardent and practical friend of the Indians than Father De Smet. He held them in the deepest affection. He sympathized with them in the wrongs they suffered. At the same time he saw their limitations; he hated their revolting uncleanliness, abhorred their cruelties, and hesitated not to point out to them the evils of their manner of life. With all of Catlin's enthusiasm for the native character, he had none of those impracticable and chimerical notions which made that writer wholly unreliable as an authority, and his plans impossible of realization.

As Father De Smet was a friend of the Indians to an extent never equaled by any other white man, so there was never another white man for whom they felt the deep personal affection and absolute trust that they did for him. Nothing is more remarkable in his eventful life than this fact. He had but to show himself to win their hearts. There was that in his benevolent manner that commanded their trust in an instant. They delighted to honor him. He was borne in triumph or escorted with imposing ceremony; given their best lodge; feasted until endurance could receive no more. And as years rolled on and they found him always true, their first impressions grew into a worshipful love. He was the only white man, they were wont to say, who never talked to them with a forked tongue.

His interviews with them were full of exquisite incidents,

and he knew perfectly how to impress their minds with the wonders of life and pave the way to the reception of religious truth. "In their hunting expeditions," he once wrote, "I used to pass the beautiful summer and autumnal evenings seated on the grass and flowery meadows of their lovely mountain valleys surrounded by my dear neophytes. They took the liveliest interest in my narratives of the holy writ — on the creation, the deluge, the ark of Noah, the Maccabees, Samson, Joseph and his brethren, etc. I occasionally entertained them on American and European events and wars, on Washington and his great country, on the battles of Napoleon the First, his struggles and his final overthrow at Waterloo."

His intercourse with that wild and roving tribe of freebooters, the Crows, was always interesting. We have noted the astonished remark of a Crow chief when he found what had to be done to inherit the white man's heaven. On a subsequent occasion the good Father explained to them the greatness of the white nation. "They asked me innumerable questions; among others they wished to know the number of the whites. 'Count,' I replied, 'the blades of grass upon your immense plains, and you will know pretty nearly the number of whites.' They all smiled, saying that the thing was impossible, but they understood my meaning. And when I explained to them the vast extent of the villages inhabited by white men (New York, Philadelphia, London, Paris); the grand lodges (houses) built as near each other as the fingers of my hand, and four or five piled up, one above the other (meaning the different stories of our dwellings); when I told them that some of these lodges (speaking of churches and towers) were as high as mountains and large enough to contain all the Crows together; that in the grand lodge of the national council (the Capitol at Washington) all the great chiefs of the whole world could smoke the calumet at their ease; that the roads in these great villages were always filled with passengers, who came and went more thickly than the vast herds of buffalo that sometimes cover their beautiful plains; when I explained to them the extraordinary celerity of those moving lodges (the cars on the railroad) that leave far behind them the swiftest horse, and are drawn along by frightful machines whose repeated groanings re-echo far and wide, as they belch forth immense volumes of fire and smoke; and next those fire canoes (steamboats) which transport whole villages, with provisions, arms and baggage, in a few days, from one country to another, crossing large lakes (the seas), ascending and descending the great rivers and streams; when I told them that I had seen white men mounting up into the air (in balloons) and flying with as much agility as the warrior eagle of their mountains — then their astonishment was at its height; and all placing their hands upon their mouths, sent forth at the same time one general cry of wonder. 'The Master of Life is great,' said the chief, 'and the white men are his favorites.' "

Then he spoke to them of religion. They had dimly heard of the white man's prayer and wanted to hear how he addressed the Great Spirit. Father De Smet planted three United States flags near by; called the multitude around him, knelt beneath the ensign of his country and intoned the solemn canticles and repeated the prayers of the Church, and had them interpreted. These things made a deep impression, and the Crows, like every other tribe whom he visited, always remembered them.

Apart from the bearing of these incidents upon his religious work, Father De Smet thoroughly enjoyed this contact with the unsophisticated children of the wilderness. It was always fresh and novel, no matter how often repeated; and every new repetition evolved some new feature. It was his compensation for the hardships of savage life, so intolerable to a cultured taste. He refers again and again to the feasts to which he was subjected — the disgusting cookery and repulsive food, and he marveled that human beings could live in that way. " The stomach of the Indian has always been a riddle to me," he said; and it required all his ingenuity to devise ways and means of escaping this form of lavish hospitality without doing offense to his hosts.

The great Indian Question absorbed his thoughts perhaps more than any other. He understood it perfectly, and constantly deplores in his letters the terrible position in which the Indian was placed by the encroachment of the whites. It was the same hard question which had been wrestled with in vain since the settlement of the country began — what is to become of the Indian? It mattered comparatively little so long as they were east of the Mississippi, for they could be moved to the vast areas of the West. But now they were all there and the white man kept coming. Back and still farther went the buffalo and the Indian with him. It could not last forever, and Father De Smet saw with unerring vision the fate that must soon overtake them. That it came sooner than he expected is only because no one foresaw how rapidly settlement would occupy the West. The discovery of gold was the knell of the red man. Like a mighty flood, emigration swept over the plains and filled the mountains. Father De Smet had known of gold in the mountains since 1842, and had kept his discovery a secret because he knew that its revelation meant the practical extinction of Indian life in the West. It was yet twenty years before it should become generally known; but when it came it swept all before it. Father De Smet crossed the mountains from the Columbia to Fort Benton in 1859 just before the discovery, and he went back by the same route in 1863 in the midst of the process of discovery. The change was astonishing and ominous. He wrote on this occasion: "One cannot help being anxious for the fate of the Indians on account of the approach of the whites. The treasures concealed in the heart of the mountains will attract thousands of miners from every land; and with them will come the dregs of civilization, gamblers, drunkards, robbers and assassins."

It would be easy to state from Father De Smet's writings every possible phase of the Indian question; but we will give only a few references. The general course of events by which the Indian was compelled to never-ceasing retreat before the advance of the white man is thus described:

"Since the discovery of America a system of extermination, of moving the Indians, thrusting them further back, has been pursued and practiced by the whites, little by little at first, more and more as the European settlers multiplied and gained strength. At this day this same policy is marching with giant strides; the drama of spoliation has reached its last act, both east and west of the Rocky Mountains. The curtain will soon fall upon the poor and unhappy remnants of the Indian tribes, and they will henceforth exist only in history."

And how this irresistible process drove them to desperation and war with all its savage horrors is thus set forth:

"The unhappy war which is now raging so fiercely over all the extent of the Great Desert east of the Rocky Mountains has, like so many other Indian wars, been provoked by injustices and misdeeds on the part of the whites and even the agents of the Government. For years and years they have deceived the Indians with impunity in the sale of their lands, and by the embezzlement, or rather open theft, of immense sums paid by the Government therefor. The Indians, driven to extremity, after being swindled and robbed through a long series of years, and unable to obtain any justice against their oppressors, utter at last their terrible war cry against the whole race of the enemy."

Here follows a statement, replete with wisdom, of the situation as it appeared to thoughtful observers when our Sioux wars were at their height. Its exoneration of the Government from complicity in the wrongs practiced upon the Indians is an example of broad-mindedness which one does not often meet with among the so-called " friends " of the redmen.

"In order to form a just idea of their critical position, and of the melancholy consequences which will be the result unless restrained by special protection of divine Providence, imagine two societies coming in contact, one representing the manners and customs of barbarians, the other all the splendor of modern civilization.   How many years will elapse before there will be a perfect fusion between the two societies, before unison will exist, before they can dwell together in complete harmony?   Neither the first, nor the second, nor the third generation, notwithstanding untiring efforts, will achieve that happy result, such as it is understood in our days.   Hence, previous to a perfect fusion between the societies, the civilized society will have the advantage over the barbarous; it will have it entirely at its mercy, to make it subservient to its will and pleasure.   In a word, the barbarian can no better sustain himself in the presence of civilization, than the simplicity of childhood can contest against the malicious prudence of mature age.

" This, in my opinion, is what will be realized in the Great Desert, when the copper-colored race shall come into contact with the white.   The judgment of the savage is not sufficiently ripe to be able to compete with the wisdom of man born in the bosom of civilization.   It is this conviction which fills us with anxiety for the future of our dear neophytes in the different missions.   We confide solely in divine goodness, which, we hope, will not fail to come to the help of His children.

" It is not difficult to descry from afar the grand event which must engulf in one common wreck all the Indian tribes.   The storm which has just burst forth over their heads was long preparing; it could not escape the observing eye.   We saw the American Republic soaring, with the rapidity of the eagle's flight, towards the plenitude of her power.   Every year she adds new countries to her limits. She ambitions nothing less than extending her dominion from the Atlantic to the Pacific, so as to embrace the commerce of the whole world, and dispute with other mighty nations the glory of pre-eminence.   Her object is attained. All bend to her sceptre; all Indian nationality is at her feet.

" Far be it from us, however, to accuse the noble Republic

of injustice and inhumanity in her late treaties.   It seems
to us, on the contrary, that no nation has ever furnished
more means of civilization.   If any one must be blamed on
this point, it is rather private persons, new colonists, who act
and place themselves in direct opposition with the good intentions of the Government in behalf of the savages."

But while he recognized that the change must come, he de-
plored the fact that it must be so harsh and accompanied
with so much of injustice and wrong.   He did all he could
to soften the cruelty of it and he always advised the Indians
to submit to the Government and not incur its displeasure.
His greatest grief was that, in giving this advice, which was
followed on more than one occasion, he was compelled to
see the promises made them unfulfilled and his advice lead
ever to new suffering.   The Government, always a friend
to the Indian, was weak in the execution of its laws and
treaties with them.   Exactly there was the fault — that it
did not enforce the fulfillment of its promises.   There is no
more impressive scene in our Indian history than Father
De Smet's visit to Sitting Bull's band in 1868.   To the Indians he was the representative of truth, the Great Father
in Washington that of falsehood.   When they saw the banner of Father De Smet they first thought it the flag of the
United States and would have massacred every white man
in the party; but when they saw it to be the simple emblem
of Christ, borne by the valiant missionary, their hatred
changed to joy and their hostile attitude to the most enthusiastic friendliness.   It was the faithlessness of the Great
Father in his promises to them that embittered their minds
and called forth all that was savage in their nature.[1]

The Indians revered and loved Father De Smet to the
last.   They were always looking for him to return among
them.   From every tribe in the northwest he received peti-

[1] " Commissioners and agents of the Government come to us every
year.   They are affable and prodigal of words and promises on behalf
of our Great Father.   What is the reason that so many fine words and
pompous promises always come to nothing, nothing, nothing."

tions to have a black-robe sent them, and whenever he passed through their country in later years it was like a triumphal march. They came to see him and pour out their grievances and to have their children baptized. All in all their love and veneration for this man present one of the most touching spectacles in the history of the native races in America.

Father De Smet planned his work among the Indians on a far greater scale than he was able ever to realize. This was due in the first place to lack of resources. The Jesuits never had either the workers or the funds that were necessary. In the second place the field itself was entirely swept away. In 1846 Father De Smet no doubt anticipated that the seed he had sown in Oregon would grow into a mighty harvest. But what man proposes is rarely realized. In 1863, as he passed over the country again, he found it occupied by a new race, the hunting grounds of his neophytes filled with settlers; the Indians struggling in vain for their lands and being rapidly huddled together on small reservations. The whole opportunity for a great work had gone in the twinkling of an eye. The work of the missionary among the Indians was confined to a few small localities whose influence upon the general community was wholly inappreciable.

This is not saying that their work so far as it went was not a success. There is no finer example of an Indian mission than St. Ignatius in Montana; but a few individual successes were not a vast field. The truth is the Indian was gone, swallowed up in the flood of settlement, and no longer a factor in the life of that country.

It is a reasonable conclusion from the history of the Catholic missions in Oregon, that if the Indians had remained in a state of primitive wildness, the missionaries would have accomplished their conversion to the Christian religion; and that, without interfering with their native customs to any great extent, they would have lessened the wars among the tribes, promoted cleanliness and virtue among them, and at the same time have left them free in the exercise of all their manly sports, the chase, the nomadic life, and the gathering of furs by which their conveniences and comforts could be promoted through trade with the white man.

As a missionary force among the Indians there is no doubt of the superiority of the Catholic method. It appealed to the Indians, they liked it, and they had greater confidence in the black-robes than in Protestant ministers. The reasons for this are numerous and convincing, but chiefly two: (1) The sublime and exalted forms of Catholic worship appealed to the imagination of the Indian and he was attracted by them where abstract preaching made no impression.

(2) The black-robe came to the Indian unfettered by outward ties. His life was devoted solely to his calling. Poverty was his portion and no suspicion could exist that his devotion to his work was tainted with motives of self-aggrandizement. He was without wife or children and there was nothing to come between him and his work. His very personality was separate and distinct from that of ordinary men and he came to be universally known among the Indians as the " *robe noire* " or " black gown."

The Protestant clergyman came under different auspices. He had no distinguishing dress that marked him off in his calling. His personal appearance was like that of other white men who cheated and deceived them. The minister brought his wife and children who must needs come first in his heart. Then he taught more by abstract methods and devoted little time to those forms and ceremonies which appealed with peculiar power to the childlike mind of the Indian.

From these and other causes, the choice of the Indian, whenever he had means of acquaintance with both parties, was always for the black-gown, and there is no doubt that the Catholics were the most successful missionaries among the Indian tribes.[2] It was a deep grief to Father De Smet

2 " You are aware that I have filled the office of agent of the United States Government among the Indians for fifteen years. During all

in the closing years of his life, when called to Washington
for consultation about the apportionment of the missions
among different religious bodies, that the Indians were not
consulted at all, but the missions were parceled out on a
wholly different basis.   It was then that he saw his great
work, cut down as it already was by the influx of settlers,
practically swept away.[3]

Father De Smet made a profound study of the Indian
character as it related to his missionary work among them.
He never sought to minimize or conceal the natural difficulties in the way.   In a long letter written late in life he reviews the whole question in an exhaustive manner.[4]   From
this most valuable essay one readily discovers that he did not
then view the subject with the same enthusiasm as thirty
years before.   In his early work, fortune threw him among
a tribe which above all others was susceptible to religious
teaching.   They received him with a sincere desire to learn
his religion, and everything then looked as if the field had
only to be occupied to become permanently fruitful.   His

this time I have noticed with the greatest interest that the efforts made
by good Christians to establish missions and schools, to instruct the
Indians in spiritual and temporal matters, have contributed the most to
civilizing and pacifying them.   Furthermore, I take pleasure in testify-
ing that the Catholic Church, to which you belong, has everywhere
obtained the most pre-eminent success.   The Catholic missionaries have
always succeeded in gaining the Indian's hearts, in controlling their
brutal outbreaks and ameliorating their condition in every respect."
Letter from Alfred Vaughan, Indian agent, to Father De Smet.

[3] " I have been called to Washington by the Secretary of the Interior, where a great council has been held on Indian affairs in general.
I then learned that forty-three Indian stations were to be divided
among different denominations in the various sections of the country
inhabited by the Indians, of which only four are assigned to the
Catholics, viz : One in Dakota (the mission we intend to establish in
the spring among the Sioux), one in New Mexico, another in Montana
(Flathead) and a fourth in Idaho.   *In the whole of this affair the
Indians have not been consulted as to the religion they desired to belong to."*   Father De Smet, 1870.

[4] See page 1062 of the *Letters*.

great confidence at that time is shown in the following extract from his letters: " How consoling it is to pour the regenerating waters of baptism on the furrowed and scarred brows of these desert warriors,— to behold these children of the plains and forests emerging from that profound ignorance and superstition in which they have been for so many ages enveloped; to see them embrace the faith and all its sacred practices with an eagerness, an attention, a zeal, worthy the pristine Christians."

But all the Indians were not like the Flatheads, and the problem grew in complexity as the good missionary's experience increased. He found the Indians a fickle people. It was hard for them to stick to a thing, particularly when it ran counter to their immemorial customs. Their religious beliefs and social ethics were very different from those of Christian peoples. It was not a lack of intellectual capacity nor of a susceptibility to religious teachings that stood in the way; but the inertia of long-established customs. It was therefore Father De Smet's conclusion that the full " conversion of these poor heathens is the work of the Lord, for it implies the entire regeneration of the adult Indian which would be next to a miracle of grace."

There were other obstacles to missionary success among the Indians which are thus stated by Father De Smet: " The principal ones are the immoderate use of strong drink, polygamy, superstitious practices and prejudices, a language very difficult to acquire, and their inclination to a wandering life. This inclination is so strong that they become melancholy and morose if they stay three months in the same place."

We have several times referred to Father De Smet's work in providing ways and means for carrying on the missions. One important resource which was available for many years ought to be referred to. The American Fur Company gave the missionaries free transportation, both for passengers and freight, on the company's boats plying the Missouri river. It was a most valuable contribution, for which

the Jesuits were indebted to Charles P. Chouteau, to whom
Father De Smet refers in his letters as a benefactor of the
missions.   After the American Fur Company withdrew
from the upper river the same privilege was occasionally
enjoyed at the hands of Captain Joseph La Barge, Father
De Smet's personal friend.

CHAPTER XII.

Father De Smet an active observer of public events — The growth
of the United States — Its future — The Oregon Question — The anti-
Catholic movement — The radical party — The Test Oath in Missouri.

FATHER DE SMET was an interested observer of
public affairs and of the progress of his adopted
country. His letters to his European correspondents are
full of references to these subjects. In regard to the
growth of the United States he held the most enthusiastic
views, and often expressed his wonder and admiration at
the marvelous result developing under his eyes. A few
examples of the way in which he represented this new
nation to his friends in the Old World are given here: " I
have said in Europe, and I repeat it, there is no country in
the world that has greater resources than this; none that
is making such progress; where everything is developing
in so wonderful a manner as to draw the admiration of
the civilized world. Providence has laid out this country
on a gigantic scale; its destiny is to march onward, and no
power on earth can stop it. It is a mighty country, young
and vigorous, and possesses a vast space which time will
fill with millions of men."

The vast extent of the United States appealed powerfully
to his imagination: " I shall never forget," he once wrote,
" the rapture of a traveler who left the green parks of
New Orleans early in March — that land of the orange
and the olive, then teeming with verdure, freshness and
life, and, as it were, mocking him with the midsummer of
his own northern home. He journeyed leisurely toward
the region of ice and snow, to watch the budding of the
young flowers and to catch the breezes of spring. He

[127]

crossed the Lakes Pontchartrain and Borgne and he ascended the Big Tombigbee in a comfortable steamboat. From Tuscaloosa he shot athwart the wilds of Alabama, over Indian grounds that bloody battles have rendered memorable. He traversed Georgia and the Carolinas, ranged along the base of the mountains of Virginia; and for three months more he enjoyed one perpetual, unvarying, ever-coming, spring — that most delicious season of the year — till, by the middle of June, he found himself in the fogs of the Passamaquoddy where tardy summer was even then hesitating whether it was time to come. And yet he had never been off the soil of his own country! The flag that he saw on the summit of the fortress on the lakes near New Orleans was like that which floated from the staff on the hills of old Fort Sullivan, in the easternmost extremity of Maine; and the morning gun that startled his slumbers among the rocky battlements of the Bay of Fundy, was not answered till many minutes after on the shores of the Gulf of Mexico, and hours after on the shores of the Bay of San Francisco in California."

The political unity of the United States appeared to him quite as wonderful as its territorial extent. " What nation on earth presents such a spectacle as the United States of North America of a confederated government over such a vast extent of territory so complicated, with so many varied interests, and yet moving so harmoniously? I went within the walls of the Capitol at Washington, and there, under the star-spangled banners that wave amid its domes. I found the representatives of thirty States — nations, in many senses, they may be called — that have within them each the germ of a greater people than many of the proud, now tottering, principalities of Europe; all speaking or learning the same language, all acting with one heart and all burning with the same enthusiasm — the love and glory of this great Republic."

The " manifest destiny " of this nation, as arbiter of the political fortunes of the Western Hemisphere, did not escape him. "I have seen an old geographical chart," he wrote a friend, "which shows the eagle soaring in the air above the great extent of North America, with the numerous islands adjacent to both coasts. He is casting a penetrating and greedy look over the vast Canada and all its dependencies, and his open beak seems ready to snatch them up. All those immense regions of which the United States occupy the center rest under his shadow. His fine widespread tail covers all of Mexico and the adjoining regions as far as the Gulf of Darien and the Bay of Panama; and the tips of his wings are dipped in the two oceans beyond San Domingo and the Sandwich Islands. And that is the grand future, perhaps not far off, to which the great American Republic aspires, and which she will attain if she is wise."

Many pages might be quoted from his letters to show how well he foresaw the future development of the West, but the following brief reference must suffice: "Are these vast and innumerable fields of hay forever destined to be consumed by fire, or perish in the autumnal snows? How long shall these superb forests be the haunts of wild beasts? And these inexhaustible quarries, these abundant mines of coal, lead, sulphur, iron, copper and saltpetre — can it be that they are doomed to remain forever undeveloped? Not so. The day will come, etc."

It was quite natural, considering Father De Smet's intimate acquaintance with the Columbia Valley, that he should take an active interest in the Oregon Question. Like his co-worker in those parts, Doctor Marcus Whitman,[1] he wanted to see this region fall into the hands of the United States. He was thrown a great deal with the

[1] Father De Smet and Marcus Whitman are the most distinguished names in the history of Protestant and Catholic missionary work in Oregon. There is now in possession of George H. Himes of Portland, Oregon, a "Douay Bible," dated "Belfast, 1839," with the following inscription in Father De Smet's hand: "Presented to Dr. M. Whitman by P. J. De Smet."

9

British traders, and they were not altogether discreet in
setting forth their schemes of empire on the Pacific slope.
It aroused Father De Smet's indignation that such things
should be going on and his country not bestir itself. He
did not like the comparison of our lethargy with the activity of Great Britain, and a little incident serves to show
us that he did not conceal his opinion.

In 1845 he met on the upper Columbia two engineer
officers of the British army on their way to the mouth of
that stream. After a brief interchange of courtesies and
news each party went on its way; but Father De Smet had
observed enough to set him thinking, and he placed his
reflections upon record:

" I received with gladness the recent news from Europe,
but the Oregon Question seemed to me somewhat alarming; for it was not curiosity or pleasure that had led these
two officers to cross the ocean and so many desert wastes
and that was hastening their course toward the mouth of
the Columbia. They were under orders from their Government to take possession of Cape Disappointment, to
unfurl the flag of England and to build a fort there in
order to control the entrance to the river.   In the Oregon
Question John Bull, without talking too much, goes
straight to the point and seizes the most important strat-
egical sites in the country. Uncle Sam, on the other
hand, wastes his time in words, fumes and threatens.
Years have passed in this way in debates and fruitless controversies, without a practical effort to secure his real or
pretended rights in Oregon."

Father De Smet, on another occasion, furnished Sen-
ator Thomas H. Benton with a report of a conversation
which he heard among British naval officers, disclos-
ing an official intention to take possession of Oregon.[2]

But while Father De Smet was an enthusiastic believer
in the future material greatness of his country, he had

[2] See page 486 of the *Letters*.

many misgivings about its moral and religious destiny. This arose almost entirely from the hostile feeling that prevailed extensively throughout the country at a certain period against the Roman Catholic religion. The crusade against the Church — for it practically amounted to that — attained its greatest power during the existence of the so-called Know-nothing party, between 1850 and 1860. This ephemeral organization, characteristic of the nervous energy of a rapidly developing country, was founded in 1852. It was at first a secret, oath-bound, political fraternity, whose object it was to exclude aliens from office. It was the first formidable expression of public alarm at the rapid influx of immigrants and the growth of Roman Catholicism in the United States. Opposition to the extension of slave power was another of its tenets. When it entered the political arena, it did so under the name of the American Party, and its motto was, "Americans must rule America." It was popularly known as the Know-nothing party, because, in its earlier history, its members, when questioned about the doings of their organization, answered "I don't know." In 1854 it carried several northern states, including New York, and in 1856 elected thirty-two "American" governors. In the latter year it ran a candidate for the presidency, but carried the electoral vote of only one state, Maryland. Thereafter its fortunes rapidly declined and by 1860 it had practically passed out of existence.

During the active history of this organization public feeling against the Roman Catholics ran high and in many cases amounted to outrageous persecution, wholly inconsistent with the principle of religious liberty which is fixed in the foundation of our government. It made a deep and lasting impression upon Father De Smet, as we now know from his personal letters to his friends in Europe. We might quote at great length from his expressions upon this subject, some of which disclose a degree of bitterness quite as extreme as the persecution at which they were aimed. The following show the general tenor of all: " I cannot say much of the United States. This vast land, with all its advantages, must grow great and mighty, * * * but the American liberty and tolerance, so highly boasted, exist less in this great Republic than in the most oppressed country of Europe."

Here is another extract which shows to what a degree Father De Smet's vision was clouded by the sinister events of the time: " Let me say, *entre nous,* this country is marching rapidly toward anarchy. I dare say we are already there in some degree. Everything indicates that it will be preceded by a violent persecution of our holy religion. This Republic, where mobs are the order of the day, cannot long endure. Liberty here is a perversion of the word; it is license pure and simple. * * * Oh, little Belgium! She is truly free, prosperous and happy, because she is profoundly Catholic. Protestantism, in all its phases, has always been given to persecution."

At this period in his life, Father De Smet earnestly discouraged migration to America. As he saw the vast numbers of Catholics coming to these shores, and no possibility of supplying them with teachers, he felt that they could not long withstand the influence of Protestanism and that apostacy would exceed the number of conversions. He also advised some of his more intimate friends not to send their children here on account of the total change from the life to which they were accustomed. In Europe they were to a large degree born to their station in life. They would not work in well where boys commenced at the very foot of the ladder, doing the commonest service for the sake of getting a start. Their language would furthermore be against them until they could gain a command of English; and on the whole they would stand little show in competition with the universal adaptability of the American boy.

We have already noted Father De Smet's attitude toward the questions of the Civil War. If he had taken any part in politics he would doubtless have been what was called a " War Democrat " — a Unionist, when it was a question of the unity of the country, but opposed to the extreme measures adopted by the Republicans at the close of the war. In his letters are several extended reviews of the causes of the war, which are generally judicious and enlightened. After the war came to a close, he became imbued with a fear of the radical element in the dominant party and looked upon its success as fraught with great danger to the Republic. He favored the milder policy of President Johnson toward the South and deprecated the hostility of Congress toward his reconstruction measures.

His feeling on these questions was doubtless largely controlled by the turn things took in the State of Missouri after the close of the war. The radical party for a time held control of the State and proceeded to extreme measures in order to perpetuate it. In 1865 a new constitution was adopted. The convention which drafted it was under the control of a few extremists. Among the more drastic features was the requirement of a test oath as condition precedent to voting, holding office, teaching school, preaching the gospel, solemnizing marriage, practicing law, sitting as a juror, or holding property in trust for any church, religious society or congregation. The principal condition of the oath was that the individual had never sympathized with or aided the South. There were some forty-five offenses that he must never have committed; and so sweeping were its provisions that no one could truthfully take it.

This provision of the new constitution was a failure almost from the start. The better sentiment of the community rebelled against it. Prominent men refused to be bound by it. Finally its validity was passed upon by the Supreme Court of the United States in January, 1867, and it was declared to be unconstitutional.

In one of his letters to friends in Europe, written while the test-oath was still in force, Father De Smet thus sets forth the attitude of his Church upon the question: "The old proverb says *sunt bona mixta malis,* and that is the case today in Missouri. Upon emerging from the war and at the beginning of the return of peace we find ourselves in fresh trouble and in a state of cruel uncertainty. This is the way of it. The radical party has installed itself, *per fas et nefas,* at the head of the state government. The new constitution, which has been adopted by a slender majority and which is publicly denounced as fraudulent, requires the clergy of all denominations, all professors of seminaries and colleges and all school teachers of either sex (including nuns) to take the following oath: 'that they have at no time in the past uttered a word nor sympathized in any manner in favor of the Rebellion,' etc. Preaching and performing the marriage ceremony are expressly forbidden to the clergy by this law.

"The priests are generally agreed that, on principle, such an oath cannot be taken, because our authority does not emanate from the state and we cannot, without compromising the ecclesiastical estate, consent to take it. No Catholic priest in Missouri will take it; the Protestant ministers have generally done so. The penalty for those who refuse to take this abominable *ex post facto* oath is a fine of $500 and imprisonment. The governor has announced in a speech 'that he has had the state prison enlarged and that the law shall be executed. If this cruel law is really enforced, our churches will have to be closed and our schools and colleges will be ruined."

Father De Smet naturally had little love for a political party capable of a *faux pas* like that and he looked with deep dread upon the prospect of Grant's election in 1868. He felt that the great general shared the Protestant antagonism to his Church, and that he could not withstand the more radical element in his party who would use his great authority among the people to further their extreme measures. When the election came and Grant uttered his famous manifesto, "Let us have peace," it lifted a heavy load from Father De Smet's mind and he hoped that every semblance of religious persecution would be purged from the politics of the country.

In all that we have said of Father De Smet's attitude on the subject of religious persecution, it should be borne in mind that it has come to us only through his private correspondence. He was always particularly careful not to enter in any way into political controversy, and no one could have told his real feelings nor their deep intensity. "I am keeping my mouth shut about politics," he wrote to a friend, "and I wish some of our other brethren would do the same." It is now a most interesting revelation to learn what the good priest thought on these disturbing questions; and to know how wisely he conducted himself, calmly waiting for the Providence on which he relied to bring all things to a just result.

CHAPTER XIII.

LITERARY WORK.

Description of the Missouri River — Father De Smet's map — Fauna and Flora — Indian history and traditions — Origin of Father De Smet's letters — Methods of writing — Unfounded aspersions — Literary records and data — The Linton album — Father De Smet's style — List of publications.

FATHER De SMET'S writings are a distinct contribution to human knowledge. They abound in descriptions of the regions through which he passed, and although this information has been superseded by the more thorough work of later years, it served a useful purpose in its time. A particular example of his descriptive work is found in his notes upon the Missouri river, its tributaries, scenery, characteristics, navigation, etc. Very few, except pilots, knew that river as well as he, and they only knew its channel, while he was acquainted with its whole wonderful valley and with the wild inhabitants who occupied it. He had been at its very source in Red Rock lake on the Continental Divide and he had passed over every foot of its length except the distance between the Three Forks and Sun river in Montana. The information which he has left us on this subject will always possess a high historic value.

He made an early observation in regard to Great Salt lake which later researches have fully verified. " The lake, which is now only seventy miles long and thirty-five wide, probably filled, at a remote epoch, the whole valley. On all sides, on the slopes of the mountains, at a uniform height, are traces which water alone could have made." The Quaternary Lake Bonneville of the scientists filled a large part of the Great Basin and overflowed to the north into Snake river, making the watershed of the lake, geologically at least, a part of the Columbia Basin.

Father De Smet did a great deal of work in the line of map-making. He thus refers to this matter in one of his letters: " During the ten years I spent in the Indian country I occupied myself occasionally in drawing maps of the countries through which I passed. I availed myself of the best information I could obtain from trappers and intelligent Indians who were well acquainted with the mountain passes and the course of the rivers. Not having had instruments with me, the maps were necessarily only an approximation to the true positions." Before his death he gathered together into an ordinary stub-file all his manuscript maps. They are not executed with a degree of technical skill in draftsmanship to justify their reproduction; but they are extremely interesting and valuable historically. We may cite, as a single instance, that, although the Yellowstone Park country was not made known to the world until 1870, these maps, prepared before 1850, show nearly every feature of interest in that wonderful region.[1] In 1851 Father De Smet, at the request of D. D. Mitchell, drew a map of the western country for the Government, and it is now presumably on file in the Bureau of Indian Affairs in Washington.

The writings of Father De Smet are full of references to the fauna and flora of the country. There is not much original matter in these descriptions, and the changes in scientific nomenclature since they were written are so great that it is hardly worth while to attempt to utilize them. In a general way, however, there is a great deal of interest in his notes on the larger animals, such as the buffalo, beaver and bear, and the large space that these animals filled in the life of the Indian and of the early pioneers.

The fund of Indian lore contained in the *Letters* has permanent value. It includes descriptions of the manners and customs of the Indians, their traditions and notable

[1] See pages 182 and 661 of the *Letters*.

exploits, comments upon their intellectual and spiritual
nature, and a great variety of other subjects. The history
of the native races of North America can never be fully
written without consulting the writings of Father De
Smet.

Coming now to the vehicle by which Father De Smet
transmitted to the public the information he had collected,
it remains to note the most important feature of his career, his literary work. The vast magnitude of this labor
can best be judged by the bulk of material contained in
the present edition of his letters. The industry and application necessary to produce such a result were prodigious;
yet in spite of the great quantity of matter its quality
was such as always to interest the reading public.

The primary purpose of his writings was to interest the
Catholic public both in Europe and America in his missionary work and thus aid in securing the necessary funds
for the missions. This duty fitted in perfectly with Father
De Smet's natural tastes, for there is no doubt that he
loved the work and would have achieved fame as a writer
even without the specific motive above referred to. Concerning this primary motive Father De Smet has left the
following definite statement: "I have been more or less
engaged in the Indian missions for something like thirty
years. The Reverend Father [General] Roothaan, of
blessed memory, imposed it upon me as a duty to write
very fully and to enter into minute details upon everything that concerned them — the diverse countries inhabited by the Indians, the manners, customs, beliefs, etc.,
of these strange and unfortunate tribes. My numerous
letters, consisting of five volumes, bear witness that I have
at least endeavored to discharge the duty laid upon me,
and with humility and assurance, I hope that I can add
that I have tried to do it faithfully. The present Very
Reverend Father General encourages me by his letters to
continue to give the details of my missionary labors year
after year. All the superiors and provincials of Missouri

have also called for them, and I have always been submissive to their requests in the spirit of obedience."

Nearly all of Father De Smet's writings are in the form of letters, published mainly in Europe where they would be most effective in securing generous aid for the missions. They were later translated in large part into English and published in the United States. These letters were extensively edited before publication, by Father De Smet's express request, and were shorn of whatever might possibly offend in America. They were not letters in the strict sense of the term, but careful dissertations, often addressed to several different parties, and they contain little of a personal character. The style bears evidence of this editorial revision. While it is more polished, particularly in the English translations, than in the genuine letters not written for publication, it has less of the freedom and vigor which were so characteristic of whatever Father De Smet said or did.

The correspondence of Father De Smet is in both French and English, with a line or two of vernacular Flemish (if writing to his family) whenever he was saying something that he did not want read if it fell into the wrong hands. He did not have a very perfect command of English. He was frequently mixed up on his tenses and occasionally on his prepositions and pronouns. He indulged in excessively long sentences, some of which are so involved that they cannot be disentangled except by breaking them up into separate parts. Yet in spite of these drawbacks there was a freshness, vigor and originality of expression that make his personal letters more attractive than those written expressly for publication.

Like all men who attain positions of prominence in the public eye, Father De Smet provoked the jealousy of inferior natures who were envious of a career which they could not equal. Elsewhere we have noted the accusations presented to the Father General at Rome concerning the subject-matter of Father De Smet's writings.

He was later accused of crookedness in regard to the purely literary features of his work. The nature of these charges is thus stated by Father De Smet: "For some years past I have been subjected to criticisms, often personal and malevolent, on the part of several German priests, who are saying in America, on the testimony of one or several fathers of your Province, that my name is only an assumed name in the letters which are printed and the books that are published afterwards bearing my name."

To Father De Smet's sensitive and guileless nature these false accusations brought genuine sorrow, as he could not understand why any human being should bear him ill-will on so slender a provocation. Nothing in the present editorial studies of his writings has been discovered that can give the slightest color to the charge, unless it be a single instance in which Father De Smet consulted a friend in preparing his reply to certain inquiries from Europe in regard to the Indian Question, and transmitted as his own his adviser's answers.[2]

In the last two or three years of his life, Father De Smet spent considerable time in collecting material for a history of the religious Province of Missouri. Here is a personal reference to this work: "Whilst confined to my room by sickness, I take great pleasure in my leisure moments in collecting whatever I can concerning the history of the Province. I have commenced at the beginning of our leaving Belgium in 1821, of our coming to Missouri in 1823, with all its traveling incidents and digging the first spadeful of earth on 31st of July, 1823, the feast day of St. Ignatius, of the Novitiate in Florissant. I have already written eighty pages from notes in the archives of the Province, from personal recollections, and from such other information as I am able to obtain."

Father De Smet did not live to complete this work, and even the partial narrative to which he refers is apparently lost.

[2] See page 1208 of the *Letters*.

Father De Smet's methods of writing were those of any careful investigator. The following reference to his study of the Missouri river is a good example of all his work: "I spend my leisure hours in reading and taking notes upon the Missouri and its tributaries and upon the immense territory of 500,000 square miles that it drains. I investigate, I draw upon my own fund of information, and then I write." He drew from many sources, particularly the traders at the remote posts with most of whom he was on terms of close friendship. Among those whom we know to have furnished him information which found its way into his letters are Alexander Culbertson and E. T. Denig, distinguished traders of the American Fur Company, Zephyr Rencontre and Charles E. Galpin, interpreters, and Joseph La Barge, pilot. It was his constant habit to pick up information from every source available and jot it down for future use.

We have already referred to the great volume of Father De Smet's literary work. Considering the absence of extraneous mechanical aids which are now regarded as indispensable, as, for example, stenography and typewriting, the actual physical labor involved in his work appears incredible. Many of his longer letters were copied several times in his own hand, showing that in large degree he had to depend upon himself even for the purely mechanical labor of making necessary copies. He wrote a clear hand, and at times reduced it to a degree of fineness which is simply marvelous. The Jesuit training cultivated a fine hand, and the necessity of economy when paper was scarce and postage high accentuated the habit. To cite a single example, one of the letters is so finely written that a single page of ordinary letter size contains 1,231 words whereas a modern hand would fill it with from 150 to 250 words.

Father De Smet kept copies of nearly all his published letters and these are now scattered through several letter-books without any careful index. He apparently did not begin to keep copies of his personal letters until about

1850, but from that time on the file seems to be complete except of those letters written when he was in Europe. He preserved comparatively few of his letters received, or if he did, the files have been lost. All of the papers now known to exist are preserved in the archives of the St. Louis University.

One of these old records deserves more than a passing notice. It may be called the Linton Album from the name of the owner, though now it is a part of the Father De Smet papers. Dr. Moses L. Linton was for many years connected with the St. Louis University and was besides one of the prominent citizens of St. Louis.[3] In the course of his professional career one of his patients, a lady, made him a present of an album as "a souvenir of professional kindness." It was not an album to be devoted exclusively to the reception of pictures, but one to be written in, with frequent pages of a specially ornate character on which, presumably, matters of particular interest could be set down.

Dr. Linton devoted the present to a unique purpose the great importance of which he doubtless did not at the time fully realize. He gave it over to Father De Smet with the request that he would fill it with the record of his life. In carrying out this arrangement Father De Smet did nearly all the work with his own hand. The book is filled, in the most faultless writing, with a great variety of matters. There are Indian legends, poems, the Lord's Prayer in many different Indian dialects, and a variety of other interesting curiosities. It contains a complete account of the great work of 1868 which we have narrated elsewhere. Throughout the

[3] Dr. Moses Linton was born in Kentucky in 1812 and died in St. Louis June 1, 1872. His early education was partly under Catholic influence and he formally united with that church in 1841. He went to Europe to perfect his education and in 1842 became a member of the medical faculty of the St. Louis University, retaining the place until his death. He took an active interest in public affairs, and was a recognized force in the politics of his city and state.

book are photographs and sketches, the most important being a series of water colors by one Matthew Hastings, an
amateur artist of very pronounced merit. Some of these
sketches, particularly those of the expedition of 1868, are
of great historical value.

But the most interesting and important feature of this
album is the itinerary of Father De Smet's journeyings.
He was a great traveler, and he early gained wide celebrity
as such. He fell into the habit of keeping a record of the
distances traveled each year and it finally became a matter
of no little personal vanity. There are several photographs
of himself on which he has written the years of his life
since 1821 around the border with the distances traveled
each year. There are in his letter books two other similar
records. Considering the means of travel in the earlier
years of Father De Smet's life the simple statement of
180,000 miles traveled gives an impressive idea of his untiring activity.

The album is a beautiful and costly book, in enameled
covers and rich leaves of different tints, with ornamental
pages scattered here and there. Father De Smet was proud
of it and succeeded in making it a memento of rare value.
Whenever he returned to St. Louis Dr. Linton would get
him to bring it up to date. We find this reference to it
among the *Letters:* " You ask me for a fresh letter, or
rather for the continuation of my itinerary. For the last
twelve years, at each of my returns to St. Louis, you have
joyously placed your album upon my table. Each recurring
sight of it has been a fresh pleasure, like the meeting of
a familiar acquaintance, and immediately I have resumed
my pen with gladness to lengthen out the old sketch with
one more page." It is very rarely that a public character
has left behind him so valuable a collection of personal
data as this Linton Album contains.

Father De Smet indulged in verse a good deal and his
efforts in this line are expressed in English, French and
Latin. Some of his verse merits perusal, but it is evident

that prose was the true medium for the expression of his thought. His prose style was simple and direct, and never monotonous. It is in many places overburdened with religious phraseology, and the frequent recurrence of the terms peculiar to the work of the Church detracts somewhat from its pleasure to the general reader. This trait is more apparent in the earlier letters intended for publication with a view to influencing missionary contributions, than in his later official and personal correspondence.

In his personal letters Father De Smet indulges in a great deal of pleasantry, as this was about the only opportunity in his order of life for the natural exuberance of his nature to find expression. Like other men he had his idiosyncrasies of style, one of which was a fondness for the use of a word under different meanings, often carrying the practice to an extreme length.

Finally all his literary work is characterized by a lofty sense of purity and honor, and there is little in it to which the most scrupulous taste could take exception. The uprightness of his life found expression in his writings and this is the highest encomium that can be bestowed upon them.[4]

[4] The following is a list of the more important publications of Father De Smet's writings:

Published during his lifetime.

Pamphlet, by Father Verhaegen, entitled *The Indian Missions in the United States of America, under the Care of the Missouri Province of the Society of Jesus.* Comprises 34 pages, 26 of which are devoted to two letters of Father De Smet's, one on the Potawatomi Mission and one giving a brief account of the 1840 Journey.

Letters and Sketches: with a Narrative of a Year's Residence Among the Indian Tribes of the Rocky Mountains. M. Fithian, 61 N. Second Street, Philadelphia, 1843.

French edition of the above, entitled *Voyages aux Montagnes-Rocheuses, et une Année de Séjour chez les Tribus Indiennes du Vaste Territoire de l'Orégon dépendant des Etats-Unis d'Amérique.* P. J. Hanicq, Malines, 1844.

Second French edition, entitled *Voyages aux Montagnes Rocheuses chez les Tribus Indiennes du Vaste Territoire de l'Orégon, Dependant des Etats-Unis d'Amérique.* Deuxième Edition. L. Lefort, Imprimeur-Libraire, Lille, 1850.

Dutch edition of the same, entitled *Reis naar het Rotsgebergte (Rocky Mountains), door Eerw. vader De Smet, Belgisch zendeling in de Vereenigde Staten.* J. W. Robijns en comp., Deventer; n. d.

German edition of the same, entitled *Reisen zu den Felsengebirgen und ein Jahr unter den Wilden Indianerstämmen des Oregon Gebietes.* St. Louis, 1865.

The preface to the *Western Missions and Missionaries* makes mention of a further edition in Italian, issued by Louis Prevete, Palermo, 1847.

Oregon Missions and Travels Over the Rocky Mountains, in 1845–46. Edward Dunigan, 151 Fulton-Street, 1847.

French edition of the above, entitled *Missions de l'Orégon et Voyages aux Montagnes-Rocheuses, aux Sources de la Colombie, de l'Athabasca et du Sascatshawin; pendant l'année 1845–46.* Ouvrage orné de 16 Gravures et de 3 Cartes. Il se vend au Profit de la Mission. Veuve Vander Schelden, Gand (1848).

Second French edition (a different translation) entitled *Missions de l'Orégon et Voyages dans les Montagnes-Rocheuses en 1845–46.* Ouvrage traduit de l'anglais par M. Bourlez. Librairie de Poussielgue-Rusand, Paris and J. B. Pélagaud et Cie., Lyon, 1848.

Flemish edition of the same, entitled *Missien van den Orégon en Reizen naer de Rotsbergen en de Bronnen der Colombia, der Athabasca en Sascatshawin, in 1845–46.* Uit het fransch door een' kloosterling van Latrappe. Wwe. Vander Schelden, Onderstraet No. 37, Gent, 1849.

Voyage au Grand Desert en 1851. Imprimerie de J. Vandereydt, Bruxelles, 1853. Reprint of articles in the Précis Historiques.

Western Missions and Missionaries: a Series of Letters. James B. Kirker, late Edward Dunigan and Brother, 599 Broadway (up-stairs), New York, 1863.

Later editions from the same plates, with a defect on p. 334, are issued by P. J. Kenedy, Excelsior Catholic Publishing House, 5 Barclay Street, New York, n. d.

French edition of the same, entitled *Cinquante Nouvelles Lettres.* Publiées par Revd. Edward Terwecoren de la Compagnie de Jésus. H. Casterman, Paris et Tournai, 1858.

New Indian Sketches. D. & J. Sadlier & Co., 31 Barclay St., New York, 1865.

10

A later undated edition from the same plates, marked " Copyright 1885."

The letters of Father De Smet were also extensively published in the *Annales de la Propagation de la Foi,* Lyons; and in the *Précis Historiques,* Brussels, edited by Ed. Terwecoren, a friend and correspondent of De Smet; and in several Cathoiic periodicals in the United States.

Published after Father De Smet's death.

Father François Deynoodt, S.J., of Belgium, with the approval of Father De Smet, given a short time before his death, undertook the work of bringing out a complete edition of his writings, together with a biographical sketch. Up to the time when this work was arrested by Father Deynoodt's death the following had appeared:

Voyages aux Montagnes-Rocheuses, et Séjour chez les Tribus Indiennes de l'Orégon (Etats-Unis). Nouvelle Edition. Revue et considerrablement augmentée. Bruxelles, Victor Devaux et Cie., and Paris, H. Repos et Cie., 1873.

Voyages dans l'Amérique Septentrionale. Orégon. Troisième édition, soigneusement corrigée et augmentée de notes, d'un portrait et d'une carte. Mathieu Closson et Cie., Bruxelles, and H. Repos et Cie., Paris, 1874.

Lettres Choisies du Révérend Père Pierre-Jean De Smet de la Compagnie de Jésus, Missionaire aux Etats-Unis d'Amérique. Soigneusement Revues et corrigées d'après les manuscrits de l'auteur et Augmentées de nombreuses notes. En quatre Séries.

Première Série. 1849–1857. Bruxelles, Mathieu Closson et Cie.; Paris, H. Répos et Cie. 1875.

Seconde Série. 1855–1861. Bruxelles, F. Haenen; Paris, H. Répos et Cie. 1876.

Troisième Série. 1860–1867. Bruxelles, M. Closson et Cie.; Paris, H. Répos et Cie. 1877.

Quatrième Série. 1867–1873. Bruxelles, M. Closson et Cie. 1878.

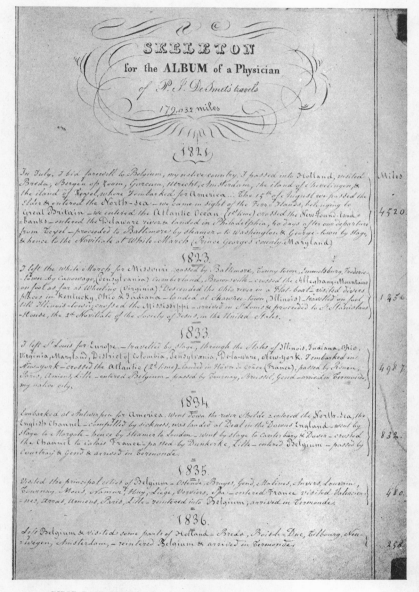

FIRST PAGE OF ITINERARY, FROM THE LINTON ALBUM.

PART I.

1838–1839.

Itinerary of Father De Smet from 1821 to 1839 inclusive.

1821.

IN the month of July Father De Smet, then in his twenty-first year, left Belgium, his native country, in company with the Very Reverend Mr. Nerinckx, missionary to Kentucky — Passed through Holland, visiting several of its cities — Embarked at the Island of Texel on board the brig *Columbus* — Sailed on August 15th — Crossed the Atlantic (first time) in forty days — Landed at Philadelphia—Went by steamer to Baltimore — Went thence to Washington and Georgetown by stage — Thence to the Novitiate of Whitemarsh, fifteen miles from Annapolis, where he and his six companions entered the Society of Jesus — Remained at Whitemarsh eighteen months.

Distance traveled during year, 4,520 miles.

1823.

Early in the spring Father De Smet and his six Belgian companions left Whitemarsh with Fathers Van Quickenborne and Timmermans, who were sent by Monseigneur Du Bourg, Bishop of Louisiana and Missouri, to St. Ferdinand, near St. Louis, to found there the first Jesuit establishment in the western portions of North America since the suppression of the Society — Passed by way of Baltimore, Fredericktown and Cumberland to Wheeling on the Ohio, all the way *" pedibus apostolorum,* staff in hand "*—* Embarked at Wheeling in two house boats and descended the Ohio to Shawneetown, Ill., where they left the river and crossed the country on foot with much fatigue to the Mississippi opposite St. Louis — Crossed the river — Rested several days at the house of the Bishop — Went to St. Ferdinand fifteen miles from St. Louis to complete their two years of probation and to found the second novitiate of the Society of Jesus in the United States, and to prosecute their studies in philosophy and theology until 1827, the year of their ordination.— Number of novices increased from year to year — Churches were erected at St. Charles and other places, and the University of St. Louis was founded in 1830.

Distance traveled in 1823, 1,256 miles.

1833.

Left St. Louis for Europe under orders of his Superior on business for the Society and on account of his health — Traveled by way of Washington to New York, where he embarked (second passage of the ocean)— Landed at Havre, France, and proceeded thence via Paris and Rouen to Belgium — Arrived at Termonde, his birthplace.

Distance traveled, 4,987 miles.

1834.

Visited the principal cities of Belgium — Embarked at Antwerp with three candidates to return to America — Was taken dangerously ill on the North Sea as a result of tempestuous weather and violent sea-sickness — Advised by physician that he could not stand journey — Landed at Deal in the Downs, England — Traveled by stage to Margate, by steamboat to London, by stage to Dover — Crossed the channel to Calais — Passed by Dunkirk and Lille into Belgium, and to Termonde.

Distance traveled, 480 miles.

1835–1836.

Father De Smet spent these years in traversing the principal cities of Belgium, Holland and France on business of the Society.

Distance traveled in the two years, 738 miles.

1837.

Left Belgium — Entered France — Embarked at Havre on an American packet — crossed the Atlantic (third time) in thirty days — Landed at New York — Went by rail and canal to Pittsburg — Thence by steamboat to St. Louis — Visited the Lazarist Seminary at the Barrens, St. Mary's County, Mo., and then repaired with three candidates to the novitiate near St. Ferdinand.

Distance traveled, 5,268 miles.

1838.

Sent by his Superior, with one father and two brothers, to found a mission among the Potawatomies — Left St. Louis May 10th — Traveled all the way by steamboat, visiting en route the Kickapoos, Sauks, Iowas, Otoes, Missouris and Omahas — Arrived at destination May 31st — Erected a residence and church several miles from the river within the limits of the modern city of Council Bluffs.

Distance traveled, 685 miles.

1839.

Father De Smet made a trip up the Missouri on a mission of peace from the Potawatomies to the Sioux, the two tribes having been at war — Traveled by steamboat — Started April 29th — Ascended as far as Vermillion — Met and conferred with the Yanktons and Sioux — Returned by canoe to St. Joseph (or St. Mary) about May 15th — Went to St. Louis in December to procure supplies for the mission — Traveled overland all the way, on foot, horseback, and by wagon.

Distance traveled, 1,322 miles.

CHAPTER I.

JOURNEY TO COUNCIL BLUFFS.

Pursuit of the steamboat — Indians by the way — Site of St. Joseph — Inconveniences of river navigation — The Otoes and their minister — First touch of Indian life — Disappointing reception by the Potawatomies — Beginning of missionary work.

Reverend Father Superior: [1]

YOUR REVERENCE will have been uneasy, and will no doubt have desired for some time to receive news from this quarter. Opportunities to get letters through to you by way of Ft. Leavenworth are rare and uncertain and besides we have all been sick for a fortnight, which we attribute to the change from the thin warm water of the river to springwater as cold as ice. Father Felix is still indisposed.

I left the village of the Kickapoos on the 25th of May for the fort [Leavenworth], meaning to wait there for a boat. When I reached there I was surprised to learn from Mr. Hamilton that the *Wilmington* had left the place two hours before. Arming myself with a good switch, I applied it to the sides of my poor Rozinante, and galloping, galloping, we made together seven miles in half an hour. I reached the path where the boat was taking on wood in time. Nothing very remarkable happened during the voyage. The first night we stopped two miles from the village of Pashishi. Here the captain bought some twenty cords of wood, cut by the Indian women. The passengers amused themselves with putting up small coins on sticks to test the skill of the little Indians in shooting with the bow: one especially, only

[1] A hitherto unpublished fragment in French, giving a description of Father De Smet's journey from the Kickapoo village to the Potawatomies in 1838. Written June, 1838, at the Potawatomi Mission, Council Bluffs.

YOUTHFUL PORTRAIT OF FATHER DE SMET.

seven or eight years old, handled his bow and arrows with admirable dexterity, for though the distance was considerable he never missed, and he always went promptly to put the little piece of money into his poor mother's hands. I rejoiced in his good success: he was the only one who had a chaplet and medal about his neck, and I learned that he had been baptized by the Rev. F. Van Quickenborne.[2] Toward evening I paid a visit to Pashishi's village, situated on the river.

The soil all around seemed to me very rich, the woods that I traversed on my way were superb and the prairie smiling and beautiful. There this good chief might live quiet and happy, if he had the courage to embrace our holy religion, for he acknowledges it to be the only true one, and he often tells how "in a dream, the ancient Fathers of the Society, who had formerly visited his tribe, appeared to him and reproached him with the hardness of heart of his nation and their perversity in stubbornly refusing to receive and follow the law of Christ; that that is the cause why the Great Spirit has abandoned them to all sorts of irregularities and to the impositions of a false prophet (Keokuk, of whom I will tell you hereafter); and that none of them should escape his wrath in the other world."

We stopped for two hours at the Black-snake Hills [St. Joseph, Mo.]. There I had a long talk with J[oseph] R[oubidoux], who keeps a store and runs his father's fine farm. He showed me a great deal of affection and kindness, and expressed a wish to build a little chapel there, if his father can manage to get some French families to come and settle near them. The place is one of the finest on the Missouri for the erection of a city.

At one of the landings or paths, where the boat had

[2] Rev. Charles Felix Van Quickenborne; born 1788 in Ghent, died near St. Charles, Mo., August 17, 1837. The first Jesuit to enter the Mississippi valley after the re-establishment of the Society. One of Father De Smet's teachers at Whitemarsh, and his conductor to Missouri.

stopped to take on wood, which generally takes an hour, I took a walk along the bank alone in search of rare plants. I had seated myself on a rock when a negro of eighty years came up to me. He seemed to stare at me attentively and with astonishment because of my black coat, and asked me if I was not a Catholic priest? Having replied that I was, he said to me with tears in his eyes " I too have the happiness of being a Catholic, but it is five years since I had that of seeing a priest of my religion. Often have I said my prayers that I might have the consolation of confessing once more before I die. Sir, would you not have the kindness to hear and help me? " I made him sit down beside me, and I had hardly uttered the words of absolution when the steamboat bell gave the signal for starting. The poor old man wept with joy and pressed my hand, unable to speak a word. I cannot express to you the consolation that this little meeting yielded me.

As we passed up by the Sauk country, the bank for more than a quarter of a mile presented nothing but groups of savages, warriors, women and children, accompanied by an army of dogs. Curiosity to see the steamboat pass had no doubt attracted them to the bank. The chiefs, who knew Father Verreydt and Brother Mazelli, saluted us in a most affectionate manner, wished us a fortunate voyage and promised to come and see us soon.

We stopped several hours at the village of the Iowas. There I talked with our former disciple Francis, called White Cloud, who since his father was killed has become chief of the nation. I made him a little present of tobacco, which he accepted with much pleasure. It seems that these Indians are very much dissatisfied with their present minister and they expressed to me their wish to have us among them. They seem poor and very drunken, sell everything they have to obtain the unlucky stuff, the great scourge of the Indians. Some days before we were there an Indian had been killed in a drunken row and several mortally wounded. I noticed among them certain young men well dressed, with silk ribbons of all colors entwined in their hair, a profusion of porcelain beads hung about their necks, and wolf-tails and little bells attached to their heels, knees and arms. Their faces too were painted with great care, in red, black, green, gray, yellow and brown according to the taste of each. In Belgium they would have been taken for fine Harlequins from the fairs. All these young men were playing on a sort of flageolet or flute. I addressed a young savage who spoke English well to learn the reason of this distinction. He laughed and told me : " Those gentlemen are in love. When any one among us desires to wed, he makes his inclination known by playing the flute, and passes whole days, and often nights too, in serenading around the girl's cabin. When the parents have arranged the affair, he passes his flute on to another comrade who has been taken with the notion." This custom seems quite general among all the tribes.

With the exception of the snags which raked and scraped us now and then and the sand-bars which opposed our passage, and which had to be crossed at all hazards, our journey was pleasant enough. The boat has to be lifted over these bars, which is not any too easy. Two heavy timbers [spars] are set in the water in front and the boat made fast to them. Then the engine is started full speed, and by means of posts it lifts the stern and shoves the boat forward a yard or two or three. Then the same thing is done over again, and so on until the bar is crossed. This often takes a whole day.

The Devil's Rake, which has to be passed through, is a place much dreaded by the rivermen. It has the appearance of a whole forest, swallowed up by the immense river. Gigantic trees stretch their naked and menacing limbs on all sides; you see them thrashing in the water, throwing up foam with a furious hissing sound as they struggle against the rapid torrent. Add to these inconveniences the fear of the boiler exploding, which often causes loss of life among the unhappy travelers. At the same time the weather was excessively hot: the warm, muddy water of the Missouri was our only drink, and myriads of mosquitos, fleas, and other insects were our traveling companions. Still every one spoke of the beautiful fortunate voyage we had made. I fear the sea, I will admit, but all the storms and other unpleasant things I have experienced in four different voyages did not inspire so much terror in me as the navigation of the somber, treacherous and muddy Missouri.

The Missouri has the same characteristic features from its mouth to Council Bluffs, and even 1,500 miles farther. After you pass the fort the prairies along the river are more extensive. The eastern shore is being settled very rapidly as far as across the Nishnabotna, insomuch that we were not once obliged to stop to have the crew cut wood. While the boat was stranded on a big sand-bar ten miles below the mouth of the Platte, I had a chance to explore the rocks, and found a great number of petrifactions scattered along the bank, among them fine specimens of the pretended vegetable-animal, the polyp, tubipores, encrini, trachitæ, columnar asteria, etc. I filled my handkerchief to send to you. I unluckily forgot on board the *Howard* the stones and minerals I had picked up below the fort.

I visited the village of the Otoes; they seem poor and miserable; steal when they can and get drunk when they have a chance. They have a Baptist minister[3] among

[3] Reverend Moses Merrill, born in Maine in 1803, died at the Otoe Mission February 6, 1840, of consumption. Baptist missionary at Sault Ste Marie, 1832, Bellevue fall of 1833. Author of hymn-book and some other works in the Otoe language. The reports of the Nebraska State Historical Society contain a biography by a son, Reverend Samuel Pearce Merrill, the first white child born in Nebraska; probably the " reverend ducky " (*poupon*) of the text; also extracts from journals of Mr. and Mrs. Merrill, in which occasional mention is made of baptisms among the Indians.

There was another Baptist mission established about 1837 by Rev. Samuel Curtis and wife, first at Bellevue, later at Blackbird Hills, among the Omahas.

them. The $600 that the Government grants every year
to this reverend gentleman; the aid which the Boston
propaganda sends his Reverence; and a fine farm which
he cultivates carefully and which brings him in a large
profit each year, are so many items which prevail on him
to remain among them; for in the five years that he has
been here he has not yet baptized a single person. Indeed, that is all that this horde of apostles of Protestantism, with which all the Indian territory is flooded, are
doing. The reverend lady of the Otoe minister, and her
reverend little ducky, were on board the same boat that
took us up.

A visit to an Indian village is worth a few words of description. Some of the interesting peculiarities that I observed among the Otoes were as follows. Groups of naked
children were amusing themselves on all sides at various
games, and painfully lean dogs without end were frolick-
ing with these young *sans culottes*. The village consists of
a number of large earthen huts, containing some ten
families each, and a few tents of tanned buffalo hides sewed
together. The women whom I met presented an appearance of the utmost misery. Some were blind, others one-
eyed, and all extremely filthy and disgusting to look at.
They were clothed in petticoats of deerskin, reaching to
the knees, jackets, leggings and shoes of the same material,
all as dirty and black as if they had been their towels for
the last century. Bracelets of polished metal were worn
at the wrists by both sexes, and around their necks they
had five or six yards of porcelain or glass beads.

I was introduced into the largest cabin, that of the first
chief; his queen put me a cushion, shining with grease,
upon a still more greasy mat, and made me the sign to
be seated. She then presented me a rudely-made wooden
dish (for everything here is done with the hatchet and knife)
and a pot-spoon of the same material, which seemed not
to have been washed since the day of their manufacture.
Then she served me with a stew of her own compounding

and a pie of a grey color and sufficiently disgusting in appearance. To refuse a savage who offers you food in his own cabin would be considered a grave affront. " Well, well," I said to myself, " you are not in Belgium; let us begin our apprenticeship in earnest, and so long as we are in the woods, howl heartily with the wolves." A dozen or more dogs, sitting on their hams in front of me, with their eyes fastened on my dish, seemed really to envy me my happiness as I approached my spoon to it, and to be offering their aid and assistance in case of need. But it was not necessary to have recourse to my canine company; I had a good appetite and the stew was excellent, a buffalo tongue with a good gravy of bear fat, mixed with flour from the wild sweet potato. I thanked my hostess, and handed her dish back much cleaner than I had received it.

It is sorrowful to see the neglected condition of the little children in all the Indian villages. Their hair seems never to have undergone the operation of the brush, so that their heads look like masses of cobwebs. Many have eye trouble, and their faces and all their limbs look as if water had never touched them. The younger ones are generally naked, and great was the alarm which my presence occasioned among this juvenile portion of the community, wherever I presented myself without warning. The dogs in these villages (all belonging to the wolf family) are the greatest torments to a stranger; the barking of one brings all the others together, of all sizes; they form a chorus, utter piercing yelps and roars and follow you in all directions.

The men seem to pass their time in complete idleness: playing cards and smoking are their only amusements. They subsist the greater part of the time on a small quantity of dried meat and a mush made of roasted and pounded corn. But this temperance and frugality are the result of necessity, not of choice, for when they have abundance you will see them thrust their whole hands into the pot and eat incessantly like starving wolves until they are ready to split; then they lie down and go to sleep. All their wealth consists of a few horses which graze at large in the uncultivated prairie. It is truly a melancholy sight to see these desolate villages surrounded by such fine country and such fertile virgin soil. The Indian at his birth is wrapped in rags; he grows up in buffalo-skins; he is raised in idleness, and industry has no attractions for him; he never tries to improve his condition, and in fact were one of them to aspire to higher enjoyments and to raise his fortune by his efforts and activity, he would soon find himself the object of universal hatred and envy, and whatever he had gathered together would speedily be pillaged or sacked.

We arrived among the Potawatomies on the afternoon of the 31st of May. Nearly 2,000 savages, in their finest rigs and carefully painted in all sorts of patterns, were awaiting the boat at the landing. I had not seen so imposing a sight nor such fine-looking Indians in America: the Iowas, the Sauks and the Otoes are beggars compared to these. Father Verreydt and Brother Mazelli went at once to the camp of the half-breed chief, Mr. Caldwell, four miles from the river. We were far from finding here the four or five hundred fervent Catholics we had been told of at the College of St. Louis. Of the 2,000 Potawatomies who were at the landing, not a single one seemed to have the slightest knowledge of our arrival among them, and they all showed themselves cold or at least indifferent toward us. Out of some thirty families of French half-breeds two only came to shake hands with us; only a few have been baptized. All are very ignorant concerning the truths of religion; they cannot even make the sign of the cross nor say a pater or an ave. This, as I suppose, is the cause of their great reserve toward us. They change wives as often as the gentlemen of St. Louis change their coats. * * * (Portion illegible.)

A fortnight after our arrival we discovered one single Catholic Indian; he came to see us and asked our blessing.

We tried to get him to stay with us; he knew his prayers well and could serve us for a catechist.

Mr. C[aldwell?], though far advanced in years, seems to be a very worthy honest man: he is well disposed toward us and ready to assist us. The half-breeds generally seem affable and inclined to have their children instructed, and we receive many tokens of affection from the Indians themselves; they come to see us every day. The chief has given us possession of three cabins, and we have changed the fort which Colonel Kearny[4] has given us into a church. On the day of Corpus Christi I put up a cross on the roof, and while I climbed the ladder to put it in place, and my flag floated from a hole in my breeches, Father Felix beheld the devil clap his tail between his legs and take flight over the big hills.

I employ my days in instructing the children: I have already baptized ————————, among them a young man of eighteen years of age. At present I am preparing for baptism twelve or fourteen of ten to twenty years. This nation is divided into different bands, living five to twenty-five miles apart. We try to visit them once a week, to instruct the children and preach to the elders, through an interpreter. Providence has placed us at some distance from any great number of these savages, for since the arrival of the steamboat, which brought a large quantity of liquor, they are quarreling and fighting from morning till night. When they are sober the most perfect harmony prevails throughout the nation: whole years often pass

4 Brigadier-General Stephen W. Kearny of the Mexican War, Governor of California, etc. " Old " Fort Kearney at Table Creek (Nebraska City) was named for him, he having chosen the site in 1838 and begun the construction of a post there in 1846; also the Fort Kearney of the emigrant period, on the Platte, opposite the present city of Kearney, upon his death in 1848. His name was Kearny, but the other spelling has become fixed in the maps.— Perhaps more frequently mentioned by contemporary travelers than any other army officer; see Catlin, Parkman, Beckwourth, Garrard, Hildreth, Bryant, etc.

without quarrels.   They are not at all addicted to the per-
nicious practice of slander; the most corrupt regard a
slanderer with disdain, while the more respectable avoid
him as they would a snake.   No one would dare make accusations against those who enjoy a good reputation, and
as for the good-for-nothings, they do not lower themselves
so far as to speak of them.   (Portion illegible.)

CHAPTER II.

COMMENTS ON THE SITUATION.

Dangers of the Missouri — Kickapoos, Sauks, Iowas and Otoes — Hindrances to conversion of Indians on the frontiers — The Pawnees prefer Catholic priests — Their opinion of liquor — The Omahas come and dance — The Indian Question in 1838 — Notes on the country — Missionary progress.

Reverend and Very Dear Father:[1]

KNOWING the great interest that you take in the Indian missions, I propose to give you some details concerning those which we have just undertaken, adding various Indian traditions and a few observations upon the manners and customs of these peoples. In these remote regions, we necessarily meet with numerous privations; but the Lord never lets himself be outdone in generosity; he repays a hundredfold the slightest sacrifice made for him; and if our privations are great, our consolations are much greater. I thank Divine Providence daily for having put me in these countries.

I set out from St. Louis on the 10th day of May, in the company of our Reverend Father Superior [Verhaegen][2] who was to visit the Kickapoos, and Father Helias, who was going to found a new mission among the Germans

[1] To the Father General, dated, Nation of the Potawatomies at the Council Bluffs, July 20, 1838. Translated from the French of Father De Smet's manuscripts. A portion of the letter was published as Letter XXVII, *Missions de l'Orégon.*

[2] Peter Joseph Verhaegen, a Belgian, one of the young men who came to America in 1821 and to Missouri in 1823, with Father De Smet; died at St. Charles July 21, 1868, at the age of sixty-eight. Father Verhaegen was very closely connected with Father De Smet throughout their lives. He was a finely educated man, and was first president of the St. Louis University, first vice-provincial of Missouri, provincial of Maryland and first president of St. Joseph's College at Bardstown.

around Jefferson City.   I made the whole journey on the
steamboat, and arrived among the Potawatomies of the
Prairies on the 31st of the same month.

To relate to you all our adventures on the old Father of
Waters, the Mississippi, and particularly on the Missouri
or " muddy water," which we ascended for a distance of
over 800 miles; to describe to you all the little towns and
villages which are born, as if by magic, upon its banks; the
vertical cliffs, several hundred feet high, the caverns, the
forests and the immense prairies which follow one another
in prodigious variety on its shores; its bed, strewn with
numberless islands one, two, three and even four leagues
in length and filled with every kind of game: this task
would carry me a great deal too far and could only interest you in a slight degree.   I will only remind you that
steam navigation on the Missouri is one of the most dangerous things that a man can undertake.   In my opinion,
the sea, despite its storms and the tribute which one is
compelled to pay, is much to be preferred.   The current
of this river is of the swiftest; high pressure is therefore
required to overcome it, and hence the continual danger
to which the traveler is exposed of finding himself overturned, and even, as happens only too often, of having his
limbs shattered and hurled here and there to a terrible
elevation.   Add the sand-bars with which the river is filled,
and upon which one is always being cast, and the innumerable snags and sawyers upon which boats are often
wrecked; all these things brought us several times within
a finger's breadth of our destruction.   Snags are trees
whose roots are imbedded in the mud at the bottom of the
river, with their branches spreading on all sides below,
above and at the water-level.[3]

I stopped three days at our residence of the Kickapoos,
to wait for Father Verreydt and Brother Mazelli, with
whom I was to continue my journey.   The head chief

[3] This excellent summary of the difficulties of Missouri river navigation is evidence of Father De Smet's habit of close observation.

Pashihi appeared much attached to us, and showed us a great deal of affection. He is a man full of wit and good sense, who needs only a little courage to become an excellent Christian; he told us several times that in a vision he had seen the "Ma-che-ta-co-ni-a" (Black-gowns) in heaven, reproaching his nation with their unfaithfulness and vices, and telling them that because they were not willing to listen to them in time, the Great Spirit had rejected them.

The Sauk Indians, who are two days' journey further north, were drawn up on the river bank to see us pass, and the chiefs, who had often visited our residence, recognizing us by our black robes, saluted us very cordially with a shout of joy, and wished us a pleasant and prosperous voyage. The Iowas, whom we visited in passing, also seemed very favorable to us, and sought to keep us among themselves. Their head chief, White Cloud, had been my disciple at St. Ferdinand a dozen years before. Before we reached our destination we traversed the villages of the Otoes.[4] They build their huts in the form of mounds and cover them with sod. These huts are so large that 150 people may be lodged in one at their ease; the interior resembles a temple; the rafters which support the sods rest upon a score of pillars or posts; a hole arranged in the top lets in light and gives an outlet to the smoke. They are a poor nation and very much addicted to thievery and drink. They are the only Indians I know of who, in their misfortunes and reverses, lay the blame upon the Great Spirit and dare to blaspheme.

One day when the boat had stopped and the crew landed to cut wood, I walked back from the river quite a distance. In my excursion I met an old man of ninety who halted as I drew near and looked at me with astonishment mingled with joy. He had judged from my garb that I was a priest, and when I had confirmed him in his idea, "Ah! my

[4] The Otoes dwelt near the mouth of the Platte, sometimes on its left bank, sometimes on the right.

Father," he cried, "I am a Catholic, and it is many years since I have had the happiness of seeing a priest. I have so ardently desired to see one before I die! Help me therefore to be reconciled with God." I hastened eagerly to comply with his request, and we both of us wept abundantly. Then he conducted me back to the boat and I parted from the good old man; but I cannot tell you the consolation that I tasted in this most fortunate meeting.

When we arrived, and while our things were being unloaded, a young man was brought on board the boat, very dangerously sick. It was late, and on account of our baggage I could not go ashore to the cabin that the head chief of the nation had caused to be made ready for us. The young man suffered a great deal during the night; though unknown, I went into his room to relieve or console him. I learned that he was a Catholic, and that he had received from an uncle, a zealous churchman, a Christian education; moreover, he had always felt a great devotion for the Mother of God. For six years he had been traveling in the mountains, among the different nations, without ever seeing a priest. I had no trouble to bring him to shrive himself, and I gave him extreme unction. I have since learned that he died the day after he reached the end of his voyage.

There are great obstacles to be overcome in converting an Indian nation; the principal ones are the immoderate use of strong drink, polygamy, superstitious practices and prejudices, a language of which it is very hard to acquire a knowledge, and their inclination to a wandering life; this inclination is so strong that they become melancholy and morose if they stay three months in the same place; their conversion is therefore altogether a work of God. This portion of the divine Master's vineyard requires from those who tend it, a life of crosses, privations and patience. Still we hope, that aided as we are by grace, and assisted by your prayers and those of all our brothers, the Lord will grant some measure of success to our feeble labors.

The results of the last four [?] months have been truly consoling; a goodly number of the savages show a desire of being instructed. We have opened a school; but for the lack of larger quarters we are only able to receive some thirty children. Twice a day we give an instruction to those whom we are preparing for baptism. We have already admitted 118, and I have had the consolation of baptizing 105. The day of the glorious Assumption of the most holy Virgin Mary will not soon be forgotten among the Potawatomies. The church where the divine service was celebrated was perhaps the poorest in the world; but twelve young neophytes, who three months before had had no idea of the law of God, sang mass in a manner truly edifying. Reverend F. Verreydt preached upon devotion to the Mother of God; afterward I gave an instruction upon the ceremonies and upon the necessity of baptism, and conferred that sacrament upon a score of adults; the wife of the head chief was among the number. This woman is very charitable, she has zeal and stands high in the esteem of her nation. It is to be hoped that her conversion will soon attract others to our holy religion. After the mass I blessed four marriages. In the evening we paid a visit to one of these converted families; all our little congregation was assembled to return thanks to God for the signal benefits with which he had overwhelmed them during this feast. These honest people are now overrunning the country in every direction to win their near relations and acquaintances, to bring them to be instructed and enjoy the same happiness with themselves. Several Indian women, whose relations, being still in paganism, would not let us know, have dragged themselves, sick as they were, for a distance of two to three leagues, to come and ask us for baptism before they died. I could tell you many other admirable anecdotes of our new converts, but the narrative would carry me too far.[5]

*   *   *   *   *   *   *

[5] For the part of this letter omitted here, see p. 1098.

Three of the head chiefs of the Pawnee Loups[6] came to pay us a visit, and lodged in our cabin. They noticed the sign of the cross that we made before and after our prayers and our meals, and when they went home, they taught all the inmates of their village to make the same sign, as something agreeable to the Great Spirit. They begged us, through their interpreter, to come and visit them. The Government had sent them a Protestant minister,[7] but they did not choose to keep him. "They knew," they told him, "that the devil accompanied such as he; and since they did not wish to have such a guest in their village, they could not admit him himself." The use of liquor is prohibited in this tribe, and when any one tries to bring them any they answer that they are crazy enough already without drink. They have also a singular custom; they eat the vermin off one another, and render the same service to those who come to visit them.

The Protestant minister of the Omahas also had to move. This tribe has a population of about 2,000 souls. Two of their chiefs, Kaiggechinke and Ohio, with two-score warriors, came to dance the calumet, or their dance of friendship for us. Such a dance is really worth seeing, but it is not easy to give one an idea of it, because everything seems confusion. They yell and strike their mouths, at the same time performing leaps of all descriptions, now on one foot, now on the other, always at the sound of the drum and in perfect time, pell-mell, without order, turning to the right and left, in every direction and in every shape, all at once. They all evinced the greatest affection for us and prayed us to smoke the calumet with

6 The Pawnee villages were on the Platte, about the present Fremont and Columbus.

7 Probably the reference is to Samuel Allis or Reverend John Dunbar, Presbyterians, who went among the Pawnees in the fall of 1834. The former attached himself to the band known as Pawnee Loups, the latter to the Grand Pawnees. They remained among them until 1846, when the hostile operations of the Sioux made the country unsafe.

them. I showed our chapel to the chiefs, who appeared to take great interest in the explanation I gave them of the cross, the altar and the images of the passion of Our Lord Jesus Christ. Afterward they urgently begged me to come and make them a visit, to baptize their children, and they made me a present of a fine beaver skin for a tobacco-bag. I in turn gave them some chaplets for the children and to each one a fair copper cross, which they received with great gratitude, kissing them respectfully and putting them around their necks. When speaking, they addressed me in the most cordial manner. They are scarcely more than a hundred miles from Council Bluffs.[8]

The new Indian territory, as lately arranged by the Government, will have as its limits the Red river on the south, and on the east the State of Arkansas and that of Missouri, with the river of the same name; so that we have already seen a good portion of it. The territory now contains the following nations: Poncas, Dourvas [?], Otoes, Kansas, Osages, Kickapoos, Potawatomies, Delawares, Shawanos, Weas, Piankishaws, Peorias, Kaskaskias, Ottowas, Senecas, Sauks, Quapaws, Creeks, Cherokees and Choctaws. There are about 100,000 of them, sad remnants of once powerful nations. When the Europeans visited the new world for the first time, they found its islands and shores extremely populous; but several tribes that were flourishing, have now disappeared from the surface of the earth; the very names of many are unknown. As fast as the whites extended their dominion in the east, the savages withdrew toward the west, leaving behind them, at every step that they took, mournful monuments of their misfortunes and decadence. Here to-day are 100,000 of them, pushed out upon the borders of the vast and uninhabitable prairie; hunting cannot suffice for their subsistence; they are unused to labor; one may well, therefore, feel serious apprehensions concerning their lot. Ah! if there were

[8] The Omahas were on the right or west bank of the Missouri river, twenty-five miles below Sioux City.

more of us, with means to correspond, this would perhaps be the moment to accomplish permanent good among them and to prevent their total extinction. There are besides many other nations on both sides of the mountains called Rocky Mountains: they number several hundreds of thousands; some of these tribes, which are very numerous, have already invited us to come and settle among them. I may say that almost all the nations of the northern part of America show a great predilection for the Catholic missionaries and seem to stretch their arms toward us in preference, notwithstanding the millions of dollars that the Protestant societies are spending to attach these poor people to themselves; for as a matter of fact, these dollars serve only to enrich the so-called ministers of the gospel, with their wives and children that they drag around with them. Meanwhile they come and occupy the ground, and wherever they are, it is very difficult to form a Catholic establishment afterward.

It is not uncommon to meet bears in our neighborhood; but this animal will seldom attack a man first, though he will defend himself when wounded. Wolves come very often to our very doors; quite lately they have carried off all our chickens. They are of all kinds; prairie-wolves, small and timid; black mountain wolves, large and dangerous. We are obliged to be continually on our guard against these bad neighbors, and so I never go out without a good knife, a tomahawk or a sword-cane. There are snakes too, among which I might name the copper-head, the garter-snake [? *couleuvre*], blacksnake and rattlesnake. Field, forest and cabin swarm with mice, which gnaw and devour the few fruits that we possess. Insects, butterflies especially, are very numerous here, and very variegated and very large. Night-moths are of all colors and of a prodigious size; they are no less than eight inches in length. We live also in the midst of horse-flies and mosquitoes; they come upon us by thousands and give us no rest day nor night.

I wish I could give Your Paternity an idea of the architecture of an Indian village; it is as outlandish as their dancing. Imagine a great number of cabins and tents, made of the bark of trees, buffalo skins, coarse cloth, rushes and sods, all of a mournful and funereal aspect, of all sizes and shapes, some supported by one pole, others having six, and with the covering stretched in all the different styles imaginable, and all scattered here and there in the greatest confusion, and you will have an Indian village.

We have a fine little chapel, twenty-four feet square, surmounted with a little belfry; four poor little cabins besides, made of rough logs; they are fourteen feet each way, with roofs of rude rafters, which protect us from neither rain nor hail, and still less from the snow in winter.

Good Brother Mazelli and myself commend ourselves urgently to the holy sacrifices and prayers of Your Paternity.

————

Very dear and Reverend Father: [9]

I think I told you, the first time I wrote you, that I had already baptized twenty-two persons. To-day the number of those upon whom I have had the consolation of conferring holy baptism amounts to seventy-six, among whom I reckon thirty-four adults of ages from twelve to sixty years. I am sure that Your Reverence would be touched to see with what fervor these good Indians assist at the holy sacrifice and with what docility they listen to our instructions. For my part, I assure you that I see the work of God in it, and that I feel penetrated with gratitude toward those who, by their prayers, cease not to obtain for us from heaven these unexpected successes. One of our first conquests for Jesus Christ was the spouse of the head chief of the Potawatomi

[9] Extract from a letter to Father Verhaegen, Superior of the Mission of Missouri. Dated Potawatomi Nation, St. Joseph [Mission], August 20, 1838. Translated from the French and hitherto unpublished.

nation. She enjoys the greatest consideration among the Indians, and I venture to hope that her example will have a great influence upon the rest of her compatriots. Since I could not at the beginning express myself with sufficient facility, I was obliged for several weeks to make use of an interpreter. As soon as I found her well enough instructed and disposed, I admitted her to the sacrament of regeneration, which she received with all signs of the liveliest faith and the most ardent piety. Eight other persons, who had imitated her example, shared her happiness.

A short time afterward, on the 9th of August, a young person of eighteen years of age, who had long been sick, came over six miles to find me. She seemed in a state of extreme exhaustion when I saw her in the church. " Father," she said, " I have a secret presentiment that my end is near; I know that you are the Great Spirit's minister, and I have made a great effort today to come and beg you to show me the road that leads to heaven." I spent several hours in instructing her in the most essential dogmas of our holy religion, and as I found her fully disposed to receive holy baptism, I thought it my duty to bestow it upon her at once. I have never seen a person so self-possessed, so modest, so deeply touched during the administration of the holy sacrament. After the ceremony, she said to me : " Oh! now, until my last breath, I shall love the Great Spirit with all my heart, and shall honor his good Mother with a daughter's love. Oh! I am happy in this moment!"

On the 13th of the same month, an Indian woman brought me her little child, who was sick, praying me to baptize it. "Alas!" said the poor woman, " I had another son, and he died without having received this favor, and it would break my heart should this one be likewise exiled from the paradise of the Great Spirit." Among those whom I have baptized are a Protestant lady and her child; she is now one of the most fervent of Catholics; all the others are Indians or half-breeds, who do not know even the name of our holy religion. There are a few families besides who are preparing to receive the same favor. My companion, Reverend Father Verreydt, lately visited a village belonging to the mission, where they promised to let him baptize all the little children.

The feast that we have just been celebrating in honor of the assumption of the glorious queen of heaven will never be forgotten in this mission; it was celebrated in a poor wooden church, but I can assure you that no place in the world ever offered a more consoling spectacle nor one more agreeable to the Almighty and his most holy mother.

In the afternoon of that day I baptized eleven adults and a little Indian girl who was sick. Three of these adults had already reached their fiftieth year; five were twenty, and three about fifteen years old. All exhibited during the ceremony a great deal of piety and fervor. Afterward we sang together several canticles to praise and bless the Lord's mercies. At the close of the ceremony, four couples received the nuptial benediction according to the Catholic rite. All who were present were so touched with what they had seen and heard that, yielding to the grace of the Holy Spirit, they demanded urgently to be instructed. Among this number was an old Indian woman belonging to the great medicine band, who, as soon as she reached home, immediately destroyed her medicine bundle. Going toward evening to visit a newly converted family, we were agreeably surprised and edified to find all the adults and several others besides assembled to recite in common the most fervent prayers, and to thank the Lord for the signal favors that he had granted them that day. I cannot conceal from you, dear Father, that in no circumstances of my life have I ever felt, myself, more joy and consolation than in this happy moment.

*   *   *   *   *   *   *   *   *

CHAPTER III.

DAILY LIFE AT THE MISSION.

A missionary journal — Major Dougherty — Indian councils — Glory of the warpath — Liquor in abundance — Murder and mutilaticn — Sale of children — Law ineffective — How the Indians spent $90,000 — Colonel Kearny — Protestant ministers leaving — Peace mission to the Sioux.

Most dear Sir: [1]

YOUR kind favors of the 6th of July and the 27th of October arrived this day. Had I known, dear friend, for what port of this vast continent you had sailed, I would have written long before this; for I am not of that class of gentry who easily forget their real friends. No! your family will be ever dear to me, and it will afford me at all times the greatest satisfaction and pleasure to hear from you, and to know that you are well and prospering. Not a day passes, but I pray the Lord for your family's welfare.

I keep a journal of the most remarkable events which take place around us. They are of a rather gloomy nature, disgusting and discouraging; a short sketch, however, of these I intend to give you, and I feel confident your regret at having left the Council Bluffs, when being made acquainted with the abominations of the place, will soon vanish.

May   10. Mr. Dougherty [2] held a council at Bellevue with the Pawnees. An Iowa waylaid a Pawnee, took his scalp and escaped. Paid the Pawnees

[1] Letter to a "most dear friend," dated Potawatomi Nation, Council Bluffs, December, 1839. Hitherto unpublished.

[2] John Dougherty, a member of Long's exploring party and for many years Government agent for the Pawnees. Somewhat famous in his time for having almost succeeded in rescuing a female captive who had been devoted to sacrifice by that tribe. A brother, Hannibal, was also at this time sub-agent at Bellevue.

a hundred dollars' worth in goods for the body. Obtained the title of a distinguished warrior among his nation.

May   12. Majors Dougherty and Davis held council with the Potawatomies and proposed an exchange of country. The Indians unanimously refused to treat, and declared upon the wampum belt (equal to an oath among the whites) they would not and could not enter into any engagements, a great majority of their brethren being absent. They expressed a desire to see all former treaty stipulations first executed: they had no confidence in a new treaty.

24. A war party of Sauks discovered three lodges of Omahas on the head waters of the Boyer consisting of nine men and twelve women. Invited them to a friendly smoke; accepted, believing them to be Potawatomies. They were treacherously murdered and their women taken prisoners. Danced nine days round the scalp post in the Sauk village. Huzza! for the Indian braves.

25. Two Potawatomies killed on the Chage [?] river in a drunken frolic.

27. Three Potawatomies drowned in the Missouri, supposed to be drunk.

28. A Potawatomie poisoned on the Mosquito while drunk. Frequently the case.

30. Arrival of the steamer *Wilmington* with provisions. A war of extermination appears preparing around the poor Potawatomies. Fifty large cannons have been landed, ready charged with the most murderous grape shot, each containing thirty gallons of whiskey, brandy, rum or alcohol! The boat was not as yet out of sight when the skirmishes com-

menced. After the fourth, fifth and sixth
discharges, the confusion became great and
appalling. In all directions, men, women and
children were seen tottering and falling; the
war-whoop, the merry Indian's song, cries,
savage roarings, formed a chorus. Quarrel
succeeded quarrel. Blows followed blows.
The club, the tomahawk, spears, butcher
knives, brandished together in the air.
Strange! astonishing! only one man, in this
dreadful affray, was drowned in the Missouri,
another severely stabbed, and several noses
lost. The prominent point, as you well
know, the Potawatomies particularly aim at
when well corned.

I shuddered at the deed. A squaw offered her
little boy four years old, to the crew of the
boat for a few bottles of whiskey.

I know from good authority, that upwards of
eighty barrels of whiskey are on the line ready
to be brought in at the payment.

No agent here seems to have the power to put
the laws in execution.

May   31. Drinking all day. Drunkards by the dozen. Indians are selling horses, blankets, guns, their
all, to have a lick at the cannon. Four dollars a bottle! Plenty at that price!! Detest-
able traffic.

June   3. A woman with child, mother of four young children, was murdered this morning near the is-
sue-house. Her body presented the most
horrible spectacle of savage cruelty; she was
literally cut up.

4. Burial of the unhappy woman. Among the provisions placed in her grave were several bottles of whiskey. A good idea if all had been
buried with her.

June   5. A drunken Potawatomi killed a Sauk. The
           murderer, after the perpetration of the deed,
           was mortally stabbed by his own father-in-
           law.   Indian way of redressing wrongs.
        6. Rumor. Four Iowas, three Potawatomies, one
           Kickapoo are said to have been killed in
           drunken frolics.
        7. Attempt at murder. A Potawatomi was dis-
           covered endeavoring to kill his aunt, our next
           neighbor.   Timely assistance, a knock down,
           prevented him.
       11. Another bluff accident. Severe scalding. An
           Iowa drew his knife to stab a companion,
           when another friend, without the least cere-
           mony or hesitation, poured over the ag-
           gressor's head a full kettle of boiling soup.
           The unhappy man escaped death, lost his hair
           only, and presents a melancholy appearance
           amongst his kindred.
       19. A monster in human shape. On the Mosquito
           [Creek], a savage returning home from a
           night's debauch, wrested his infant son from
           the breast of his mother and crushed him
           against a post of his lodge.
       17. *Tekchabe,* another Mosquito Potawatomi, shot
           an Indian through the thigh merely for the
           pleasure of killing, and finished the unhappy
           man with the butt of his gun; pounding the
           head literally to atoms. The nephew of the
           murdered individual, as a matter of course,
           stole up to Tekchabe's camp, found him lying
           down apparently composing himself to sleep
           and shot him instantly through the head.
           This whole affair was settled within twenty
           minutes' time.
       18. Arrival of a sub-agent, Mr. Cowper. His pres-
           ence seems to keep the whiskey sellers in

some awe, "Don't know what he might or will do." Secure the liquor in cages. The many murders committed act powerfully upon the minds of the Indians. They begged the agent in council to prevent the poison being brought among them.

June 20. A young brother of McPherson killed the assistant blacksmith of the Potawatomies, a Mr. Case, an old man; shot him through the head. Got clear at the court in Liberty.

July 6. A company of dragoons from Fort Leavenworth arrived at Bellevue with the Omaha women whom the Sauks had surrendered to them, and delivered them over to their relations. Three of the dragoons, in crossing the Platte opposite the Otoe village were drowned.

Aug. 4. Arrival of the *Antelope*. More whiskey landed.

6. An encounter lately took place between the Omahas and Sioux; originating in the stealing of a few horses by the latter. About forty are said to have been slain on both sides.

7. The son of the prophet of the Kickapoos killed the blacksmith of the nation. It is rumored that the white man was the aggressor.

8. Arrival of the *St. Peter's* with the annuities.

19. Annuities $90,000. Divided to the Indians. Great gala. Wonderful scrapings of traders to obtain their Indian credits.

20. Since the day of payment, drunkards are seen and heard in all places. Liquor is rolled out to the Indians by whole barrels; sold even by white men even in the presence of the agent. Wagon loads of the abominable stuff arrive daily from the settlements, and along with it the very dregs of our white neighbors and voyageurs of the mountains, drunkards,

gamblers, etc., etc. Three horses have been brought to the ground and killed with axes. Two more noses were bit off, and a score of other horrible mutilations have taken place. One has been murdered. Two women are dangerously ill of bad usage.

Sept.   15. Colonel Kearny arrived at Bellevue with 200 dragoons. Held council with the Iowas. Took four prisoners among the most distinguished for depredations on their white neighbors and missionaries. Preparations were made to whip them. The colonel reluctantly pardoned them at the intercession of their new agent, Mr. Hamilton, and after having previously consulted with experienced gentlemen living in this neighborhood. The Otoes came to the council in battle array, bows strung and arrows in hand, apparently ready for a blow. The manly conduct of the colonel, accompanied by great prudence and a great presence of mind, kept them in awe. I observed several chiefs tremble and stutter as they stood before him. Many who knew them well thought that great mischief was brewing.

A few days later, the son of old Pipestone was treacherously killed by a party of young men of his own nation. He had dared to make allusion in open council to the misconduct of the prisoners. * * * In a difference among themselves they burned most of their earthen wigwams. Otoes as bad as ever.

Oct.   15. Saw Mr. Merrill; looked very pale and sickly; was about selling out and removing. The Otoe blacksmith, Mr. Gilmore, left the Otoe station. Mr. Keis intends likewise to remove within the settlements. Made an improve-

ment already on the Nishnabotna. Messrs.
Allis, Curtis[3] and Dunbar are still in Bellevue,
waiting for their respective flocks to become
more steady and to settle permanently.

In the beginning of last November, two young Potawatomies, a grandson of old Blackfoot (who died last summer)
and a son of old Miami, were killed on the head waters of
the Des Moines. Not ascertained as yet whether the party
were Sauks, Iowas, or Santees of the St. Peters river. Mr.
Caldwell and family, P. Le Clair, the families La Framboise
are all doing very well at present. There has been a great
deal of sickness among the nation. I do not think that any-
body escaped the fever. I had my first trial of it. * * *
Mr. Harden's family well except little David who for some
time past has been much subject to fits and fever. He is
somewhat improving at present. Mrs. Scugin and her son
Ramsay, Miss Henrietta, Messrs. Dick and Allen are below
at Westport.

Dear friend, from the above statement you may easily
gather, that our prospects are not so very bright and flattering, surrounded as we are by so many evils and obstacles,
which all our efforts to the contrary are not able to stem.
Indians are weak, laws disregarded, money a powerful temptation for the wicked white man and half-breed. We have
not lost courage, however; a short sketch of our little mission will show that our endeavors have not been altogether
fruitless and unavailing. We performed the ceremonies of
marriage for twenty-three couples who have so far remained
very steady and promised to remain so till death will part
them for better or for worse. We baptized in all 242, among
whom were upward of eighty adults, most of them half-
breeds and some Indians. Forty have been admitted already
to the Lord's Supper. Some I must own have slackened,

---

[3] See previous note, page 154. "Mr. Curtis could preach a good
sermon and probably would be useful in the states, where all was
pleasant and agreeable, but did not succeed with the Indians."—*Allis*.

12

attracted by the bad examples and occasions which surround them. Our chapel is tolerably well attended on Sundays. Most of the Indians are absent, being on their hunting expeditions. * * *

I made a trip last summer to the Sioux country, visited the Yanktons and Santees, joined two couples in lawful wedlock, baptized three adults and twenty-six children. I invited them in the names of our chiefs to come and smoke the calumet with them, and, while I write to you, we have forty of them in our bluffs, and of their bravest warriors, caroling together with the Potawatomies, and behaving towards each other like true brethren and friends. Last night they honored us with their great pipe-dance, and gave a serenade before every wigwam and cabin. They appeared to be very much pleased with all the people here.

I would have wished to have entered into many more particulars, but Pascal Miller [?] is waiting with impatience for my letter. * * * He leaves for the fort. More news, and better, I hope, by the next occasion. Remember me in your good prayers to the Lord. A kiss to my little dear Clarissa and to your son. * * * My best respects to your good lady. * * * Please remember me to the honorable Dr. James,[4] the true father and friend to the Indian. Father Verreydt, Mr. Caldwell, and Mr. Hardy's family send their best love to you. Farewell.

[4] Possibly Edwin James, scientific member and historiographer of Long's expedition; who had previous to this time been agent to the Potawatomies.

CHAPTER IV.

EXCURSION TO THE SIOUX COUNTRY. [1]

First knowledge of the Sioux — Nicollet and Fremont — Acrobatic explorations — Notes on the country — Loss of vessel with mission supplies — Lights and shadows of life among the natives — Surreptitious baptism of children — Blackbird, the great Omaha chief — The recent smallpox epidemic — Honorable reception among the Yankton Sioux — Return downstream in a canoe — First experience of out-door life.

ON the 29th of April I went on board the American Company's steamboat, which makes every year the voyage from St. Louis to the Yellowstone river to furnish the Indians of those countries with whatever they need and bring down their furs in return. The year 1839 has been a very favorable one: they have obtained about 45,000 buffalo robes, besides an immense number of skins of deer, elk, antelope, beaver, otter, wildcats, etc. To my great joy I found on board the celebrated Mr. Nicollet,[2] whom I had had the honor of knowing for a long time. He is a French mathematician, well known in his own country, and I think in Belgium too, by literary men. This respectable gentleman has been traveling in the United States for seven or eight years.

[1] Fragmental journal in French of voyage of Father De Smet in 1839, from Council Bluffs to the Sioux country. Hitherto unpublished.

[2] Jean Nicolas Nicollet, born Cluses, Savoy, July 24, 1786. Came to United States, 1832, to study physical geography of North America. Explored the southern states and the great basin of the Red, Arkansas and Missouri rivers. In 1836 to sources of the Mississippi. Determined position and elevation of many important points, and collected history and dialects of Indian nations and productions and natural history of the country. On his return to Washington he was engaged by the War Department to visit the far west and make a map and reports. He died in Washington September 11, 1843. See letters from him, pp. 1549 and 1552.

At present he is making a scientific excursion upon the upper Missouri, as he did last year to the sources of the Mississippi and its tributaries. He is accompanied by an American lieutenant [Fremont], a German botanist [Charles A. Geyer], very distinguished and tireless in his researches, and several guides. His works will be a treasure for the literary world. He is a very deeply learned man, and a solid Catholic at the same time, who examines his subject on the spot and spares neither time nor pains nor his purse to go to the bottom of the matters he writes upon. He made me a present of several instruments, thermometers, barometers, compass, etc., to take observations during the summer, to aid those he was making in the upper country.

The water of the river was very low and the snags and sand-bars very numerous everywhere, so our progress was slow and we had plenty of opportunities to make excursions in the woods and prairies and over the hills in search of minerals, petrifactions and rare and new plants, which abound in those regions. In a walk of this kind which I was taking with the botanist, he led me to the top of a hill 300 feet high. The path up which we went was quite practicable, but our descent in another place was different. I followed him, thinking that I could go where he had gone, but almost the first step I took, the slippery earth gave way under my feet, and I made a third of the descent at railroad speed. It seemed dangerous and impossible to return by the way I had come, and I found that the rest of the hillside was still steeper. Hung up there 200 feet above the river, I did not find myself very well fixed for meditation or reflection. But I took careful measures and partly by jumping from rock to rock and crawling from shrub to shrub, and partly on my hind-quarters without regard to my breeches, which felt this treatment deeply, I reached *terra firma* in safety. There the lover of Flora was already waiting for me, and being highly pleased with his discoveries he told me " that he did not think there was any pleasure on earth to be compared to an excursion of this kind." He

was unconscious of the capers that I had been cutting. I
answered him in German " that I had found the promenade
fearfully pleasant." But I took good care afterwards not
to follow Mister Florist except on flat country.

In the country of the Omahas I crossed a prairie three
miles in width, full of onions of the size of a marble and
very excellent for eating. In another we found a great
deal of asparagus of the size of your thumb, which supplied the passengers for four days. Everywhere there was
abundance of strawberries, blackberries, gooseberries and
plums, nuts of various kinds, cherries and grapes: the
fruit of the red and black thorn also appeared to be quite
plentiful.

The marks which particularly characterize the immense
Missouri are: its muddy water, thin [leger] and wholesome,
and its swift and winding current, lined with islands of
various sizes formed by the sediment brought down by
the stream, and the aspect of which changes continually.
Its course is between two banks which now traverse a
level plain of either forest or prairie, containing perhaps
thousands of acres and rising ten, twenty or thirty feet
above the water, and now rise majestically from its edge
to a height of 300 to 400 feet, with promontories which,
when the mists of evening descend upon the landscape,
make the impression of lofty mountains seen at a distance.
These hills lie along both banks of the river at a distance
of six to fifteen miles. The windings of the river present
lovely views every moment, but the regular succession of
bluffs and bottoms give such a sameness to the country
that unless one were very familiar with the region he could
never tell in which one of a dozen precisely similar spots
he found himself. The Author of nature seems to have
chosen to divert himself by repeating over and over the
first forms that he applied to this charming and fertile
land.

All the country as you ascend the river seems evidently
to be of volcanic formation. In several places moreover

you can see steam and sulphurous flames escaping from the bosom of the earth. I learned from a traveler who has been all over this region for a number of years, that subterranean noises are often heard, resembling those of volcanic districts.

Very kind Mother: [8]

I received your letter of March 13th, with all your good news of Termonde, even that Charles Geyzel is made Vicar. Doubtless he will be a good vicar. All your communications give me great pleasure and consolation. I do not forget my native place. Continue, therefore, to send me very frequently the most minute details. All that a Termontois can learn of that point of the globe, even when he finds himself in an American desert, 2,000 miles away, amid Indians and wild beasts, is always charming to him. Indeed, the reception of your letter was a holiday for me.

What shall I say to you, Mother, on all that you write me of the present state of your house, and of the good Marolles whom the Lord destines to take care of so many poor and miserable, under the direction of your worthy director? Ah! I assure you, I bless God for it, in the sincerity of my heart. If he deigns to hear me, he will keep you all, your orphan boys and girls, your old men and your children, beneath his powerful and holy grace. It is my ardent and daily prayer before the altar.

I thank you all, teachers and pupils, that you do not forget me, above all, in your prayers. I hope you will continue to implore the Blessed Virgin to protect our poor

[8] Written to the Superior of the Orphanage of Termonde. Sent by her in December, 1856, to the editor of the *Précis Historiques*, Brussels, at the latter's request and with Father De Smet's permission, and published as letter XXVIII of the *Cinquante Nouvelles Letters, XXV of the Western Missions and Missionaries.* Dated Potawatomi Nation, St. Joseph [Mission], July, 1838. The date should be 1839.

missions, and obtain for us, from her Divine Son, who can refuse her naught, the grace and strength necessary to overcome the numerous obstacles which separate the savage from the path of salvation.

You no doubt expect a little recital from the depth of our wilderness. Well, I will exhibit to you the light and the shade. It is just that you who pray so much for us should know somewhat of the exact state of our affairs. Your prayers for us, I am sure, will, if possible, increase in fervor.

First I will narrate to you the great loss that we experienced towards the end of April. Our Superior sent us, from St. Louis, goods to the amount of $500, in ornaments for the church, a tabernacle, a bell, and provisions and clothes for a year. I had been for a long time without shoes, and from Easter we were destitute of supplies. All the Potawatomi nation were suffering from scarcity, having only acorns and a few wild roots for their whole stock of food. At last, about the 20th of April, they announced to us that the much-desired boat was approaching. Already we saw it from the highest of our hills. I procured, without delay, two carts to go for our baggage. I reached there in time to witness a very sad sight. The vessel had struck on a sawyer, was pierced, and rapidly sinking in the waves.[4] The confusion that reigned in the boat was great, but happily no lives were lost. The total damage was valued at $40,000. All the provisions forwarded by Government to the savages were on board of her. Of our effects, four articles were saved: a plough, a saw, a pair of boots and some wine. Providence was still favorable to us. With the help of the plough, we were enabled to

[4] This must have been the annual boat of the American Fur Company to the mouth of the Yellowstone. The name cannot be identified from the "List of Steamboat Wrecks on the Missouri River," in the Annual Report of the Missouri River Commission for 1897. From the preceding fragment the boat would seem to have been raised.

plant a large field of corn; it was the season for furrowing. We are using the saw to build a better house and enlarge our church, already too small. With my boots I can walk in the woods and prairies without fear of being bitten by the serpents which throng there. And the wine permits us to offer to God every day the most holy sacrifice of the mass, a privilege that had been denied us during a long time. We therefore returned with courage and resignation to the acorns and roots until the 30th of May. That day another boat arrived. By that same steamer, I received news from you, as well as a letter from my family and from the good Carmelite superior.

Our congregation already amounts to about 300. At Easter we had fifty candidates for the first communion. I recommend, in a very special manner, these poor Indians, that they maintain their fervor. The dangers and scandals which surround them are very great. I have remarked in one of my preceding letters that one of the principal obstacles to the conversion of the savages is drinking. The last boat brought them a quantity of liquors. Already fourteen among them are cut to pieces in the most barbarous manner, and are dead. A father seized his own child by the legs and crushed it, in the presence of its mother, by dashing it against the post of his lodge. Two others most cruelly murdered an Indian woman, a neighbor of ours, and mother of four children. We live in the midst of the most disgusting scenes.

The passion of the savages for strong drink is inconceivable. They give horses, blankets, all, in a word, to have a little of this brutalizing liquid. Their drunkenness only ceases when they have nothing more to drink. Some of our neophytes have not been able to resist this terrible torrent, and have allowed themselves to be drawn into it. I wrote an energetic letter to the Government against these abominable traffickers. Join your prayers to our efforts to obtain from Heaven the cessation of this frightful commerce, which is the misery of the savages in every relation.[5]

I visit the Indians in their wigwams, either as a missionary, if they are disposed to listen to me, or as a physician to see their sick. When I find a little child in great danger, and I perceive the parents have no desire to hear the word of God, I spread out my *vials:* I recommend my medicines strongly. I first bathe the child with a little camphor; then taking some baptismal water, I baptize it without their suspecting it — and thus I have opened the gate of heaven to a great number, notwithstanding the wiles of hell to hinder them from entering.

During the winter a chief of a neighboring nation brought me his child, attacked with a very dangerous malady; it only had a breath of life remaining. The father asked medicine from me. I gave him to understand that his child was past recovery, but that I had the means of rendering it, after death, the happiest of his nation. I explained to him the favors arising from the sacrament of baptism. The chief, quite delighted, offered me his son in order to secure its happiness, and the child died on the following day.

I might cite you a great number of other consoling traits with which Heaven favors us, but my sheet is too small to allow of it.

I will consecrate this last page to a description of the principal incidents of my excursion of 360 miles farther into the Indian Territories, through the country of the Omahas, and in the immense tract of country occupied by the Sioux.

The object of this journey was to afford the benefit of

5 Father De Smet here touches upon one of the greatest evils that has characterized the relations of the white man with the Indian under the United States Government, from the beginning until very recent times. In spite of all its efforts the Government was never able to suppress what the author very justly describes as an "abominable traffic."

baptism to some children, to give adults some ideas of our holy religion, and to establish a durable and advantageous peace between the two nations. Our savages have lived, during the last two years, in a terrible dread of this numerous and warlike nation; lately, also, two of our people had been massacred.

I embarked on the Missouri, the 29th of April, [1839] in a steamboat [the *St. Peter's*]. I met on board, to my great joy, two old friends: the one a French mathematician, Mr. Nicollet, a very learned and pious man; the other, Mr. [Chas. A.] Geyer, a German. These gentlemen are making a scientific excursion of 4,500 miles into the Indian countries. The waters of the river were low; the sand-banks and the sawyers very numerous and difficult to pass; the winds strong and contrary. Our progress was very slow. We had many an opportunity to make excursions in the woods and prairies, searching for new minerals, which abound in these wilds, and rare and curious plants, among which we made some beautiful discoveries. I thought of you, my good mother, when I found myself in those beautiful parterres. I imagined once for an instant, that you were there, with your children. I heard your exclamations: " *Potten, potten, kinderen! Wel, wel!* * * * *Dat zijn schoone bloemen! Wie zoude het konnen gelooven?* * * * *Maar ziet, maar ziet!* * * * *Komt hier, moeder; hier heb ik eene schoone,*" [6] etc., etc. Indeed it was truly the most beautiful view one could fancy. When the bell called us back to the steamer, I quitted those little parks of wild flowers with much difficulty. I gathered a great number of plants which I preserved in my herbal. We passed over several spots where there were only onions, round, and about as large as the marbles children use for play, but excellent for eating. In another place we gathered a great quantity of asparagus,

[6] " Children, get some vases! Well, well! Those are pretty flowers! Who would have thought it? Just look! Here, Mother, here is a pretty one."

as thick as a man's thumb. All the passengers of the steamboat regaled themselves with it during four days. I will tell you nothing of our little encounters with the wolves and the serpents; that would dispel the charm.

On the route, I instructed and baptized, on the vessel, a woman with her three children, and heard the confessions of a great number of Canadian voyageurs, who were going to the Rocky Mountains.

A tomb attracts attention in these regions; it is the tomb of Blackbird, the great chief of the Omahas. This chief became celebrated by the ascendancy which he possessed over his nation; he was an object of terror and respect to his people, for they believed that he could control life and death. The origin of their belief is as follows: he had procured a large quantity of arsenic, by the aid of a trader; the latter at the same time instructed him in the method of using it; but the wretch soon received his recompense. Blackbird invited him to dine with him on a day appointed, and adroitly administered to him a good dose of his terrible medicine. The trader, to the great pleasure of his host, died some hours after, in frightful torments.

Proud of his attempt, Blackbird soon meditated a perfidious blow, and made great preparation for its execution. He dispatched a party of his people to the chase, so as to kill some deer and buffalo for his banquet. The principal warriors and the minor chiefs had become jealous of the ascendancy that the great chief exercised for some time over the nation. Blackbird, informed of their discontent and murmurs, invited to his feast every one of his warriors who had murmured. He lavished his attentions upon them, and showed the most distinguished marks of cordiality to his guests, wishing apparently to be reconciled with them, and to efface the bad impression that his hard-heartedness and haughty bearing had caused. As soon as each one had emptied his plate, and the poison had begun to act on some, he threw off the mask, and

began to harangue them on the great power of his manitou or genius which guided him, and, brandishing his
tomahawk in triumph, bade them, with sarcasm and bitterness, " to intone their death songs, if any warlike blood
yet circled in their veins;" adding with the accent of
revenge " that before the sun's rising " — it was night —
" the vultures would fly above their wigwams, and that
their wives and children would mourn over their lifeless
corpses." It was a night of confusion, tears, fear and
tumult. No one escaped the poison!

The whole life of this man was a chain of crimes and
cruelties. Tired of " pouring out blood " as the Indians
say, or rather pursued by remorse and despair, he allowed
himself to die with hunger. Before expiring, he gave
orders to his faithful warriors to bury him on the highest
of the hills, an elevation of 300 feet, seated on his most
beautiful courser, facing the impetuous Missouri — " so
that," said he, " I can salute all the voyageurs." His tomb
resembles a little hillock. It is surmounted by a pole, to
which the Indians attach a flag. It can be easily distinguished eighteen miles off.[7]

Our boat passed near the village of the Omahas, composed of about 1,400 souls. It is situated at the extremity
of a beautiful prairie, about three miles in extent, at the
foot of a little range of hills. No one came to the shore
to see us pass,— fearing, it seems, that the smallpox was
on board, and might be introduced among them. Only
two years ago [1837], by an unpardonable imprudence of

[7] The story of Blackbird is a famous one in the history of the western Indians. It has been best told by Washington Irving in his
Astoria. The hill on which the grave rests is a prominent one on the
west shore of the river. Twenty-five miles distant, on a high hill
on the east shore, stands an obelisk, 100 feet high, over the
grave of the first American pioneer to die in this region — Sergeant
Charles Floyd of the Lewis and Clark Expedition, who died and was
buried here August 20, 1804. These two graves practically in sight of
each other, have a deep historic significance, denoting, as they do, the
advent into this region of one race and the exit of another.

the captain, this disease was introduced into the Indian country by the same vessel, [*St. Peter's*] and produced ravages frightful and unheard-of in Indian annals. Twenty-five or thirty thousand died in a few weeks. Of 1,200 men of the tribe of the Mandans, only seven families escaped the contagion. About eighty warriors of this little nation committed suicide in the days of calamity, some in despair at the loss of their children and friends, others through fear of becoming the slaves of their enemies, and the greater number saying that they were horrified at the idea of seeing their bodies corrupted while yet alive.[8]

On the 11th of May I reached my destination, and quitted with regret my four new children in Christ and my two friends. It would have been very gratifying to me to have accompanied these two gentlemen in their lengthy course, if my health and circumstances would have allowed me, so as to visit the numerous nations of the mountains.

On my arrival among the Sioux, the chiefs and warriors of the tribe of Yanktons invited me to feast. All were seated in a circle in a grand lodge or tent of buffalo hides. Each one rested his chin on his knees, the legs drawn close up to the body, a position that my corpulency would not allow me to assume. I therefore seated myself like a tailor on his table, with my legs crossed. Every one received a big piece of venison in a wooden trencher; those who cannot finish their portion are permitted to take away — it is their custom — the remains of the dish. I was among this number, and I had enough left for two days. I observed at this feast that when a savage had finished his dish, he rubbed his belly and breast with his two hands in sign of satisfaction, and thanked his host for having so well regaled him.

The repast concluded, I disclosed to them the principal object of my visit among them, viz: a durable peace be-

[8] For a history of this terrible scourge, see *American Fur Trade of the Far West*, p. 619.

tween the Sioux and the Potawatomies their neighbors. Having discussed the different points and refuted the false reports that divided the two nations, I persuaded the Sioux to make some presents to the children of such of our Potawatomies as they had killed, which is called *covering the dead,* and to come and smoke with them the calumet of peace. The feast and the council were terminated with the most perfect cordiality. The same evening I gave them an instruction on the Apostles' Creed, and I baptized a great number of their little children. This nation, dispersed over a wide extent, reckons 32,000 souls.

The evening before I left a number of the savages came to honor me with the calumet dance.

The object of my voyage being obtained, I seized the first opportunity of returning to my mission. The savages, besides, had already struck camp to follow the bison, which were moving away. My vessel, this time, was a tree hollowed out, which is called a canoe, ten feet in length by one and a half in width. I could just seat myself in it. Before this, I had crossed the river in this sort of craft, but never without fear, it being evidently very dangerous; now I had 360 miles to descend on the most perilous and most impetuous of rivers, and it was necessary, for I had no other way. Happily I was accompanied by two very skilful pilots, who, paddling on the right and left, darted with the fleetness of an arrow through the numerous sawyers with which the river was filled, the frail bark which the slightest shock could overturn. Judge how swift its course is: in three days, sailing from four o'clock in the morning until sunset, we had passed over 120 leagues. Two nights only I slept in the open air, having no bed but my buffalo robe, and no pillow but my traveling-bag. Yet I can assure you that my slumbers were as peaceable and profound as I ever enjoyed in my life. A good appetite, for the air on the water is fresh, prepared us for three excellent meals each day. My companions were well provided with bread, butter, coffee and sugar; game was also abundant, and we had but to select. I never saw so many ducks, geese, bustards, swans and wild turkeys, in such a short trip.

We made our evening soup with the muddy water of the Missouri, which gave the meat the singular appearance of having been seasoned with mud. It was, however, thanks to our appetites, excellent, notwithstanding this, and soup and meat swiftly disappeared.

At our last encampment, attracted without doubt by the sight of the fire which sparkled at our feet, a noble stag approached us, stamping with his feet — a little more and we might have had our skulls broken in by this enraged animal. It aroused the pilot, who, seizing the gun that was lying beside me, discharged it about two inches from my ear. This report awaked me suddenly, without, however, frightening me.

During my route, except the Sioux, I saw only one Indian hunter, and one single village, that of the Omahas. What a contrast with the beautiful, little and populous Belgium![9] The huts of the Omahas are built of earth, and are conical; their circumference at the base, 120 to 140 feet. To construct them, they plant in the ground long and thick poles, bend and join together all the ends, which are fastened to about twenty posts in the inside. These poles are afterwards covered with bark, over which they put earth about a foot in depth, and then cover the whole with turf. They look like small mounds. A large hole in the summit permits light to enter and smoke to escape. The fire-place is in the center and every hut holds from six to ten families.

A young French Creole conducted his wife to me, to have her instructed in our holy religion. He came down with her quite recently from beyond the Rocky Moun-

[9] Scarcely greater than would be the contrast with this same country to-day where within a radius of ten miles of Father De Smet's starting point on this journey are now a quarter of a million people.

tains, a distance of eleven or twelve hundred leagues. The recital that she gives me of the life led by her nation, the Ampajoots [Yampah Utes?] is truly heartrending. The soil is one of the most ungrateful; they have no game at all. If they hazard leaving their country, their more numerous neighbors kill them without mercy. They are without clothes, without habitations, and roam like wild animals in the prairies, where they live on roots, grasshoppers and large ants. They crush the last-named insects between two stones, and make a species of cake with them, which they cook in the sun or before a fire, to regale themselves with after. This poor Indian woman, aged about twenty-five years, *had never eaten meat.* Her astonishment was excessive when she first saw chickens, pigs, cows and oxen, with other domestic fowls and animals, running about our dwellings. As soon as she is sufficiently instructed to receive baptism, I will name her Isabella, and you shall be her godmother. Therefore do not forget the poor Ampajoot in your prayers.

Your letter that you mentioned, dated July, did not reach me. The distance is about 2,000 miles, and the dangers are great. My letter to the Carmelites is about the same as this.

PART II.

Itinerary for the Years 1840, 1841 *and* 1842.

1840.

FATHER De SMET left St. Louis by steamer March
27th and went as far as Westport where he joined the
American Fur Company caravan under Andrew Drips[1] —
Left Westport by land April 30th — Followed the usual
route across the country to the Platte and up that stream past
Fort Laramie, Independence Rock and South Pass[2] — Arrived at the fur company rendezvous June 30th where he met
the advance guard of the Flatheads sent out to meet him —
In company with the Flatheads he continued his route via
the head of Green river; across the divide to Jackson's Little
Hole on the head of Hoback river; down the valley of that
stream to the Snake river; across the Snake at the lower
end of Jackson Hole; across Teton Pass, and into the valley
called Pierre's Hole, where he met the main camp of the
Flatheads, Pend d'Oreilles and Nez Percés about July 12th.

Continued his route in company with the Indians up
Henry Fork of Snake river to Henry lake July 22d; across
the Divide to Red Rock lake (Mosquito lake of the trappers), the ultimate source of the Missouri; down the Stink-
ing Water river to its confluence with the Beaver Head

---

[1] A distinguished trader of the American Fur Company, and later
Indian agent for the tribes of the upper Missouri.

[2] The most noted pass across the Continental Divide. It lay between
the source of the Sweetwater river in the Missouri watershed and Big
Sandy river, a tributary of Green river, itself the main tributary of the
Colorado of the West.

river, and down the latter to Jefferson Fork which they descended to the junction of the Three Forks where the Missouri proper takes its source; August 21st.

After a brief sojourn here, he bade adieu to the Indians, and with a small escort, started August 27th on his return to St. Louis — Ascended the east fork of the Gallatin; crossed what is now called Bozeman Pass, between the valleys of the upper Missouri and Yellowstone; descended the Yellowstone along the left bank and met the Crow Indians in the Big Horn valley, some distance above the mouth of that stream — After some delay he pursued his journey down the Big Horn to the Yellowstone and down the latter stream to the mouth of the Rosebud where he crossed to Fort Alexander — Bidding good-bye to the inmates of the fort and to the Indians, he and a single companion set out down the Yellowstone along the left bank; crossed the Missouri at the mouth of the Yellowstone and arrived at Fort Union.

Leaving Fort Union September 23d, he made his way by land down the Missouri, visiting Forts Clark, Pierre (October 17th) and Vermillion — At Vermillion he took a canoe but was stopped by ice at St. Joseph Mission near Council Bluffs — Thence (December 14th) he traveled by horse back to Independence, and thence to St. Louis by stage, arriving December 31st.

Distance traveled, 4,814 miles.

1841.

Father De Smet left St. Louis April 24th for the Rocky Mountains, accompanied by two fathers and three brothers of the Society — Left Westport May 10th — The route followed was practically the same as that of 1840 as far as South Pass (July 7th)— Thence they followed the route of the Oregon trail via Bear river, Soda Springs (August 13th), across the dividing ridge and down the Portneuf river to Fort Hall on the banks of the Snake.

Left Fort Hall August 19th — Crossed the Snake river and traversed the desert in the vicinity of the Three Buttes — Continued north to the Continental Divide and crossed it about on the present line of the Oregon Short Line railroad — Entered the Beaver Head valley (August 30th) where the Flatheads were found encamped — Recrossed the Divide into the valley of Deer Lodge creek near the well-known hot springs in that vicinity — Descended the Deer Lodge creek and Hellgate river to its junction with the Bitter Root where Missoula now stands — Ascended the Bitter Root valley about thirty miles and commenced the Mission of St. Mary's, September 24th.

Set out to Fort Colville for provisions October 28th — Went to Flathead lake — Thence down the Flathead river to its junction with Missoula river; thence down Clark's Fork, passing Camas Plains, Horse Plains, and a dense forest of cedar and pine which it took four days to traverse — Passed by Pend d'Oreille lake, which he called Kalispel lake — Thence to Lake Kalispel called by him Lake de Boey — Crossed the mountains to Mill creek, and descended its valley to Fort Colville on the Columbia where he arrived November 15th.

After three days spent in procuring provisions and tools Father De Smet returned by practically the same route and arrived at St. Mary's Mission December 8th.

Distance traveled, 2,323 miles.

1842.

" In the spring of this year [about April 10th] I set out from St. Mary's to visit Fort Vancouver and the Willamette valley to confer with the Governor of the Hudson Bay Company and with the Very Reverend Mr. Blanchet, administrator of Oregon, upon the present and future interests of our missions in the mountains " — Went by way of Flathead lake and the route of the previous year most of the way arrived at Fort Colville " in the beginning of

May " — Met a Kootenai band near the head of Flathead
lake — At the Bay of the Kalispels he was invited by the
Cœur d'Alènes to visit their country and he accordingly
made a detour to Cœur d'Alène lake where the Indians
were encamped — Remained several days in their country
— Passed by the site of the modern Spokane City and thence
to the sources of Mill creek, which he descended all the way
to Fort Colville.

May 30th embarked in a skiff on the Columbia — Five
men drowned in a rapid a little above Fort Okinagan —
Stopped at Fort Okinagan — Visited Fort Walla Walla
and the Protestant mission at the Dalles — Passed the Dalles
by boat but portaged around the Cascades — Arrived safely
at Fort Vancouver on the morning of June 8th — Ascended
the Willamette valley to the Willamette Falls and thence
to the mission of St. Paul which was Reverend Blanchet's
residence.

Having completed his business with Blanchet and Mc-
Loughlin, Father De Smet set out on his return journey
June 30th — Ascended the Columbia as far as Fort Walla
Walla — Thence northerly across the Nez Percé and Spokan
deserts to the Cœur d'Alène lake — Thence via St. Joseph
river and over the mountains to Missoula river, and thence
up the Bitter Root to St. Mary's Mission.

Father De Smet had been strongly advised by the Reverend Blanchet, Governor McLoughlin and others to return
to the United States for personal and material succor for
the missions, and accordingly, after arranging for the commencement of two new residences, one among the Kalispels
of the Bay and another among the Cœur d'Alènes, he made
preparations for departure.

Accompanied by two Indians to serve as guides and hunters, Father De Smet set out on his journey July 29th — Ascended the Bitter Root to its source — Crossed the Divide
to the headwaters of the Big Hole — August 2d to August
15th spent in the plain of the Three Forks with the Flatheads

who were on a buffalo hunt — August 16th set out for St. Louis — Followed practically the same route as in 1840 — Left Fort Alexander about August 25th, and arrived at Fort Union about September 10th — Set out in a skiff for St. Louis but on third day out met steamboat and went on board — Was forty-six days making the down trip and arrived in St. Louis the last Sunday in October.

Distance traveled, 4,529 miles.

CHAPTER I.

ST. LOUIS TO GREEN RIVER RENDEZVOUS.[1]

Steamboat journey to Westport — Passengers and scenery — Start overland with Fur Company caravan — Kansas Indians — Chills and fever — The picturesque Platte — Antelope, prairie-dogs, buffalo and wolves — Chimney Rock — Camp of the Cheyennes on Laramie Fork — Boiled dog — First view of the Rocky Mountains — Red Butte — Sweetwater river — Independence Rock — South Pass.

NO doubt you are looking for some interesting details of my long, very long, journey from St. Louis to the other side of the Rocky Mountains. It took me sixty days to cross the famous American desert, and nearly four months to effect my return by a new and very hazardous road.

Sent out by the right reverend bishop and by my provincial, to gain knowledge of the disposition of the savages and of the success that might probably be looked for from founding a mission among them, I left St. Louis[2] on the 27th of March, 1840, in a steamboat, and ascended the Missouri a distance of 500 [390] miles to reach the state frontier. The craft on which I had embarked was (like all of them in this land, where emigration and commerce have grown to such an extent) encumbered with freight and passengers from every state of the Union; I may even say from the

[1] The text of the following two chapters is taken from the first 82 pages of the *Voyages aux Montagnes-Rocheuses* where it is addressed to M. le Chanoine Charles de la Croix (a former missionary to the Osage Indians) at Ghent, under date of February 4, 1841. Letter II of the *Letters and Sketches* is apparently a translation into English of another copy of the same letter, transmitted to the Father General (Roothaan) three days later; but much matter being omitted, the editors have preferred to follow the French copy.

[2] Accompanied by " Young " Ignace, of the fourth Flathead deputation; the other member, Peter Left Hand, having gone on ahead to announce their coming.

various nations of the earth, white, black, yellow and red, with shadings of all these colors.   The boat was like a little floating Babel, on account of the different languages and jargons that were heard upon it.   These passengers drop off here and there on the river, to open farms, construct mills, build factories of every kind; they increase day by day the number of the inhabitants of the little towns and villages that spring up as if by magic, on both sides of the river.

As we went on up, we found the country full of charm and interest, diversified with vertical rocks and very high clay hills, often cut-faced.   The bottoms exhibit a great variety of trees and bushes, oaks, and walnuts of a dozen different species; the sassafras and the *acacia triacanthus,* whose flowers load the air with their delicious perfume; the maple, which is the first to clothe itself in the livery of spring; and the sycamore, king of the western forest, which erects itself in the most graceful forms, with vast spreading branches, covered with a brilliant white bark, and adds a distinctive note of grandeur to the imposing beauty of the woods.   I have seen them fifteen feet and a half in diameter.   The cottonwood, (*populus deltoides,*) is another giant, growing to a prodigious height: the *bignonia radicans* seems to prefer it to all others, climbs to its very top and lets loose a profusion of great flame-colored trumpet-shaped blossoms. Here the traveler is struck by the thousand lofty columns of the cottonwood, enveloped, from the ground to the branches, by a drapery of dark green vines.   It is one of nature's charms that one never wearies of contemplating.[3]

The dogwood, (*cornus florida,*) and the redbud, (*cercis canadensis,*) fill the gap betwixt tree and shrub.   The first has a handsome heart-shaped leaf and spreads out its

[3] Father De Smet does not overstate the natural beauty of the lower Missouri valley. With its lofty bluffs of white limestone, its varied and luxuriant foliage, and its rich cultivated bottom land, it exhibits one of the most perfect examples of landscape beauty to be found anywhere.

branches like an umbrella: in spring they are covered with brilliant white flowers: in the fall they exhibit lovely scarlet berries. The other is the first shrub that one sees in blossom the length of the Missouri.

These shrubs are scattered everywhere throughout the woods, and in the earliest spring their masses of brilliant flowers form a delicate contrast with the dominant brown of the forest. The redbud gives to the landscape a charm that the traveler who sees it for the first time can never forget. The wild cherry, mulberry and ash are very common. In all these bottoms the soil is prodigiously rich, and strongly impregnated with saline substances and decomposed limestones.

The banks, however, are very unstable and crumble continually: which renders the river water, otherwise very pure and wholesome, muddy and disgusting as a drink. Sandbars and submerged trees are so numerous that one becomes used to them and scarcely thinks of the risks that he is running every minute. It is interesting to observe how deep the roots thrust themselves into this fertile soil; where the bank has crumbled you may observe the whole length of them; as a rule there is only one main tap root, which penetrates ten or twelve feet, with other smaller ones round about it.

After ten days' navigation, I reached Westport,[4] a little

[4] *Independence* and *Westport,* progenitors of the present Kansas City. Independence was the older of the two towns. It was located on the 29th of March, 1827. Its early growth was largely due to the Sante Fe trade.

The rise of Westport so close to Independence was due to the caprices of the Missouri river. That erratic stream destroyed the steamboat landing of Independence. Farther up stream there was a stable bank and here the steamboats went. The place was called Westport landing, and was the true beginning of the future Kansas City. Westport itself was back some distance from the landing. It was laid out in 1833 and grew rapidly, diverting much of the trade from Independence.

The early life of both of these towns depended almost entirely upon town on the Indian frontier, whence I was to strike out for the mountains. On the 30th of April, [1840] I set out from Westport with the annual expedition of the American Fur Company, [Captain Andrew Drips][5] which was on its way to Green river, one of the branches of the Colorado. Until the 17th of May we traveled westward over immense plains, destitute of trees or shrubs, except along the streams, and broken by deep ravines, where our voyageurs lowered and raised the carts by means of ropes. The heat of summer was already commencing to make itself felt; still the weather was favorable; often the thermometer would be as low as 27° in the morning, though it might rise to 90 by noon. The strong winds that prevail unceasingly in these vast plains make the heat supportable. Game was scarce; still my hunter supplied my tent abundantly with ducks, snipe, prairie-chickens, cranes, pigeon, badgers, deer and antelope.

The only men that I met in these first days were some Kansas Indians, who were on their way to Westport to sell their peltries. They dwell upon the Kansas river. Their territory begins sixty miles west of the state of Missouri, and their villages are at a distance of eighty miles. Their language, customs and manners are the same as those of the Osages.

In peace and in war, these two nations unite their interests, and form, so to speak, a single nation of some 1,700 souls. They live in villages, wherein their huts, which may be made of bark, like the wigwams of the Potawatomies, or of rushes like those of the Osages, or of earth like the *akozos* of the Pawnees and Otoes, are placed at random and

the trade along the Oregon and Santa Fe trails, and that with the numerous tribes of Indians located in the surrounding country. Both were outstripped at a later date by Kansas City, which was laid out in 1838.

5 Andrew Drips, born in Pennsylvania, 1789, died Kansas City, September 1, 1860. In the fur trade at least as early as 1820; member of Missouri and American Fur Companies; trader at Bellevue; Indian agent under President Tyler.

without order.   These last are round and shaped like a
cone; the wall is near three feet thick; the whole work is
supported within by sundry posts.   In all their huts, the
hard ground is the floor; the fire-place is in the middle and
the smoke escapes through a hole arranged in the summit.
The door is so low and narrow that one can enter only by
crawling; it consists merely of a dried skin hung up.   These
savages seemed to me very poor and miserable.   The greater
part of them were on foot; just before we met them, the
Otoes had stolen twenty-five of their horses.   They expressed an ardent longing to have a mission of our fathers
among them.

As we advanced toward the west, we crossed elevated
ridges, which now and then gave us extensive and very
beautiful views.   The great plain was dotted with groves of
old and large trees; especially noticeable was the *wakarusa,*
or cottonwood,[6] a plant which is abundant in this region,
and on which the Indians feed.   It is found along a river
that bears the same name, and which flows into the Kansas.
Both these rivers have rich and fertile bottoms and are well
wooded.   All the summit of the Divide is full of petrifactions.   The surface of the earth over a considerable part of
this region is covered with great flat grey and yellow stones,
lying in confusion as if they had been brought forth from
the bosom of the earth by some subterranean agitation.

I had been no more than six days in the wilderness, when
I was overcome by intermittent fever, with the chills that
ordinarily precede the attacks of heat.   This fever never
left me until I reached the Yellowstone, on my way back
from the mountains.   I cannot give you any idea of my
deplorable state.   My friends advised me to go back; but my
desire of seeing the nations of the mountains prevailed over
all their good reasons.   I therefore followed the caravan as
best I could, sticking on my horse as long as I had the
strength; after that I would go and lie in a cart on the

[6] *Waggère-roussé, ou la fleur du cotonnier.*   [Wakarusa is commonly said to mean " hip deep."]

boxes, where I was jolted about like a malefactor; very often we would have to cross deep and perpendicular ravines, throwing me into the most singular positions; now my feet would be in the air, now I would find myself hidden like a thief between boxes and bundles, cold as an icicle or covered with sweat and burning like a stove. You might add that during the three days when my fever was at its highest, I had no water but what was stagnant and dirty.

On the 18th of May, after crossing a beautiful plain thirty miles in width, we arrived upon the banks of the Nebraska[7] or Deer river (rivière au Cerf), which the French designate by the less appropriate name of Platte, or Rivière-Plate. The Platte is the chief tributary of the Missouri, and may be considered the most wonderful and most useless of the rivers of North America; for it is 2,000 yards in width from one bank to the other, and its depth is seldom more than two to six feet; the bottom is quicksand. It comes from an immense distance, through a wide and green valley, and receives the great abundance of its waters from various branches that come down from the Rocky Mountains. The mouth of this river is 800 [650] miles from St. Louis by water, and forms the dividing point between the Lower and the Upper Missouri. I was often struck with admiration at sight of the picturesque scenes which we enjoyed all the way up the Platte. Think of the big ponds that you have seen in the parks of European noblemen, dotted with little wooded islands; the Platte offers you these by thousands, and of all shapes. I have seen groups of these islands that one might easily take, from a distance,

[7] Father De Smet's explanation of the meaning of "Nebraska" (*r. au Cerf* in French, Big Horn in English version) is unique. All the early explorers accounted for it as an Indian equivalent for "shallow water," French *la Platte*. Many geographical names for streams, derived from Siouan languages, contain the root "ne" or "minne:" Minnehaha (laughing water), Nehawka (weeping water), Niobrara (running water), Nemaha (river of the Omahas), etc. It is said, however, that *nebra-ska* means "fine white sand," such as flies from the bars of the Platte and Missouri, in the Sioux language.

for fleets under sail, garlanded with verdure and festooned with flowers; and the rapid flow of the river past them made them seem to be flying over the water, this appearance of motion completing the charm of the illusion. Neither bank of the river is wooded; the trees which the isles chiefly produce are a species of white poplar, commonly called cottonwoods; the savages cut them down in winter and the bark serves as fodder for their horses.

Antelope are very plentiful in the plain of the Platte; I have often seen several hundred in sight at one time. It is the most agile animal of the prairies. Hunters make use of a trick to come near him: they run at him full gallop, and the animal is off like a flash, leaving the horseman far behind; but soon it stops to look at him, being a very curious creature; meanwhile the hunter dismounts and lays himself flat on the ground; here he makes all kinds of flourishes with his arms and legs, now and then waving his handkerchief, or a red cap, on the end of his ramrod. The antelope draws slowly near, to watch and investigate him; and as soon as it is within gunshot, the hunter fires and lays it low. Often one will get as many as six before the band scatters. Other animals are rare in this region, but there are evident indications that game has not always been lacking.

For several days' journeys, we found the whole plain covered with buffalo bones and skulls arranged in circles or half-moons and painted with various devices. It is in the midst of these skulls that the Pawnees are wont to practice their superstitious divinations, when they go forth to war or to the chase. After a long sea-voyage, the sailor rejoices at the sight of floating weeds, or of some little land birds that may alight for rest on the ship's cordage, sure signs to him that the end of his voyage is near. Even so in this desert, the traveler, wearied of living so long on salt meat, is rejoiced at sight of these weather-bleached bones, which announce to him the vicinity of the buffalo. Nothing, accordingly, but shouts of joy was heard in our camp; our hunters perceived that the buffalo plains were not far off, and they saluted with noisy cheers the hope of soon spreading destruction among those peaceful herds.

In these same places we found moreover the *wistonwish* of the Indians, the prairie-dog, more accurately called by the voyageurs the American squirrel. These animals appear to have a kind of civil government established in their society. Their towns are generally located on the slope of a hill, sometimes near a little lake or stream; but more often far from any water, that the earth in which they dwell may not be exposed to floods. They are of an earthy brown color, except the belly, which is white; their tail is not so long as that of the grey squirrel, but they have exactly the same form; the teeth, the head, the claws and the body are perfect squirrel, except that they are bigger and plumper than that animal. The voyageurs believe that their only food is the roots of the grass, and the dew of heaven their sole drink.

As we went on, we saw here and there the solitary burial-places of the Pawnees; probably those of some chiefs or warriors who had fallen in combat with their hereditary foes, the Sioux, Cheyennes or Osages. These tombs were adorned with buffalo skulls painted red; the body is put, in a sitting position, into a little cabin made of reeds and branches of trees, strongly interwoven to keep the wolves out. The face is daubed with vermilion, the body is covered with its finest war-ornaments, and beside it one sees provisions of every kind, dried meat, tobacco, powder and lead, gun, bow and arrows. For several years the families will come back every spring to renew these provisions. Their idea is that the soul hovers for a long time about the spot where the body reposes, before taking its flight to the land of souls.

After marching for seven days alongside the Platte, we reached the plains inhabited by the buffalo. I left the camp alone, very early one morning, to see them more at my ease; I approached them by way of the ravines, without showing myself or allowing them to get the wind of me. This is the most keen-scented of animals; he will detect the presence of a man at a distance of four miles, and take flight at once, since that odor is insupportable to him. I gained, without being perceived, a high bluff, resembling in shape the Waterloo monument; from it I enjoyed a view of perhaps a dozen miles. This vast plain was so covered with animals, that the markets or fairs of Europe could give you only the feeblest idea of it. It was indeed like a fair of the whole world assembled in one of its loveliest plains. I looked with wonder upon the slow and majestic walk of these heavy wild cattle, marching silently in single file, while others cropped with avidity the rich pasturage, which is called the short buffalo grass. Whole bands were lying amidst flowers on the grass; the scene altogether realized in some sort the ancient tradition of the holy scriptures, speaking of the vast pastoral countries of the Orient, and of the cattle upon a thousand hills.

I could not weary of gazing upon this delightful scene, and for two hours I watched these moving masses in the same state of astonishment. Suddenly the immense army seemed startled; one battalion gave the panic to another, and the whole multitude was in flight, running in every direction. The buffalo had caught the scent of their common enemy; the hunters had rushed among them on the gallop. The earth seemed to tremble under their steps, and the dull sounds that came back were like the mutterings of distant thunder. The hunters shot to right and left; they made a great slaughter among the fattest of these animals. I returned to camp with them. They had a number of horse-loads of tongues, humps, ribs, etc., all the rest being left to the wolves and vultures [turkey buzzard]. We camped not far from this scene of butchery, and every one in camp busied himself straightway about the cooking. There being no wood on the banks of the Platte, our people made use of the dry dung of the buffalo, which burns like peat. We were often obliged to have recourse to the same expedient in the prairies of the Black Hills.

In the middle of the night frightful sounds, howlings and

barkings awoke me; one would have thought the four tribes of the Pawnees were assembled to dispute our passage over their territory.   I woke my guide, to learn the cause of the noise, and that he might aid in resisting the enemy's attack. He laughed and answered, " Don't be scared; that is nothing.   It is the wolves celebrating after their long winter's fast; they are feasting on the carcasses of the cows that the hunters have left on the prairie."   Wolves are very numerous in this region.   According to the Indians, they kill every year a third of the buffalo calves; often when they are in strong bands, they will even attack full-grown bulls or cows, hurling themselves all together upon a single buffalo, pulling him down very skilfully and devouring him.

To give you an idea of the great number of buffaloes upon the Missouri, I will here add that in this year of 1840, the Fur Company has brought down 67,000 robes to St. Louis.   The number of buffalo that the savages of the Missouri kill for their own needs, for their tents, clothing and saddle-covers, is estimated, one year with another, at 100,000 besides this.

On the 28th, we forded the South Fork of the Platte. All this region, clear up to the great mountains, is a veritable barren, rocky and sandy, covered with scoria and other volcanic substances, with no fertile spots save on the rivers and creeks.

This region, says one modern traveler,[8] resembles the deserts of Asia with its vast undulating and treeless plains, and its uncultivated, sandy, lonely expanses, which weary the eye by their monotonous extent.   It is a land wherein no man dwells; at certain seasons of the year, even the hunter and his horse lack food there.   All herbage is burnt up; the rivers and creeks are dry; the buffalo, elk and deer withdraw to distant spots, keep upon the edge of the expiring verdure, and leave behind them only a vast uninhabited solitude, cut up by ravines and old beds of

[8] Irving.   This paragraph and the next are from chapter XXII of *Astoria*, very little modified.

streams, which only serve now to torment the traveler and augment his thirst. At long intervals the monotony of this great desert is interrupted by heaps of stones, piled in confusion, like ruins; or perhaps it is traversed by ridges of rocks, rising up before the traveler like insurmountable barriers; such are the Black Hills. Beyond rise the Rocky Mountains, the boundaries of the Atlantic world. The gorges and valleys of this vast chain give a refuge to a great number of savage tribes, some of which are but the mutilated remainders of different peoples, formerly peaceful possessors of the prairies, now driven back by war into almost inaccessible defiles, where the spoiler ceases at length to pursue them.

It seems that this western desert, such as I have described it, must forever defy the industry of civilized man. There are perhaps some places, more fortunately situated upon the banks of rivers, where agriculture could be successfully practiced; others might be converted into grazing lands as fertile as those of the east; but it is to be feared that, with very little exception, this immense region is nothing more than an ocean between civilization and barbarism, where bands of malefactors, organized like the caravans of the Arabs, may work their depredations with impunity. Some day perhaps it may be the cradle of a new people, composed of the old savage races and of this class of adventurers, of the fugitive and the banished, thrust out from the bosom of society, a heterogeneous and menacing population, which the American Union is piling up like a sinister cloud upon its frontiers, increasing continually its strength and its irritation by transporting whole tribes of Indians from their birthplace on the banks of the Mississippi, into the places of exile assigned them among these western solitudes. These savages bring with them an implacable hatred of the whites, who, they say, have driven them from their own country, far from the burial-places of their fathers, that they may take unjust possession of their heritage. If some of these tribes should some day form into hordes like the nomadic peoples, half shepherd, half warrior, who range the plateaus of Asia with their herds, is it not to be feared that in time others may organize themselves into bands of robbers and assassins, with the swift horses of the prairies for coursers, the desert for the theater of their brigandage, and inaccessible rocks for a safe refuge for their lives and their booty?

On the 31st of May we camped two miles and a half from one of the most remarkable curiosities of this savage region.   It is a cone-shaped eminence of not far from a league in circumference, gashed by many ravines and standing upon a smooth plain.   From the summit of this hill rises a square shaft, thirty to forty feet through by 150 in height; the form of this column has given it the name of the Chimney; it is 175 yards above the plain, and may be perceived from thirty miles away.   The Chimney is composed of clay in a petrified state, interspersed with layers of white and grayish sandstone.   It seems to be the remnant of a lofty mountain which the winds and the storms have been wearing down for ages; a few years more and this great natural curiosity will crumble away and make only a little heap on the plain; for when it is examined near at hand, an enormous crack appears in its top.[9]   In the neighborhood of this wonder, all the hills present a singular aspect; some have the appearance of towers, castles and fortified cities.   From a little distance, one can hardly persuade himself that art is not mingled in them with the fantasies of nature.   Bands of the *ashata,* an animal called also *grosse-corne,* or bighorn, have their abode in the midst of these bad lands.   The Chimney, with its castles and fantastic cities, forms the termination of a high ridge, which runs from south to north.   We found a narrow passage through between two perpendicular cliffs 300 feet in height.

[9] The Chimney, though still crumbling, remains a conspicuous object in 1903.

14

This region abounds in magnesia, insomuch that Glauber's salt is found almost everywhere, and in several places in great quantities in a crystallized state. Rattle-snakes and other dangerous reptiles, which are met with at every step, would be a scourge to the country, if the savages had not discovered, in a root that is very common in these parts, an infallible specific against all poisonous bites.[10]

Although we were still three days' journey from the Black Hills,[11] they were already distinctly visible. Everywhere we were in the midst of buffalo. If the earth is thankless and yields but little, Providence has provided in a different way for the subsistence of the Indians and travelers who traverse these regions. We killed without any trouble six buffalo a day for the forty persons who constituted our camp. In all my travels I have never wearied of watching with admiration these truly majestic animals, with their rugged necks, shoulders and heads. If their peaceable nature was not known, their aspect alone would terrify one. But they are timid and without malice, and never offer to do any harm, except in their own defense, when they are wounded and hard pressed. Their strength is extraordinary, and though they appear clumsy, they run notwithstanding with great speed; it takes a good horse to follow them very far.

In this same region, bands of wild or runaway horses are very numerous; much skill and a long-winded horse are required to catch them. The Spanish-Mexicans and, as a rule, the Indians, are expert in this kind of chase; it is seldom that they miss casting their lasso about an animal's neck, though at full speed.

On the 4th of June, we crossed the Fourche-à-la-Ramée,[12] [Laramie fork] one of the principal tribu-

[10] Probably the blackroot, spoken of on p. 663.

[11] This term, at present practically restricted to the Black Hills of South Dakota, was at first applied to all the secondary mountain systems of southeastern Wyoming.

[12] Laramie river takes its name from a trapper by the name of

taries of the Platte, in a buffalo canoe, or bull-boat. Here we found some forty lodges of the Cheyennes, who received us with all the signs of good will and esteem; they were polite, cleanly and decent in their manners. The men in general are of great stature, straight and vigorous; they have aquiline noses and strongly marked chins. The history of this nation[13] is that of all the wild tribes of the prairies; they are the remnant of the powerful nation of the Shaways that once dwelt upon that Red river which flows into Lake Winnipeg. The Sioux, their irreconcilable enemies, forced them after a long war to cross the Missouri and take refuge on a little river called Warrikane, where they fortified themselves; but the conquerors again attacked them there, and drove them from post to post, to the midst of the Black Hills, upon the waters of the Big Cheyenne. In the course of these reverses, the tribe lost even its name; it is at present known only by that of the river which they frequent. They make no more efforts to establish a permanent abode, for fear of another attack from their cruel enemies. They have embraced the nomadic life, live by the chase and follow the buffalo in his migrations.

The head chiefs of this village invited me to a feast, and put me through all the ceremonies of the calumet, as follows: first they give the Great Spirit to smoke, holding the pipe toward the heavens, then toward the sun, the earth and the water; then the calumet goes the rounds of the lodge three times; it passes from hand to hand, and every one takes half a dozen puffs. Then the chief embraced me and greeted me, saying, " Black-robe, my heart was very glad when I learned who you were. Never has

Laramé, Joseph Laramée, as one writer gives it, who lost his life on the stream in 1821. The name was a frequent one among the voyageurs, and is often met with in the American Fur Company correspondence.

[13] From chapter XXIII of *Astoria*. The " Shaways " are not known to present-day ethnologists.

my lodge seen a greater day.   As soon as I received the news of your coming, I had my big kettle filled to give you a feast in the midst of my warriors.   Be welcome.   I have had my three best dogs killed in your honor; they were very fat." Do not wonder when I tell you that this is their great feast, and that the flesh of the wild dog is very delicate and extremely good; it much resembles that of a young pig.   The portion bestowed upon me was large; the two thighs and the paws, with five or six ribs; the law of the feast required me to eat it all, but it was too much for me.   Finally I learned that one may get rid of his dish by passing it to another guest, with a present of tobacco.

I took the opportunity to speak to them of the principal points of religion; I explained to them the ten commandments of God and several articles of the creed.   I made known to them the object of my journey to the mountains, asking whether they also did not desire to have Black-robes among them, to teach their children to know and serve the Great Spirit.   The proposition seemed to please them greatly, and they answered that they would do what they could to render the stay of the Black-robes among them agreeable.   I believe that a zealous missionary would meet with very good success among these savages.   Their language is said to be very difficult; they are about 2,000 in number.   The neighboring nations consider these Indians the most courageous warriors of the prairies.

Fort la Ramée [Laramie][14] is at the foot of the Black

[14] Fort Laramie dates from 1834.   In that year William L. Sublette built a fort at the mouth of the Laramie river and called it Fort William.   Soon after it fell into the hands of the American Fur Company and was christened Fort John for John B. Sarpy.   In 1846 it seems to have been abandoned and another built in its stead a mile farther up stream, and to this the name Fort Laramie was given.   About 1849 the post was sold to the United States and the famous military post of Fort Laramie began its career.

Hills. There is nothing observable, either in the color of the soil of these mountains or in that of the rocks, that can have given them this name; they owe it to the sombre verdure of the little cedars and pines that shade their sides. The vegetable soil along the rivers and in the valleys is rather good; the uplands are very sterile and almost entirely covered with blocks of granite, quartz, marcasite[15] and other kinds of rock commingled, showing clearly that at some remote time there have been great subterranean convulsions in this region.

From la Ramée [Laramie] a range of the Rocky Mountains forty miles away is visible. It stands 5,000 feet above the plain. Every day the thermometer rose to 80° and 90° in the valleys of these mountains; while their summits were covered with snow. I was often deceived in regard to distances; sometimes I wished to examine more closely a big rock or an odd-looking hill; I started for it expecting to reach it in an hour; and it took me at least two or three hours. This must be due to the great purity of the atmosphere in the prairies of this high region.

Absinthe [artemisia; sage-brush] is a spontaneous product of this country; it grows to a height of eight to ten feet, and in so great abundance that it makes traveling in carts quite inconvenient. Wild cherries, gooseberries and service berries (an excellent little black fruit) are also very plentiful. The elder grows in ravines. Two kinds of cottonwood are common in the bottoms. On the banks of rivers and the slopes of mountains, groves of pines and cedars are seen.

On the 14th, [June, 1840] we camped at the foot of the Red Butte. This is a very lofty hill, of a red ochre color, composed of clay in a petrified state, and is a central point for the savages, who pass and repass it on their travels westward and northward. The northern branch of the Platte, which we had been following thus far, here takes

---

[15] Native bisulphide of iron; prismatic iron pyrites.

a southerly direction; its source is 150 miles farther up. From the Red Butte we crossed over a high ridge to the Sweetwater,[16] or Rivière-de-l'Eau-douce, so called from the great purity of its waters. The most remarkable spot upon this river is the famous Independence Rock;[17] it is the first massive rock of that famous mountain chain which divides North America, and which travelers call the backbone of the universe. It is composed of granite *in situ* of a prodigious thickness, and covers several miles of ground; it is entirely exposed from top to bottom. It is the great register of the desert; the names of all the travelers who have passed by are there to be read, written in coarse characters; mine figures among them, as that of the first priest to reach this remote spot.

For several days now we had on our right a chain of those naked rocks, so properly called Rocky Mountains. They are nothing but rocks heaped upon rocks; you think

[16] The name of this stream dates from the period of Ashley's expeditions. A fitting explanation of its origin might easily be given even in the absence of any historic data. The water in the adjacent country for many miles around is so impregnated with alkaline salts as to be unfit to drink. The thirsty traveler, coming suddenly upon this stream of pure mountain water, would very naturally by contrast call it the Sweetwater. But the French name, as first given, was not *Eau Douce,* but *Eau Sucré,* sugared water, and arose, according to Ferris, from the fact that in the very early years, certainly before 1830, a pack mule laden with sugar was lost in the stream.

[17] Independence Rock was a famous landmark. It is an immense oblong block of oval, but irregular shape, along the southern base of which lay the river and along the northern base the old Trail. It covers an area of over twenty-seven acres and its highest point is 155 feet above the level of the river. It is wholly isolated and looks as if it had been dropped there in the midst of the plain. The site of the rock became from the first a great camping place, and the custom early arose of inscribing on it the names of travelers who passed it. It was named before 1830 from the circumstance of a party of American trappers having celebrated the Fourth of July at its base.

The granite of the rock is not durable, and though a multitude of names appear upon it, few, if any, dating back more than twenty-five or thirty years are now legible (1903).

you have before your eyes the ruins of a whole world, covered with the eternal snows as with a shroud. On the 19th, we descried the Wind [or Wind River] Mountains, in which is the rendezvous of the caravan and its point of separation as well; but we were still nine days' journey from the place. Every day we became aware that it was growing colder and colder, and on the 24th [of June] we traversed plains covered with snow. On the day following we passed [South Pass] from the waters tributary to the Missouri to those of the Colorado, which flows into the Pacific Ocean by way of California, two degrees farther south than New Orleans. The pass across the mountains is almost imperceptible; it is five to twenty-five miles in width, and eighty in length. These mountains are calculated to be twenty to twenty-four thousand feet above the Atlantic Ocean.[18]

[18] The Wind River range constitutes a massive and rugged system of mountains between Wind and Green rivers. It was a very noted range during all the period of Father De Smet's travels. Their altitude, however, is greatly overstated by Father De Smet who here follows Captain Bonneville. Fremont Peak, the highest of the range, is only 13,790 feet high.

CHAPTER II.

The rendezvous on Green river — First meeting with the Flatheads — Makes friends also with the Snakes — Their manners and customs — Four days' rest on Green river — Sets out with the Flatheads for their country — A veteran of Napoleon's — Jackson's Little Hole — Crossing Snake river in a bag — Pierre's Hole — The home camp — Amiable Indians — Religious labors — Gratifying results — Across the mountains into Montana — The plain of the Three Forks.

ON the 30th I came to the rendezvous,[1] where a band of Flatheads, who had been notified of my coming,[2] were already waiting for me. This happened, as I said further back, on Green river, a tributary of the Colorado; it is the place whither the beaver-hunters and the savages of different nations betake themselves every year to sell their peltries and procure such things as they need.

I will now give you a short account of the customs, characters and locations of the several mountain tribes, according to my own observations and the best information that I have been able to obtain.

The Shoshones, or Root-diggers, called also Snakes, were present at the rendezvous in great numbers. They

[1] The rendezvous was one of the most interesting developments of the fur trade in the Rocky Mountains. It arose from the necessity of carrying the trade into regions remote from navigable rivers, where boats could not carry the annual merchandise nor bring back the furs. The transportation was done by annual caravans from the States, and rendezvous were appointed for each year at points convenient for the trappers and Indians to meet the traders. These meetings were great events and form one of the most picturesque features of early frontier life in the Far West.

[2] By Peter Left Hand, one of the two members of the fourth " Flathead embassy," who preceded him to announce his coming, while the other envoy, Young Ignace, remained to accompany Father De Smet.

inhabit the southern part of the territory of Oregon, in the vicinity of upper California. Their population of about 10,000 souls is divided into several bands, scattered here and there over the barrenest country in all the region west of the mountains; almost all the surface is covered with scoria and other volcanic products. They are called Snakes by reason of their poverty, which reduces them to burrow in the ground like those reptiles and to live upon roots. Occasionally a hunting-party will come east of the mountains to hunt buffalo, and at the season when the fish come up from the sea, they go down to the banks of Salmon river and its tributaries to lay in their winter stock. They are pretty well provided with horses. At the rendezvous they gave a parade to greet the whites that were there. Three hundred of their warriors came up in good order and at full gallop into the midst of our camp. They were hideously painted, armed with their clubs, and covered all over with feathers, pearls, wolves' tails, teeth and claws of animals, outlandish adornments, with which each one had decked himself out according to his fancy. Those who had wounds received in war, and those who had killed the enemies of their tribe, displayed their scars ostentatiously and waved the scalps they had taken on the ends of poles, after the manner of standards.

After riding a few times around the camp, uttering at intervals shouts of joy, they dismounted and all came to shake hands with the whites in sign of friendship. I was invited to a council by some thirty of the principal chiefs. Just as among the Cheyennes, we had first to go through all the ceremonies of the calumet. To begin, the chief made a little circle on the ground, placed within it a small piece of burning dried cow-dung, and lit his pipe from it. Then he offered the pipe to the Great Spirit, to the sun, to the earth and the four cardinal points. All the others observed a most profound silence and sat motionless as statues. The calumet passed from hand to hand, and I noticed that each one had a different way of taking it.

One turned the calumet around before putting the stem to his mouth; the next made a half-circle as he accepted it; another held the bowl in the air; a fourth lowered it to the ground, and so on.   I am naturally inclined to laughter, and I must confess that on this occasion I had to make serious efforts not to break out, as I watched the gravity observed by these poor savages in the midst of all these ridiculous affectations.   These forms of smoking enter into their superstitious religious practices; each one has his own, from which he would never dare deviate all his life long, for fear of displeasing his Manitous.

I made known to them the motives of my visit, the commandment which God had given the Black-robes to go and preach his holy law to all the nations of the earth, the obligation that all peoples were under to follow it as soon as it was known to them, the everlasting happiness which it brings to all who follow it faithfully unto death, and hell with all its torments, which would be the lot of whomsoever should close his ears to the word of Jesus Christ. I laid before them the advantages which they would receive from a mission, and I ended by preaching to them the principal points of Christianity.

The savages paid the greatest attention, and appeared struck with wonder at the holy doctrine that I had been explaining to them.   They then took counsel among themselves for the space of half an hour, when the spokesman, in the name of all the chiefs, addressed me in the following words: " Black-gown, your words have entered our hearts; they will never go out from them.   We wish to know and practice the sublime law that you have just made known to us, in the name of the Great Spirit, whom we love.   All our country is open to you, you need only choose to settle an establishment.   We will all of us leave the plains and the forests, to come and put ourselves under your orders, about you."   I advised them, while awaiting that happy day, to choose wise men in their several camps, to perform the prayers in common evening and morning;

since thereby the good chiefs would find occasion to incite all the people to virtue. That very evening they assembled, and the head chief promulgated a law, that whoever in future should steal or commit any other scandal should be punished in public.

The Snakes believe the especial residence of the Great Spirit to be in the sun, in fire and in the earth. When they make a solemn promise, they take the sun, the fire and the earth to witness their undertaking. When a chief or warrior of the nation dies, his wives, children and nearest relatives cut off their hair; that is their full mourning. They even clip the manes and tails of all the dead man's horses, giving the poor animals a most sorry appearance. Then they make a pile of all his possessions in the middle of the lodge, cut the poles that support it into little pieces and burn all his property at once. The corpse is tied upon his favorite horse, and led down to the edge of the neighboring river. There the warriors chase the animal, surround him closely and utter such horrible yells that they force him to leap into the current with his master's body. Then, yelling all the louder, they tell him to transport his master without delay to the land of souls. Nor is that all: to testify to their sorrow, they cut themselves in all the fleshy parts of their bodies; and the greater their attachment to the departed the deeper are the gashes. I have been assured that they claim that their sorrow escapes through these wounds. Would you believe that these same people, who feel the death of a relative so keenly, have, like the Sioux, the Pawnees and most nomadic tribes, the barbarous custom of abandoning the old and the sick pitilessly to the ferocious beasts of the desert, as soon as they begin to be in the way in their hunting expeditions?

While I was in their camp, the Snakes were making ready for an expedition against the Blackfeet. As soon as the chief had announced to all the young warriors his resolution to carry the war into the enemy's country, all who proposed to follow him prepared their rations, moccasins, bows and arrows. The evening before their departure, the chief, at the head of his soldiers, performed his farewell dance at every lodge; everywhere he received a piece of tobacco or some other present. If they take any women prisoners on these expeditions, they carry them to camp and hand them over to their wives, mothers and sisters. These women immediately butcher them with their hatchets and knives, vomiting upon the poor wretches, in their frantic rage, the most crushing and outrageous language. "Oh! Blackfoot bitches," they cry: "If we could only eat the hearts of all your young ones, and bathe in the blood of your cursed nation!" [3] * * *

Never in my life have I enjoyed so many consolations as during my stay among these good Flatheads and Pend d'Oreilles; the Lord has amply compensated for all the privations and sufferings that I had endured in this long and laborious journey. I have spoken further back of having found a deputation from these two tribes at the rendezvous on Green river. Those good Indians had come to meet me to serve as an escort in this country, so dangerous to travel. Our meeting was not that of strangers, but of friends; it was like children running to meet their father after a long absence. I wept with joy at embracing them, and they also, with tears in their eyes, welcomed me with tenderest expressions. With a truly patriarchal simplicity, they told me all the little news of their nation, their almost miraculous preservation in a fight between sixty of their warriors and 200 Blackfeet, a fight that lasted five days, and in which they had killed fifty of their enemies without losing a single man. "We fought like brave men," they told me, "in the desire to see you; the Great Spirit took pity on us, he helped us to remove dangers from the path that is to lead you to our camp. The Blackfeet will not trouble us again

[3] For omitted portion of the letter, see p. 989.

for a while; they went away weeping. Our brothers are burning with impatience to see you." We thanked the Lord together for having preserved us thus far in the midst of so many dangers, and implored his protection in the long journey that we had yet to make.

I had stayed four days on Green river to allow my horses time to recover from their fatigue, to give good, wholesome advice to the Canadian hunters, who seem to be in great need of it, and to talk with the Indians of various nations. On the 4th[4] of July, I resumed my travels, with my Flatheads; ten brave Canadians also chose to accompany me. A good Fleming from Ghent, Jean-Baptiste de Velder, an old grenadier of Napoleon, who had left his fatherland thirty years ago, and had passed the last fourteen in the mountains in the capacity of beaver-hunter, generously offered to serve and aid me in all my journeyings. He was resolved, he told me, to pass the rest of his days in the practice of his holy religion. He had almost forgotten the Flemish language, except his prayers and a hymn in Flemish verses in honor of Mary, which he had learned as a child on his mother's knees, and which he recited every day.

Three days we ascended Green river, and on the 8th we crossed it, heading for an elevated plain which separates the waters of the Colorado from those of the Columbia. In this plain, as in all mountain valleys that I have traversed, flax grows in the greatest abundance; it is just the same as the flax that is cultivated in Belgium, except that it is an annual; the same stalk, calix, seed and blue flower, closing by day and opening in the evening. On leaving this plain, we descended several thousand feet by a trail and arrived in Jackson's Hole.[5] The slope of the surrounding mountains abounds in the rarest plants, and offers the amateur botanist a superb collection. The val-

[4] 6th in one of the English letters.
[5] This was not Jackson's Hole, but a much smaller valley near the head of Hoback river, called Jackson's Little Hole.

ley is seventeen miles long by five or six wide. Thence we passed into a narrow and extremely dangerous defile, which was at the same time picturesque and sublime. Mountains of almost perpendicular cliffs rise to the region of perpetual snow, and often overhang a rugged and narrow path, where every step threatens a fall. We followed it for seventeen miles, upon a mountain side inclined at an angle of 45° over a torrent which rushed uproariously in cascades, hundreds of feet below our route. The defile was so narrow, and the mountains on either hand so high, that the sun could scarcely penetrate it for an hour or two of the day. Pine forests like those of Norway, balsam firs, ordinary poplars, cedars, mulberry trees and many other varieties cover the sides of these mountains.

On the 10th, after crossing the lofty mountain, we arrived upon the banks of Henry's Fork, [Snake river] one of the principal tributaries of Snake [Columbia] river.[6] The mass of snow melted during the July heat had swollen this torrent to a prodigious height. Its roaring waters rushed furiously down and whitened with their foam the great blocks of granite which vainly disputed the passage with them. The sight intimidated neither our Indians nor our Canadians; accustomed to perils of this sort, they rushed into the torrent on horseback and swam it. I dared not venture to do likewise. To get me over, they made a kind of sack of my skin tent; then they put all my things in and set me on top of it. The three Flatheads who had jumped in to guide my frail bark by swimming, told me, laughing, not to be afraid, that I was on an excellent boat. And in fact this machine floated on the water like a majestic swan; and in less than ten minutes I found myself on the other bank, where we encamped for the night.

The next day we had another high mountain to climb through [Teton Pass] a thick pine forest, and at the top we found snow, which had fallen in the night to the depth

[6] Father De Smet is in error here and later on, page 228, in applying the name Henry to the main Snake river.

of two feet. This is a very remarkable thing in this region; when it rains in the valley in summer, snow falls in big flakes on the mountains. In descending into the great valley known as Pierre's Hole,[7] we found the trail very steep and slippery. The horses and mules of the mountains are very skilful in these kinds of dangerous passages; just let them alone and you are safe; a rider who should persist in guiding them in these circumstances would be at every step in danger of breaking his neck.

In the mountain valleys, the soil is generally nearly black, but sometimes yellow. It is often found mixed with marl and marine substances in a decomposed state. This kind of soil extends to a great depth, as may be seen in the vast cuttings of the ravines and upon the banks of rivers. The vegetation in these valleys is very abundant. It is a land where the geologist beholds evidences of the extensive action of volcanic forces, and much also that is of interest in the various formations of lava, etc.

One day's travel in the great valley of Pierre's Hole brought us to the camp of the Flatheads and the Pend d'Oreilles. The poles were already up for my lodge, and at my approach men, women and children came all together to meet me and shake hands and bid me welcome; the number of them was about 1,600. The elders wept with joy, while the young men expressed their satisfaction by leaps and shouts of happiness. These good savages led me to the lodge of the old chief, called in his language Big Face. He had a truly patriarchal aspect, and received me in the midst of his whole council with the liveliest cordiality. Then he

[7] Pierre's Hole is one of the most beautiful, and in early times was one of the most celebrated, valleys of the Rocky Mountains. The trappers always called the mountain valleys "holes." Pierre's Hole lies just west of the Teton Mountains and is about twenty-five miles long by five to fifteen broad. It was named from an Iroquois trapper who discovered it. It was a favorite resort for the traders, trappers and Indians and several rendezvous were held there. The famous battle of Pierre's Hole, between the Blackfeet Indians on one side and the trappers and Flathead Indians on the other, took place in 1832.

addressed me the following remarks, which I report to you word for word, to give you an idea of his eloquence and his character: "Black-robe, you are welcome in my nation. Today Kyleêeyou[8] (the Great Spirit) has fulfilled our wishes. Our hearts are big, for our great desire is gratified. You are in the midst of a poor and rude people, plunged in the darkness of ignorance. I have always exhorted my children to love Kyleêeyou. We know that everything belongs to him, and that our whole dependence is upon his liberal hand. From time to time good white men have given us good advice, and we have followed it; and in the eagerness of our hearts, to be taught everything that concerns our salvation, we have several times sent our people to the great Black-robe at St. Louis (the bishop) that he might send us a Father to speak with us.— Black-robe, we will follow the words of your mouth."

Then I had a long talk on religion with these honest folk; I explained to them the object and advantages of my mission, and the necessity of settling permanently in a fertile and suitable spot. All expressed the greatest satisfaction and showed much eagerness to exchange the bow and quiver for the spade and plow. I set a schedule of spiritual exercises for them, particularly for the morning and evening prayers in common, and for the hours of instruction. One of the chiefs at once brought me a bell to give the signals, and on the first evening I gathered all the people about my lodge. I made known to them my conversation with their chiefs, the plan which I meant to follow for their instruction, and the necessary frame of mind that the Great Spirit required of them to comprehend and practice the holy law of Jesus Christ, who alone could save them from the torments of hell, make them happy on earth and procure them after this life eternal happiness with God in heaven. After that I said the evening prayers, and finally they sang together, in a harmony which surprised me very much, and which I

8 Kaikolinzoeten (Our God) in the English version. The word in the text means Our Father.

thought admirable for savages, several songs of their own composition, on the praise of God. It would be impossible to describe to you the emotions that I felt at this moment. How touching it is for a missionary to hear the benefactions of the Most High proclaimed by poor children of the forests, who have not yet had the happiness of receiving the light of the gospel!

Every morning, at daybreak, the old chief was the first to rise; then mounting a horse he rode up and down the camp to harangue his people. This is a custom that he has always observed, and I think it has kept these Indians in the great unity and admirable simplicity that are observed among them. These 1,600 persons, thanks to his fatherly care and good advice, seemed to form but a single family, in which order and charity reigned in a truly surprising manner. " Come, courage, my children," he cried, " open your eyes. Address your first thoughts and words to the Great Spirit. Tell him that you love him, and ask him to take pity on you. Courage, for the sun is about to appear, it is time you went to the river to wash yourselves. Be prompt at our Father's lodge, at the first sound of the bell; be quiet when you are there; open your ears to hear and your hearts to hold fast all the words that he says to you." Then he would administer fatherly rebukes for anything he and the other chiefs had observed that was out of order in their conduct the day before. At the voice of this old man, whom all love and respect like a tender father, they would hasten to arise; all would be in motion in the village, and in a few minutes the banks of the river would be covered with people.

When all were ready, I rang the bell for prayer, and from the first day to the last they continued to show the same avidity to hear God's word. Their eagerness was so great that they would run to get a good place; even the sick got themselves carried thither. What a lesson for the cowardly and pusillanimous Christians of the old Catholic countries, who have always plenty of time for coming to the divine services, and think they do enough if they are in time for

15

the first gospel and get the benediction at the *Ite missa est;* or for those who make a pretext of the least sickness, or of a show of bad weather to excuse themselves from attending the holy mass and their pastors' sermons!

This zeal for prayer and instruction (and I preached to them regularly four times a day) instead of declining, increased up to the time of my departure. They told me often that it was their delight to hear the word of God. The day after my arrival among them, I had nothing more urgent to do than to translate the prayers into their language, with the aid of a good interpreter [Gabriel Prudhomme]. Fifteen days later, at instructions, I promised a medal to the first who should be able to recite without a mistake the *Pater,* the *Ave,* the *Credo,* the ten commandments of God and the four acts. A chief rose: " Father," he said, " your medal belongs to me." And to my great surprise, he recited all these prayers without missing a word; I embraced him and made him my catechist. The good savage put so much zeal and perseverance into his task that in less than ten days the whole nation knew their prayers.

During my stay among this good people, I have had the happiness of regenerating nearly 600 of them in the saving waters of baptism; all [the others] ardently desired to obtain the same favor; and their dispositions were without doubt excellent; but since the absence of missionaries could only be momentary, I thought it prudent to put them off until the following year, to give them a high idea of the dignity of the sacrament, and to try them in regard to the indissolubility of the bonds of marriage, which is an unknown thing among the Indian nations of America; for they often part for the most frivolous causes. Among the adults baptized were the two head chiefs of the Flatheads and Pend d'Oreilles, both octogenarians. Before bestowing the holy sacrament upon them, as I was urging them to renewed repentance for their sins, Walking Bear, the second of the two named, answered me: " When I was young, and even as I became old, I was plunged in profound ignorance of good

and evil, and in that period I must no doubt have displeased
the Great Spirit; I sincerely implore pardon of him. But
every time I have perceived that a thing was bad, I have
at once banished it from my heart. I do not remember ever
in my life to have deliberately offended the Great Spirit."
Are there in our Europe many Christians who could give
this testimony of themselves?

I was not able to discover among these people the slightest
blameworthy act, unless it was their gambling, in which
they often venture everything they possess. These games
were unanimously abolished, as soon as I had explained to
them that they were contrary to the commandment of God,
saying: "Ye shall not covet anything that is your neighbor's." They are scrupulously honest in their buying and
selling; they have never been accused of having committed
a theft; everything that is found is taken to the lodge of the
chief, who cries the articles and returns them to the owner.
Slander is unknown even among the women; lying is hateful
to them beyond anything else. They fear, they say, to
offend God, and that is why they have only one heart, and
they abhor a "forked tongue;" a liar. Quarrels and fits
of rage are severely punished. No one suffers without his
brothers interesting themselves in his trouble and coming to
his succor; accordingly, they have no orphans among them.
They are polite, always of a jovial humor, very hospitable,
and helpful to one another in their duties. Their lodges are
always open to any one; they do not so much as know the use
of keys and locks. One single man, by the influence which
he has justly acquired by his bravery in fight and his wisdom in the council, leads the whole tribe; he has no need of
guards, nor bolts, nor iron bars, nor state prisons. I have
often asked myself: "Is it these people whom the civilized
nations dare to call by the name of savages?" Wherever
I have met Indians in those remote regions, I have found
them very teachable in everything adapted to better their
condition. The vivacity of their young people is surprising,
and the amiability of their characters and their dispositions

among themselves are remarkable. People have too long been accustomed to judge the savages of the interior by those of the frontier; these last have learned the vices of the whites, who, guided by the insatiable thirst for sordid gain, endeavor to corrupt them and encourage them by their example.

I found the camp of the Flatheads and Pend d'Oreilles in the valley called Pierre's Hole. This valley is situated at the foot of the three Tetons,[9] sharp-peaked mountains of a prodigious height, rising almost perpendicularly more than 10,000 feet, and covered with perpetual snow. There are five of them, but only three can be seen at any great distance. Thence we ascended one of the principal forks of Henry's [Fork of Snake] river,[10] making every day little camps nine or ten miles apart. Often, in these little stages, we passed and repassed high hills, wide and swift torrents, narrow and dangerous defiles. Often also we came upon lovely valleys, level and open, rich in pasture grounds of a beautiful verdure, dotted with flowers, and where the mountain balsam (the travelers' tea) abounds. This tea, even after it has been crushed beneath the feet of thousands of horses, still perfumes the air with its delicious scent. In the valleys and defiles which we traversed, several more mountains drew our attention; some were in the form of cones, rising to a height of several thousand feet at an angle of forty-five to fifty degrees, very smooth and covered with a fair verdure; others represented domes; others were red as well-burned brick, and still bore the imprints of some great convulsion of nature; there were scoria and lava so porous that they floated on water; they were found scattered in all

[9] The Teton Mountains are the most interesting, historically and otherwise, in the United States. The principal summit, the Grand Teton, is 13,691 feet high. Jackson Hole (named for the fur trader, David Jackson), is a very celebrated valley at the eastern base of the range.

[10] Named for Andrew Henry, a fur trader, who built a fort in its valley in the fall of 1810.

directions, and so abundantly in some places that they seemed to have filled whole valleys. In several places the openings of ancient craters were still to be distinguished. The argillaceous and volcanic strata of the mountains are generally horizontal; but in several places they hang perpendicularly, or else they are curved or wavy; often one might take them for artificial works.

On the 22d of July the camp came to Henry's lake, one of the principal sources of the Columbia; it is about ten miles in circumference. We climbed on horseback the mountain that parts the waters of two great rivers; the Missouri, which is properly speaking the main branch of the Mississippi and flows with it into the Gulf of Mexico, and the Columbia, which bears the tribute of its waters to the Pacific Ocean. From the elevated spot at which I was I could easily distinguish Mosquito lake,[11] source of one of the main branches of the north fork of the Missouri, called Jefferson River.

The two lakes are scarce eight miles apart. I started for the summit of a high mountain, for a better examination of the fountains that give birth to these two great rivers; I saw them falling in cascades from an immense height, hurling themselves with uproar from rock to rock; even at their source they formed already two mighty torrents, scarcely more than a hundred paces apart. I was bound to get to the top. After six wearisome hours, I found myself exhausted; I think I must have climbed more than 5,000 feet; I had passed snow drifts more than twenty feet deep, and still the mountain top was at a great height above me. I therefore saw myself compelled to give up my plan, and I found a place to sit down. The fathers of the Company who are in the missionary service on the banks of the Mississippi and its tributaries, from Council Bluffs to the Gulf of Mexico, came to my mind. I wept with joy

[11] Le lac des Maringouins; Red Rock lake. This lake is the most distant from the sea, by river channel, of any lake upon the globe. It is the ultimate source of the Missouri.

at the happy memories that were aroused in my heart. I thanked the Lord that he had deigned to favor the labors of his servants, scattered over this vast vineyard, imploring at the same time his divine grace for all the nations of Oregon, and in particular for the Flatheads and Pend d'Oreilles, who had so recently and so heartily ranged themselves under the banner of Jesus Christ. I engraved upon a soft stone this inscription in large letters: *Sanctus Ignatius Patronus Montium. Die Julii* 23, 1840.

I said a mass of thanksgiving at the foot of this mountain, surrounded by my savages, who intoned chants to the praise of God, and installed myself in the land in the name of our holy founder. Let us implore his aid, that through his intercession in heaven, this immense desert, which offers such great hopes, may speedily be filled with worthy and unwearying laborers. To-day is the accepted time to preach the gospel to these different nations. The apostles of Protestantism are beginning to crowd in and pick out the best places, and soon the cupidity and avarice of civilized man will make the same inroads here as in the east, and the abominable influence of the vices of the frontier will interpose the same barrier to the introduction of the gospel, which all the savages seem to have a great desire to know, and which they will follow with fidelity, like the Flatheads and Pend d'Oreilles.

During all my stay in the mountains, I said the holy mass regularly Sundays and feast-days, as well as on days when the Indians did not break camp in the morning; the altar was made of willows; my blanket made an altar cloth, and all the lodge was adorned with images and wild flowers; the Indians knelt without in a circle of about 200 feet, surrounded by little pines and cedars, set out expressly; they took assiduous part with the greatest modesty, attention and devotion, and since various nations were among them, they chanted the praises of God in the Flathead, Nez Percé and Iroquois languages. The Canadians, my Fleming and I sang chants in French, English and Latin. The Flatheads had already had for some years a custom of never breaking camp on Sunday, but of passing that day in devotional exercises.

On the 24th of July, the camp crossed the mountain and moved from Henry's lake to Mosquito [Red Rock] lake. Until the 8th of August, we were still traveling through a great variety of country. Now we would find ourselves in open, smiling valleys, now in sterile lands beyond lofty mountains and narrow defiles, sometimes in extensive high plains, profusely covered with blocks and fragments of granite.

On the 10th we camped on Jefferson river. The bottom is rich in lovely pasture lands and wooded with trees of thin growth. We went down it, making twelve to fifteen miles a day, and on the 21st of the same month we came to the junction of the three forks of the Missouri, where that river first takes this name; we camped on the middle branch [Madison Fork]: In this great and beautiful plain were buffalo in numberless herds. From Green river to this place, our Indians had made their food of roots and the flesh of such animals as the red and black-tailed deer, elk, gazelle, bighorn or mountain sheep, grizzly and black bear, badger, rabbit and panther, killing also occasionally such feathered game as grouse, prairie-hens (a kind of pheasant), swans, geese, cranes and ducks. Fish abounded besides in the rivers, particularly salmon trout. But cow-meat is the favorite dish of all the hunters, and as long as they can find it, they never kill any other animals. Finding themselves therefore in the midst of abundance, the Flatheads prepared to lay in their winter supply; they raised willow scaffolds about their lodges for drying meat, and every one made ready his fire-arm, his bow and his arrows. Four hundred horsemen, old and young, mounted on their best horses, started early in the morning for their great hunt. I chose to accompany them in order to watch this striking spectacle from near at hand. At a given signal, they rode at full gallop among the herds; soon everything appeared confusion and flight all over the plain; the hunters pursued the fattest cows, discharged their guns and let fly their arrows, and in three hours they killed more than 500.   Then the women, the old men and the children came up, and with the aid of horses carried off the hides and the meat, and soon all the scaffolds were full and gave the camp the aspect of a vast butcher-shop.   The buffalo are hard to kill; they must be wounded in the vital parts.   A ball that strikes a bull's forehead produces no other effect than a movement of the head and a greater exasperation; on the other hand, one that strikes the forehead of a cow penetrates.   Several bulls, mortally wounded in this hunt, defended themselves furiously.[12]

*   *   *   *   *   *   *   *   *

[12] For omitted portion of this letter, see p. 1001.

CHAPTER III.

RETURN FROM THREE FORKS TO ST. LOUIS.

Affecting departure from the Flatheads — Across Bozeman Pass to the Yellowstone — Danger from prowling Indians — Meets a camp of the Crows — Two days' observations of that tribe — More Crows on the Big Horn — Their poor prospects in the next world — Flathead escort returns from first trading post — Alone with the grenadier in the desert — Fort Union — Mandan village — Geological curiosities — An account of the Aricaras — Medicine feats — Encounters with the Sioux — Their friendliness — Ten days in a canoe among floating ice — Council Bluffs, Westport and St. Louis.

*T*HE 27th of August [1840] was the day I had set for my departure. Seventeen warriors, selected braves of the two nations, stood early in the morning at the entrance to my lodge with three chiefs. The council of the elders had deputed them to serve as my escort for so long as I should find myself in the country of the Blackfeet and Crows, two nations so hostile to the whites,[1] that the first give them no quarter when they meet them, but massacre them in the cruelest manner; the second take from them everything they have, strip them to the shirt and leave them in the desert to perish of hunger and misery; sometimes they grant them life but make them prisoners. Long before sunrise all the nation was assembled around my lodge; no one spoke, but grief was painted on each face. The only thing I could say that seemed to console them was a formal promise of a prompt return in the following spring, and of a reinforcement of several missionaries. I performed the morning prayers amid the weeping and sobs of those good

[1] This is true of the Blackfeet but not of the Crows, who were always friendly to the whites, except that they never hesitated to rob them of horses.

savages. They drew from me despite myself the tears that I would gladly have stifled for the moment. I made them see the necessity for my voyage; I urged them to continue serving the Great Spirit with fervor and to put from them every cause of scandal; I recalled to them the principal truths of our holy religion. After this I gave them for their spiritual head a very intelligent Indian, whom I had taken pains to instruct myself in a most particular manner; he was to represent me in my absence, call them together evening and morning, as well as Sundays, say the prayers to them, exhort them to virtue, and anoint the dying, and, in case of need, little children. There was but a single voice, a unanimous assent to all my recommendations. With tears in their eyes they all wished me a fortunate journey. Old Big-Face rose and said: " Black-robe, may the Great Spirit accompany you in your long and dangerous journey. We will offer vows evening and morning that you may arrive safe among your brothers at St. Louis. We will continue to offer vows until you return to your children of the mountains. When the snows disappear from the valleys, after the winter, when the grass begins to be green again, our hearts, so sad at present, will begin to rejoice. As the grass grows higher, our joy will become greater; but when the flowers appear, we will set out to come and meet you. Farewell."

Full of trust in the Lord who had preserved me thus far, I started with my little band and my faithful Fleming, who chose to continue sharing my dangers and my labors. For two days we were going up the Gallatin, the southern [eastern] fork of the Missouri; thence we crossed by a narrow pass[2] thirty miles in length to the Yellowstone river, the second of the great tributaries of the Missouri. Here it

[2] Father De Smet crossed Bozeman Pass, the immemorial route of of travel between the Gallatin fork of the Missouri and the Yellowstone river, at the point where the latter stream turns sharply east from its long northerly course. The Northern Pacific railroad crosses the divide by means of a tunnel 3,600 feet long near the pass.

was needful to take the greatest precautions; this is why we formed only a little band. We had to cross plains that stretched out of sight, sterile and arid lands, cut up with deep ravines, where at every step one might come upon enemies lying in wait. Scouts were sent out in every direction to reconnoiter the country; all traces, whether of men or of animals, were attentively examined. It is here that one cannot but admire the sagacity of the savage; he will tell you what day an Indian has passed by the spot where he sees his tracks, he will calculate the number of men and of horses, he will make out whether it was a war or hunting party; he will even recognize, from the impression of their footgear, to what nation they belonged. Every evening we chose a favorable place to pitch our camp, and built in haste a little fort with trunks of dead trees, to shelter us from a sudden attack.

This region is the range of the grizzly bear, the most terrible animal of this desert; at every step we came upon their terrifying tracks. One of our hunters killed one and brought him to camp; his paws were thirteen inches in length, and each claw seven. The strength of this animal is surprising; an Indian has assured me that with a single blow of his paw he has seen one of these bears tear away four ribs from a buffalo, which fell dead at his feet. Another of my company was passing on the run near a dense willow thicket (the retreat of the bears when they have their young) when a she-bear rushed furiously upon his horse, put her formidable paw upon his croup, and rending the flesh to the bone overturned him with his rider. Luckily for my man, he gained his feet in a flash, gun in hand, and had the satisfaction of seeing his terrible adversary retreat into the willows as hastily as she had come forth. It is, however, rare for a bear to attack a man, unless the latter comes suddenly upon him or wounds him. If he is allowed to pass without harm, he retires, showing that the fear of man is upon him, as upon all the other animals.

For several days our route lay through the Yellowstone

bottoms. Buffalo were scarce, for war-parties had traversed the same plains a few days previously. All the country along this river is very gravelly and full of round and oblong boulders, shaped by the water; here and there little patches of woods were seen in the distance on the banks of rivers.

Below the mouth of Clark's Fork the Yellowstone is hemmed in by high cliffs. We climbed them by a narrow trail to gain the uplands, or rather a chain of rough hills, which we were six days crossing. In this march we suffered much from thirst. We found all the springs exhausted and the beds of the streams dry. The whole region was covered with loose fragments of volcanic rocks; scarcely a trace of vegetation could be observed. Little elevations and banks of sand appeared at intervals, lightly covered with red cedars of a slim growth; but as a rule we saw no other vegetation than a small and stunted weed, *pommes de raquette* (a kind of thorny cactus) and some varieties of plants, which, like the cactus, grow best in the driest and most ungrateful soil. Fragments from the high hills and rocks, angular slabs of sandstone, were everywhere heaped upon the ground as ice-cakes are found heaped up on the sand-bars and banks of rivers; often they rose in lone pyramids or resembled obelisks of different forms.

As we went on, we perceived frequent tracks of horses. On the 5th of September we came to a place where numerous troop of horsemen had passed an hour before. Were they allies or enemies? Right here I will remark that in these solitudes, though the howling of wolves, the hissing of venomous serpents and the roaring of the tiger and grizzly bear are capable of freezing one with terror, this fear is nothing in comparison with that which fresh tracks of men and horses can arouse in the soul of the traveler, or the columns of smoke that he sees rising round about him. In an instant the escort came together to deliberate; every one examined his fire-arm, whetted his knife and the points of his arrows and made all preparations for a resistance to the death; for to surrender in such an encounter would be to expose one's self to perish in the most frightful torments. We resolved to follow the trail, determined to know who were ahead of us; it led us to a heap of stones piled up on a little eminence. Here more signs were manifest; these stones were colored with freshly shed blood; my savages surrounding them, examined them with serious attention. The head chief, a man with much sense, presently said to me, "Father, I think I can explain to you what we see before us. The Crows are not far away; we shall see them in two hours. If I am not mistaken, we are upon one of their battlefields; their nation will have met with some great loss here. This heap of stones has been raised to the memory of the warriors who have fallen under the blows of their enemies. Here the mothers, wives, sisters, daughters of the dead (you see their traces) have come to weep over their graves. It is their custom to tear their faces, cut their arms and legs and shed their blood upon these stones, rending the air at the same time with their cries and lamentations."

He was not mistaken; presently we perceived a considerable troop of savages some three miles off. They were in fact Crows returning to their camp, after having paid the tribute of blood to forty of their warriors, massacred two years before by the Blackfeet. Since they are just at present allies of the Flatheads, they received us with the greatest transports of joy. Soon we met groups of women covered with dried blood, and so disfigured that they aroused at once compassion and horror. They repeat this scene of mourning for several years, whenever they pass near the tombs of their relations and so long as the slightest spot of blood remains on their bodies they may not wash themselves.

The Crow chiefs received us with cordiality and gave us a great feast. The conversation was really pleasing; the languages of the two nations being different, it was carried on by signs. All the tribes of this part of America know the system and understand one another perfectly. Presently the Crows desired to buy the Flathead's handsome horses.

This is how a bargain was concluded before my eyes. A young Crow chief, of gigantic stature and covered with his gayest raiment, advanced to the midst of the gathering, leading his horse by the bridle, and placed it in front of the Flathead, as if to offer it in exchange for his. The latter giving no sign of approval, the Crow then laid at his feet his gun, then his scarlet robe, then all his ornaments one after another, then his leggings too, and finally his moccasins. Then the Flathead took the horse by the bridle, picked up the goods, and the bargain was concluded without a word being said. The Crow chief, though despoiled of all his fine clothes and plumage, leaped with joy upon his new courser and ran him around the camp several times, uttering yells of triumph and trying the horse at all his gaits.

The main wealth of the western Indians consists of horses; every chief and warrior owns a great number of them, which may be seen grazing in herds about their camps. They are objects of trade for them in time of peace and of booty in war, so that they often pass from one tribe to another at a very great distance. The horses that the Crows have are principally from the wild races of the prairies; but they had stolen some from the Sioux, the Cheyennes and other tribes of the southwest, who in turn had got them from the Spanish in their raids into the Mexican territory. The Crows are considered the most indefatigable marauders of the plains; they cross and recross the mountains in every direction, carrying to one side what they have stolen on the other. This is how they get the name of *Absaroka,* which signifies " Crow." [3] From their childhood they are practiced in this kind of larceny; they acquire an astonishing ability in it; their glory increases with the number of their captures, so that an accomplished robber is in their eyes a hero. Their country seems to stretch from the Black Hills [of Dakota] to the Rocky Mountains, embracing the Wind River Moun-

[3] Sparrow-hawk, not crow.

tains and all the plains and valleys watered by that stream, as well as by the Yellowstone and Powder rivers and the upper waters of several branches of the Platte. The soil and climate of this country are very diverse; there are vast plains of sand and clay; there are springs of hot water and mines of coal; game is very abundant throughout. These are the best-formed savages I have met on my travels.

I rode with this tribe for two days; they had plenty of everything, and according to their custom were passing the time in feasts and rejoicings. Since I hide nothing from you, I hope you will not be scandalized at learning that in a single afternoon I took part in twenty different banquets; hardly was I seated in one lodge, when somebody would come and call me to another. But as my stomach was not as accommodating as those of the Indians, I satisfied myself with tasting their messes, and for a little piece of tobacco the *eaters,* whom I had had the foresight to take with me, emptied the dishes carefully in my stead.

From this camp we made our way to the Big Horn, the largest tributary of the Yellowstone; it is a fair broad river, whose waters are pure as crystal. It traverses very extensive plains, well wooded on both banks, and offering beautiful grazing grounds. There we found another camp of Crows, to the number of about 1,000 souls. They too received us with the greatest demonstration of friendship, and again it was necessary to pass the day in going from one feast to another. I took a favorable occasion to speak to them upon various points of religion. As I was vividly depicting to them the torments of hell, and telling them how the Great Spirit had prepared it for those who evade his laws, one of the chiefs uttered an exclamation which I could not think of translating to you and said: " I think there are only two in all the Crow nation who will not go to that hell you speak of; those are the Otter and the Weasel; they are the only ones I know who have never killed, nor stolen, nor been guilty of the excesses which your law forbids. Still I may be mistaken about them, and in that case we will all go to hell in company." The next day I set out; one of the head chiefs made me a present of a handsome bell and hung it on my horse's neck. He invited me to make the tour of the camp with him; I followed him, my animal sounding his bell, and afterwards he accompanied me, out of civility, to the distance of six miles from his village.[4]

After having spent several more days in surmounting the difficulties of the passage, across sterile and broken hills, we came at last to the Fur Company's first fort.[5] It is called the Fort of the Crows. The Americans who reside there received us with a great deal of benevolence and friendliness, and I quickly recovered from my fatigue. Not until then did the intermittent fever entirely leave me. At this place the Flatheads edified all hands by their piety. In the fort as well as in the camp, and when we were on the road, we never failed to assemble morning and evening to say the prayers in common, and to sing some canticles to the praise of God. I had set my departure from the fort for the 13th of September. Here I decided to part from my faithful Flatheads. I told them

[4] Father De Smet found himself again among the Crows upon his return journey to St. Louis in the fall of 1842. He was equally well received by them, but as on the present occasion, no conversions nor baptisms resulted. Father Palladino records that Father Point baptized twelve children, believed to have been Crows, among the Grosventres in the winter of 1846–47 (see page 955), and Father De Smet baptized a number in 1863, as related hereafter. No other missionary work seems to have been done among them by Catholic priests until the year 1880.

[5] There were four "Crow posts" built by the American Fur Company in this vicinity.— Fort Cass, at the mouth of the Big Horn, built in 1832; Fort Van Buren, on the right bank of the Yellowstone near the mouth of Tongue river, in 1835; Fort Alexander on the left bank of the Yellowstone opposite the mouth of the Rosebud, about 1839; and Fort Sarpy on the right bank of the Yellowstone about twenty-five miles below the mouth of the Big Horn, in 1850. These posts were built for the trade of the Crow Indians.

that the country I was about to enter was yet more dangerous than that which we had just traveled together, since it was ranged incessantly by war-parties of the Blackfeet, Assiniboins, Grosventres, Aricaras and Sioux, nations which had always been hostile to them; that I durst not expose their lives further; that I entrusted my own preservation to Providence, and that aided by that divine protection I had nothing to fear.　I exhorted them at the same time to continue to serve the Great Spirit with fervor; and reiterating my promises of a prompt return, accompanied by other missionaries, I embraced them all and wished them a fortunate journey.

My Fleming and I set out with courage upon the solitary and dangerous trip of several hundred miles that we had to make together across an unknown desert, in which there was no trail, nor any other guide than the compass. For a long time we followed the course of the Yellowstone [left bank], except in some places where chains of rocks intercepted our march and obliged us to make long circuits, crossing rough hills four or five hundred feet high.　At every step we were aware of the forts that war-parties put up for their times of raid, murder and pillage; they might contain lurking enemies at the moment we passed them.　Such a solitude, with all its horrors and dangers, has notwithstanding one very real advantage; it is a place where one is constantly looking Death in the face, and where he presents himself incessantly to the imagination in the most hideous forms.　There one feels in a very special manner that he is wholly in God's hands. It is then easy to offer him the sacrifice of a life which belongs less to you than to the first savage who may see fit to take it; and to form the most generous resolutions a man is capable of.　That was, in fact, the best " retreat " that I have ever made in my life.　My only consolation was the object for which I had undertaken the journey; my guide, my support, my refuge, was the fatherly Providence of my God.

16

On the second day of the journey, I espied, upon waking very early in the morning, the smoke of a great fire a quarter of a mile away; only a rocky point separated us from a savage war-party. Without losing time, we saddled our horses and started at full gallop; at last we gained the hill, and crossing the ravines and the dry bed of a torrent, we reached the top without being perceived. That day we made forty to fifty miles without a halt, and did not camp until two hours after sunset, for fear of the savages coming upon our trail and following us. The same fear prevented our lighting a fire, and so we had to do without supper. I rolled myself in my blanket and stretched myself on the sod, commending myself to the good God. My grenadier, braver than I, was soon snoring like a steam engine in full swing; running through all the notes of the chromatic scale, he closed each movement of his prelude with a deep sigh, by way of modulation. As for me, I turned and rolled, but spent a sleepless night; what they call a *nuit blanche*. At dawn next morning we were already under way; we had to use the greatest precautions, because the country we had to traverse was most dangerous. Towards noon, a fresh cause for alarm; a buffalo had been killed, not more than two hours before, in a spot by which we had to pass; his tongue, marrowbones and some other delicate morsels had been taken. We trembled at this sight, thinking the enemy was not far away; but we ought rather to have thanked the Lord, who had thus prepared food for our evening meal. We turned in the opposite direction to the tracks of the savages, and that night we camped among rocks that are the resort of bears and tigers. There I had a good sleep. This time the music of my companion's snoring did not trouble me.

We always took the road early in the morning; but it was to confront fresh dangers each time, to meet here and there recent foot-prints of men and horses. Towards ten o'clock we came to an abandoned camp of forty lodges; the fires were not yet out; but luckily we saw no one. At last we came to the Missouri, but at a place where 100 lodges of Assiniboins had crossed an hour before. This is only a feeble outline of my dangerous transit from the Fort of the Crows to Fort Union at the mouth of the Yellowstone.

I related these particulars one day to an Indian chief, who at once answered: " The Great Spirit has his manitous (guardian spirits); he sent them out to you on your way, to stupefy and put to flight the enemies who might have harmed you." A Christian could not better have recalled the fine text of the Psalms: *"Angelis suis mandavit de te, ut custodiant te in omnibus viis tuis."* I have never seen a plainer instance of the special Providence that protects the poor missionary.

The Yellowstone country abounds in game; I do not believe that there is in all America a region better adapted to the chase. I was for seven days among innumerable herds of buffalo. Every moment I perceived bands of majestic elk leaping through this animated solitude, while clouds of antelopes took flight before us with the swiftness of arrows. The ashata or bighorn alone seemed not to be disturbed by our presence; these animals rested in flocks or frolicked upon the projecting crags, out of gunshot. Deer are abundant, especially the black-tailed deer, which is hardly found elsewhere than in mountainous country. It is a noble and beautiful animal, covered with a dark brown *pelisse;* you will see him jump with all four feet at once, and his movements are so quick that he hardly seems to touch the ground. All the rivers and streams that we crossed in our course, gave evident signs that the industrious beaver, the otter and the muskrat were still in peaceable possession of their solitary waters. There was no lack of ducks, geese and swans. This country abounds in coal and in iron-mines. The Yellowstone appeared to me to be full of currents; it is not navigable, unless in the middle of summer, when the water from the melting snows rushes down in torrents from the mountains.

Fort Union[6] is the vastest and finest of the forts that the Fur Company has upon the Missouri; it is situated 2,200 [1,765] miles from St. Louis. The gentlemen residing there overwhelmed us with civilities; they could not get over their astonishment at the dangerous journey which we had just concluded so fortunately. During our stay among them, they supplied all our wants most liberally, and at our departure for the village of the Mandans they loaded us with all sorts of provisions. I shall be most thankful to them all my life.

After having regenerated sundry half-breed children in the holy waters of baptism, I left the fort on the 23d of September. It took us ten days to reach the village of the Mandans. The soil along the great river is much more fertile than that of the Yellowstone; but it is still the same vast prairie, diversified with high hills, or rather mountains, guttered with ravines. The river beds are dry through part of the year; but they are swollen to a prodigious height in the rainy season. On the hillsides and in the bottoms, on the banks of the rivers, handsome groves are found here and there; but the general aspect of the region is nothing but an undulating plain, covered with sod and various plants. The soil is strongly impregnated with sulphur, copperas, alum and Glauber's salts; the strata of earth give a strong color to the rivers that traverse them, and together with the crumbling of the banks of the Missouri, impart to the water of that immense stream the materials that render it muddy.

There are some sandy places in that region,[7] full of natural curiosities; I noticed great trunks of trees petrified, and

[6] Fort Union, the most important and the most celebrated of the American Fur Company posts on the upper Missouri, was founded in the fall of 1828, by the distinguished trader Kenneth McKenzie.

[7] This is the region which the distinguished geologist, Doctor F. V. Hayden, afterward made peculiarly his own. He made his first explorations here in 1854, and, confirming Father De Smet's belief, found matter for years of labor and many subsequent expeditions.

the skeletons of various species of animals; among other things I found a big buffalo-skull, changed to stone as red as porphyry. I carried it a long way, but the trouble that this burden caused me, and the fatigue of the horses, who at that season of the year hardly found whereon to live, soon forced me to abandon it regretfully in the prairie, as I had been obliged to do before in the Black Hills and Rocky Mountains with all the other curiosities I had picked up.

We met on our way a war-party of fifteen Assiniboins, returning from a fruitless expedition against the Grosventres of the Missouri. It is chiefly on such occasions as this that it is dangerous to meet the savages. To come home without horses, prisoners, scalps, is for them the climax of dishonor and shame; accordingly they showed us much displeasure, and their looks were nothing if not sinister. These Indians are, however, cowards, and this particular band were poorly armed. I was accompanied by three men from the fort, who were going to the Aricaras with a herd of horses, and though we were only five, each of us laid his hand upon his weapon, assuming an air of determination, and we had a little talk with them and continued our route without being molested. The next day we passed through a forest on the banks of the Missouri which had been in 1835 the winter quarters of the Grosventres, Aricaras and Mandans; it was there that these unfortunate nations had been attacked by that epidemic, which, in the course of a year, made such ravages among the Indian tribes; several thousand of the savages died of smallpox. We observed in passing that the corpses, wrapped in buffalo hides, had remained bound to the branches of the largest trees. This savage burial-ground offered a very sad and mournful sight, and gave my traveling companions occasion to relate several anecdotes as deplorable as they were tragic. Two days later we came to the miserable remnants of these three unfortunate tribes. The Mandans, who to-day scarce number ten

families, have united with the Grosventres, who themselves
had joined the Aricaras; altogether there are about 3,000
of them.   Some of the young men having perceived us
afar off, gave notice to the chiefs of the approach of
strangers.   At once they rushed out by hundreds to meet
us; but the three men from Fort Union made themselves
known, and presented me to their chiefs as a Black-robe
of the Frenchmen.   They received us with the greatest
signs of friendliness and forced us to pass the afternoon
and night in their camp.   The kettles were soon filled in
all the lodges, and the roasting pieces were set to the fire
to celebrate our arrival.   Here again, as among the Crows,
it was a succession of invitations to feasts that we had to
undergo until midnight.   To refuse would have been the
height of rudeness, and besides they believe us as capable
as themselves of eating hugely and at any hour of the day
or night.   An Indian is a singular being in this respect; he
is insatiable and indefatigable; he is always ready when
eating is in question; but I must say also that he is of an
admirable patience in time of dearth, and keeps the most
rigorous fast for whole weeks.

These savages helped us next day to cross the Missouri in their bull-boats.   These are shaped like a round
basket, made of willows as thick as one's thumb interwoven and covered with a buffalo skin.   The women manage these boats of their own manufacture with much skill.
The weight and number of persons that they will carry is
truly astonishing.   Our horses, that had followed us swimming, became mired to the neck on the opposite bank; it
took a half day's work to get them out of the mud.

The same evening we came to the first permanent village of the Aricaras.   Their houses are very commodious
and roomy; they are made with four great crotched tree-
trunks set on end, supporting the beams and a roof of
stout poles interwoven with osiers; the whole structure is
covered with earth.   A hole dug in the ground in the
middle of the lodge serves for a fireplace, and an opening

contrived in the top lets the smoke out and admits the light. Inside the lodge is surrounded with alcoves, resembling the bunks on a ship and concealed by skins in place of curtains. At the extremity of each lodge, or else upon the summit, you will see a kind of hunting or war trophy, consisting of two or more buffalo heads painted in an odd manner, and surmounted with shields, bows, quivers and other weapons.

[8]These Aricaras commonly wear no other garment than a loin-cloth. On feast days, they put on a handsome tunic, leggings and moccasins of gazelle-skin embroidered with porcupine quills of lively colors; then they envelope themselves in a buffalo robe loaded with ornaments and colors, throw their quiver filled with arrows over the left shoulder, and cover their head with a bonnet of eagle feathers. He who kills an enemy on his own ground is distinguished by tails of animals which he attaches to his legs. He who kills a grizzly bear wears the claws of that animal in the form of a collar, and it is the most glorious trophy of an Indian hunter. The warrior who returns from the enemy with one or several scalps, paints a red hand across his mouth, to show that he has drunk enemies' blood.

The warriors of the Aricaras and Grosventres, before starting on the warpath, keep a strict fast, or rather they abstain totally from drinking and eating for four days. In this interval their imagination is exalted to the point of delirium; whether it is the enfeebling of their organs or the natural effect of the warlike plans they are nursing, they claim to have strange visions. The elders and wise men of the tribe, being called in to interpret these dreams, draw from them auguries more or less favorable to the success of the enterprise; their explanations are received as oracles by which the expedition is to be regulated. While the preparatory fast continues, the warriors make incisions in their bodies, thrust pieces of wood into their flesh be-

[8] Much of this is from *Astoria,* chapter XXI.

neath the shoulder blade, tie leather straps to them and let themselves be hung from a post fastened horizontally upon the edge of a chasm 150 feet deep; often they even cut off one or two fingers, which they offer as a sacrifice to the Great Spirit, that he may grant them scalps in the warfare that they are about to undertake. In one of their last skirmishes with the Sioux, the Aricaras killed twenty of the enemy and placed their bodies in a heap in the middle of their village. Then began their grand war dance; many women and children took part. After having celebrated for a long time the exploits of their braves, they rushed like wild beasts upon the inanimate bodies, hacked them to pieces and stuck the scraps on the ends of long poles, with which they danced several times around the village.

One can form no idea of the cruelty of a great number of these savage tribes in the continual warfare that they wage with their neighbors. When they know that the warriors of a rival tribe have gone for a hunt, they come unexpectedly upon their village, massacre the children, women and old men, and carry away prisoners all the men they can lead. Sometimes they put themselves in ambush and let part of the band pass quietly, then all at once they give a hideous yell and shower upon the enemy a hail of bullets and arrows. A deadly combat begins instantly, they rush upon one another, war-club and ax in hand, and make a horrible butchery, boasting of their valor and spewing a torrent of insults upon the unhappy vanquished; death shows himself in a thousand hideous forms, the sight of which, though it would freeze with horror any civilized man, only inflames the rage of these barbarians. They insult and trample under foot the mutilated corpses; they tear off the scalps, roll in the blood like ferocious beasts, and often even devour the quivering members of those who still breathe. The conquerors return to their village dragging with them the prisoners destined to torment.

The women come to meet them, uttering frightful howls on the supposition that they will have to weep the death of their husbands or brothers. A herald calls out the circumstantial details of the expedition; the roll of the warriors is called, and their silence indicates that they have succumbed. Then the piercing cries of the women are renewed and their despair presents a scene of rage and grief that passes imagination. The last ceremony is the announcement of the victory; forgetting at once their own troubles, they [the women] hasten to celebrate the triumph of their nation; by an inexplicable transition, they pass in an instant from frantic sorrow to the most extravagant joy.

I could not find words to describe to you the torments that they [the men] inflict upon the poor prisoner devoted to death; one tears out his nails by the roots, another chews the flesh off his fingers, sticks the torn finger into his pipe and smokes its blood; they crush their toes between two stones, apply red-hot irons to all parts of their bodies, skin them alive and feed upon their quivering flesh. These cruelties continue for several hours, sometimes for a whole day, until the victim succumbs to so many fearful torments. The women, like veritable furies, often outdo the men in cruelty in these scenes of horrors. During all this horrible drama, the chiefs of the tribe are tranquilly seated about the stake where the victim is writhing; they smoke and look on at these tragic scenes without the slightest emotion. Often the prisoner dares to brave his executioners with a coolness truly stoical: "I do not fear death," he cries; "those who dread your torments are cowards, they are lower than women. May my enemies be confounded; they shall not draw a groan from me; let them rage and despair. Oh! if I could devour them and drink their blood in their own skulls to the last drop!"

At last we came to the big village of the Aricaras, which is only ten miles from that of the Mandans. The Fur

Company has a fort here also [Fort Clark].[9] I was surprised to find around the dwellings fair fields of maize, cultivated with the greatest care. These Indians continue to make the same earthen vessels (and every lodge has several of them) that are found in the ancient tombs scattered through the United States, and which the antiquarians of the country assume to have belonged to an earlier race than the savages of to-day. The jugglers or conjurers of the Aricaras enjoy a high reputation among the Indians, by reason of the astonishing tricks that they perform to give themselves greater importance; they pretend to have communications with the spirit of darkness. They plunge their arms to the elbows in boiling water, by means of the juice of a certain root wherewith they rub their arms. They eat fire and shoot arrows at one another without injury. One trick surprised me greatly, though the savage was unwilling to perform it in my presence, saying that my medicine (religion) was stronger than his.

He had his hands, feet, legs and arms bound with a thousand knots; he was then enclosed in a big net and afterwards in a buffalo robe. The man who tied him promised him a horse if he got rid of his bonds; but in a minute he came forth free from all his fetters, to the great surprise of all the spectators. The commandant of the fort offered him another horse if he would communicate his secret to him. " Let yourself be tied," said the sorcerer to him; " I have ten invisible spirits that are at my orders; I

---

[9] Fort Clark was built to accommodate the trade of the Mandans, Minnetarees and other tribes. It was located on the right bank of the Missouri fifty-five miles above the point where the Northern Pacific now crosses the river at Bismarck, N. D. This had been an important trading point from the earliest times. A post had been built there as early as 1822. Several other temporary posts were built in the vicinity but were succeeded by Fort Clark in 1831. This post was built by James Kipp under the orders of Kenneth McKenzie and was named after William Clark of the Lewis and Clark expedition.

will detach three of my band and give them to you; they
will untie you; but don't be afraid of them, for they will
accompany you everywhere." The commandant was dis-
concerted by this statement of the savage and durst not
accept the offer.

On the 6th of October I started on again for the fort of
the Little Missouri,[10] or Fort Pierre. This is the company's
great warehouse for goods destined for the wants of the
savages inhabiting the river. As upon the Yellowstone, I
was again without a guide in this ten days' journey. A
Canadian who was going the same way accompanied us.
One becomes by degrees accustomed to braving dangers.
Full of confidence in the protection of God, we sought our
way in a country where there is no trodden path, guided
through these desert expanses like the mariner upon the
vast ocean. The inhabitants of the fort had carefully
recommended to us to avoid meeting the Yanktonnais,
the Santees, the Hunkpapas, the Ogallalas, and the Blackfeet Sioux. Still we had to traverse the plains where they
range. On the third day, a party of Yanktonnais and
Santees, who were in hiding behind a butte, suddenly surprised us; but they were so far from meaning any harm
that they loaded us with kindnesses, and after smoking the
calumet of peace with us, furnished us provisions for the
road. The next day we met several other parties who
showed us the same friendliness and the same attentions;
they shook hands with us and we smoked with them.

On the fifth [Eng. ninth] day we found ourselves in the
neighborhood of the Blackfeet Sioux, a detached tribe of
the Blackfeet of the mountains.[11] Their name alone and
the race from which they descend terrified us; we therefore traveled as much as possible in the ravines, to con-

[10] This stream has been variously known as the Little Missouri, the
Teton, and Bad river. It was formerly generally known by the second
name, but now only by the third.

[11] Wrong. There is no relationship between the two tribes.

ceal ourselves from the piercing eye of the savages who were roaming in the plains. Toward noon we stopped near a lovely spring to dine and take a moment's rest. As we were congratulating ourselves on not having yet met those redoubtable Blackfeet, all at once a fearful noise was heard on the hill that overlooked the spot where we had halted; a band of Blackfeet, who had been following our tracks in the ravines for several hours, came at us in a gallop. They were armed with guns, bows and arrows, almost naked, and painted in the most outlandish manner. I rose at once and presented my hand to him whom I believed to be the chief of the band; he said coldly, "Why are you hiding in this ravine?" I answered him that we were hungry and that the spring had invited us to take a moment's repose. He looked at me with wonder, and addressing the Canadian, who could speak the Sioux language a little better, said to him, "I have never seen such a man in my life. Who is he?" My long black robe and the missionary's cross that I bore upon my breast especially excited his curiosity. The Canadian answered him (and under the circumstances he was prodigal of his titles) "It is the man who talks to the Great Spirit. It is a chief or Black-gown of the Frenchmen." His fierce look at once changed; he ordered his warriors to put away their weapons and they all shook hands with me. I made them a present of a big twist of tobacco, and everybody sat down in a circle and smoked the pipe of peace and friendship. He then besought me to accompany him and to pass the night in his village, which was at no great distance. I followed him, and on coming in sight of the camp, which comprised some hundred lodges, or about 1,000 souls, I stopped a quarter of a mile away in a fair meadow on the bank of a fair river, and there pitched my camp. I had the head chief invited to sup with me. When I said the *Benedicite,* he asked the Canadian what I was doing. He answered that I was speaking to the Great

THE MISSIONER'S WELCOME.

An engraving in the life of Father De Smet, S. J.

Spirit to thank him for having procured us whereof to eat. He uttered an exclamation of approval.

Twelve warriors and their chief, in full costume, shortly afterward presented themselves before my lodge and spread a large and fine buffalo robe. The head chief took me by the arm and leading me to the skin made me a sign to be seated. I had no idea of the meaning of this ceremony, but I sat down, thinking that it was an invitation to smoke the calumet with them. Judge of my surprise when I beheld the twelve warriors seize this kind of carpet by the ends, lift me from the ground and, preceded by their chief, carry me in triumph to the village, where everybody was instantly afoot to see the Black-robe. The most honorable place in the chief's lodge was assigned to me, and he, surrounded by forty of his principal warriors, harangued me in these terms: "Black-robe, this is the happiest day of our lives. To-day for the first time we see among us a man who comes so near to the Great Spirit. Here are the principal braves of my tribe. I have bidden them to the feast that I have had prepared for you, that they may never lose the memory of so happy a day." Then he requested that I would speak again to the Great Spirit before commencing the feast; I made the sign of the cross and said the prayer. All the time it lasted, all the savage company, following their chief's example, held their hands raised toward heaven; the moment it was ended, they lowered their right hands to the ground. I asked the chief for an explanation of this ceremony. "We raise our hands," he replied, "because we are wholly dependent on the Great Spirit; it is his liberal hand that supplies all our wants. We strike the ground afterward, because we are miserable beings, worms crawling before his face." Then he took from my dish a piece of *pomme blanche* (a root that they use for food) and put it in my mouth with a little piece of buffalo meat.

I desired to speak to these honest folk of the main points

of Christianity;[12] but the interpreter was not sufficiently skilled in the language to render my words into the Sioux. The next day, though we were still five days' journey from the fort, the chief had his son and two other young men go with me, praying me to instruct them. He desired absolutely, he said, to know the words I had to impart to them in behalf of the Great Spirit; and at the same time these young men would be a safeguard for me against evil-disposed savages.

Two days afterward we met an Indian loaded with cow's meat. Seeing that we were without provisions, he threw his load on the ground, begging that we would accept it; " For," he said, " you are going toward the fort, where game is very scarce." We reached Fort Pierre[13] on the 17th of October.

These are the names of the principal chiefs whom we met on our route: Iron Crow, Good Bear, Dog Hand, Black Eyes, Won't Eat Cow and Goes Barefoot. The last named is the chief of the Blackfeet. The principal

[12] It was Father De Smet's lifelong ambition to establish a mission among the Sioux. This ambition he never realized, although his influence over those tribes, the foundation of which was laid on the present journey, never lapsed, but on the contrary came to be the greatest ever wielded by any white man.

[13] Fort Pierre, next to Fort Union, the most important of the American Fur Company posts on the Missouri river, was built for the trade of the great tribe of the Sioux. It was located at an important bend in the stream where it turns east from its long southerly course after leaving Fort Clark. It was conveniently located for the trade of the whole Dakota country as far west as the Black Hills. Many posts have been built in its vicinity, where the Teton river empties into the Missouri. Fort Tecumseh, the predecessor of Pierre, was built in 1822 by the Columbia Fur Company, and passed to the American Fur Company when the latter bought out the Columbia Fur Company in 1827. Owing to the encroachments of the river which threatened the destruction of the fort, it was rebuilt in 1831, and christened Fort Pierre about June 1, 1832, in honor of Pierre Chouteau, the head of the company.

rivers we crossed on this stretch are the Heart, Cannon-
ball, Grand, Moreau and Big Cheyenne rivers. [La rivière
du Cœur, la rivière au Boulet, la rivière Grande, le Moreau
et la grande Cheyenne.]

After spending several days at Fort Pierre, I set out
again for Fort Vermillion, in company with two Canadians. The plains that we crossed were almost entirely
bare of timber; often we were obliged to cook our meals
with dry grass, which we had to keep in a constant flame.
We met very few Indians in this journey of nineteen days;
the plain was burnt up. We crossed the Medicine, Chapelle, James and Vermillion rivers. [La rivière de Méde-
cine, la rivière de la Chapelle, la rivière à Jacques et le
Vermillon.]

The Sioux nation is very numerous and warlike and is
divided into several tribes. According to the best information I could obtain, the Santees and Yanktons number
3,000; the Yanktonnais, 4,300; the Blackfeet, 1,500; the
Hunkpapas, 2,000; the Brûlés, 2,500; the Sans arcs, 1,000;
the Minneconjous, 2,000; the Ogallalas, 1,500; the Two-
kettles, 800; the Saones, 2,000; the Unkepatines, 2,000.[14]
These are the Sioux of the Missouri. Eight to ten thousand more of them are found on the Mississippi, dispersed
in different bands, from the Des Moines to the Red river.

The shape of the Indian lodges is worthy of attention;
each tribe has a different form which it is easy to recognize. The Sioux lodges have a gay exterior; they are
painted in wavy red, yellow and white lines, or decorated
with figures of horses, deer and buffalo, moons, suns and
stars.

Among the Sioux, as among the Aricaras, warriors preparing for an expedition undergo a very rigorous fast of

---

[14] The Unkepatines and Saones cannot be identified. The latter
name was in common use during the period of the fur trade, but seems
to have lapsed entirely. There was a Teton-Saone band, and a Sawon
(Saone) trading post.

several days. They have for this purpose a "medicine" lodge where they spread a buffalo robe and plant a red-painted post; at the top of the lodge is tied a calf-skin containing all sorts of devices. There, to obtain the aid of the Great Spirit, they pierce their breasts, pass leather cords through, attach themselves to the post, and dance thus several times around the lodge to the sound of the drum, singing their warlike exploits and flourishing their warclubs over their heads. Others make deep cuts under their shoulder-blades, run cords through the gashes, and drag two great buffalo heads to an eminence about a mile away from the village; there they dance until they drop senseless. A last offering before setting out consists in cutting off little pieces of flesh from different parts of their bodies, which they offer to the sun, the earth and the four cardinal points, to render the Manitous, or tutelary spirits, of the different elements favorable.

The Sioux who quarrels or dies in a state of drunkenness, or falls victim to the vengeance of a compatriot, does not receive the usual honors of burial; he is interred without ceremony and without provisions. To die in combat with the enemies of the nation is for them the most glorious death. In that case their bodies are wrapped in buffalo skins and placed upon scaffolds near to their camps or to the highways. I have every reason to believe, from several conversations upon religion that I have had with the chiefs of the different tribes, that a mission among them would have the most consoling results.

When I reached Fort Vermillion, a Santee war-party was just back from an excursion against my dear Potawatomies; they brought one scalp with them. The murderers had blackened themselves from head to foot with the exception of their lips, which were rubbed with vermilion. Proud of their victory, they performed their dance in the midst of the camp, carrying the scalp on the end of a long pole. I appeared all at once in their presence and invited them to meet in council. There I reproached them vigorously with their unfaithfulness to the solemn promise they had made me the year before, to live in peace with their neighbors the Potawatomies. I made them feel the injustice they were guilty of in attacking a peaceable nation that wished them nothing but good, and who had even prevented their hereditary foes, the Otoes, Pawnees, Sauks, Foxes and Iowas from coming to invade them. Finally I advised them to employ all means to effect a prompt reconciliation and avoid the terrible reprisal which could not fail to come upon them; being well assured that the Potawatomies and their allies would come soon to take vengeance for their perjury, and perhaps to wipe out their whole tribe. Abashed at their fault and dreading its consequences, they conjured me to serve once more as their mediator, and to assure the Potawatomies of their sincere resolution to bury the hatchet forever.

The next day, the 14th of November, accompanied by an Iroquois half-breed, I embarked upon the Missouri in a canoe; for my horse, worn out with fatigue, was unable to carry me farther. The snow and the cold that followed filled the stream with ice-cakes, which, striking upon the snags of which the river is full, rendered navigation doubly dangerous. We were still 300 miles from Council Bluffs, the first establishment one comes to below the Vermillion, and in a region where all the prairie grasses and plants of the forest had been burned by the Indians to the very banks of the river, and from which in consequence all the animals had withdrawn. We did, however, kill a fine deer, which seemed embarrassed and stood motionless upon the bank of the river as if to receive the mortal blow. Five times we were on the point of perishing by being overturned among the numerous snags, upon which the ice-floes dragged us despite all our efforts. We passed ten days in this dangerous and disquieting navigation, sleeping on sand-bars at night and taking only two meals, even-

ing and morning; besides, we had nothing in the way of
food but frozen potatoes and a little fresh meat. The very
night of our arrival among our Fathers at Council Bluffs,
the river closed. It would be in vain for me to attempt
to tell what I felt at finding myself once more amidst our
brothers, after having traveled 2,000 Flemish leagues, in
the midst of the greatest dangers and across the territories
of the most barbarous nations. I had, however, the grief
of observing the ravages which unprincipled men, liquor-
sellers, had caused in this budding mission; drunkenness,
with the invasions of the Sioux on the other hand, had
finally dispersed my poor savages. While awaiting a more
favorable turn of events, the good Fathers Verreydt and
[Christian] Hoeken[15] busy themselves with the cares of
their holy ministry among some fifty families that have
had the courage to resist these two enemies. I discharged
my commission to them from the Sioux, and I venture to
hope that in future they will be quiet in that quarter.

I left Council Bluffs on the 14th of December for Westport, a frontier town of Missouri. I met neither obstacle
nor accident in the country of the Otoes, Iowas, Sauks,
Kickapoos, Delawares and Shawanos, which I traversed.
On the night of the 22d I found myself at Father Point's
at Westport. On the day following I took the stage in
the town of Independence, and on New Year's eve I arrived among my dear brothers at the University of St.
Louis.

I am now preparing to return to that untended vineyard
of the Lord. I shall start early in the spring, accompanied
by two fathers and three brothers of our community. You
know that such an undertaking cannot be carried out with-

---

[15] The name of this missionary and his brother Adrien, constantly
recurring throughout this work, was sometimes spelled " Hoeken " by
Father De Smet and his associates, and sometimes " Hoecken." The
present editors have preferred to adopt the briefer form, though aware
that Father Adrien Hoeken, at least, used the longer in his signature.

out proportionate means, and it is a fact that I have nothing assured; all my hope is in Providence and in my friends' zeal; I hope that they will not fail me. I know that you take much interest in this deserving work; this is why I take the liberty of recommending it to your generosity and to that of your friends; the smallest contribution will be a material help.

I commend myself, as well as my dear neophytes, to your fervent and holy sacrifices, and am, etc.

CHAPTER IV.

A SECOND ACCOUNT OF THE JOURNEY OF 1840.[1]

The start from Westport again — Andrew Drips — The Cheyennes willing to receive missionaries — The polyglot mass at the rendezvous — How the Flatheads and Pend d'Oreilles welcomed him — They learn their prayers and many receive baptism — The return journey eastward — The Crows — Michael Insula — Across the desert and down the river.

Reverend and Dear Sir:

I PRESUME you are aware that in the beginning of last spring I was sent by the Right Reverend Bishop of St. Louis, and my Provincial, on an exploring expedition to the Rocky Mountains, in order to ascertain the dispositions of the Indians and the prospects of success we might have if we were to establish a mission among them. It is truly gratifying to me to have so favorable a report to make. My occupations do not allow me to enter into all the details; I shall therefore be satisfied at present with giving you a brief sketch of my journey and its result.

I started from Westport on the 30th of April, in company with the annual expedition of the American Fur Company, which for this year had appointed the rendezvous on Green river, a tributary of the Rio Colorado of the West. Captain Drips, who commanded the caravan, treated me on all occasions with the most polite attention. On the sixth day of our journey I was seized with the fever and ague, and have been subject to it for nearly five months. Nothing particularly worth noticing occurred during the journey, except when we halted in the village of the Cheyennes. I was introduced to the chiefs as a minister of the Great Spirit: they showed me great deference, and I was invited

[1] To the Reverend F. J. Barbelin. Dated St. Louis University, February 4, 1841. Published as Letter I of the *Letters and Sketches.*

to a feast. I had to pass at first through all the ceremonies of the calumet; the great chief approached me to shake hands, and gave me a heartfelt " How do you do." " Black-gown," said he, " my heart was filled with joy when I learned who you were. My lodge never received a visitor for whom I feel a greater esteem. As soon as I was apprised of your coming, I ordered my great kettle to be filled, and in your honor I commanded that my three fattest dogs should be served up." The bravest warriors of the nation partook of the repast, and I availed myself of the opportunity to explain to them the most important tenets of Christianity. I told them the object of my visit, and enquired whether they would not be satisfied to have also Black-gowns among them, who would·teach them to love and serve the Great Spirit, as he wished. " Oh yes," they eagerly answered, " we will gladly provide for everything that they stand in need of; they will not die of hunger amongst us." I have no doubt but a zealous missionary would do a great deal of good among them.[2] They are about 2,000 in number. Their language, it is said, is very difficult.

On the 30th of June we arrived at the rendezvous. An escort of warriors had been provided for me by the Flat-heads. Our meeting was that of children who came to meet their parent, and in the effusion of their heart, they bestowed upon me the fondest names with a simplicity truly patriarchal. They told me of all the interesting particulars of their nation, and of the wonderful preservation of sixty of their men, in a battle against 200 Blackfeet, which lasted five whole days, and in which they killed fifty of their enemies, without losing a single man of their number. " The Great Spirit watched over them;" they said, " he knew that

[2] No formal movement for the conversion of the Cheyennes was, however, made by Catholic priests until 1882. Father De Smet baptized 253 children of the Cheyennes at the Grand Council of 1851. " There are in their midst those still living who remember the great Black Robe and take a pardonable pride in the fact that they were baptized by him."— *Palladino.*

we were to guide you to our camp, and he wanted to clear
the road of all the obstacles that you might have found on
your way. We trust we will not be annoyed any more by
the Blackfeet; they went off weeping like women." We
thanked heaven for the signal preservation, and implored
its assistance for the new and perilous journey we were on
the point of undertaking. The Indians of different nations
and the trappers had assembled at the rendezvous in great
numbers, for the sake of the trade. On Sunday, the 5th
of July, I had the consolation of celebrating the holy sacrifice of mass *sub dio*. The altar was placed on an elevation,
and surrounded with boughs and garlands of flowers; I
addressed the congregation in French and in English, and
spoke also by an interpreter to the Flatheads and Snake Indians. It was a spectacle truly moving for the heart of a
missionary, to behold an assembly composed of so many
different nations, who all assisted at our holy mysteries with
great satisfaction. The Canadians sang hymns in French
and Latin, and the Indians in their native tongue. It was
truly a Catholic worship. * * * This place has been
called since that time, by the French Canadians, *la prairie de
la Messe*.

About thirty of the principal chiefs of the Snake Indians
invited me to a council. I explained to them the Christian
doctrine in a compendious manner — they were all very attentive — they then deliberated among themselves for about
half an hour, and one of the chiefs, addressing me in the
name of the others, said: " Black-gown, the words of thy
mouth have found their way to our hearts; they never will
be forgotten. Our country is open for thee; come to teach
us what we have to do, to please the Great Spirit, and we
will do according to thy words." I advised them to select
among themselves a wise and prudent man, who, every
morning and evening, should assemble them to offer to Almighty God their prayers and supplications; that there the
good chiefs should have an opportunity of exhorting their
warriors to behave as they ought. The meeting was held

the very same evening, and the great chief promulgated a law, that for the future, the one who would be guilty of theft, or of any other disorderly act, should receive a public castigation. On Monday, the 6th, we proceeded on our journey. A dozen Canadians wished to accompany me, to have an opportunity, as they said, to practice their religion. Eight days afterward we arrived safely in the camp of the Flatheads and Ponderas, or Pend d'Oreilles.

Immediately the whole village was in commotion; men, women and children, all came to meet me and shake hands, and I was conducted in triumph to the lodge of the great chief Tjolizhitzay (Big Face). He has the appearance of an old patriarch. Surrounded by the principal chiefs of the two tribes, and the most renowned warriors, he thus addressed me: " This day Kaikolinzoeten (the Great Spirit) has accomplished our wishes, and our hearts are swelled with joy. Our desire to be instructed was so great, that three times had we deputed our people to the Great Black-gown (the bishop) in St. Louis, to obtain a father. Now, Father, speak, and we will comply with all you will tell us. Show us the road we have to follow, to come to the place where the Great Spirit resides." Then he resigned his authority to me; but I replied that he mistook the object of my coming among them; that I had no other object in view but their spiritual welfare; that with respect to temporal affairs, they should remain as they were, till circumstances should allow them to settle in a permanent spot. Afterward we deliberated on the hours proper for their spiritual exercises and instructions. One of the chiefs brought me a bell, with which I might give the signal.

The same evening about 2,000 persons were assembled before my lodge to recite night prayers in common. I told them the result of my conference with the chiefs; of the plan of instructions which I intended to pursue; and with what disposition they ought to assist at them, etc. Night prayers having been said, a solemn canticle of praise, of their own composition, was sung by these children of the mountains to the Author of their being. It would be impossible for me to describe the emotions I felt at this moment; I wept for joy, and admired the marvelous ways of that kind Providence, who, in his infinite mercy, had deigned to depute me to this poor people, to announce to them the glad tidings of salvation. The next day I assembled the council, and with the assistance of an intelligent interpreter [Gabriel Prudhomme], I translated into their language the Lord's Prayer, the Hail Mary, the Apostles' Creed, the Ten Commandments, and four Acts. As I was in the habit of reciting these prayers morning and evening, and before instructions, about a fortnight after I promised a beautiful silver medal to the one who would recite them first. One of the chiefs rising immediately, " Father," said he, smiling, " that medal is mine," and he recited all the prayers without missing a word. I embraced him, praised the eagerness which he had evinced of being instructed, and appointed him my catechist. This good Indian set to work with so much zeal and perseverance, that in less than a fortnight all knew their prayers.

Every morning, at the break of day, the old chief is the first on horseback, and goes round the camp from lodge to lodge. " Now, my children," he exclaims, " it is time to rise; let the first thoughts of your hearts be for the Great Spirit; say that you love him, and beg of him to be merciful unto you. Make haste, our Father will soon ring the bell, open your ears to listen, and your hearts to receive the words of his mouth." Then, if he has perceived any disorderly act on the preceding day, or if he has received unfavorable reports from the other chiefs, he gives them a fatherly admonition. Who would not think that this could only be found in a well-ordered and religious community, and yet it is among Indians in the defiles and valleys of the Rocky Mountains!!! You have no idea of the eagerness they showed to receive religious instruction. I explained the Christian doctrine four times a day, and nevertheless my lodge was filled, the whole day, with people eager to hear more. At night I related those histories of the holy scriptures that were best calculated to promote their piety and edification, and as I happened to observe that I was afraid of tiring them, " Oh, no," they replied, " if we were not afraid of tiring you, we would gladly spend here the whole night."

I conferred the holy sacrament of baptism on 600 of them, and if I thought it prudent to postpone the baptism of others till my return, it was not for want of desire on their part, but chiefly to impress upon their minds a greater idea of the holiness of the sacrament, and of the dispositions that are required to receive it worthily. Among those baptized were the two great chiefs of the Flatheads and of the Ponderas. As I excited the catechumens to a heartfelt contrition of their sins, Walking Bear, chief of the Ponderas, answered: " Father, I have been plunged for a number of years in profound ignorance of good and evil, and no doubt, during that time, I have often greatly displeased the Great Spirit, and therefore I must humbly beseech his pardon. But when I afterward conceived that a thing was bad, I banished it from my heart, and I do not recollect to have since deliberately offended the Great Spirit." Truly, where such dispositions are found, we may well conclude that a rich harvest is to be gathered.

I remained two months among these good people, and every day they were adding to my consolations, by their fervor in prayer, by their assiduity in coming to my instructions, and by their docility in putting into practice what they had been taught.

The season being far advanced, and as I had waited in vain for a safe opportunity to return to St. Louis, I resolved to commit myself entirely to Providence, and on the 27th of August I took leave of my dear neophytes. I appointed one of the chiefs to replace me during my absence, who should preside in their evening and morning devotions, and on the Sabbath exhort them to virtue, baptize the little children, and those who were dangerously ill. Grief was depicted on the features of all, and tears were glistening in every eye. The old chief addressed me, saying, " Father, the Great Spirit accompany thee in thy long and dangerous voyage; every day, morning and evening, we will address to him our humble supplications, that thou mayest arrive safely among thy brethren. And we will continue to do so, till thou be again among thy children of the mountains. We are now like the trees that have been spoiled of their verdure by winter's blast. When the snow will have disappeared from these valleys, and the grass begins to grow, our hearts will begin to rejoice; when the plants spring forth our joy will increase; when they blossom, it will still be greater, and then we will set out to meet you. Farewell, Father, farewell."

The chiefs would not suffer me to depart by myself — thirty of the bravest warriors were deputed as a safeguard to traverse the country of the Blackfeet, who are very hostile to the whites, and they were instructed to accompany me as far as need would be of their assistance. I resolved to take on my return a different route from the one I had taken in coming. I was induced to do so, in order to visit the forts of the American Fur Company on the Missouri and on the Yellowstone, to baptize the children. After five or six days traveling, we fell in with a war-party of the Crow Indians, who received us very kindly, and we traveled together for two days. Then we directed our course to the Big Horn, the most considerable of the tributary streams of the Yellowstone. There we met another party of the same nation, who were also amicably disposed toward us. As there was question about religion, I availed myself of the opportunity to express to them the main articles of the Christian faith, and as I was depicting in lively colors the torments of hell, and had told them that the Great Spirit had kindled this fire of his wrath for those who did not keep the commandments I had explained to them, one of the chiefs uttered a horrid shriek. " If this be the case," said he, " then I believe there are but two in the whole nation who will not go to that place; it is the Beaver and the Mink; they are the only Crows who never stole, who never killed, nor committed all the excesses which your law prohibits. Perhaps I am deceived, and then we must all go together." When I left them on the next day, the chief put a fine bell on my horse's neck, and invited me to take a turn round the village. Next, he accompanied me for six miles.

After several days of a painful journey over rocks and cliffs, we arrived at last at the Fort of the Crows. It is the first the American Fur Company possessed in that country. My dear Flatheads edified all the inhabitants by their fervor and their piety. As well in the fort as on the road, we never missed performing in common our evening and morning devotions, and singing canticles in honor of the Almighty. Frequently, during my stay with them, they had given me abundant proofs of their trust in Providence. I cannot forbear mentioning one instance that occurred during my travels in this place. One day as dinner was preparing and provisions scarce, a countryman of mine, who accompanied me, suggested the propriety of keeping something in reserve for supper. " Be not uneasy," said the chief called Ensyla,[3] " I never missed my supper in my life. I trust in the mercy of the Great Spirit, he will provide for all our wants." We had just camped at night, when the chief

[3] " Michael" Ensyla or Insula, called also Little Chief and Red Feather; conspicuous throughout Father De Smet's relations with the Flatheads. He had gone in 1835 to Green river to meet Parker and Whitman, and according to Palladino, " discovering in those gentlemen none of the signs of the Black-robe, would not consent to have them come among his people." Parker's journal contains the following mention of him: " Next arose Insala, the most influential chief among the Flathead nation, and said, ' he had heard, a man near to God (meaning a minister of the gospel) was coming to visit them, and he, with some of his people, together with some white men, went out three days' journey to meet him, but missed us. A war-party of Crow Indians came upon them, and took away some of their horses, and one from him which he greatly loved, but now he forgets all, his heart is made so glad to see a man near to God.' There was a short battle, but no lives were lost."

killed two stags. " Did I not tell you right? " he remarked, smilingly, to my companion. " You see the Great Spirit does not only provide for our wants of this evening, but he gives us also a supply for to-morrow."

Now began the most difficult and most perilous part of our journey. I had to pass through a country supposed to be overrun by war-parties, of the Blackfeet, Assiniboins, Grosventres, Aricaras and Sioux. All these nations entertained the most hostile dispositions toward the Flatheads. I therefore dispensed with their services any farther. I again excited them to continue the good work they had begun; to be steadfast in their faith; regular in their devotions; charitable toward one another. I embraced them all and took my leave. Mr. John de Velder, a native of Ghent in Belgium, had volunteered his services to me at the rendez-vous. In consideration of the bad state of my health, I deemed myself very happy to accept of them; he has never left me since. He was now to be my only traveling companion. As there is no road, we followed the direction of the river; at intervals we were obliged to make immense circuits to avoid the steep and craggy hills that defied our passage. For 200 miles, we had continually death before our eyes. On the second day, I discovered before daylight a large smoke at a distance of about a quarter of a mile. We hastily saddled our horses and following up a ravine we gained a high bluff unperceived. At night we did not dare to make fire for fear of attracting notice. Again about dinner time, we found on the road the carcase of a buffalo, killed only two hours before; the tongue and the marrow-bones with some other dainty pieces had been taken away. Thus the kind Providence of our God took care to supply our wants.

We took a direction contrary to the tracks of the Indians, and spent a safe night in the cliffs of the rocks. The next day we struck upon a spot where forty lodges had been encamped, the fires were yet in full blaze.

Finally, we crossed the Missouri at the same place where,

only an hour before, a hundred lodges of ill-minded Assiniboins had passed, and we arrived safe and unmolested at Fort Union, situated a few miles above the mouth of the Yellowstone. In all these forts great harmony and union prevail; Mr. Kipps, [James Kipp] the present administrator of them, is a gentleman well worthy of his station. Everywhere I was treated by these gentlemen with the greatest politeness and kindness, and all my wants were liberally supplied. As I was relating the particulars of this dangerous trip to an Indian chief, he answered: " The Great Spirit has his Manitous; he has sent them to take care of your steps and to trouble the enemies that would have been a nuisance to you." A Christian would have said: *Angelis suis mandavit de te, ut custodiant te in omnibus viis tuis.*

On the 23d of September we set out for the village of the Mandans, in company with three men of the fort, who had the same destination. We met on the road a party of nineteen Assiniboins, who were returning to their country from an unsuccessful expedition against the Grosventres. Their looks indicated their bad intentions: although we were but five in number, we showed a determined countenance, and we passed unmolested. Next day we crossed a forest, the winter quarters of the Grosventres and Aricaras in 1835. It was there that those unfortunate tribes were nearly exterminated by the smallpox. We saw their bodies wrapped up in buffalo robes, tied to the branches of the largest trees. It was truly a sad and mournful spectacle. Two days later we met the miserable survivors of these unhappy tribes. Only ten families of the Mandans, once such a powerful nation, now remain. They have united with the Grosventres and Aricaras. They received me with great demonstrations of friendship; I spent that night in their camp, and the next day crossed the Missouri in their canoe, made of a buffalo skin. The next day we came to the first village of the Aricaras, and on the following day to their great village, consisting of about a hundred earthen wigwams. This tribe also received me very kindly. On the 6th of October we started from the Mandan village, for Fort Pierre, on the little Missouri; a Canadian, whose destination lay in the same direction, accompanied us,[4] * * * In due time we arrived at Fort Pierre. Thence I traveled through prairies for nineteen days successively. We were often obliged to cook our victuals with dried herbs — not a stick was to be found. When I arrived at Fort Vermillion, * * * I had lost two horses on the road; the one I was riding could hardly support me any longer, and I was yet 300 miles distant from the Council Bluffs. I resolved of course to embark on the Missouri, and engaged a native Iroquois to be my pilot. At first we were favored with fine weather, but this lasted only a few days. Very soon inclement weather set in, with frost and snow; and several times as we drifted down the rapid stream, our frail canoe was on the point of being dashed to pieces against the numberless snags that obstruct its navigation. This dangerous trip lasted ten days. We generally spent the night on a sand-bar. We had only a few frozen potatoes left when we perceived a beautiful deer gazing at us, and apparently waiting to receive its mortal blow. We shot at it. At last we arrived safe at the bluffs, and on the same night the river was closed by ice.

So many escapes from the midst of so many dangers thoroughly convinced me that this undertaking is the work of God — *omnia disponens fortiter et ad finem suam conducens suaviter*. I am now preparing for my return, and will start early in spring, accompanied by three fathers and as many brothers. You are aware such expeditions cannot be undertaken without the necessary means, and the fact is, I have no other reliance than Providence and the kindness of my friends. I hope they will not be wanting. I know that you must feel deeply interested in this meritorious good work, I therefore take the liberty of recommending it to your generosity, and that of your friends — every little con-

---

[4] The portions omitted here are nearly identical with corresponding passages in the previous letter.

tribution will help. I will be very grateful to you, if you have the kindness to forward to my address at the St. Louis University, Mo., before the end of March, or middle of April, the amount you have collected.

I recommend myself and my dear neophytes to your good prayers and holy sacrifices, and rest assured that we shall not forget our benefactors.

CHAPTER V.

How Father De Smet raised the money to keep his promises to the Flatheads — Delays at Westport — The mixed company that started — The missionary party — A visit to the Kansas Indians in their village — Father Point's whiskers — White Plume — Catholic and Protestant — The Pawnees.

To the Editor the *Catholic Herald,*
Steamboat *Oceana,* Mo. River,
May 1, 1841.

Reverend and Dear Sir:

¶ CANNOT set out for my distant mission, without expressing through the medium of your excellent paper, my grateful thanks to the friends who have come forward with such noble and disinterested generosity, and offered the means of carrying the gospel of peace and salvation to the uninstructed savage of the mountains. You, Reverend Sir, who are engaged in the same sublime vocation, the salvation of souls, may form an idea from my former letter of my ardent desire to labor among the poor forsaken children of the Oregon; among whom I resided three months and who hailed my arrival with so much joy; listened with so much eagerness and docility to my instructions, and exhibited in their whole conduct the wonderful fruits which the word of God produced in a few weeks in hearts well disposed.

[1] This chapter consists of Letter III, *Letters and Sketches,* and Letter I, Second Voyage, *Voyages aux Montagnes Rocheuses,* dated as above in both and addressed respectively to the Father Provincial and to Father De Smet's brothers Charles and Francis. The published letters also contain a brief account of a case of human sacrifice among the Pawnees, which is omitted here because described more fully elsewhere in this work. The English text is followed in the main.

I had visited them only for the purpose of ascertaining the prospect of forming a permanent establishment for their entire conversion. I was, of course, obliged to return, in order to report the result of my observations to my superior. When about to leave, my good neophytes crowded around me, as children around a beloved parent; their tears and sobs told how truly they grieved for our separation. The only consolation that I could offer then was the assurance that I would return in the spring. This was my promise; this, their hope. "Father," said they in their simple and beautiful language, "Father, when the snow shall have disappeared from these hills, we shall think of your return; when the plants begin to spring forth, we shall set out to meet you. Farewell!"

We parted. I repassed the mountains, traversed the prairies and forests under the guidance of the good angels who had charge to watch over me. On my arrival at St. Louis, I gave an account to my superior of my journey and of the flattering prospects which the mission beyond the Rocky Mountains held out. You will easily believe me when I tell you that my heart sank within me on learning from him that the funds at his disposal for missionary purposes would not enable him to afford me scarcely the half of what would be necessary for the outfit and other expenses of an expedition. The thought that the undertaking would have been given up, that I would not be able to redeem my promise to the poor Indians, pierced my very heart and filled me with the deepest sorrow. I would have desponded had I not already experienced the visible protection of the Almighty in the prosecution of this great work. My confidence in him was unabated. Whilst in this state of mind one of my friends encouraged me to appeal to the zealous and learned coadjutor of Philadelphia and to his indefatigable clergy. I immediately acted upon the thought. I did appeal and with what success the Catholic public already know. To the Bishop who gave his sanction to the plan of a general and simultaneous collection throughout his

18

diocese; to the clergy of the different churches of the city who so kindly interested themselves in this good work and proposed it to their congregations; to the generous people of Philadelphia who so liberally responded to the call of their pastors, I return my sincere thanks and will daily beg the father of mercies to reward them with his choicest blessings.

I must not omit to mention of other generous contributors. After having written to Philadelphia I was advised to visit New Orleans and recommend the cause of the Indians to the good Bishop of that city and to his clergy and people. I did so. The Bishop received me with great kindness; gave his approbation to a collection, and placed his name first on the list. His clergy followed his example. As I had only a few days at my disposal, I thought it was best to solicit subscriptions through several generous ladies who offered themselves for this purpose. In the space of three or four days, they collected nearly $1,000. You have no idea with what spirit the pious portion of the people entered into the affair. Almost every moment of my stay persons came to offer me something for the Indian mission. Several ladies gave me various trinkets, such as ear-rings, bracelets, and ornaments of every description; others brought implements and articles, which will be of great use in the Indian country. In a word, Reverend Sir, I left New Orleans with $1,100 in cash and six boxes full of various and most useful articles. From the Reverend Mr. Durbin of Kentucky I received $300, and the Reverend Jno. O'Reilly remitted $140, the amount collected in St. Paul's Church, Pittsburg. St. Louis supplied the balance of what was necessary for the outfit, the expenses of the journey and the commencement of the establishment in the Indian country. To the Bishops and to the zealous clergy and laity of Philadelphia and New Orleans; to the clergy and laity of other places who aided the good cause; in a word, to all the benefactors of the mission beyond the Rocky Mountains, I again return my sincere thanks. Myself and my fellow-laborers will teach our neophytes to pray for those who have been instrumental in procuring them so much good. In conclusion, Reverend Sir, I would solicit your fervent prayers and those of all good Christians, who may read this account. Our journey is perilous in the extreme. We must pass through the countries of hostile tribes — tribes that thirst for the blood of the white man. I hope, therefore, that reverend brethren will not forget us at the holy altar; and that the pious Christians who are interested in our mission will sometimes offer up for us a Pater and Ave. The expedition will leave Westport about the 12th of May.

Your obedient servant, etc.

Reverend and Very Dear Father Provincial:

Behold us at last on our way toward the long-wished for Rocky Mountains, already inured to the fatigues of the journey and full of the brightest hopes. It is now afternoon and we are sitting on the banks of a river which, it is said, has not its equal in the world. The Indians call it Nebraska or Big Horn; the Canadians give it the name of la Platte;[2] and Irving designates it, as the most magnificent and useless of rivers. The sequel will show that it deserves these various affixes. It was to enjoy the freshness and beauty of its scenery that we traveled more than twenty miles this morning, without breaking our fast, through a wilderness without a single rivulet to water our jaded horses, who must therefore rest where they are till to-mor-

[2] The name Platte is characteristic and arises from the extremely shallow character of the stream. Its use dates from 1739. In that year two brothers, Mallet, with six companions, undertook to reach Santa Fe from a point on the Missouri somewhere near the present site of Sioux City. They left the river on the 29th of May and arrived at the Platte June 2. (*Le 2 Juin ils tombèrent sur une rivière qu' ils nommèrent la Rivière Platte."* De Margry.) The party ascended the main stream and the South Fork to the mountains and reached Santa Fe on the 22d of July.

row. I am far from regretting the delay, as it will give me an opportunity of commencing a letter which, I know, will interest you.

Like all the works of God, our humble beginnings have not been unattended with trials : our journey had even well nigh been indefinitely deferred by the postponement of two caravans on which we had confidently relied; one of hunters, for the American Fur Company; the other an exploring expedition belonging to the United States, at the head of which we expected to see the celebrated M. Nicollet. Happily God inspired two estimable travelers, [named Romaine and Baker] of whom more hereafter, and afterward some sixty others,[3] to take the same route as ourselves, some for health, others for science or pleasure; but the greater number to seek their fortune in the too highly boasted land of California. This caravan formed an extraordinary mixture of different nations, every country of Europe having in it a representative, my own little band of eleven persons hailing from eight.

The difficulties of setting out once overcome, many others followed in succession. We had need of provisions, fire-arms, implements of every kind, wagons, guides, a good hunter, an experienced captain,— in a word, whatever becomes necessary when one has to traverse a desert of 800 leagues, and expects nothing but formidable obstacles to surmount, and thieving, and sometimes murderous, enemies to combat,— and swamps, ravines and rivers to cross, and mountains to climb, whose craggy and precipitous sides suddenly arrest our progress, compelling us to drag our beasts of burden up their steep ascents. These

[3] The remains of the "Western Emigration Society," organized in Weston, Missouri, the preceding winter, with 500 members, all but one of whom (John Bidwell) withdrew before the time set for starting — discouraged, it is said, by Thomas J. Farnham's published account of California. The party as made up was composed of emigrants from Missouri, an invalid named George Henshaw from Illinois, three families from Arkansas, and others. It was commanded by John Bartleson, and guided by Thomas Fitzpatrick.

things are not done without toil and money, but thanks
to the generous charity of our friends in Philadelphia, Cin-
cinnati, Kentucky, St. Louis and New Orleans, which
place I visited in person and which is always at the head
of the others when there is a question of relieving the
necessities of the poor, or showing compassion and munifi-
cence to any who may be in need of assistance, we were
enabled by the resources thence supplied, and by a portion
of the funds allowed by the Lyons Association in behalf of
the Indian Missions, to undertake this long journey.

You have already learned from my letters of the past
year, that I was specially sent among the Flatheads to
ascertain their dispositions toward the Black-gowns,
whom they had so long desired. I therefore started from
St. Louis in April, 1840, and arrived on the banks of the
Colorado precisely at the moment when a band of Flatheads reached that point on their way to meet me. It was
the rendezvous I had given them. Besides the Flatheads,
I visited during that journey many other tribes, such as
the Pend d'Oreilles (Ear Rings) or Kalispels, Nez Percés
(Pierced Noses) or Sapetans, Cheyennes, Snakes or Shoshones, Crows or Absarokas, Grosventres or Minnetarees,
Aricaras, Mandans, Kansas, the numerous nations of the
Sioux or Dakotas, the Omahas, Otoes, Iowas, etc. Finding everywhere such good dispositions, I resolved, notwithstanding the approach of winter and frequent attacks
of fever, in order to second the visible designs of the divine
mercy in favor of so many souls, to commence my journey
across the immense ocean of mountains and prairies. I
have traveled without any other guide than a compass,
without any protection from nations hostile to the whites,
but a veteran from Ghent, formerly a grenadier of the
Empire, any other provisions, in an arid desert, than what
powder and ball and a strong confidence in God might
procure us.

I shall not here repeat what I have already communicated to you, of my adventures and the result of this mis-

sion. It will suffice to say that the unexpected quickness of my return to St. Louis, the excellent health I enjoyed, even though it was the midst of winter, and the consoling accounts I had to give of my reception by the Flatheads, etc., etc., all contributed to make the most lively impression on the hearts of our brethren. Almost every one thought himself called to share the labors of a mission which offered so many attractions to their zeal. After due deliberation, the fellow-laborers allotted me were five in number, namely, two Fathers, Reverend Nicolas Point[4] of La Vendée, as zealous and courageous for the salvation of souls as his compatriot, La Roche Jacquelin, was in the service of his lawful sovereign. Reverend Gregory Mengarini,[5] recently from Rome, specially selected by the Father General himself for this mission, on account of his age, his virtues, his great facility for languages and his knowledge of medicine and music; and three lay-brothers, two Belgians, William Claessens[6] and Charles Huet, and one German, Joseph Specht,[7] of whom the first is a blacksmith, the second a carpenter, and the third a tinner, or a sort of *factotum;* all three industrious, devoted to the missions and full of good will. They had long ardently desired to be employed on these missions and I thank God

[4] Father Point remained among the Blackfeet until the spring of 1847, when an order from his superiors in France, which had, according to Palladino, been three years on the road, recalled him to the missions of Upper Canada. It was his desire, as appears from letters in Father De Smet's correspondence, in later years to return to the Northwest. He died at Quebec, July 4, 1868. A volume of Indian drawings, apparently his work, is preserved at the University of St. Louis.

[5] Father Mengarini was transferred to California in 1850 and died at Santa Clara September 23, 1866.

[6] Brother Claessens remained among the Indians until 1891, when he was ordered to California. He died at Santa Clara on the 11th of October of that year at the age of eighty.

[7] Brother Specht died at St. Ignatius Mission June 17, 1884, aged seventy-six.

that had the choice been left to myself, I could have made
none better. Thus launched into the midst of this interminable Far West, how often did I repeat these beautiful
lines of Racine:

> O Dieu, par quelles routes inconnues aux mortels
> Ta Sagesse conduit 'tes desseins eternels!

In seven days from my departure from St. Louis, namely
on the 30th of April, I arrived at Westport, a frontier town
on the west of the United States. It took us seven days,
on board a steamboat, to perform this journey of 500
[390] miles, no unfair average of the time required to
travel such a distance on the Missouri at the breaking up
of the winter, when, though the ice is melted, the water
is still so low, the sand-banks so close together and the
snags so numerous that boats cannot make greater head-
way. * * * We landed on the right bank of the river,
and took refuge in an abandoned little cabin, where a poor
Indian woman had died a few days before, and in this retreat, so like to that which once merited the preference of
the Savior and for which was thenceforth to be substi-
tuted only the shelter of a tent in the wilderness, we took
up our abode until the 10th of May — occupied as well
we might be in supplying the wants created by the burning
of our baggage wagon on board the steamboat, the sickness of one of our horses which we were compelled to
leave after us, and the loss of another that escaped from
us at the moment of landing.

We started, then, from Westport, on the 10th of May,
and after having passed by the lands of the Shawnees and
Delawares, where we saw nothing remarkable but the college of the Methodists, built, it is easy to divine for what,
where the soil is richest; we arrived after five days' march
on the banks of the Kansas river, where we found those of
our companions who had traveled by water, with a part
of our baggage. Two of the relatives of the grand chief
had come twenty miles from that place to meet us, one of

whom helped our horses to pass the river in safety, by swimming before them, and the other announced our arrival to the principal men of the tribe who waited for us on the opposite bank. Our baggage, wagons and men crossed in a pirogue, or hollowed tree trunk, which, at a distance, looked like one of those gondolas that glide through the streets of Venice. As soon as the Kansas understood that we were going to encamp on the banks of the Soldier's river, which is only six miles from the village, they galloped rapidly away from our caravan, disappearing in a cloud of dust, so that we had scarcely pitched our tents when the great chief presented himself with six of his bravest warriors, to bid us welcome. After having made me sit down on a mat spread on the ground, he, with much solemnity, took from his pocket a portfolio containing the honorable titles, bestowed by the American Congress, that gave him a right to our friendship, and placed them in my hands. I read them, and having, with the tact of a man accustomed to the etiquette of savage life, furnished him the means of smoking the calumet, he made us accept for our guard the two braves who had come to meet us. Both were armed like warriors, one carrying a lance and a buckler, and the other a bow and arrows, with a naked sword and a collar made of the claws of four bears which he had killed with his own hand. These two braves remained faithful at their post during the three days and three nights that we had to wait the coming up of the stragglers of the caravan. A small present which we made them at our departure secured us their friendship.

On the 19th we continued our journey to the number of seventy souls, fifty of whom were capable of managing the rifle — a force more than sufficient to undertake with prudence the long march we had to make. Whilst the rest of our company inclined to the west, Father Point, a young Englishman [Romaine] and myself turned to the left, to visit the nearest village of our hosts. At the first sight

of their wigwams, we were struck at the resemblance they
bore to the large stacks of wheat which cover our fields
in harvest time.   There were of these in all no more than
about twenty, grouped together without order, but each
covering a space of about 120 feet in circumference, and
sufficient to shelter from thirty to forty persons.   The entire village appeared to us to consist of from seven to eight
hundred souls — an approximation which is justified by
the fact that the total population of the tribe is confined
to two villages, together numbering 1,500 inhabitants.

These cabins, however humble[8] they may appear, are
solidly built and convenient.   From the top of the wall,
which is about six feet in height, rise inclined poles, which
terminate round an opening above, serving at once for
chimney and window.   The door of the edifice consists of
an undressed hide on the most sheltered side, the hearth
occupies the center and is in the midst of four upright
posts destined to support the *rotunda;* the beds are ranged
round the wall and the space between the beds and the
hearth is occupied by the members of the family, some
standing, others sitting or lying on skins, or yellow
colored mats.   It would seem that this last-named article
is regarded as a piece of extra finery, for the lodge assigned
to us had one of them.

It would be impossible to describe all the curiosities we
beheld during the hour we passed among these truly,
strange beings; a Teniers would have envied us.   What
most excited our attention was the strongly characterized
physiognomy of the greater number of these personages,
their vivacity of expression, singular costume, diversity of
amusement and fantastic attitudes and gestures.   The
women alone were occupied, and in order to attend to
their various duties with less distraction, they had placed
those of their papooses who were unable to walk, on beds
or on the floor, or at their feet, each tightly swathed and
fastened to a board, to preserve it from being injured by

8 Fr. humides.

surrounding objects. This machine, which I shall not
call either cradle or chair, is carried, when they travel,
either on the back, after the fashion of the gypsies and
fortune-tellers in Europe, or at their side, or more frequently suspended from the pommel of the saddle, while
they lead or drive their ponies, laden with the rest of their
goods and chattels. With such encumbrances they manage to keep pace with their husbands, who generally keep
their horses at a gallop; and the babies are rarely heard
to cry. But let us return to our wigwam. How were
the men occupied? When we entered, some were preparing to eat, (this is their great occupation when they
are not asleep) others were smoking, discharging the
fumes of the tobacco by their mouths and nostrils, re-
minding one of the funnels of a steamboat; they talked,
they plucked out their beard and the hair of their eye-
brows, they made their toilette; the head receiving particular attention. Contrary to the custom of the other
tribes, who let the hair on their heads grow, (one of the
Crows has hair eleven feet long) the Kansas shave theirs,
with the exception of a well curled tuft on the crown,
destined to be wreathed with the warrior's plume of
eagle's feathers, the proudest ornament with which the
human head can be adorned. While we were smoking
I could not help watching the motions of a young savage, a sort of dandy, who ceased not to arrange, over and
over again, his bunch of feathers before a looking glass,
apparently unable to give it the graceful finish he intended. Father Point, having suffered his beard to grow,
soon became an object of curiosity and laughter, to the
children — a beardless chin, a shaved head and well picked
brows and eye-lashes being, among them, indispensable to
beauty. Next come the Plume and Slit-ears, with their
pendants of beads and other trinkets. This is but a part
of their finery, and the pains thus taken to reach the *beau-
ideal* of personal decorations, are but a faint specimen of

their vanity. Do you wish to have an idea of a Kansa satisfied with himself in the highest degree? Picture him to yourself with rings of vermilion encircling his eyes, with white, black or red streaks running down his face, a fantastic necklace, adorned in the center with a large medal of silver or copper, dangling on his breast; bracelets of tin, copper or brass, on his arms and wrists; a cincture of white around his waist, a cutlass and scabbard, embroidered shoes or moccasins on his feet; and, to crown all, a mantle, it matters not for the color, thrown over the shoulders and falling around the body in such folds or drapery as the wants or caprice of the wearer may direct, and the individual stands before you as he exhibited himself to us.

As for dress, manners, religion, modes of making war, etc., the Kansas are like the savages of their neighborhood, with whom they have preserved peaceful and friendly relations from time immemorial. In stature, they are generally tall and well made. Their physiognomy is manly, their language is guttural, and remarkable for the length and strong accentuation of the final syllables. Their style of singing is monotonous, whence it may be inferred that the enchanting music heard on the rivers of Paraguay never cheers the voyager on the otherwise beautiful streams of the country of the Kansas.

With regard to the qualities which distinguish man from the brute, they are far from being deficient. To bodily strength and courage they unite a shrewdness and address superior to other savages, and in their wars or the chase they make a dexterous use of fire-arms, which gives them a decided advantage over their enemies.

Among the chiefs of this tribe are found men really distinguished in many respects. The most celebrated was White Plume, whom the author of the *Conquest of Granada*[9] represents as a man of great powers of mind and chival-

[9] Irving in *Captain Bonneville*, chapter II.

rous character. He was endowed with uncommon intelligence, frankness, generosity and courage. He had been particularly acquainted with Reverend Mr. De la Croix,[10] one of the first Catholic missionaries that visited that part of the West, and conceived for him and his colleagues, the "Black-robes," profound esteem. His feelings toward the Protestant missionaries were far different. He had neither esteem nor veneration for them or their reformation. When on a certain occasion one of them spoke to him of conversion; "conversion," said the unsophisticated savage, " is a good thing when the change is made for something good. For my part, I know none such but what is taught and practiced by the Black-robes. If then you desire me to change, you must first quit your wife and then put on the habit I shall show you, and then we shall see further." This habit was a priest's cassock, which a missionary had left him with the memory of his virtues. We presume we need not add that these hard conditions were not complied with by the preacher.

It is not to be inferred from the apparent pleasantry of this remark that the chief spoke lightly of religion; on the contrary, the Kansas, like all the Indian tribes, never speak on the subject without becoming solemnity. The more they are observed the more evident does it become that the religious sentiment is deeply implanted in their souls, and is, of all others, that which is most frequently expressed by their words and actions. Thus, for instance, they never take the calumet, without first rendering some homage to the Great Spirit. In the midst of their most infuriate passions they address him certain prayers, and even in assassinating a defenseless child, or a woman, they invoke the Master of life. To be enabled to take many a

[10] Charles De la Croix, born in 1792 in Flanders: came to America in 1817. Besides filling a number of posts for the Society in the west, he made two sojourns among the Osage Indians as missionary. He returned to Ghent in 1839 and died August 20, 1869.

scalp from their enemies, or to rob them of many horses, becomes the object of their most fervid prayers, to which they sometimes add fasts, macerations and sacrifices. What did they not do last spring, to render the heavens propitious? And for what? To obtain the power, in the absence of their warriors, to massacre all the women and children of the Pawnees! And in effect they carried off the scalps of ninety victims, and made prisoners of all whom they did not think proper to kill. In their eyes, revenge, far from being a horrible vice, is the first of virtues, the distinctive mark of great souls, and a complete vindication of the most atrocious cruelty. It would be time lost to attempt to persuade them that there can be neither merit nor glory in the murder of a disarmed and helpless foe. There is but one exception to this barbarous code; it is when an enemy voluntarily seeks a refuge in one of their villages. As long as he remains in it, his asylum is inviolable — his life is more safe than it would be in his own wigwam. But woe to him if he attempt to fly — scarcely has he taken a single step, before he restores to his hosts all the imaginary rights which the spirit of vengeance had given them to his life!

However cruel they may be to their foes, the Kansas are no strangers to the tenderest sentiments of piety, friendship and compassion. They are often inconsolable for the death of their relations, and leave nothing undone to give proof of their sorrow. Then only do they suffer their hair to grow — long hair being a sign of long mourning. The principal chief apologized for the length of his hair, informing us of what we could have divined from the sadness of his countenance, that he had lost his son. I wish I could represent to you the respect, astonishment and compassion expressed on the countenances of three others, when they visited our little chapel at Westport [where Father Point had been stationed] for the first time. When we showed them an " Ecce Homo " and a statue of our Lady of the seven Dolours, and the interpreter explained to them that that head crowned with thorns, and that countenance defiled with insults, were the true and real image of a God who had died for the love of us, and that the heart they saw pierced with seven swords was the heart of his mother, we beheld an affecting illustration of the beautiful thought of Tertullian, that the soul of man is naturally Christian! On such occasions, it is surely not difficult, after a short instruction on true faith and the love of God, to excite feelings of pity for their fellow creatures in the most ferocious bosoms.

What were the Iroquois before their conversions, and what have they not since become? Why do the Kansas and so many other tribes on the confines of civilization still retain that savage ferocity of manners? Why have the great sums expended in their behalf by Protestant philanthropy produced no satisfactory results? Why are the germs of civilization so thickly scattered by their learned societies among these tribes, as it were, stricken with sterility? Ah! it is doubtless because something more than human policy and zeal of Protestantism is necessary to civilize the savage and make them Christians. May the God of Mercies, in whom we alone place all our trust, bless our undertaking and enable us to predict that our sweat, mixed with the fertilizing dew of heaven, will fall auspiciously on this long barren earth, and make it produce something else besides briars and thorns!

When we took leave of our hospitable hosts, two of their warriors, to one of whom they gave the title of Captain, escorted us a short distance on the road, which lay through a vast field which had been cleared and planted for them by the United States, but which had been ravaged before the harvest home — sad proof of what we have stated above. Our escort continued with us until the day following, and would have remained with us still longer, did they not fear the terrible reprisals of the Pawnees for the massacre committed some months previously. Having therefore received our thanks and a portion of tobacco, they resumed the road to their village, just in time to escape the vengeance of a party of Pawnees, whom we met two days later, in quest of the Kansas!

The Pawnees are divided into four tribes,[11] scattered over the fertile borders of the Platte and upon the upper branches of the Kansas rivers. Though six times more numerous than the Kansas, they have almost on every occasion been conquered by the latter, because they are far inferior to them in the use of arms, and in strength and courage. Yet as the party just mentioned seemed to have adopted decisive measures, and as their thirst of revenge had been stimulated to the highest degree by the still fresh recollection of what their mothers, their wives and children had suffered, we had reason to fear for the Kansas. Already we fancied that we saw the blood streaming on all sides, when, two days after we had passed them, we saw them returning. The two first who approached us excited our attention, the one by a human scalp which hung suspended from the neck of his horse, the other by an American flag, which he had wrapped around his body in the form of a cloak. This kind of attire made us tremble for the fate of our hosts; but the captain of the caravan having asked them by signs concerning the result of their expedition, they informed us that they had not even seen the enemy, and that they suffered much from the cravings of hunger. We gave to them, and to about fifteen others who followed them, both victuals and tobacco. They devoured the victuals, but did not smoke; and, contrary to the custom of the Indians, who generally expect to get a second meal after the first, they left us in a manner which indicated that they were dissatisfied. The sudden-

11 The Grand, Republican, Tapage and Wolf or Loup bands; names explained in various ways, like most Indian names that the white man has tried to account for.

ness of their departure, their refusal to smoke the calumet, the unexpected return of their party, the neighborhood of their villages, and their well-known love of plunder — in short, everything induced us to fear that they had some design to make an attempt, if not upon our persons, at least upon the horses and baggage; but, God be praised, not one reappeared after the departure of the party.

*   *   *

CHAPTER VI.[1]

FROM THE PLATTE RIVER TO THE BITTER ROOT VALLEY.[2]

The " Flathead Embassies "— Meeting with the forerunners of the tribe — Their enthusiasm — Frank Ermatinger — Parting from the American emigrants — Friendly though disagreeing — Devil's Gate on the Sweetwater — Halt on Green river — Mountain trails and amateur teamsters — More Snake Indians — Features of Bear river — Over the divide to Fort Hall — Meeting with the Flathead escort — Insula and Big Face — Northward to the Deer Lodge valley — Perils of western travel — River crossings and Indian alarms — Interview with the Bannocks.

Fort Hall, Aug. 16, 1841.

IT was on the eve of the beautiful festival of the Assumption that we met the vanguard of the Flatheads. We met under the happiest auspices, and our joy was proportionate. The joy of the savage is not openly manifested — that of our dear neophytes was tranquil; but from the beaming serenity of their looks, and the feeling manner in which they pressed our hands, it was easy to perceive that, like the joy which has its source in virtue, theirs was heartfelt and profound. What had they not done to obtain a mission of " Black-gowns? " For twenty years they had not ceased to supplicate the Father of Mercies; for twenty years, in compliance with the counsels of some poor Iroquois, who had established themselves in their tribe, they had conformed, as nearly as they could, to our creed and manners, and even

---

1 This chapter consists of Letters V and VI, *Letters and Sketches,* addressed to the Father Provincial and dated respectively Fort Hall, August 16, 1841, and Big Face's Camp (Beaver Head river), September 1, 1841; paralleled by Letters III and IV, Second Voyage, *Voyages aux M.-R.,* dated as above and without address. The English text is followed in the main.

2 For original chapter omitted here, see p. 1345.

19

to our religious practices. In what Catholic parish was tl
Sunday, for example, ever more religiously observed? -
During the ten years just elapsed, four deputations, eac
starting from the banks of the Bitter Root, on which the
usually assemble, had courageously ventured to St. Loui
over a space of 3,000 miles,— over mountains and valley
infested by Blackfeet and other hostile tribes.

Of the first deputation, which started in 1831, three die
of diseases produced by the change of climate. The secon
embassy reached its destination; but owing to the great wai
of missionaries in the Diocese of St. Louis, received nothin
but promises. The third, which set out in 1837, consiste
of five members, all of whom were unmercifully massacre
by the Sioux. All these crosses, however, were insufficier
to abate their zeal. In 1839, they sent two Iroquois depu
ties, one of whom was named Peter, and the other Youn
Ignatius, to distinguish him from another called Old Igna
tius. These they earnestly advised to make still more press
ing entreaties to obtain the long-sought blessing, a " Black
gown, to conduct them to heaven." Their prayers were, a
length, heard, even beyond their hopes. One Black-gow
was granted, together with a promise of more, if necessar
for their greater good. While Peter returned in haste to th
tribe to acquaint them with the complete success of thei
mission, Ignatius remained at Westport, to accompany th
promised missionary. I had the happiness to be that mis
sionary; I visited the nation, and became acquainted, i
person, with their wants, their dispositions, and the neces
sities of the neighboring tribes. After an absence of
year, I was now returning to them, no longer alone, but witl
two Fathers, three artisan brothers, and all that was essen
tial to the success of the expedition. They themselves ha
traveled upwards of 800 miles to meet us, and now that w
were together, both parties were full of vigor and hope
What joy must not these good Indians, at that moment, hav
experienced? Being unable, however, to express their hap
piness, they were silent : their silence surely could not b

ascribed to a deficiency of intelligence or a want of sentiment, for the Flatheads are full of feeling, and many are
truly intelligent. These, too, were the *élite* of the nation.
Judge of it by what follows.

The chief of this little embassy, named Wistilpo, portrayed himself in the following address to his companions,
a few days subsequently, on viewing the plan of the first
hamlet [réduction] : " My dear children," said he, " I am
but an ignorant and wicked man, yet I thank the Great
Spirit for the favors which he has conferred on us,—(and
entering here into an admirable detail, he concluded thus :)
Yes, my dear friends, my heart has found content; notwithstanding my wickedness I despair not of the goodness of
God.   Henceforth, I wish to live only that I may pray; I
will never abandon prayer (religion) ; I will pray until the
end of my life, and when I die I will commit myself into
the hands of the Author of life; if he condemn me, I shall
submit to his will, for I have deserved punishment; if he
save me, I shall bless him forever.   Once more, then, my
heart has found content.— What shall we do to evince the
love we bear our Fathers? "   Here he made practical resolutions, but I must hasten to commemorate the zeal of each
of those who formed the embassy.

Simon, who had been baptized the preceding year, was
the oldest of the nation, and was so burdened with the weight
of years, that even when seated, he needed a stick for his
support.   Yet, he had no sooner ascertained that we were
on our route to join the tribe, than mounting his horse and
mingling with the young warriors who were prepared to
go forth to meet us, he said : " My children, I shall accompany you; if I die on the way, our Fathers, at least, will
know the cause of my death."   During the course of the
journey, he repeatedly exhorted his companions : " Courage,
my children," he would say, " remember that we are going
to the presence of our Fathers;" and urging his steed forward, whip in hand, he led on his youthful followers, at the
rate of fifty miles per day.

Francis, a boy from six to seven years old, grandson of Simon, was an orphan from the very cradle. Having served at the altar, the preceding year, he would not be refused permission to accompany his grandfather: his heart told him that he was about to recover father and mother, and enjoy all the happiness that loving parents can bestow.

Ignatius, who had advised the fourth deputation, and had been a member of it,— who had succeeded in his mission, and introduced the first Black-gown into the tribe,— who had just recently exposed himself to new dangers, in order to introduce others, had crowned his zealous exertions by running for days without eating or drinking, solely that he might reach us the sooner.

Pilchimo, his companion and brother to one of the martyrs of the third deputation, was a young warrior, already reputed brave among the brave. The preceding year, his presence of mind and his courage had saved seventy of his brethren in arms from the fury of nearly 1,900 Blackfeet who had surrounded them.

Francis Xavier[3] was the son of old Ignatius, who had been the leader of the second and third deputation, and had fallen a victim to his devotion to the cause of religion and of his brethren. Francis Xavier had gone to St. Louis at the age of ten, in the company of his courageous father, solely that he might have the happiness of receiving baptism. He had finally attached himself without reserve to the service of the mission, and supplied our table with a daily mess of fish.

Gabriel, [Prudhomme] who was of mixed blood, but an adopted child of the nation, was interpreter for the missionaries. Being the first to join us on the banks of Green river, he merited the title of precursor of the Flatheads. His bravery and zeal had four[4] times induced him to travel

[3] Still living (1903) near Arlee, Montana, where his ranch may be seen from passing trains. He is commonly called François Saxa (meaning Iroquois) or Lamousse, and is a most respected citizen.

[4] Fr. three.

for our sakes, over a space of 400 miles, which separated us
from the main camp.

Such were they who now greeted us.   Let them tell their
own story.

They had prayed daily to obtain for me a happy journey
and a speedy return.   Their brethren continued in the same
good disposition; almost all, even children and old men,
knew by heart the prayers which I had taught them the
preceding year.   Twice on every week day, and three times
on each Sunday, the assembled tribe recited prayers in common.   Whenever they moved their camp, they carried with
them, as an ark of safety, the box of church ornaments
left in their custody.   Five or six children, whom I had
baptized, had gone to heaven during my absence; the very
morrow of my departure, a young warrior whom I had
baptized the day previous, died in consequence of a wound
received from the Blackfeet about three months before.—
Another, who had accompanied me as far as the Fort of the
Crows, and was as yet but a catechumen, died of sickness
in returning to the tribe, but in such happy dispositions that
his mother was perfectly consoled for his loss by the conviction that his soul was in heaven.   A girl, about twelve
years of age, seeing herself on the point of dying, had solic-
ited baptism with such earnestness that she was baptized
by Peter the Iroquois, and received the name of Mary.—
After having sung a canticle in a stronger voice than usual,
she died, saying: " Oh, how beautiful! I see Mary, my
mother."   So many favors from heaven were calculated to
instigate the malice of hell.   The enemies of salvation had
accordingly attempted to sow the cockle among the good
grain, by suggesting to the chiefs of the tribe that my conduct would be like that of so many others, who, " once gone,
had never returned."   But the head chief had invariably
replied: " You wrong our Father; he is not double-tongued,
like so many others. He has said: ' I will return,' and he
will return, I am sure."   The interpreter added that it was
this conviction which had impelled the venerable old man,

notwithstanding his advanced age, to place himself at the head of the detachment bound for Green river; that they had arrived at the rendezvous on the 1st of July, which was the appointed day; that they had remained there till the 16th, and would have continued to occupy the same position, had not the scarcity of provisions obliged them to depart. He stated also that the whole tribe had determined to fix upon some spot as a site for a permanent village; that, with this view, they had already chosen two places which they believed to be suitable; that nothing but our presence was required to confirm their determination, and they relied with such implicit confidence on our speedy arrival, that the head chief, on starting from Green river, had left there three men to await us, advising them to hold that position until no longer tenable.

Here, I have much to relate that is not less edifying than curious; but before I enter upon the chapter of noble actions, I must conclude what I had commenced in my preceding letter. But I feel bound, before all, to pay Mr. Ermatinger,[5] the captain of Fort Hall, the tribute of gratitude which we owe him.

Although a Protestant by birth, this noble Englishman gave us a most friendly reception. Not only did he repeatedly invite us to his table, and sell us, at first cost, or at one-third of its value, in a country so remote, whatever we required; but he also added, as pure gifts, many articles which he believed would be particularly acceptable. He did more: he promised to recommend us to the good will of the Governor of the honorable English Hudson Bay Com-

[5] Francis or Frank Ermatinger (often spelled Ermantinger), an Englishman by birth, prominent as an agent of the Hudson Bay Company; met with at Fort Okinagan, Oregon City, on Red river and elsewhere; connected by marriage with Dr. John McLoughlin; probably at Fort Hall at this time to compete for the Flathead and Nez Percé trade with the American companies. Said to have died in Canada, and to have had a brother, who may be confused with him in some places.

pany, who was already prepossessed in our favor; and, what is still more deserving of praise, he assured us that he would second our ministry among the populous nation of the Snakes, with whom he has frequent intercourse. So much zeal and generosity give him a claim to our esteem and gratitude. May heaven return to him a hundredfold the benefits he has conferred on us!

It was at Fort Hall that we took our final leave of the American colony, with which we had, till then, pursued the same route. It was previously to this, while we were yet at Green river, that those who came to that wild region merely for information or pleasure, had turned back, with some fewer illusions than when they started out upon the journey. They were five or six in number.[6] Among them was a young Englishman, who had been our messmate from St. Louis. In taking leave of us, this young man, who was in many respects estimable, assured us that, if Providence should ever again throw us together, the meeting would give him the highest satisfaction, and that he would always be happy to do us all the service in his power. He was of a good English family, and like most of his countrymen, fond of travel: he had already seen the four quarters of the globe; but *qui multum peregrinantur.* * * * He cher-- ished so many prejudices, however, against the Catholic re- ligion, that, despite all our good wishes, we were of no service to him in the most essential relation. We recom- mended him to our friends. I have treasured up one of his beautiful reflections: "One must travel in the desert to wit- ness the watchful care of Providence over the wants of man."

They who had started purely with the design of seek- ing their fortune in California, and were pursuing their enterprise with the constancy which is characteristic of Americans, had left us, but a few days before our arrival at the fort, in the vicinity of the boiling springs which empty

[6] Bidwell names three — Peyton, Rodgers and Amos E. Frye — from the emigrants.

into Bear river.   There now remained with us but few of the party, who had come to the fort in order to revictual. Among the latter were the leader of the colony,[7] and a reputed deacon of the Methodist Episcopalian sect [named Williams].   Both were of a peaceable disposition, and manifested for us the highest regard; but the former, like so many others, being very indifferent as to religious matters, held as a maxim, " that it was best to have no religion, or else to adopt that of the country in which we live;" and wishing to display his great Bible erudition, he in proof of his paradox, cited as a text of St. Paul the ancient proverb: *Si fueris Romæ, Romano vivite more.*   The minister was of the same opinion, but yet he wished some religion, it being well understood that his was the best.   I say *his,* because he was neither a Methodist, a Protestant nor a Catholic — not even a Christian; he maintained that a Jew, a Turk, or an Idolater may be as agreeable as any other in the sight of God.   For the proof of his doctrine, he relied (strange to say) on the authority of St. Paul, and particularly on this text: *Unus Dominus una fides.*   In fact, these were the very words with which he greeted us, the first time we saw him, and which formed the subject of a long valedictory discourse that he delivered in one of the meeting-houses of Westport, previous to his departure for his western mission. By whom was he sent?   We have never ascertained.   His zeal frequently induced him to dispute with us; it was not difficult to show him that his ideas, with the exception of one, were vague and fluctuating.   He acknowledged it himself; but after having wandered from point to point, he always returned to his favorite tenet, which, according to him, was the fundamental principle of all true belief: " that the love of God is the first of duties, and that to inculcate it we

---

[7] "A man named Bartleson, from Jackson county, Missouri. He was not the best man for the position, but we were given to understand that if he was not elected captain he would not go; and as he had seven or eight men with him, and we did not want the party diminished, he was chosen."— *Bidwell.*

must be tolerant." This was his strongest point of support, the foundation of all his reasoning, and the stimulus of his zeal. The term Catholic, according to him, was but another word for " love and philanthropy." He carried his absurdities and contradictions so far that he excited the hilarity of the whole camp. His ingenuous simplicity was even greater than his tolerance. For example, he once said to me: " Yesterday one of the members of my persuasion returned to me a book which I had lent him, stating that it contained an exposition of the Roman creed. When I asked him his opinion of it, he replied, ' that the book was full of errors;' yet it was an exposition of Methodist principles that I had given him. Witness," said he, with emphasis, " the blinding influence of prejudice."

I had daily conversations with some one of the caravan, and frequently with several. And although Americans are slow to change their creed, we had the consolation to relieve our traveling companions of a heavy load of prejudice against our holy religion. They parted from us exhibiting signs of respect and veneration; nay, even of preference for Catholicity. These controversies so completely engrossed my mind, my heart and my senses, that I arrived almost unconsciously on the banks of Snake river. Here a great danger and a profitable lesson awaited us; but before speaking of the adventures of our journey, I shall conclude what remains to be related of the country we traversed.

We halted with our narrative upon the shore of the Sweetwater. This stream is one of the most beautiful tributaries of the Platte. It owes its name, indeed, to the purity of its waters.[8] It is distinguished from its fellow tributaries by the numerous wanderings of its current — a proof that the fall of its bed is but slight. But suddenly changing its course, we see or rather hear it rushing impetuously through a long cleft in a chain of mountains. These mountains, which harmonize well with the torrent, exhibit the most picturesque scenes; travelers have named this spot the

8 See p. 214.

Devil's Entrance [Devil's Gate, Wyoming]. In my opinion, they should have rather called it Heaven's Avenue, for
if it resembles hell on account of the frightful disorder which
frowns around it, it is still a mere passage, and it should
rather be compared to the way of heaven on account of the
scene to which it leads. Imagine, in short, two rows of
rocks, rising perpendicularly to a wonderful height, and at
the foot of these shapeless walls a winding bed, broken, encumbered with trunks of trees, with rubbish, and with timber
of all dimensions; while, in the midst of this chaos of obstacles, the roaring waves force a passage, now rushing
with fury, then swelling with majesty, and anon spreading
with gentleness, accordingly as they find in their course a
wider or more straitened passage. Above these moving
and noisy scenes, the eye discerns masses of shadow, here
relieved by a glance of day, there deepening in their gloom
by the foliage of a cedar or pine, till finally, as the sight
travels through the long vista of lofty galleries, it is greeted
by a distant perspective of such mild beauty, that a sentiment of placid happiness steals upon the mind. Such is the
spectacle we admired at the distance of nine or ten miles
from Independence Rock, on the morning of the 6th of
July. I doubt whether the solitude of the Carthusian mon-
astery, called La Grande Chartreuse, of which so many
wonders are related, can, at least at first sight, offer greater
attractions to him whom divine grace has called to a con-
templative life. As for me, who am not called to such a
state, at least exclusively, after an hour of raptures, I began
to understand the expression of the Carthusian friar, *pul-
chrum transeuntibus;* and I hastened to proceed.

Hence we directed our course more and more toward
the heights of the Far West, ascending, sometimes clam-
bering, until we reached the summit, from which we discovered another world. On the 7th of July we were in
sight of the immense Oregon Territory. I will not presume to add to the many pompous descriptions which have
been given of the spectacle now before us. I shall say

nothing either of the height, the number or the variety of
those peaks, covered with eternal snows, which rear their
heads with menacing aspect to the heavens. Nor will I
speak of the many streams descending from them and changing their course with unexpected suddenness; nor of the
extreme rarification of the air with the consequent effect
upon objects susceptible of contraction, at so great an elevation. All this is common; but to the glory of the Lord,
I must commemorate the imperious necessity I experienced
of tracing his holy name upon a rock, which towered pre-
eminent amid the grandeur around. May that ever-ador-
able name be to travelers a monument of our gratitude, and
a pledge of salvation!

Henceforth we descended toward the Pacific — first by
following, then by crossing the Little and the Big Sandy
rivers. In the vicinity of the latter, as the captain had
mistaken one road for another, the caravan wandered for
three days at random. I myself, on a fine evening, strayed
from the rest. I thought myself entirely lost; how was I
to act? I did what every sincere believer would have done
in the same circumstances, I prayed; and then urging on my
horse, I traveled several miles, when it struck me that it
would be prudent to retrace my steps. I did so instantly,
and it was fortunate, for the caravan was far behind. I
found it encamped; still ignorant however of its position,
and on a soil so arid that our jaded beasts were necessitated
to fast for the night. Days follow, but resemble not each
other; two days subsequently, we were surrounded with
abundance, filled with joy, all once more united, and on the
banks of a river not less celebrated among the hunters of
the West than the shores of the Platte. This river loses
itself not far below, in clefts of rocks said to be no less than
200 miles in extent, among which there are countless swarms
of beavers, although the trapper has never ventured to hunt
them, on account of the extreme peril of the enterprise.

At a certain period of the year, both trappers and Indians
flock to this spot, for the purpose of bartering all kinds of

merchandise. It was here, but eight years ago, the wagons that first undertook to cross the Rocky Mountains found the Pillars of Hercules, and it was here too that we found the messenger of the Flatheads, to whom I have already alluded. This river is the Rio Colorado of the West [Green river]. * * * We rested two days upon its banks, with the company of Captain F[raeb],[9] who had just returned from California. What they told us concerning that distant country dissipated many illusions, and caused some of our companions, who traveled for amusement, to return.

On the 26th of July we seriously thought of continuing our journey. With a train like ours it was no small matter. The remembrance of the Bonneville expedition was still fresh in the minds of all; but our object gave us courage. Although we had with us only such articles as were strictly necessary, they could be transported conveniently only by wagons. We put our confidence in God; the teamsters lashed their mules, the mules did their duty, and presently the river was crossed, and the line of our wagons spread out as best it could, twisting and straying in almost every direction, amid a labyrinth of mountains and valleys, obliged to open a road, now in the bottom of a ravine, now on the slope of a cliff, often through the brush; in one place the mules would have to be unhitched, in another teams must be doubled, and again all hands would be called upon to support the wagons on the inclined edge of an abyss or hold them back in some too rapid descent, to prevent what after all was not always prevented, for how many overturnings did we not behold? Our good Brothers especially, who had become teamsters from necessity much more than from

[9] Fraeb (always called Frapp by the trappers) was one of the members of the old Rocky Mountain Fur Company about 1830.

"They came and camped on Green river very soon after our arrival, buying the greater part, if not all, of our alcohol. Years afterward we heard of the fate of that party; they were attacked by Indians the very first night after they left us and several of them killed, including the captain of the trapping party, whose name was Frapp. The whisky was probably the cause."— *Bidwell.*

choice; how often were they not astonished at finding themselves, one upon the croup, another on the neck, another
among the hoofs, of their mules, without any clear idea of
how they had come there, but thanking the God of the
traveler that they had gotten off so easily. The same protection covered the horsemen; in the course of the journey,
Father Mengarini had six tumbles and Father Point quite
as many; once while riding at full gallop my horse fell and
I flew over his head, and not one of us in these various
occurrences received the least scratch.

We traveled in this manner for ten days, to reach Bear
river, which flows through a wide and beautiful valley,
surrounded by lofty mountains and often intersected by
inaccessible rocks.[10] We continued our march through it
during eight successive days. The river resembles in its
course the form of a horseshoe, and falls into the Great Salt
lake, which is about 300 miles in circumference, and has
no communication with the sea.   On our way, we met several families of Shoshones or Snake Indians, and Soshocos
or Root-diggers. They speak the same language, and are
both friends to the whites. The only difference we could
observe between them was that the latter were by far the
poorer. They formed a grotesque group, such as is not to
be seen in any other part of the Indian Territory.   Represent to yourself a band of wretched horses, disproportionate
in all their outlines, loaded with bags and boxes to a height
equal to their own, and these surmounted by rational beings
young and old, male and female, in a variety of figures and
costumes, to which the pencil of a Hogarth or a Breugel
could scarcely do justice, and you will have an idea of the

10 In his itinerary from the Linton Album, Father De Smet says that
his party traveled by way of Brown's Hole. He does not refer to it
in his letters, though the time consumed in going from Green river to
Bear river would make such a wide detour from the regular route
possible. It is doubtful, however, if he went there, for, if he had, the
remarkable natural beauty of this valley would not have escaped com-
ment in his letters. This was two years before the founding of Fort
Bridger.

scene we witnessed. One of these animals, scarcely four
feet high, had for its load four large sacks of dried meat,
two on each side, above which were tied several other objects, terminating in a kind of platform on the back of the
living beast; and, on the summit of the whole construction,
at a dangerous elevation, was seated cross-legged on a bear
skin a very old person smoking his calumet. At his side,
on another Rozinante, was mounted an old one-eyed Goody,
probably his wife, seated in the same manner on the top of
sacks and bags, that contained all sorts of roots, dried beans
and fruits, grains and berries; in short, all such comestibles
as the barren mountains and the beautiful valleys afford.
These are carried to their winter encampment. Sometimes
we have seen a whole family on the same animal, each according to his age, the children in front, the women next,
and the men behind. On two occasions I saw thus mounted
five persons, of whom two at least had the appearance of
being as able to carry the poor horse as the horse was to
support the weight of these two Soshocos gentlemen.

Some places on Bear river exhibit great natural curiosities. A square plain of a few acres in extent presents an
even surface of fuller's earth of pure whiteness, like that of
marble, and resembling a field covered with dazzling snow.
Situated near this plain are a great many springs, differing
in size and temperature. Several of them have a slight
taste of soda, and the temperature of these is cold. The
others are of a milk-warm temperature, and must be wholesome; perhaps they are not inferior to the celebrated waters
of the Spa, or of the lime springs in Belgium. I am inclined to believe so, though I am not firm in the opinion;
at all events, they are surrounded by the mountains over
which our wagons found it so difficult to pass. I therefore
invite neither sick nor sound to test them. In the same
locality there is a remarkable spring, which has made for
itself a little mound, of a mixed stony and sulphurous substance, in the shape of an inverted kettle. It has only a
small opening in the top, through which one can hardly pass

his hand; from this hole issue alternately a jet of water and a gush of steam. The earth for some distance around resounds like an immense vault, and is apt to frighten the solitary traveler as he passes along.

It was here that we left Bear river. On the 14th of August our wagons, having proceeded ten hours without intermission, arrived at the outlet of a defile which seemed to us the end of the world. On our right and left were frightful mountains; in our rear a road which we were by no means tempted to retrace; in front a passage through which rushed a torrent; but so small that the torrent itself seemed with difficulty to force its way. Our beasts of burthen were, for the first time, exhausted. Murmurs arose against the captain, who, however, was imperturbable, and as he never shrank from difficulties, advanced to reconnoitre the ground. In a few moments he made us a sign to approach; one hour after we had surmounted every obstacle, for we had traversed the highest chain of the Rocky Mountains and were nearly in sight of Fort Hall. On the evening previous to the departure of the camp from the Soda Springs, I directed my course toward the fort, to make a few necessary arrangements. The young Francis Xavier was my only companion. We were soon involved in a labyrinth of mountains, and about midnight we were on the summit of the highest chain. My poor guide, being able to see nothing by the weak light of the moon but frightful precipices, was so pitifully embarrassed that after veering about for a while, like a weather-cock, he confessed himself lost. That was not a place, nor was it a time, to wander at random; I therefore took what I considered the only alternative, that of waiting for the morning sun to extricate us from our embarrassment. Wrapped up in my blanket and with my saddle for a pillow, I stretched myself upon the rock, and immediately fell into a sound sleep. Early the next morning we descended by a small cleft in the rocks, which the obscurity of the night had concealed, and arrived on a plain watered by the Portneuf, one of the tributaries of Snake

river.   We trotted or galloped over fifty miles in the course
of the day.   The whole way presented evident remains
of volcanic eruptions; piles and veins of lava were visible
in all directions, and the rocks bore marks of having been
in a state of fusion.   The river, in its whole length, exhibits a succession of beaver ponds, emptying into each other
by a narrow opening in each dike, thus forming a fall of
between three and six feet.   All these dikes are of stone,
evidently the work of the water (the trappers call them
the work of the beaver) and of the same character and
substance as the stalactites found in some caverns.[11]

We arrived late in the evening, within half a mile of the
Fort, [Hall][12] but being unable to see our way in the darkness, and not knowing where we were, we encamped for the
night among the bushes, near the margin of a small brook
and amid a cloud of mosquitoes.

Beaver Head, Camp of the Big Face, 1st Sept. 1841.

Reverend and Dear Father Provincial:

Nearly four months had elapsed since our departure
from Westport, when we met the main body of the nation to which we had been sent.[13]   Here we found the
principal chiefs, four of whom had advanced a day's journey to welcome us.   They met us at one of the sources of
the Missouri called Beaver Head, where we had encamped

11 They do bear a close resemblance to beaver dams, but are built
up of mineral deposit.   They are easily visible from the railroad trains
on the Oregon Short Line.

12 Fort Hall was built by Nathaniel J. Wyeth in the year 1834 on
the left bank of the Snake river, a little above the mouth of the
Portneuf.   Its history as a trading post is almost entirely associated
with the Hudson Bay Company, to whom Wyeth sold it in 1836.   It
was an exceedingly important point during the emigration period,
and later became a military post of considerable note.

13 Led by Little Chief, Insula, afterward baptized Michael, " on
account of his fidelity and courage."

with some Bannocks, of whom I will tell hereafter. Having crossed the small river under the direction of these new guides, we came to an extensive plain, at the western part of which the Flatheads lay encamped. This was on the 30th of August, and it was only toward night that we could distinctly discern the camp. A number of runners who rapidly succeeded each other informed us that the camp was not far distant. Contentment and joy were depicted on their countenances. Long before, the Flathead warrior who is surnamed the Bravest of the Brave sent me his finest horse to Fort Hall, having strongly recommended that no one should mount him before he was presented to me. Soon after the warrior himself appeared, distinguished by his superior skill in horsemanship, and by a large red scarf, which he wore after the fashion of the Marshals of France. He is the handsomest Indian warrior of my acquaintance. He came with a numerous retinue. We proceeded at a brisk trot, and were now but two or three miles from the camp, when at a distance we descried a warrior of lofty stature. A number of voices shouted Paul! Paul! and indeed it was Paul, the head chief, [Big Face] who had just arrived after a long absence, as if by special permission of God, to afford him the satisfaction of introducing me personally to his people. After mutual and very cordial demonstrations of friendship, the good old chief insisted upon returning to announce our arrival. In less than half an hour all hearts were united and moved by the same sentiments. The tribe had the appearance of a flock crowding with eagerness around their shepherd. The mothers offered us their little children, and so moving was the scene that we could scarcely refrain from tears. This evening was certainly one of the happiest of our lives. We could truly say that we had reached the peaceful goal. All previous dangers, toils and trials were at an end and forgotten. The hopeful thought that we would soon behold the happy days of the primitive Christians revive among these Indians, filled our minds, and the main subject of our conversations became the question:

20

" What shall we do to comply with the requisitions of our signal vocation? "

I engaged Father Point, who is skilled in drawing and architecture, to trace the plan of the missionary stations. In my mind, and still more in my heart, the material was essentially connected with the moral and religious plan. Nothing appeared to us more beautiful than the Narrative of Muratori.[14] We had made it our Vade Mecum. It is chiefly to these subjects that we shall devote our attention for the future, bidding farewell to all fine perspectives, animals, trees and flowers, or favoring them only with an occasional and hasty glance.

From Fort Hall we ascended Snake river, also called Lewis' Fork, as far as the mouth of Henry's Fork. This is unquestionably the most barren of all the mountain deserts. It abounds in absinthe, cactus, and all such plants and herbs as are chiefly found on arid lands. We had to resort to fishing for the support of life, and our beasts of burden were compelled to fast and pine; for scarcely a mouthful of grass could be found during the eight days which it took us to traverse this wilderness. At a distance we beheld the colossal summits of the Rocky Mountains. The Three Tetons were about fifty miles to our right, and to the left we had the Three Buttes at a distance of thirty miles.[15]

[14] Muratori is the historian of the Jesuit missions in Paraguay, to which frequent references are made throughout the present work. The first South American missions were established in 1610, and in the 150 years in which the missionaries continued their labors a large part of the native population came under their influence. They had nearly a clear field during this time, thanks to laws which made it difficult for strangers to introduce the vices of Europe, and appear to have been building up an exemplary Christian community. The name " réduction " comes from their system, where it was applied to the settled abodes which they induced their wandering neophytes to adopt. The Society was expelled from Paraguay in 1757, and ten years later from all Spanish America, and the entire promising structure fell to the ground.

[15] The Three Buttes have always been notable landmarks on the Snake River plain.

From the mouth of Henry's Fork we steered our course toward the mountains over a sandy plain furrowed by deep ravines, and covered with blocks of granite. We spent a day and night without water. On the following day we came to a small brook, but so arid is this porous soil that its waters are soon lost in the sand. On the third day of this truly fatiguing journey we entered into a beautiful defile, where the verdure was both pleasing and abundant, as it is watered by a copious rivulet. We gave to this passage the name of "the Father's Defile," and to the rivulet that of St. Francis Xavier. From the Father's Defile to the place of our destination the country is well watered, for it abounds with small lakes and rivulets, and is surrounded by mountains, at whose base are found numberless springs. In no part of the world is the water more limpid or pure, for whatever may be the depth of the rivers, the bottom is seen as if there were nothing to intercept the view. The most remarkable spring which we have seen in the mountains is called the Deer Lodge. It is found on the bank of the main fork of the Bitter Root or St. Mary's river; to this fork I have given the name of St. Ignatius.[16] This spring is situated on the top of a mound thirty feet high, in the middle of a marsh. It is accessible on one side only, and is formed of a stony crust deposited by the spring, which has risen as the mound has grown. The water bubbles up on the top, and escapes through a number of openings at the base of the mound, the circumference of which seems to be about sixty feet. The waters at the base are of different temperatures — hot, lukewarm and cold — though but a few steps distant from one another. Some indeed are so hot that meat may be boiled in them. We actually tried the experiment.[17]

[16] Now called Deer Lodge Creek.

[17] Warm Springs, Deer Lodge county, Montana; now the site of a sanitarium and of the state asylum for the insane.

Hell Gate, 21st Sept., 1841.[18]

"It is on a journey through the desert that we see how attentive Providence is to the wants of man." I repeat with pleasure this remark of my young Protestant friend, because the truth of it appears through the narrative which I have commenced, and will appear still more evidently in what is to follow. Were I to speak of rivers, the account would be long and tedious, for in five days we crossed as many as eighteen, and crossed one of them five times in the space of a few hours. I shall only mention the most dangerous among them. The first which we found it very difficult to cross was the South Fork of the Platte. But as we had been long apprised of the difficulty, we took our precautions beforehand, and some of our Canadians had explored it with so much care that we forded it, not without great difficulty, but without any serious accident. The greatest distress was felt by the dogs of the caravan. Left on the bank when all had crossed, nothing but fidelity toward their masters could have induced them to swim over a river but little less than a mile wide, and having so rapid a current that it would have carried away wagons and carts, had they not been supported on all sides, while the mules exerted all their strength to pull them onward. The poor dogs did not attempt to cross till they found that there was no choice left between encountering the danger and losing their masters. The passage over these rivers is generally effected by means of a bull-boat, the name given to a kind of boat, constructed on the spot with buffalo hides. They are indispensable when the current is impetuous, and no ford can be found. Thanks to our Canadians, we wanted them neither on this nor any other occasion.

[18] Letter VIII, *Letters and Sketches* and Letter VI, Second Voyage, *Voyages aux Montagues-Rocheuses,* both dated as above and addressed respectively to the Father Provincial and to Father De Smet's sister, Mme. Rosalie van Mossevelde, Termonde. The English text is followed for the most part.

The second difficult passage was over the North Fork, which is less wide, but deeper and more rapid than the Southern. We had crossed the latter in carts. Having mustered a little more courage, we determined to cross the North Fork on horseback. We were induced to do so, on seeing our hunter drive before him a horse on which his wife was mounted, whilst at the same time he was pulling a colt that carried a little girl but one year old. To hold back under such circumstances would have been a disgrace for Indian missionaries. We therefore resolved to go forward. It is said that we were observed to grow pale, and I am inclined to believe we did; yet, after our horses had for some time battled against the current, we reached the opposite shore in safety, though our clothes were dripping wet. Here we witnessed a scene which, had it been less serious, might have excited laughter. The largest wagon was carried off by the force of the current, in spite of all the efforts, shouts and cries of the men, who did all they could to keep themselves from being drowned. Another wagon was literally turned over. One of the mules showed only his four feet on the surface of the water, and the others went adrift entangled in the gears. On one side appeared the American captain,[19] with extended arms, crying for help. On the other, a young German traveler was seen diving with his beast, and soon after both appearing above water at a distance from each other. Here a horse reached the shore without a rider; further on, two riders appeared on the same horse; finally, the good Brother Joseph dancing up and down with his horse, and Father Mengarini clinging to the neck of his, and looking as if he formed an indivisible part of the animal. After all our difficulties, we found that only one of the mules was drowned. As the mule belonged to a man who had been the foremost in endeavoring to save both men and horses, the members of the caravan agreed to make him a

[19] Bartleson.

present of a horse, as a reward for his services. We offered thanks to God for our escape from danger.

I mentioned before that great dangers awaited us on Snake river. This stream being much less deep and wide than the other two, and having such limpid waters that the bottom can everywhere be seen, could only be dangerous to incautious persons. It sufficed to keep our eyes open, for any obstacle could easily be distinguished and avoided. But whether it were owing to want of thought or attention, or to the stubborn disposition of the team, Brother Charles Huet found himself all at once on the border of a deep precipice, too far advanced to return. Down went mules, driver and vehicle, and so deep was the place that there scarcely appeared any chance to save them. Our hunter, at the risk of his life, threw himself into the river to dive after the poor brother, whom he had to pull out of the carriage. All the Flatheads who were with us tried to save the vehicle, the mules and the baggage. The baggage, with the exception of a few articles, was saved; the carriage was raised by the united efforts of all the Indians, and set afloat; but after this operation it was held by but one of them, who found that his strength was inadequate to the task, and crying that he was being drowned, let go his hold. The hunter plunged in after him, and was himself at the point of losing his life, on account of the efforts which the Indian made to save his own. Finally, after prodigies of valor, exhibited by all the Flatheads, men, women and children, who all strove to give us a proof of their attachment, we lost what we considered the most safe, the team of the carriage. The gears had been cut to enable the mules to reach the shore, but it is said that these animals always perish when once they have had their ears under water. Thus we lost our three finest mules. This loss was to us very considerable, and would have been irreparable, had it not been for the kindness of Captain Ermatinger. Whilst the people of the caravan were drying our baggage, I returned to the fort, where the generous captain repaired our loss for a sum truly inconsiderable, when compared with what must be paid on such occasions to those who wish to avail themselves of the misfortunes of others. We had escaped the danger, and were besides taught a very useful lesson, for it was remarked that it was the first day since we began our journey, on which, by reason of the bustle occasioned by our departure from the fort, we had omitted to say the prayers of the itinerary.

We had dangers of another description to encounter, from which we were also delivered by the aid of God's grace. Once as we traveled along the banks of the Platte, several young members of the caravan separated from the main body, contrary to the express orders of Captain Fitzpatrick,[20] who, together with Father Point and myself, had started a little ahead to look out for a place of encampment. We succeeded in finding a proper site, and we had already unsaddled our horses, when all at once we heard the alarm cry: *Indians! Indians!* And in fact a body of Indians, appearing much larger than it really was, was seen in the distance, first assembling together and then coming full gallop toward our camp. In the mean time a young American, unhorsed and unarmed, makes his appearance, complaining of the loss he had sustained, and indignant at the blows he had received. He seizes the loaded rifle of one of his friends, and rushes forward to take signal vengeance on the offender. The whole camp is roused; the American youth are determined to fight; the colonel, as a man of war, orders the wagons to be drawn up in double file, and places between them whatever may be exposed to plunder. All preparations are made for a regular defense. On the other hand, the Indian squadron, much increased, advances and presents a formidable front.

[20] Thomas Fitzpatrick, " a prominent member of the Rocky Mountain Fur Company, and later much in the service of the Government during the era of exploration. Frequently mentioned in narratives of travel of that period."— *American Fur Trade of the Far West.*

They manœuvre as if they intend to hem in our phalanx, but at sight of our firm position and of the assurance of the captain, who advanced toward them, they checked their march, finally halted, and came to a parley, of which the result was that they should return to the American whatever they had taken from him, but that the blows which he had received should not be returned. After this, both parties united in smoking the calumet. This band consisted of eighty Cheyenne warriors, armed for battle.[21] The Cheyennes are looked upon as the bravest Indians on the prairie. They followed our camp for two or three days. As the chiefs were admitted to our meals, both parties separated with mutual satisfaction.

On another occasion we were in company with the vanguard of the Flatheads, and had penetrated into an impassable defile between the mountains, so that after having traveled the whole day, we were forced to retrace our steps. At night the rumor was spread that a party of Bannock Indians lay encamped in the neighborhood. The Bannocks had this very year killed several white men; but it soon appeared that they were more frightened than ourselves, for before daybreak they had removed from the place.

Without being aware of it, we had escaped a much greater danger on the banks of Green river. We did not know the particulars of this danger till after we had arrived at Fort Hall. There we heard that almost immedi-

[21] "There were only forty of them, but they were well mounted on horses, and were evidently a war-party, for they had no women except one, a medicine woman. They came up and camped within a hundred yards of us. When they had put up their lodges Fitzpatrick and John Gray, the old hunter, went out to them and by signs were made to understand that the Indians did not intend to hurt the man or take his mule or gun, but that he was so excited when he saw them that they had to disarm him to keep him from shooting them. They surrendered the mule and the gun, thus showing that they were friendly. They proved to be Cheyenne Indians. Ever afterward that man went by the name of Cheyenne Dawson."— *Bidwell.*

ately after our separation from the travelers who were on their way to California, and with whom we had till then lived as brothers, they divided themselves into two bands, and each band again subdivided into two parties, one to attend to the chase, the other to guard the horses. The hunter's camp was guarded only by five or six men and some women, who had also to keep watch over the horses and baggage of the others. A booty so rich and so much exposed could not but tempt the Indians who roamed in the neighborhood, and waited, as is their custom, till a seasonable opportunity should offer to commence the attack. When least expected, they fell first upon the horses and then upon the tents, and though the guardians made a courageous defense and sold their lives dearly, yet they burned and pillaged the camp, taking away whatever might be serviceable to them; thus giving a terrible lesson to such as expose themselves to lose all, by not remaining united to withstand the common enemy.[22]

But a few days after we had received this sad intelligence we ourselves were much alarmed. We apprehended lest we should have to defend our lives against a large body of Blackfeet Indians, whose warriors continually infest the country through which we were then traveling. It was reported that they were behind the mountain, and soon after that they were in sight. But our brave Indians, glowing with the desire to introduce us to their tribe, were undaunted, and would have attacked them had they been a hundred times more numerous.

[22] The massacre of these travelers gave rise to several vague reports. As we had started together it was supposed by many that we had not yet separated when this unfortunate accident took place. Hence it was circulated in the United States, and even in some parts of Europe, that the Catholic Missionaries had all been killed by the Indians.— *Author's Note.*

John Bidwell, a member of this party, contributing to the *Century* of November, 1890, says of the Oregon party, " we heard that the party arrived safely in Oregon." He remained with the California contingent and makes no mention of any trouble with Indians.

Pilchimo, brandishing his musket in the air, started off with the greatest rapidity, and was followed by three or four others. They crossed the mountain and disappeared, and the whole camp made ready to repel the assailants. The horses were hitched and the men under arms, when we saw our brave Indians return over the mountain, followed by a dozen others. The latter were Bannocks, who had united rather with a mind to fly than to attack us. Among them was a chief, who showed the most favorable dispositions. I had a long conference with him on the subject of religion, and he promised that he would use all his endeavors to engage his men to adopt religious sentiments. Both he and his retinue left us the day after the arrival of the Flatheads, who came to wish us joy for the happy issue of our long journey. We here remarked how the power of reason acts upon the heart of the savage. The Bannock chief was brother to an Indian of the tribe who had been killed by one of the Flathead chiefs present on this occasion. They saluted each other in our presence and separated as truly Christian warriors would have done, who show enmity to each other only on the field of battle. Yet as the Flatheads had more than once been basely betrayed by the Bannocks, the former did not offer to smoke the calumet. I hope that we shall have no difficulty to bring on a reconciliation. The Flatheads will undoubtedly follow the advice we shall give them, and I feel confident that the Bannocks will be satisfied with the conditions.

CHAPTER VII.[1]

FOUNDING OF ST. MARY'S MISSION.

Arrival on banks of Bitter Root river and founding of St. Mary's mission — Cœur d'Alène Indians solicit missionaries — Other well-disposed tribes — The problem of the Blackfeet — Prowess of the Flatheads — Their exemplary piety — Plan to make them the nursery for a vast Christian community — Working details — Church and farm buildings — Futile opposition of the devil — Baptisms and marriages — First Blackfoot convert — Father Point goes to the winter hunt.

Bitter Root, the Place selected for the first Reduction, October 18, 1841.

AFTER a journey of four months and a half on horseback through the desert, and in spite of our actual want of bread, wine, sugar, fruit, and all such things as are called the conveniences of life, we find our strength and courage increased, and are better prepared than ever to work at the conversion of the souls that Providence entrusts to our care. Next to the Author of all good things, we returned thanks to her whom the Church reveres as the Mother of her Divine Spouse, since it has pleased the divine goodness to send us the greatest consolations on

[1] This chapter consists of Letter IX, *Letters and Sketches,* dated St. Mary's, October 18, 1841, and addressed to the Father Provincial, paralleled by Letter VII, Second Voyage, *Voyages aux Montagnes-Rocheuses,* dated "Bitter Root, place selected for First Reduction," October 26th and addressed to the Theresian Nuns of Termonde; Letters X, *Letters and Sketches,* and VIII, *Voyages aux Montagnes-Rocheuses,* dated St. Mary's, October 26th and addressed respectively to the Provincial and to A Father of the Company of Jesus; Letters XII, *Letters and Sketches,* and XI, *Voyages aux Montagnes-Rocheuses,* dated respectively December 30th and December 31st, and addressed to A Father; and two pages from Book II, *Letters and Sketches.* The English text has mainly been adhered to.

several days consecrated to her honor. On the feast of her glorious Assumption we met the vanguard of our dear neophytes. On the Sunday within the octave, we, for the first time since my return, celebrated the holy mysteries among them. On the following Sunday our good Indians placed themselves and their children under the Immaculate Heart of Mary, of which we then celebrated the feast. This act of devotion was renewed by the great chief in the name of his whole tribe, on the feast of her Holy Name. On the 24th of September, the feast of our Lady of Mercy, we arrived at the river called Bitter Root, on the banks of which we have chosen the site for our principal missionary station.[2] On the first Sunday of October, feast of the Rosary, we took possession of the promised land, by planting a cross on the spot which we had chosen for our first residence. What motives of encouragement does not the gospel of the present Sunday add to all these mentioned before? Today too we celebrate the Divine Maternity, and what may we not expect from the Virgin Mother who brought forth her Son for the salvation of the world? On the feast of her Patronage we shall offer by her mediation to her Divine Son, twenty-five young Indians, who are to be baptized on that day. So many favors have induced us unanimously to proclaim Mary the protectress of our mission, and give her name to our new residence.[3]

[2] The site of St. Mary's Mission was on the right bank of the Bitter Root river, about twenty-eight miles above its mouth, between old Fort Owen and the modern town of Stevensville.

[3] *Further history of St. Mary's Mission.* — In the spring of 1850, owing to increasing indifference and estrangement of the Flatheads, Father Mengarini recommended the temporary closing of the mission, and Father Joset repaired thither from St. Paul to make the necessary arrangements. "The improvements were leased to Major John Owen, with the proviso that they should revert to the Fathers, should they return, as was their intention, within a stated time. In the meanwhile everything was to be preserved in the same condition, good order and repair by the lessee." (*Palladino.*) This conveyance was dated November 5, 1850. — It was not practicable, however, to reopen

THE ORIGINAL ST. MARY'S MISSION AMONG THE FLATHEADS.

These remarks may appear silly to such as attribute everything to chance or necessity, but to such as believe in the wise dispensations of the Providence of God, by which all things are governed and directed, all these circumstances, together with the wonderful manner in which we have been called, sent and led to this new mission; and still more the good dispositions manifested by the Indians, will appear very proper motives to inspire us with fresh courage, and with the hope of establishing here, on a small scale, the order and regularity which once distinguished our missions in Paraguay. This hope is not founded on imagination, for whilst I am writing these lines, I hear the joyful voices of the carpenters, re-echoing to the blows on the smith's anvil, and I see them engaged in raising the house of prayer. Besides, three Indians, belonging to the tribe called Cœur d'Alènes, having been informed of our arrival among the Flatheads, have just come to entreat us to have pity on them. "Father," said one of them to me, "we are truly deserving your pity. We wish to serve the Great Spirit, but we know not how. We want some one to teach us. For this reason we make application to you." Oh, had some of my brethren, now so far distant from us, been present here last Sunday, when toward night we raised the august sign of salvation, the standard of the cross, in this small but zealous tribe; how their hearts would have been moved on seeing the pious

the mission for a long time, and in the interval many changes had taken place, among the Indians and in their country. In 1862, Father Giorda succeeded Father Congiato as Superior of the Rocky Mountain Missions, and by 1866 he saw his way clear to the re-establishment of the old mission on the Bitter Root. This was accomplished in September of that year, and among the missionaries who were assigned to the post was Father Ravalli, who was one of the staff who had quitted it sixteen years earlier, and who resided there thenceforth until his death in 1884. The mission was finally closed in 1891, upon the removal to the Jocko reservation of the remnant of the Flatheads, under the chief Charlot.— Father Ravalli's church still stands, and services are occasionally held by a visiting priest from Missoula.

joy of these children of the forest! What sentiments of
faith and love did they exhibit on this occasion, when,
headed by their chief, they came to kiss the foot of the
cross, and then, prostrate on their knees, made a sacred
promise, rather to suffer death a thousand times, than to
forsake the religion of Jesus Christ! Who knows how
many of this chosen band may be destined to become
apostles and martyrs of our holy religion! Were we more
numerous, I feel confident that many other tribes would
become members of the kingdom of God; perhaps more
than 200,000 might be converted to Christ. The Flatheads and the Cœur d'Alènes, it is true, are not numerous
tribes, but they are surrounded by many others who evince
the best dispositions.

The Pend d'Oreilles are very numerous, and live at a distance of four or five days' journey from our present establishment. The chief who governed them last year and
who has been baptized and called Peter, is a true apostle.
In my first visit to them I baptized 250 of their children.
Many other tribes have the same origin, and though differing in name, their languages are nearly allied. Next
to these are found the Spokans, who would soon follow
the example of the neighboring tribes; the Nez Percés,
who are disgusted at the conduct of the Protestant ministers that have settled among them; the Snakes, the
Crows and the Bannocks whose chief we have seen. Last
year I visited the Cheyennes, whom I twice met on the
banks of the Platte; the numerous nation of the Sioux, and
the three allied tribes called Mandans, Aricaras and Minnetarees, who all have given me so many proofs of respect
and friendship; the Omahas, with whom I have had so
many conferences on the subject of religion, and many
others who seem inclined to embrace the truth.

The Blackfeet are the only Indians of whose salvation
we would have reason to despair, if the ways of God were
the same as those of man, for they are murderers, thieves,
traitors, and all that is wicked. But were not the Chiqui-

tos, the Chiriquans, the Hurons, and the Iroquois equally wicked before their conversion, which required much time and great help from above? And is it not to the last, that, under God, the Flatheads owe their desire of becoming members of his Church, and the first germs of the copious fruit that has been produced among them? What is more, the Blackfeet are not hostile to Black-gowns. We have been assured by other Indians that we would have nothing to fear, if we presented ourselves amongst them as ministers of religion. When last year I fell into the hands of one of their divisions, and it was ascertained that I was an interpreter of the Great Spirit, they carried me in triumph on a buffalo robe to their village, and invited me to a banquet, at which all the great men of the tribe assisted. It was on this occasion, that, whilst I said grace, I was astonished to see that they struck the earth with one hand and raised the other toward heaven, to signify that the earth produces nothing but evil, whilst all that is good comes from above. From all this you will easily conclude that the harvest is great, whilst the laborers are few.

It is the opinion of the missionaries who accompany me, and of the travelers I have seen in the Far West, in short, of all those who have become acquainted with the Flatheads, that they are characterized by the greatest simplicity, docility and uprightness. Yet, to the simplicity of children is joined the courage of heroes. They never begin the attack, but woe to such as provoke them or treat them unjustly. A handful of their warriors will not shrink from an enemy twenty times more numerous than they; they will stand and repel the assault, and at last put them to flight, and make them repent their rashness. Not long before my first arrival among them, seventy men of the tribe, finding themselves forced to come to an engagement with a thousand Blackfeet warriors, determined to sustain the attack, and rather to die than retreat. Before the engagement they prostrated themselves and addressed such prayers as they had learned to the Great Spirit. They rose full of courage, sustained the first shock, and soon rendered the victory doubtful. The fight, with several interruptions, was continued five successive days, till at last the Blackfeet, astounded at the boldness of their antagonists, were panic-struck, and retreated from the scene of action, leaving many killed and wounded on the field of battle, whilst not one warrior of the Flatheads was killed. But one died of the wounds he had received, and his death happened several months after the engagement, on the day succeeding his baptism — (though the point of an arrow had pierced his skull). It was on the same occasion that Pilchimo, whom I have already mentioned, gave remarkable proofs of valor and attachment to his fellow warriors. All the horses were on the point of falling into the enemy's hand. Pilchimo was on foot. Not far off was a squaw on horseback; to see the danger, to take the squaw from her horse and mount it himself, to gallop to the other horses, and bring them together, and drive them into the camp, was the affair of a few minutes. Another warrior, named Sechelmeld, saw a Blackfoot separated from his company, and armed with a musket. The Blackfoot, taking the warrior for one of his own tribe, asked the Flathead to let him mount behind him. The latter, wishing to make himself master of the musket, agreed to the proposal. They advance on the plain, till Sechelmed seeing that the place favored his design, seizes his fellow rider's weapon, exclaiming: " Blackfoot! I am a Flathead, let go your musket." He wrests it from his hands, dispatches him, remounts the horse, and gallops off in pursuit of the enemy.[4]

The following feat equally deserves to be recorded: A Blackfoot warrior was taken and wounded whilst in the act of stealing a horse. The night was dark and the wound had rendered him furious. He held his loaded gun, and threatened death to any one that should approach him.

[4] This Flathead was Ambrose. A drawing by himself, representing this feat, is among Father De Smet's papers.

Peter, one of the chiefs already mentioned, though diminutive in size, and far advanced in years, felt his courage revived; he runs up to the enemy, and with one blow fells him to the ground. This done he throws himself on his knees, and raising his eyes toward heaven, he is reported to have said: " Great Spirit! thou knowest that I did not kill this Blackfoot from a desire of revenge, but because I was forced to it; be merciful to him in the other world. I forgive him from the bottom of my heart all the evils which he has wished to inflict upon us, and to prove the sincerity of my words I will cover him with my garment." This Peter was baptized last year, and became the apostle of his tribe. Even before baptism, his simplicity and sincerity prompted him to give this testimony of himself: " If ever I have done evil it was through ignorance, for I have always done what I considered good." It would be tedious to give an account of his zealous endeavors. Every morning, at an early hour, he rides through the whole village, stops at every hut, speaks a few words of encouragement and reproof, as circumstances require, and exhorts all to be faithful in the performance of their religious and social duties.

I have spoken of the simplicity and the courage of the Flatheads; I shall make some other remarks concerning their character. They little resemble the majority of the Indians, who are, generally speaking, uncouth, importunate, improvident, insolent, stubborn and cruel.— The Flatheads are disinterested, generous, devoted to their brethren and friends; irreproachable, and even exemplary, as regards probity and morality. Among them, dissensions, quarrels, injuries and enmities are unknown. During my stay in the tribe last year, I have never remarked anything that was contrary to modesty and decorum in the manners and conversation of the men and women. It is true that the children, whilst very young, are entirely without covering, but this is a general custom among the Indians, and seems to have no bad effect upon them; we are determined, however, to abolish this custom as soon as we shall be able to do it.

With respect to religion, the Flatheads are distinguished by the firmness of their faith, and the ardor of their zeal. Not a vestige of their former superstitions can be discovered. Their confidence in us is unlimited. They believe without any difficulty the most profound mysteries of our holy religion, as soon as they are proposed to them, and they do not even suspect that we might be deceived, or even could wish to deceive them. I have already mentioned what exertions they have made to obtain Black-robes for their tribe; the journeys, undertakings, the dangers incurred, the misfortunes suffered to attain their object. Their conduct during my absence from them has been truly regular and edifying. They attend divine service with the greatest punctuality, and pay the most serious attention to the explanation of the Catechism. What modesty and fervent piety do they not exhibit in their prayers, and with what humble simplicity they speak of their former blindness, and of such things as tend to reflect honor upon their present conduct. On this last subject their simplicity is truly admirable: "Father," some will say, with downcast eyes, "what I tell you now I have never mentioned to any one, nor shall I ever mention it to others; and if I speak of it to you, it is because you wish and have a right to know it."

The chiefs, who might be more properly called the fathers of the tribe, having only to express their will, and are obeyed, are always listened to, and are not less remarkable for their docility in our regard than for the ascendancy they possess over their people. The most influential among them, surnamed "The Little Chief," from the smallness of his stature, whether considered as a Christian or a warrior, might stand a comparison with the most renowned character of ancient chivalry. On one occasion, he sustained the assaults of a whole village, which, contrary to all justice, attacked his people. On another oc-

casion, when the Bannocks had been guilty of the blackest
treason, he marched against them with a party of warriors
not one-tenth the number of their aggressors. But, under
such a leader, his little band believed themselves invincible,
and invoking the protection of heaven, rushed upon the
enemy, and took signal vengeance of the traitors, killing
nine of their number. More would have been killed, had
not the voice of Little Chief arrested them in the very
heat of the pursuit, announcing that it was the Sabbath,
and the hour of prayer. Upon this signal, they gave over
the pursuit, and returned to their camp. Arrived there,
they immediately, without thinking of dressing their
wounds, fell upon their knees in the dust, to render to the
Lord of Hosts the honor of the victory. Little Chief had
received a ball through the right hand, which had entirely
deprived him of its use; but seeing two of his comrades
more severely wounded than himself, he with his other
hand rendered them every succor in his power, remaining
the whole night in attendance upon them. On several
other occasions, he acted with equal courage, prudence
and humanity, so that his reputation became widely
spread.

The Nez Percés, a nation far more numerous than the
Flatheads, came to offer him the dignity of being their
head chief. He might have accepted it without detriment
to the rights of any one, as every Indian is free to leave his
chief, and place himself under any other head he may
think proper, and, of course, to accept any higher grade
that may be offered to him. But Little Chief, content with
the post assigned him by Providence, refused the offer,
however honorable to him, with this simple remark, " By
the will of the Great Master of Life I was born among the
Flatheads, and if such be his will, among the Flatheads I
am determined to die;"— a patriotic feeling, highly honorable to him. As a warrior, still more honorable to his
character are the mildness and humility manifested by him.
He said to me once: " Till we came to know the true

God, alas, how blinded were we! We prayed, it is true —
but to whom did we address our prayers? In truth, I
know not how the Great Spirit could have borne with us
so long." At present his zeal is most exemplary; not content with being the foremost in all the offices at chapel, he
is always the first and last at the family prayers, and even
before break of day he is heard singing the praises of his
Maker. His characteristic trait is mildness; and yet he can
assume due firmness, not to say severity of manner, when
he sees it necessary to exercise more rigorous discipline.
Some days before our arrival, one of the young women
had absented herself from prayer, without a sufficient
reason. He sent for her, and after reading her a lecture
before all the household, enforced his motives for greater
attention in future, by a smart application of the cane.
And how did the young offender receive the correction?
With the most humble and praiseworthy submission.

The Flatheads are fond of praying. After the regular
evening prayer, they will assemble in their tents to pray or
sing canticles. These pious exercises will frequently be
prolonged till a late hour; and if any wake during the
night, they begin to pray. Before making his prayer, the
good old Simeon gets up and rakes out the live coals upon
his hearth, and when his prayer is done, which is always
preceded and followed by the sign of the cross, he smokes
his calumet and then turns in again. This he will do three
or four times during the night. There was a time, also,
when these more watchful spirits of the household, not
content with praying themselves, would awaken the sleep-
ers, anxious to make them partakers of the good work.
These pious excesses had sprung from a little piece of advice I had given them on my first visit, that " on waking
at night it was commendable to raise the heart to God."
It has since been explained to them how they are to understand the advice. This night, between the 25th and
26th, the prayers and canticles have not ceased. Yesterday, a young woman having died who had received bap-

tism four days previously, we recommended them to pray for the repose of her soul. Her remains were deposited at the foot of the Calvary, erected in the midst of the camp. On the cross upon her grave might confidently be inscribed the words: *In spem Resurrectionis* — In hope of a glorious Resurrection. We shall shortly have to celebrate the commemoration of the faithful departed; this will afford us an opportunity of establishing the very Christian and standing custom of praying for the dead in their place of interment.

On Sundays, the exercises of devotion are longer and more numerous, and yet they are never fatigued with the pious duty. They feel that the happiness of the little and of the humble is to speak with their Heavenly Father, and that no house presents so many attractions as the house of the Lord. Indeed, so religiously is the Sunday observed here, that on this day of rest, even before our coming, the most timorous deer might wander unmolested in the midst of the tribe, even though they were reduced by want of provisions to the most rigorous fast. For, in the eyes of this people, to use the bow and arrow on this day, would not have appeared less culpable than did the gathering of wood to the scrupulous fidelity of the people of God. Since they have conceived a juster idea of the law of grace, they are less slaves to "the letter that killeth;" but still desirous to be faithful to the very letter, they are studious to do their best, and when any doubt arises, they hasten to be enlightened thereon, soliciting in a spirit of faith and humility that permission of which they may think themselves to stand in need.

The principal chief is named "Big Face," on account of the somewhat elongated form of his visage; he might more nobly and more appropriately be named the Nestor of the Desert, for as well in years as in stature and sagacity he has all the essentials of greatness. From his earliest infancy, nay, even before he could know his parents, he had been the child of distress. Being left a helpless orphan, by the death of his mother, with no one to protect him, it was proposed to bury him with her in the same grave — a circumstance that may serve to give some idea of the ignorance and brutality of his tribe. But the Almighty, who had other purposes in his regard, moved the heart of a young woman to compassionate his helpless condition, and offer to become a mother to him. Her humanity was abundantly recompensed by seeing her adopted son distinguished above all his fellows by intelligence, gentleness, and every good disposition. He was grateful, docile, charitable, and naturally so disposed to piety, that, from a want of knowing the true God, he more than once was led to place his trust in that which was but the work of his own hands. Being one day lost in a forest, and reduced to extremity, he began to embrace the trunk of a fallen tree, and to conjure it to have pity upon him. Nor is it above two months since a serious loss befel him; indeed one of the most serious that could happen to an Indian — the loss of three calumets at the same time. He spent no time in retracing his steps, and to interest heaven in his favor, he put up the following prayer : " O Great Spirit, you who see all things and undo all things, grant, I entreat you, that I may find what I am looking for; and yet let thy will be done." This prayer should have been addressed to God. He did not find the calumets, but in their place he received what was of more incomparable value — simplicity, piety, wisdom, patience, courage and cool intrepidity in the hour of danger. More favored in one respect than Moses, this new guide of another people to God, after a longer sojourn in the wilderness, was at length successful in introducing his children into the land of promise. He was the first of his tribe who received baptism, and took the name of Paul, and like his patron, the great Apostle, he has labored assiduously to gain over his numerous children to the friendship and love of his Lord and Master.

St. Mary's, Rocky Mountains, 26th Oct., 1841.

Reverend and Dear Father Provincial:

This last letter will contain the practical conclusions of what has been stated in the preceding. I am confident that these conclusions will be very agreeable and consoling to all persons who feel interested in the progress of our holy religion, and who very prudently refuse to form a decided opinion, unless they can found it on well attested facts.

From what has hitherto been said, we may draw this conclusion, that the nation of the Flatheads appear to be a chosen people —" the elect of God;" that it would be easy to make this tribe a model for other tribes,— the seed of 200,000 Christians, who would be as fervent as were the converted Indians of Paraguay; and that the conversion of the former would be effected with more facility than that of the latter. The Flatheads have no communication with corrupt tribes; they hold all sects in aversion; they have a horror of idolatry; they cherish much sympathy for the whites, but chiefly for the Black-robes (Catholic priests), a name, which, in consequence of the prepossessions and favorable impressions, which they have received from the Iroquois, is synonymous with goodness, learning, and catholicity. Their position is central; their territory sufficiently extensive to contain several missions; the land is fertile, and the country surrounded by high mountains. They are independent of all authority except that of God, and those who represent him. They have no tribute to pay but that of prayer; they have already acquired practical experience of the advantages of a civilized over a barbarous state of life; and in fine, they are fully convinced and firmly persuaded that without the religion that is announced to them, they can be happy neither in this world nor in the next.

From all these considerations, we may again draw the conclusions, that the best end which we can propose to ourselves is that which our Fathers of Paraguay had in view when they commenced their missionary labors; and that the means to attain this end should be the same, chiefly because these means have been approved by the most respectable authorities, crowned with perfect success, and admired even by the enemies of our religion.

The principle being admitted, it only remains to form a correct idea of the method employed by our Fathers in Paraguay to improve the minds and hearts of their neophytes, and to bring them to that degree of perfection of which they conceived them susceptible. After having seriously reflected on what Muratori relates of the establishments in Paraguay, we have concluded that the following points should be laid down, as rules to direct the conduct of our converts.

1. *With regard to God.*— Simple, firm, and lively faith with respect to all the truths of religion, and chiefly such as are to be believed as theologians express it, *necessitate medii et necessitate præcepti.* Profound respect for the only true religion; perfect submission to the Church of God, in all that regards faith and morality, discipline, etc. Tender and solid piety toward the Blessed Virgin and the saints. Desire of the conversion of others. Courage and fortitude of the martyrs.

2. *With regard to our neighbor.*— Respect for those in authority, for parents, the aged, etc. Justice, charity, and generosity toward all.

3. *With regard to one's self.*— Humility, modesty, meekness, discretion, temperance, irreproachable behavior, industry or love of labor, etc.

We shall strenuously recommend the desire of the conversion of others, because Providence seems to have great designs with respect to our small tribe. In one of our instructions given in a little chapel, constructed of boughs, not less than twenty-four nations were represented, including ourselves. Next, the courage and fortitude of the martyrs, because in the neighborhood of the Blackfeet there

is continual danger of losing either the life of the soul, or
that of the body. Also, industry or the love of labor, because idleness is the predominant vice of Indians; and even
the Flatheads, if they are not addicted to idleness, at least
manifest a striking inaptitude to manual labor, and it will
be absolutely necessary to conquer this. To ensure success,
much time and patience will be required. Finally and chiefly,
profound respect for the true religion, to counteract the ma-
nœuvres of various sectaries, who desirous as it would seem,
to wipe away the reproach formerly made by Muratori, and
in our days by the celebrated Doctor Wiseman, use all
their efforts to make proselytes, and to appear disinterested,
and even zealous in the propagation of their errors.

4. *With regard to the means.*— Flight from all contami-
nating influence; not only from the corruption of the age,
but from what the gospel calls the world. Caution against
all immediate intercourse with the whites, even with the
workmen, whom necessity compels us to employ, for though
these are not wicked, still they are far from possessing the
qualities necessary to serve as models to men who are humble
enough to think they are more or less perfect, in proportion
as their conduct corresponds with that of the whites. We
shall confine them to the knowledge of their own language,
erect schools among them, and teach them reading, writing, arithmetic and singing. Should any exception be made
to this general rule, it will be in favor of a small number,
and only when their good dispositions will induce us to
hope that we may employ them as auxiliaries in religion.
A more extensive course of instruction would undoubtedly
prove prejudicial to these good Indians, whose simplicity is
such that they might easily be imposed upon, if they were
to come in contact with error, whilst it is the source of all
truth and virtue when enlightened by the flambeau of faith.
La Harpe himself, speaking of the apostolic laborers of our
Society, says that the perfection of our ministry consists in
illumining by faith the ignorance of the savage.

To facilitate the attainment of the end in view, we have

chosen the place of the first missionary station, formed the plan of the village, made a division of the lands, determined the form of the various buildings, etc. The buildings deemed most necessary and useful at present are a church, schools, workhouses, storehouses, etc. Next, we have made regulations respecting public worship, religious exercises, instructions, catechisms, confraternities, the administration of the sacraments, singing, music, etc. All this is to be executed in conformity with the plan formerly adopted in the missions of Paraguay.

Such are the resolutions which we have adopted, and which we submit to be approved, amended or modified, by those who have the greater glory of God at heart, and who, by their position and the graces of their state of life, are designed by the Most High to communicate to us the true spirit of our Society.

———

St. Mary's, Dec. 30, 1841.

Reverend Father:

I have given you the happy and consoling result of my journey in November. Before the close of the year I have yet to make you acquainted with what has passed during my absence, and since my return, among the Flatheads; all goes to prove what I have advanced in my preceding letters.

The Reverend Fathers Mengarini and Point were not idle during my absence. The following will give you some idea of the state of affairs on my return, both in regard to material and spiritual matters, as well as the practices and usages established, which could not but tend to strengthen, more and more, our good neophytes.

The plan mentioned in my letters, and unanimously approved, and which we were urged to carry into execution, was, to commence with what appeared to be the most urgent.

We enclosed the field destined to become God's portion of the settlement. We started the buildings intended to be hereafter dependencies of the farm, but serving temporarily for a church and residence, on account of the approach of winter, and our wish to unite the whole colony. These works were indispensable, and were carried on with such spirit that in the space of a month the new buildings could shelter from 400 to 500 souls.

The Flatheads, assisting us with their whole heart and strength, had, in a short time, cut from 2,000 to 3,000 stakes; and the three Brothers, with no other tools than the axe, saw and auger, constructed a chapel with pediment, colonnade and gallery, balustrade, choir, seats, etc., by St. Martin's day; when they assembled in the little chapel all the catechumens, and continued the instructions which were to end on the 3d of December, the day fixed for their baptism. In the interval between these two remarkable epochs, there was on each day one instruction more than usual. This last instruction, intended chiefly for grown persons, was given at eight o'clock in the evening and lasted about an hour and a quarter. These good savages, whose ears and hearts are alike open when the word of God is addressed to them, appeared still better disposed in the evening; the silence being unbroken by the cries of infants or children. Our Heavenly Father so graciously heard their prayers, that on St. Francis Xavier's day the good Fathers had the consolation of baptizing 202 adults.

So many souls wrested from the demons was more than enough to excite their rage,— seeds of distrust, hindrances occasioned by the best intentioned, the sickness of the interpreter and sexton, at the very moment their assistance was most required; a kind of hurricane, which took place the evening before the baptism, and which overturned three lodges in the camp, the trees torn from their roots, and everything in appearance about to be uprooted, even to the foundations of the church — the organ unintentionally broken by the savages, on the eve of being applied to so beautiful a purpose — all seemed to conspire against them; but the day for baptism arrives, and every cloud disappears.

The Fathers had intended to solemnize the marriages of the husbands and wives on the same day as their baptism. They had even announced that the ceremony would take place after baptism; but the sacred rite having occupied a much longer time than they supposed, on account of the necessity of interpreting all that was said, they were obliged to defer this sacrament until the next day, trusting to God and the new Christians for the preservation of their baptismal innocence.

As our former missionaries have left nothing in writing on the conduct we should observe with regard to marriage, it may, perhaps, be useful to relate here what has been our course, in order that our conduct may be rectified if it has not been judicious.

We hold the principle that, generally speaking, there are no valid marriages among the savages of these countries; and for this reason, we have not found one, even among the best disposed, who, after marriage had been contracted in their own fashion, did not believe himself justified in sending away his first wife, whenever he thought fit, and taking another. Many even have several wives in the same lodge. It is, however, true, that many when entering the marriage state promise that nothing but death will ever separate them; that they will never give their hand to another. But what impassioned man or woman has not said as much? Can we infer from this that the contract is valid, when it is universally received that even after such promises they have not the less right to do as they please, when they become disgusted with each other? We are then agreed on this principle, that among them, even to the present time, there has been no marriage, because they have never known well in what its essence and obligation consisted. To adopt an opposite view would be to involve one's self in a labyrinth of difficulties, from which it would be very difficult to escape. This was, if I am not mistaken, the conduct of St. Francis Xavier in the Indies, since it is said in his *Life* that he praised before the married those whom he supposed to be dearest to them, that they might be more easily induced to keep to one alone. Secondly, supposing then that there were material faults in their marriages, the necessity of a renewal was not spoken of but for the time which followed baptism, and this took place the day following that happy occasion.

After the Fathers had gained the necessary information respecting the degrees of relationship, and had given the necessary dispensations, the marriage ceremony, preceded by a short instruction, was performed, and contributed greatly to give the people a high idea of our holy religion.

The twenty-four marriages then contracted presented that mixture of simplicity, of respectful affection and profound joy, which are the sure indications of a good conscience. There were among the couples good old men and women; but their presence only rendered the ceremony more respectable in the eyes of those assembled; for among the Flatheads all that relates to religion is sacred; unhappy he who would so express himself before them as to lead them to believe that he thought otherwise. They left the chapel, their hearts filled with sentiments purified by that grace which constitutes the charm of every state of life, and especially of those in wedlock.

The only thing that appeared strange to them was when the Fathers spoke of taking the names of witnesses; but when they were told that this was only done because the church so ordained, to give more authority and dignity to the marriage contract, they no longer saw in it anything but what was reasonable, and the question was, who should be witness for the others?

The same astonishment was manifested with regard to godfathers. The interpreter had translated the word godfather, a term which is not in their language, by second father. The poor savages not knowing what this meant, or what consequences this title would imply, were not eager to make a choice. To be a godfather moreover offered no great attraction. As soon as we made them understand it, their difficulties vanished, and the more easily; for not to multiply spiritual affinities, a godfather only was given to the men, and a godmother to the women; and as to the obligations attached to the honor of being sponsors, they were much less here than elsewhere, the Black-robes promising to take upon themselves the greatest part of the burden. For the first baptisms our choice of sponsors was very limited; only thirteen grown persons were qualified to act in this capacity — but the most aged persons being baptized before the others, they, without laying aside the lighted candle, (the symbol of faith) were chosen for the second division; and so in like manner with the rest.

The day preceding the baptism, the Fathers, on account of their labors, were only able to collect the colony twice; besides Father Mengarini was indisposed. In the evening, however, he assembled the people, and great was their astonishment on beholding the decorations of the chapel. Some days previously the Fathers had engaged all who were willing, to make mats of rushes or straws. All the women, girls and children assembled eagerly for this good work, so that they had enough to cover the floor and ceiling and hang around the walls. These mats, ornamented with festoons of green, made a pretty drapery around the altar. On a canopy was inscribed the holy name of Jesus. Among the ornaments they placed a picture of the Blessed Virgin over the tabernacle; on the door of the tabernacle a representation of the heart of Jesus. The pictures of the way of the cross, in red frames; the lights, the silence of night, the approach of the important day, the calm after the hurricane, which had burst on them only a few moments before — all these circumstances united had, with the grace of God, so well disposed the minds and hearts of our Indians, that it would have been scarcely possible to find on earth an assembly of savages more resembling a company of saints.

This was the beautiful bouquet which the Fathers were permitted to present to Saint Francis Xavier. The next day they were engaged from eight o'clock in the morning until half-past ten at night, in the church, excepting only one hour and a half, which they gave to repose. The following was the order followed. First, they baptized the chiefs and married men. These were chosen as godfathers for the young men and little boys; then the married women, whose husbands were living with them; afterward the widows and wives who had been cast off; and lastly the young women and girls.

It was gratifying to hear with what intelligence these good savages replied to all the questions addressed to them, and to see them praying at the moment of receiving baptism. At the end, each received a taper whose blended light beautifully illuminated our humble chapel.

But let us come to something still more edifying. I shall not speak of their assiduous attendance at the instructions — of their eagerness to hear our words — of the evident profit they received from them; all this is common in the course of a mission; but rarely do we witness the heroic sacrifices which these Indians have made. Many who had two wives have retained her whose children were most numerous, and with all possible respect dismissed the other. One evening, a savage came to seek the Fathers at the lodge, which was filled with Indians, and unabashed by any merely human consideration, asked what he should do in his present circumstances? On the instant he acted according to the instructions given him; he dismissed his youngest wife, giving her what he would have wished another to give to his sister, if in the same situation, and was reunited to his first wife, whom he had forsaken. After an instruction, a young woman, asking to speak, said that "she desired very much to receive baptism, but that she had been so wicked she dared not make the request." Each one would have made a public confession. A great number of young mothers, married according to the mode of

the savages, but abandoned by their husbands, who were
of some other tribe, renounced them most willingly, to have
the happiness of being baptized.

The ordinary regulations observed in the village are as
follows: When the Angelus rings, the Indians rise from
sleep; half an hour after, the morning prayers are said in
common; all assist at mass and at the instruction. A
second instruction is given at evening, toward sunset, and
lasts about an hour and a quarter. At two o'clock in the
afternoon we have the regular catechism for the children,
at which grown persons may assist if they think proper.
The children are formed into two divisions: the first is
composed exclusively of those who know the first prayers;
the second of the smaller children. One of the Fathers
each morning visits the sick, to furnish them with medicines,
and give them such assistance as their wants may require.

We have adopted the system of instruction and bestowing
rewards, in usage in the schools of the brothers of the Christian doctrine. During catechism, which lasts about an hour,
we have recitations and explanations, intermingled with
canticles. Every day, for each good answer, tickets of
approbation are given; one or more, according to the difficulty of the question proposed. Experience has proved
that these tickets given at once, are less embarrassing than
when we mark their names on a list; the former plan takes
less time, and interests the children more, rendering them,
besides, more assiduous and careful. These tickets serve,
at the same time, as certificates of attendance at catechism,
and as tokens of intelligence and good will, they please the
parent not less than their children. The former are in-
cited to make their children repeat what has been said at
catechism, to render them capable of answering better the
following day; and also with a desire of improving themselves. The wish to see their children distinguish themselves, has attracted almost the whole colony to catechism;
none of the chiefs who have children fail to be there; and
there is not less emulation among the parents than among

the children themselves. A still greater value is attached to the tickets, from the exactitude and justice with which the deserving are rewarded. They who have obtained good tickets during the week, are rewarded on Sunday with crosses, medals, or ribbons, publicly distributed. On the first Sunday of every month they distribute to those who have received the most good tickets in the course of the month, medals or pictures, which become their private property. These pictures, preserved with care, are great stimulants, not only to the study of their catechism but also to the practice of piety. They are monuments of victory, examples of virtue, exhortations to piety, and models of perfection. Their rarity, and the efforts necessary to obtain them, also enhance their worth. As we desire to inspire the savages, who are naturally inclined to idleness, with a love for work, it has been judged suitable to reward their little efforts in the same manner as we recompense their improvement in, and knowledge of their catechism.

To maintain order, and promote emulation among them, the catechism children are divided into seven or eight sections, of six each; the boys on one side, the girls on the other. At the head of each section there is a chief, who must assist the children placed under him to learn their catechism; that thus every child may indulge the hope of meriting a reward at the end of the week or month. They are so divided that the competitors, to the number of five or six in each section, may be of nearly equal capacity.

Father Point, who was, immediately after Christmas, to accompany the assembled camps of Flatheads, Pend d'Oreilles, Nez Percés, etc., prepared for his new campaign by a retreat of eight days. Twenty-four marriages, as I have already said, had been celebrated during my absence, and 202 adults, with little boys and girls from eight to fourteen years of age, had been baptized. There were still thirty-four couples, who awaited my return to receive the sacraments of baptism and marriage, or to renew their marriage vows. The Nez Percés had not yet presented their

22

children for baptism. There was an old chief of the Blackfeet nation, in the camp, with his son and his little family,
five in all, who had been hitherto very assiduous in their
attendance at prayers and catechism. The day succeeding
my arrival I commenced giving three instructions daily, besides the catechism, which was taught by the other Fathers.
They profited so well that, with the grace of God,
115 Flatheads, with three chiefs at their head, thirty
Nez Percés with their chief, and the Blackfoot chief and his
family, presented themselves at the baptismal font on Christmas day. I began my masses at seven o'clock in the morning; at five o'clock P. M. I still found myself in the chapel.
The heart can conceive, but the tongue cannot express the
emotions which such a consoling spectacle may well awaken.
The following day I celebrated a solemn mass of thanksgiving for the signal favors with which our Lord had deigned
to visit his people. From six to seven hundred new Christians, with bands of little children, baptized in the past year
— all assembled in a poor little chapel, covered with rushes
— in the midst of a desert, where but lately the name of God
was scarcely known; offering to the Creator their regenerated hearts, protesting that they would persevere in his
holy service even to death, was an offering, without doubt,
most agreeable to God, and which, we trust, will draw down
the dews of heaven upon the Flathead nation and the neighboring tribes.

On the 29th the large camp, accompanied by the Fathers,
left us for the great buffalo hunt, and joined the Pend
d'Oreilles, who awaited them at two days' journey hence;
there will be above 200 lodges. I am filled with
hope for the success and fresh victories, with which, I trust,
God will deign to reward the zeal of his servant. In the
meantime we occupy ourselves (Father Mengarini and myself) in translating the catechism into the Flathead tongue;
and in preparing 150 persons for their first communion.

Our good Brothers and the Canadians are engaged at the
same time in erecting around our establishment a strong

palisade, fortified with bastions, to shelter us from the incursions of the Blackfeet, whom we daily expect to visit us. Our confidence in God is not weakened; we take the precautions which prudence dictates, and remain without fear at our post.

A young Sinpoil[5] has just arrived in our camp, and these are his words: " I am a Sinpoil, my nation is compassionate. I have been sent to hear your words, and learn the prayer you teach the Flatheads. The Sinpoils desire also to know it, and to imitate their example." This young man proposes to pass the winter in our camp, and return in the spring to his own nation, to sow among them the seeds of the gospel.

The whole Flathead nation converted — 400 Kalispels baptized — eighty Nez Percés, seven Cœurs d'Alène, many Kootenais, Blackfeet, Snakes and Bannocks — the Sinpoils, the Chaudières, who open their arms to us, and eagerly ask for Fathers to instruct them; the earnest demands from Fort Vancouver on the part of the Governor [Doctor McLoughlin], and of the Reverend Mr. Blanchet, assuring us of the good desires and dispositions of a great number of nations, ready to receive the gospel — in a word, a vast country, which only awaits the arrival of true ministers of God, to rally round the standard of the cross — behold the beautiful bouquet, Reverend Father, which we have the happiness of presenting you at the close of 1841. It is at the foot of the crucifix that you are accustomed to ask counsel of heaven for the welfare of the nations entrusted to your children. Our number is very far from sufficient for the pressing and real wants of this people. The Protestants are on the *qui vive*. Send us then some Fathers and Brothers to assist us, and thousands of souls will bless you at the throne of God for all eternity.

[5] A tribe of the Salishan family is evidently meant, whose name is commonly spelled Cinq Poils or Sans Puells — both French transliterations of a native name.

Madison Fork, August 15, 1842.

Reverend and Dear Father:

*   *   *   *   *   *   *   *   *

Our only building as yet was a wooden house, without a roof, and the winter had already set in. We began by recommending our wants to God, and with God's assistance we found ourselves, on St. Martin's day, in possession of a temporary chapel, large enough to contain all the colony, with about 100 of the Nez Percés tribe, whom curiosity had attracted to the neighborhood. Since that period they have been so careful in avoiding sin, so exact in attending our instructions, and the fruit of the divine word has been so visible in our settlement that on the 3d of December 202 catechumens were ranged in our chapel, waiting for baptism. This was too beautiful an offering to St. Francis Xavier, apostle of the Indians, not to excite the fury of man's great enemy. Accordingly, for a few days previously we encountered multiplied trials. To speak only of the most visible, the prefect, interpreter and sexton fell sick. The very eve of the great day the environs were laid waste by a sort of hurricane — the church windows were broken, large trees were rooted up, and three huts were thrown down; but these obstacles, far from prejudicing the triumph of religion, served only to render it still more striking.

The catechumens having assembled in the chapel, which had been adorned with its most beautiful ornaments, and where they had been conducted for the more immediate preparations of their hearts prior to receiving the great sacrament of baptism, were so struck by the imposing appearance of the chapel and the melodious sounds of the organ, now heard for the first time in the wilderness, that they were not able to express their admiration. The next day, with the exception of the time the Fathers took for their dinner, they were in church from eight o'clock in the morning until half-past ten in the evening. How delightful it was to listen to the intelligent answers of the good savages to all the questions proposed to them. Never will those who were present forget the pious spirit of their replies. The rehabilitations of their marriages succeeded baptism, but not without great sacrifices on their part, because until that time the poor Indians had been ignorant of the unity and indissolubility of the conjugal tie. We could not help admiring the mighty effects of the sacrament of baptism in their souls. One poor husband hesitated as to which of his wives he should select. The oldest of them, perceiving his irresolution, said to him: " You know how much I love you, and I am also certain that you love me, but you cherish another more; she is younger than I am. Well, remain with her; leave me our children, and in that manner we can all be baptized." I could cite many such traits.

*   *   *   *   *   *   *   *.   *

CHAPTER VIII.[1]

JOURNEY TO FORT COLVILLE AND RETURN.

Autumn of 1841.

Need of provisions and seeds — Start for Fort Colville — Hell Gate — Animals of the country — The ingenious carcajou — Meetings with Indians — Kalispels raising potatoes — Scenery and dangers of Clark's Fork — Large timber — Lake Pend d'Oreille — Arrival at Colville — Hospitality of Macdonald — Return journey — Adam and Eve and the buffalo fat — Hell unchained among the Kalispels — Sixty baptisms.

¶ HAVE just finished a little journey to Fort Colville on the Columbia river, about 320 miles from our establishment. Although the season was far advanced, two reasons determined me to make the journey: First, we had to have provisions for the winter; seeds for the coming spring; tools for the Indians so well disposed to work; cattle, and in short whatever the establishment of our first réduction required: second, my desire to visit the Pend d'Oreilles who generally spend the autumn upon Clark's Fork.

On the eve of my departure I informed the Flatheads of my intentions. I requested them to procure some horses, and a small escort, in case I should meet with any of their enemies, the Blackfeet. They brought to me seventeen horses, the number I had asked them; and ten young and brave warriors, who had already been often pierced with

---

[1] This chapter comprises a portion of Book II, *Letters and Sketches,* purporting to have been written at the Madison Forks, August 15, 1842, and Letter IX, Second Voyage, *Voyages aux Montagnes-Rocheuses,* dated St. Mary's, December 28, 1841, and addressed " To A Father of the Company of Jesus." The two are parallel, but the French narrative contains additional matter, here translated for the first time. Aside from this, the English text is followed.

balls and arrows in different skirmishes, presented themselves to accompany me on my journey. With pleasure I
bear testimony to their devotedness, their childlike simplicity and docility, politeness, complaisance and rare hilarity;
but, above all, to their exemplary piety. These good Flatheads endeavored in every manner to divine and anticipate
all my wants.

On the afternoon of the 28th of October, as I have already said, we commenced our march, and made about forty
miles down the valley of the Bitter Root. That day we met
no one but a solitary hunter, who was carrying a buck, the
half of which he offered to us with great eagerness. This
furnished us with an excellent supper, and a good breakfast for the next morning. The 29th, snow fell in large
flakes, notwithstanding which we continued our march. We
crossed, in the course of the day, a fine stream, without a
name [Lolo Fork] — the same one which the famous travelers, Lewis and Clark, ascended in 1805, on their way to the
section of country occupied by the tribe of the Nez Percés.
I will call it the river of St. Francis Borgia. Six miles
further south we crossed the beautiful river of St. Ignatius
[Hell Gate]. It enters the plain of the Bitter Root — which
we shall henceforward call St. Mary's — by a beautiful defile, commonly called, by the mountaineers or Canadian
hunters, the Hell Gate; for what reason, however, I know
not. These gentlemen have frequently on their lips the
words devil and hell; and it is perhaps on this account that
we heard so often these appellations. Be not then alarmed
when I tell you that I examined the Devil's pass, went
through the Devil's gate, rowed on Satan's stream, and
jumped from the Devil's horns. The "rake," [2] one of the
passes, the horns, and the stream, really deserve names that
express something horrible — all three are exceedingly dangerous. The first and second, on the Missouri, on account
of the innumerable snags which fill their beds, as there are
entire forests swallowed up by the river. The third pass of

[2] See *ante*, p. 153.

which I spoke, adds to the difficulties of the others a current still stronger. A canoe launched into this torrent flies over it with the speed of an arrow, and the most experienced pilot trembles in spite of himself. Twice did the brave Iroquois, who conducted our light canoe, exclaim: " Father, we are lost;" but a loud cry of " Courage — take courage, John, confide in God, keep steady to the oar," saved us in that dangerous stream, drew us out from between the horns and threatening teeth of this awful " rake."

But let us return to our account of the journey to Colville. We spread our skins on the borders of a little river at the foot of a high mountain, which we were to cross the next day, having traversed St. Mary's valley, a distance of about forty miles. This valley is from four to seven miles wide, and above 200 long. It has but one fine defile, already mentioned, and which serves as the entrance to, and issue from, the valley. The mountains which terminate it on both sides appear to be inaccessible; they are piles of jagged rocks, the base of which presents nothing but fragments of the same description, while the Norwegian pine grows on those that are covered with earth, giving them a very sombre appearance, particularly in the autumn, in which season the snow begins to fall. They abound in bucks, buffalo and sheep, whose wool is as white as snow and as fine as silk; also in all kinds of bears, wolves, panthers and carcajoux (an animal with short paws, some four feet long and remarkably powerful; when he has killed his prey, deer, antelope or bighorn, he tears off a piece of skin big enough to stick his head through after the fashion of a hood, and thus drags it off whole to his den). There are also found tiger cats, wild cats and whistlers, a species of mountain rat. The moose is found here, but is very seldom caught, on account of its extraordinary vigilance, for on the slightest rustling of a branch it leaves off eating, and will not return to its food for a long time afterward.

The soil of the valley is, with some few exceptions, very light; it contains, however, some good pastures. The whole course of the river is well lined with trees; especially with the pine, the fir, cottonwood and willow trees.

Amongst the most remarkable birds we distinguished the Nun's eagle (so called by travelers on account of the color of its head, which is white, whilst the other parts of the body are black), the black eagle, buzzard, waterfowl, heron, crane, pheasant and quail.

The 30th, three horses were found to have strayed off while grazing freely during the night (a liberty which they rarely abuse) and we could not start until eleven o'clock in the morning. We then ascended a gap in the mountain. The two sides were very lofty and studded with large pines, all the branches of which were covered with a black and very fine moss, that hung in festoons, or in the shape of mourning garlands, and added to the already funereal appearance of this pass. We here filed off by a little path, scarce worthy, however, of the name, for a distance of six miles. The road was filled with large blocks of stone and trunks of trees, placed as if on purpose to render the pass difficult and impracticable. The summit once attained, we proceeded to cross a smiling little plain, called the Camas Prairies, where the Flatheads come every spring to dig up that nourishing root, which, together with the game they are able to procure, forms their chief nourishment. We very soon descended the mountain in a zigzag direction, and reached a beautiful plain, which is watered by two rivers, the St. Aloysius and St. Stanislaus. They unite in this plain, whence they go to join the forks at Clark's, otherwise called the Flathead river. This valley extends about ten miles. While the tents were being set up I perceived one of those formidable Blackfoot Indians in the act of hiding himself. I did not speak of it to my young companions, fearing that I might not be able to prevent a bloody struggle between them. I, however, took the precaution of having a good watch kept over our horses.

The next day was Sunday, a day of rest. I celebrated the holy sacrifice of the mass, and baptized three little children of the Pointed Hearts' tribe, whose parents had joined us on the road. The rest of the day was spent in prayer and instructions. The chief of our band, Técousten, twice addressed his companions, and spoke with much force and precision on the different portions of our religion, which he already had heard explained.

The 1st of November — All Saints' Day — after having celebrated the holy sacrifice under a large poplar tree, we proceeded on our journey through a defile of about six miles. At the ford of Clark's Fork, we met two encampments of the Kalispel tribe, who, having heard of our approach, had come thither to see us. Men, women and children ran to meet us, and pressed our hands with every demonstration of sincere joy. The chief of the first camp was called Chalax. As we had a barren country ahead of us, he procured six bales of buffalo meat for us. I baptized twenty-four children in his little village, and one young woman, a Kootenai, who was dying. The chief of the second camp was named Hoy-telpo; his band occupied thirty huts. I spent the night amongst them; and, although they had never seen me before, they knew all the prayers that I had taught the Flatheads on my first journey. The fact is, on hearing of my arrival in the mountains, they deputed an intelligent young man to meet me, and who was also gifted with a good memory. Having learned the prayers and canticles, and such points as were most essential for salvation, he repeated to the village all that he had heard and seen. He had acquitted himself of his commission so well, and with so much zeal, that he gave instructions to his people during the course of the winter. The same desire for information concerning religion had communicated itself to the other small camps, and with the same cheering success. It was, as you can easily imagine, a great consolation for me to see the sign of the cross and hear prayers addressed to the great God, and his praises sung, in a desert of about 300 miles extent, where a Catholic priest had never been before. They were overjoyed when they heard that I hoped before long to be able to leave a missionary amongst them. They had already taken a step toward the civilized life by attempting the cultivation of potatoes. They offered me some, which were the first I had seen since I left the United States. Their lodges are made of mats of rushes, like those of the Potawatomies, east of the mountains.

I cannot pass over in silence a beautiful custom that is observed by these good people: every evening, after prayers, the chief instructs his people, or gives them some salutary advice, to which they all listen with most profound attention, respect and modesty. To see them at their devotions one would be more apt to mistake them for members of a religious order than savages. The next day, before my departure, I baptized twenty-seven children of the tribe.

That morning we crossed a mountain and entered the great Camas plain. Wolves are very numerous and very ferocious here; last spring they carried off and devoured more than forty of the Kalispels' horses. There is a boiling spring a short distance to the northeast. A mountainous defile ten miles long led us thence to the lovely Horse Prairie. A fine little lake, about six miles around, at the entrance to this prairie, I called the Lake of Souls, in honor of the church festival celebrated to-day. On that evening we alighted amongst fifteen huts of the same nation, who received us with equal kindness. Their chief had come several miles to meet me. He acknowledged frankly that having become acquainted with some American ministers, in the course of the summer — he had been told by them that my prayer (religion) was not a good one. "My heart is divided," said he, "and I do not know what to adhere to." I had no trouble in making him understand the difference between those gentlemen and priests, and the cause of their calumnious attacks against the only true church of Christ, which their ancestors had abandoned.

On the 3d of November, after prayers and instructions to the savages, we continued our march. We were on the borders of Clark's Fork, to which we were obliged to keep close during eight days, whilst we descended the country bordering the stream. The river is at this place of a greenish blue, very transparent, caused probably by the deposit of a great quantity of oxigen of iron [*sic*]. Our path during a great part of the day was on the declivity of a lofty, rocky mountain; we were here obliged to climb a steep rough pass from 400 to 600 feet high. I had before seen landscapes of awful grandeur, but this one certainly surpassed all others in horror. My courage failed at the first sight; it was impossible to remain on horseback, and on foot my weight of 211 pounds was no trifle. This, therefore, was the expedient to which I resorted: my mule Lizette was sufficiently docile and kind to allow me to grasp her tail, to which I held on firmly: crying at one moment aloud, and at other times making use of the whip to excite her courage, until the good beast conducted me safely to the very top of the mountain. There I breathed freely for a while, and contemplated the magnificent prospect that presented itself to my sight. The windings of the river with the scenery on its banks were before me; on one side hung over our heads rocks piled on rocks in the most precipitous manner, and on the other stood lofty peaks crowned with snow and pine trees: mountains of every shape and feature reared their towering forms before us. It really was a fine view and one which was well worth the effort we had made. On descending from this elevation I had to take new precautions. I preceded the mule, holding her by the bridle, while she moved cautiously down to the foot of the " Bad Rock " (as it is called by the savages), as though she feared stumbling and rolling with her master into the river which flowed beneath us.

At this place Clark's Fork runs through a narrow defile of rocky mountains; at times the soft murmurings of the waters charm the traveler, at others it spreads out and presents a calm surface clear as crystal. Wherever it is narrowed or intercepted by rocks it forms rapids, with falls and cascades; the noise of which, like that caused by a storm in the forest, is heard at a great distance. Nothing can be more diversified than this fine river. There is in this vicinity a great variety of trees, bushes and different species of the tamarisk tree. The lichnis, a medicinal plant mentioned by Charlevoix in his history of Canada, grows here abundantly.

We met in the course of that day with only one family, and that was of the Kalispel tribe. Whilst the women were rowing up the river their light canoe, made of fir-tree bark, which contained their children and all the baggage, the men followed along the bank with their rifles or bows in their hands in pursuit of game. In all the little meadows or bottom-lands that we traversed, we saw a great number of horses, which the savages leave there, unguarded, often for months at a time; this they call "caging" the horses; in fact, they seldom wander very far away.

On the 4th we entered a cedar and pine forest so dense that in its whole length we could scarcely see beyond the distance of twenty yards. Our beasts of burden suffered a great deal in it from the want of grass. We scarcely got through it after three days' march. It was a real labyrinth; from morning till night we did nothing but wind about to avoid thousands of trees, fallen from either fire, storms or age. On issuing from this forest we were charmed by an interesting prospect: Our view extended over the whole surface of the lake called Pend d'Oreille, studded with small islands covered with woods: over its inlets and the hills which overlook them, and which have for the most part their base on the borders of the lake and rise by gradual terraces or elevations until they reach the adjoining mountains, which are covered with perpetual snow. The lake is about thirty miles long and from four to seven wide. Another spectacle, still more magnificent, had arrested our attention before we reached the lake. At the head of it we traversed a forest, which is certainly a wonder of its kind; there is probably nothing similar to it in America. The savages speak of it as the finest in Oregon, and really every tree which it contains is enormous in its kind. The birch, elm and beach, generally small elsewhere, like the toad of

La Fontaine, that aimed at being as large as the ox, swell out here to twice their size. They would fain rival the cedar, the Goliath of the forest, who, however, looking down with contempt upon his pitiful companions,

> " Elève aux cieux
> Son front audacieux."

The birch and beech at its side resemble large candelabra placed around a massive column. Cedars of four and five fathoms in circumference are here very common; we saw some six, and I measured one forty-two feet in circumference. A cedar of four fathoms, lying on the ground, measured more than 200 feet in length. The delicate branches of these noble trees entwine themselves above the beech and elm; their fine, dense and ever-green foliage forming an arch through which the sun's rays never penetrate; and this lofty vault, supported by thousands of columns, brought to the mind's eye the idea of an immense temple, reared by the hand of nature to the glory of its Author.

Before entering the forest we crossed a high mountain by a wild winding path. Its sides are covered with fine cedars and pines, which are, however, of smaller dimensions than those in the forest. Several times whilst ascending the mountain I found myself on parapets of rocks, whence, thanks to my safe-footed mule, I retired in safety. Once I thought my career at an end. I had wandered from my companions, and following the path, I all at once came to a rocky projection which terminated in a point about two feet wide; before me was a perpendicular descent of three feet; on my left stood a rock as straight as a wall, and on my right yawned a precipice of about a thousand feet. You can conceive that my situation was anything but pleasant. The slightest false step would have plunged the mule and her rider into the abyss beneath. To descend was impossible, as on one side I was closed in by the rock, and suspended over a dreadful chasm on the other. My mule had stopped at the commencement of the descent, and not having any time to lose, I recommended myself to God, and as a last expedient sank my spurs deeply into the sides of my poor beast; she made one bold leap and safely landed me on another parapet much larger than that I had left.

The history of the fine forest, and my leap from the dangerous rock, will be treated with incredulity by many of your acquaintance. If so, tell them that I invite them to visit both these places: "*Venite et videte.*" I promise them beforehand that they will admire with me the wonders of nature. They will have, like me, their moments of admiration and of fear.

I cannot pass over in silence the pleasant meeting I had in the depth of the forest. I discovered a little hut of rushes, situated on the banks of the river. Raising my voice to its highest pitch, I tried to make its inhabitants hear me, but received no answer. I felt an irresistible desire to visit it, and accordingly made my interpreter accompany me. We found it occupied by a poor old woman, who was blind and very ill. I spoke to her of the Great Spirit, of the most essential dogmas of our faith and of baptism. The example of the Apostle St. Philip teaches us that there are cases when all the requisite dispositions may entirely consist in an act of faith, and in the sincere desire to enter heaven by the right path. All the answers of the poor old woman were respectful, and breathing the love of God. "Yes," she would say, " I love the Great Spirit with my whole heart; all my life he has been very kind to me. Yes, I wish to be his child, I want to be his forever." And immediately she fell on her knees and begged me to give her baptism. I named her Mary, and placed around her neck the miraculous medal of the Blessed Virgin. After leaving her, I overheard her thanking God for this fortunate adventure.

I had scarcely regained the path, when I met her husband, almost bent to the earth by age and infirmity; he could hardly drag himself along. He had been setting a trap in the forest for the bucks. The Flatheads who had preceded me had told him of my arrival. As soon, therefore, as he perceived me, he began to cry out, with a trembling voice: " Oh, how delighted I am to see our Father before I die. The Great Spirit is good — oh, how happy my heart is." And the venerable old man pressed my hand most affectionately, repeating again and again the same expressions. Tears fell from my eyes on witnessing such affection. I told him that I had just left his hut, and had baptized his wife. " I heard," said he, " of your arrival in our mountains, and of your baptizing many of our people. I am poor and old; I had hardly dared to hope for the happiness of seeing you. Black-gown, make me as happy as you have made my wife. I wish also to belong to God, and we will always love him." I conducted him to the borders of a stream that flowed near us, and after a brief instruction, I administered to him the holy sacrament of baptism, naming him Simon. On seeing me depart, he repeated, impressively: " Oh, how good is the Great Spirit. I thank you, Skylax (Black-robe), for the favor you have conferred on me. Oh, how happy is my heart. Yes, I will always love the Great Spirit. Oh, how good the Great Spirit is; how good he is."

During that same journey, I discovered in a little hut of bulrushes five old men, who appeared to be fourscore years old. Three of them were blind, and the other two had but one eye each; they were almost naked, and offered a real personification of human misery. I spoke to them for a considerable time on the means of salvation, and on the bliss of another world. Their answers edified me much, and affected me even to tears; they were replete with the love of God, a desire of doing right and of dying well. You might have heard these good old men crying out from different parts of the hut, forming together a touching chorus, to which I sincerely wished that all the children of St. Ignatius could have listened. " O Great Spirit, what a happiness is coming to us in our old days! We will love you, O Great Spirit. *Le-mele Kaikolinzoeten; one le-mele eltelill.* We will love you, O Great Spirit. Yes, we will love you till death."

When we explained to them the necessity of baptism, they demanded it earnestly, and knelt down to receive it. I have not found as yet amongst these Indians, I will not say opposition, but not even coldness or indifference.

These little adventures are our great consolation. I would not have exchanged my situation, at that moment, for any other on earth. I was convinced that such incidents alone were worth a journey to the mountains. Ah, good and dear fathers, who may read these lines, I conjure you, through the mercy of our Divine Redeemer, not to hesitate entering this vineyard; its harvest is ripe and abundant. Does not our Savior tell us: " *Ignem veni mittere in terram et quid volo nisi ut accendatur?* " It is amidst the poor tribes of these isolated mountains that the fire of divine grace burns with ardor. Superstitious practices have disappeared; nor have they amongst them the castes of East India. Speak to these savages of heavenly things; at once their hearts are inflamed with divine love; and immediately they go seriously about the great affair of their salvation. Day and night they are at our sides, insatiable for the Bread of Life. Often, on retiring, we hear them say, " Our sins, no doubt, rendered us so long unworthy to hear these consoling words."

As to privations and dangers, the Oregon missionaries must expect them, for they will certainly meet them, but in a good cause. Sometimes they will be obliged to fast, but a better appetite will be their reward. Their escapes from the many dangers of the road, or from enemies always on the alert, teach them to confide in God alone,

23

and ever to keep their accounts in order. I here feel the full application of that consoling text of the scripture: "My yoke is sweet, and my burden is light." At the last day it will be manifest that the holy name of Jesus has performed wonders amongst these poor people. Their eagerness to hear the glad tidings of salvation is certainly at its height. They came from all parts and from great distances, to meet me on my way, and presented all their young children and dying relatives for baptism. Many followed me for whole days, with the sole desire of receiving instructions. Really our hearts bled at the sight of so many souls who are lost for the want of religion's divine and saving assistance. Here again may we cry out with the scripture: "The harvest indeed is great, but the laborers are few." What Father is there in the Society whose zeal will not be enkindled on hearing these details? And where is the Christian who would refuse his mite to such a work as that of the Propagation of the Faith? that precious pearl of the Church, which procures salvation to so many souls who otherwise would perish unaided and forever.

During my journey, which lasted forty-two days, I baptized 190 persons, of whom twenty-six were adults, sick, or in extreme old age; I preached to more than 2,000 Indians; who, thus evidently conducted into my way by Providence, will not, I trust, tarry long in ranging themselves under the banner of Jesus Christ. With the assistance of my catechists, the Flatheads, who were as yet but catechumens, the conversion of the Kalispel tribe was so far advanced that when the time came round for the winter's hunting, the Reverend Father Point enjoyed the consolation of seeing them join the Flathead tribe, with the sole desire of profiting by the missionary's presence. This gave him an opportunity to instruct and baptize a great number on the Purification and on the feasts of the Canonization of St. Ignatius and St. Francis Xavier.

I found among these Indians several little children that

had been baptized by the reverend and zealous M. Demers,[3] a Canadian priest resident at Willamette, not far from the Pacific, and who has made a number of excursions as far as Fort Colville.

We spent Sunday, the 7th of November, in devotional practices with three Kalispel families on the shore of the lake of that name, where we had arrived the evening before, as I related above. Two boats loaded with merchandise, in charge of eight half-breeds in the employ of the Hudson Bay Company, also arrived in time to assist at the divine offices. Among them was Charles, the Flathead interpreter who had rendered me such great services the year before. I gave thanks to God for this fortunate meeting; he was on his way to join me again for this year. I owe this excellent interpreter to the worthy and respectable governor of the Hudson Bay Company, Mr. McLoughlin,[4] in whose service Charles was engaged.

[3] Modeste Demers, born near Quebec in 1808; crossed the continent with Reverend F. N. Blanchet in 1838, to make a beginning of Catholic work on Puget Sound; first bishop of Vancouver Island; died at Victoria, July 28, 1871. Frequently mentioned in the present work.

[4] Doctor John McLoughlin is one of the grand historic characters of Oregon. He was born in Canada, October 19, 1784. Educated in Paris, but entered the fur trade in the Northwest Company service at an early age. About 1818 he married a Scotch-Indian half-breed, widow of Alexander McKay who was killed in the Tonquin massacre. In 1824 he was transferred to the Columbia river, where he soon rose to the position of Chief Factor, or "Governor." He selected the site of Fort Vancouver and transferred his headquarters there from Astoria in 1825-6. He was brought up in the Anglican Church, but became a Catholic after the missionaries of that faith came to Oregon. He resigned from the Hudson Bay Company service in 1845 and retired to private life at Oregon City. He became a naturalized citizen of the United States. His later years were embittered by land controversies, where his claims to important holdings were challenged by the immigrants. He died September 7, 1857.

He was a man of great dignity and force and of an extraordinarily fine presence. He was always scrupulously just and generous to the immigrants from the States and drew upon himself the criticism of his own people for his course in this respect. Many are the instances

We were three days in reaching the traverse of the Kalispels. Along the river we found at intervals a great number of little Indian camps of four to six lodges. These poor folk are obliged to scatter in winter to procure food by fishing and hunting. The Pend d'Oreille Traverse offers a fine location for a mission. There is a large and fertile prairie, wood will never fail, the river abounds in fish. At the bottom of the prairie is a little lake or marsh, about six miles in circumference, which is a rendezvous for all sorts of aquatic birds. A large number of Indian tribes would there be close at hand; the Cœur d'Alènes, the Spokans, the Kettles, the Simpoils,[5] the Kootenais, the Gens-du-lac, the Nez Percés and several others, are scarce more than two or three days' travel away. Besides Fort Colville is within a long day's ride, which would make it very easy to procure victuals, tools and clothing.

On the 13th we were eight hours in crossing a lofty snow-covered mountain. That evening, we had no more than made our camp, upon a little stream [Mill creek] which runs into the Columbia river, when we received a visit from several Kalispels. I was agreeably surprised by the petition of one of them: " I am just in from a hunt," he said, " where I have killed a deer; it is too late now to go after it, and to-morrow is the day of the Great Spirit (Sunday); would you permit me, Black-robe, to bring it home to-morrow, because my little children are fasting?" Admirable lesson for the Christians of Europe! This savage had never seen a priest but once in his life. Another made me a present of a goose that he had killed, a third gave me a little basket full of camas. I spent Sunday with them, to their great satisfaction.

After dinner next day [November 15th] we went on to the fort [Colville]. There we passed three days in repairing our saddles and packing our provisions and seeds. Wher-

recorded of his noble acts to those who were in need, even when they came to his country on missions of commercial rivalry.

[5] Native form Snpuelish or Snpoiliqiq.

ever one finds the gentlemen of the Hudson Bay Company, one is sure of a good reception. They do not stop with demonstrations of politeness and affability, they anticipate your wishes in order to be of service to you. In this case, the commandant of the fort, Mr. Macdonald,[6] a Scot by birth, went so far as to have his lady prepare and put among our provisions, without my knowledge, all sorts of little extras, such as sugar, coffee, tea, chocolate, butter, crackers, flour, poultry, ham and candles.

Besides the instruction that I gave during mass to the Canadians employed at the fort, I had several conferences with the chief of the Skoyelpi or Kettle Indians, an intelligent man, who invited me to come and evangelize his nation. We left the fort on the 18th. Nothing very noteworthy happened during the return journey, unless it be a matter, which I will set down for the instruction of any who might be going our way; it only shows how useful it is sometimes to be distrustful, and that children of Eve are to be found everywhere. We had left with the Pend d'Oreilles five bales of dried meat. On our return we found only two; I asked the chief what had become of the others. "I am ashamed, Black-robe," he answered; "I am afraid to speak to you. You know that I was absent when you left your bales in my lodge. My wife opened them to see whether the meat had molded; the dépouilles (that is, the fat) looked so fair and so good that she tasted. When I came in, she offered me thereof, and to our children as well; the news was spread through the village; the neighbors came, and we all ate together." A few days more, and we would have found none at all. If this honest man had tried to imitate the history of our first parents, he could not have played his part better. This adventure

___

[6] Archibald Macdonald, for twenty years previous to this time in the service of the Hudson Bay Company; founder of Fort Nisqually; entrusted with many important positions. In 1828 he accompanied George Simpson (later Sir George) on his tour of inspection, and afterward published a journal of the voyage.

gave me my occasion to instruct them in regard to this first of prevarications and its sad consequences. When I had finished the chief spoke again, and after scolding his wife well he protested in the name of all concerned that it would not happen again. Then these poor people tried as best they could to indemnify us, and offered us two bags of wild roots and a basket full of cakes of pine-moss, as hard as glue. Necessity compelled us to accept these novel cakes; they are prepared by boiling in water; they then form a thick elastic soup, having the appearance and the taste of soap. It can be eaten, if seasoned with a good appetite and a prolonged absence of other nourishment.

On the 1st of December I found myself again in Horse Prairie, among the Kalispels, who had repaired thither from different parts of the mountains to see me as I returned. I stayed with them three days, instructing and exhorting them from morning till evening. My ten young Flatheads all assumed the functions of catechists, and went about it with a zeal which could be equaled only by the assiduity, attention and eagerness to learn of the savages who listened to them. On the 3d, the feast of St. Francis Xavier, I baptized sixty persons in this place, of whom thirteen were adults. The night preceding had been very stormy, as if hell had been unchained against us. A terrible gust of wind carried my tent away and cast it into the branches of a great pine. As I could not replace it, I found myself exposed for the rest of the night to hail, snow and rain; but there is a remedy for every evil; I found one under a thick buffalo robe, where I passed the time that was left me for sleep agreeably enough.

On the 8th we reached once more our little establishment of St. Mary's, amid shooting and shouting from our good Indians running to meet us.

CHAPTER IX.[1]

Miraculous apparition to Flathead youth on Christmas eve—Point's hardships on the buffalo hunt — Visitors from the Blackfeet — Fame of the Flatheads growing — Their modesty.

*   *   *   *   *   *   *   *   *

ON my return, the 8th of December, I continued instructing those of the Flatheads who had not been baptized. On Christmas day I added 150 new baptisms to those of the 3d of December, and thirty-two rehabilitations of marriage; so that the Flatheads, some sooner and others later, but all, with very few exceptions, had, in the space of three months, complied with everything necessary to merit the glorious title of true children of God. Accordingly on Christmas eve, a few hours before the midnight mass, the village of St. Mary was deemed worthy of a special mark of heaven's favor. The Blessed Virgin appeared to a little orphan boy named Paul, in the hut of an aged and truly pious woman. The youth, piety and sincerity of this child, joined to the nature of the fact which he related, forbade us to doubt the truth of his statement. The following is what he recounted to me with his own innocent lips: " Upon entering John's hut, whither I had gone to learn my prayers, which I did not know, I saw some one who was very beautiful — her feet did not touch the earth, her garments were as white as snow; she had a star over her head, a serpent under her feet; and near the serpent was a fruit which I did not recognize. I could see her heart, from which rays of light burst forth and

1 This chapter and that following are taken from Book II of the *Letters and Sketches,* purporting to have been written to a Father of the Society from the Madison Forks, August 15, 1842.

shone upon me. When I first beheld all this I was frightened, but afterward my fear left me; my heart was
warmed, my mind clear, and I do not know how it happened, but all at once I knew my prayers." (To be brief
I omit several circumstances.) He ended his account by
saying that several times the same person had appeared to
him whilst he was sleeping; and that once she had told
him she was pleased that the first village of the Flatheads
should be called "St. Mary." The child had never seen
or heard before anything of the kind; he did not even
know if the person was a man or woman, because the appearance of the dress which she wore was entirely unknown to him. Several persons having interrogated the
child on this subject, have found him unvarying in his
answers. He continues by his conduct to be the angel of
his tribe.

On the 23d of December, Father Point, at the head of
the inhabitants of forty lodges, started for the buffalo
hunt.[2] On the road they met with huntsmen of five or six

[2] "The plan of accompanying the Indians on these long hunting
excursions had seemed advisable to the Fathers at first, and was
adopted by them a few times at the beginning of the missions. The
object the missionaries had in view, was that the Indians might not
be left so long a time without instruction and the comforts of religion;
that assistance be rendered to such as might fall sick and die during
the hunt; also, that the presence and influence of the Black-robe
among them might restrain the Indians from the disorders and excesses, of which the great hunts were always the cause or the occasion.
All good and solid reasons.

"But, notwithstanding, the position in which the missionary was
here placed was a most delicate one. The buffalo plains were not
only the common hunting-grounds of many hostile tribes, but their
ordinary battle-fields, and the presence of the Father with any one
tribe under these circumstances, was very apt to commit him alike to
the friendly and the hostile, greatly to the detriment of his authority
and efficiency in promoting the spiritual welfare of the Indians: to
the hostile, since from the fact of his being in the enemy's camp, he
would naturally be looked upon as being in league with the enemy.
On the other hand, in the case of prisoners, his advice to the Indians

different tribes, some of whom followed him to the termination of the chase, from the desire of learning their prayers. The Flatheads having prolonged their stay at St. Mary's as long as they possibly could, so as not to depart without receiving baptism, experienced such a famine, the first weeks of January, that their poor dogs, having not even a bone to gnaw, devoured the very straps of leather with which they tied their horses during the night. The cold moreover was so uninterruptedly severe that during the hunting season, which lasted three months, such a quantity of snow fell that many were attacked with a painful blindness, vulgarly called " snow disease." One day when the wind was very high, and the snow falling and freezing harder than usual, Father Point became suddenly very pale, and would no doubt have been frozen to death in the midst of the plain, had not some travelers, perceiving the change in his countenance, kindled a large fire. But neither wind, ice, nor famine prevented the zealous Flatheads from performing on this journey all they were accustomed to do at St. Mary's. Every morning and evening they assembled around the missionary's lodge, and more than three-fourths of them without any shelter but the sky, after having recited their prayers, listened to an instruction, preceded and followed by hymns. At daybreak and sunset the bell was tolled three times for the Angelical Salutation. The Sunday was religiously kept; an observance which was so acceptable to God, that once especially it was recompensed in a very visible manner.

whom he was accompanying would always be, as a matter of course, for lenity and mercy. But lenity and mercy were seldom, if ever, practiced by the natives toward an enemy captured in war. The Father was, therefore, liable to be suspected even by these, and thus his efficiency among them would be impaired. * * * Further, it was not long before the Fathers found out by their own experience that the Indians, whilst on the great hunts, were a prey to the wildest excitement, which left little, if any, room for religious instruction. The plan of accompanying them on their buffalo hunts was, therefore, very soon after abandoned."— *Palladino.*

The following is what I read in the Journal kept by Father Point during the winter's hunt.

"*Sixth February.*— To-day, Sunday, a very high wind, the sky greyish, and the thermometer at the freezing point; no grass for the horses; the buffaloes driven off by the Nez Percés. The 7th, the cold more piercing — fcod for our horses still scarcer — the snow increasing; but yesterday was a time of perfect rest, and the fruits of it show themselves to-day in perfect resignation and confidence. At noon we reach the summit of a mountain, and what a change awaits us. The sun shines, the cold has lost its intensity; we have in view an immense plain, and in that plain good pasturages, which are clouded with buffaloes. The encampment stops, the hunters assemble, and before sunset 155 buffaloes have fallen by their arrows. One must confess that if this hunt were *not* miraculous, it bears a great resemblance to the draught of fishes made by Peter when casting his net at the word of the Lord, he drew up 153 fishes.— St. John, xxi. 11. The Flatheads confided in the Lord, and were equally successful in killing 153 buffaloes. What a fine draught of fishes! but what a glorious hunt of buffaloes! Represent to yourself an immense amphitheatre of mountains, the least of which exceeds in height Montmartre, and in the midst of this majestic enclosure a plain more extensive than that of Paris, and on this magnificent plain a multitude of animals, the least of which surpasses in size the largest ox in Europe. Such was the park in which our Indians hunted.

"Wishing to pursue them," continues Father Point, in his journal, "I urged on my horse to a herd of fugitives, and as he was fresh, I had no difficulty in getting up to them. I even succeeded in compelling the foremost to abandon his post, but enraged, he stopped short, and presented such a terrible front, that I thought it more prudent to open a passage and let him escape. I acted wisely, as on the same day one of these animals, in his fall, overturned a horse and his rider. Fortunately, however, the latter was more dexterous than I should have been in such a perilous situation; he aimed his blows so promptly and well, that of the three who were thrown, only two arose. On another occasion, a hunter who had been also dismounted, had no other means to avoid being torn to pieces than to seize the animal by the horns just at the time he was about to trample him to death. A third hunter, fleeing at all speed, felt himself stopped by the plaited tail of his horse hooked on the buffalo's horn; but both, fearing a trap, made every effort to disengage themselves."

The buffalo hunt is attended with dangers, but the greatest of these does not consist in the mere pursuit of the animal, but proceeds rather from the bands of Blackfeet who constantly lurk in these regions, especially when there is some prospect of meeting with the larger game, or stealing a number of horses. Of all the mountain savages the Blackfeet are the most numerous and wicked and the greatest thieves. Happily, however, from having been often beaten by the smaller tribes, they have become so dastardly, that unless they are twenty to one they confine their attacks to the horses, which, thanks to the carelessness of their courageous enemies, they go about with so much dexterity and success, that this year, while our good Flatheads were asleep, they discovered their animals as often as twenty times, and carried off more than 100 of them.

During the winter, about twenty of these gentlemen visited the Flatheads in the daytime, and without stealing anything, but in this manner. There resided in the camp an old chief of the Blackfeet tribe, who had been baptized on Christmas day, and named Nicholas; this good savage, knowing that the missionary would willingly hold an interview with his brethren, undertook himself to harangue them during the night, and so well did he acquit himself, that upon the calumet's being planted on the limits of the camp, and the messenger being admitted to an audience, singing was heard in the neighboring mountains, and soon after a band of these brigands issued, armed as warriors, from the gloomy defile. They were received as friends, and four of the principals were ushered into the missionary's lodge; they smoked the calumet and discussed the news of the day. The missionary spoke of the necessity of prayer, to which subject they listened most attentively; nor did they manifest either surprise or repugnance. They told him that there had arrived recently in one of their forests a man who was not married, and who wore on his breast a large crucifix, read every day in a big book, and made the sign of the cross before eating anything; and in fine, that he was dressed exactly like the Black-robes at St. Mary's.[8] The Father did everything in his power to gain their good will — after which they were conducted to the best lodge in the encampment. It certainly would seem that such hosts were worthy of better guests. However, toward the middle of the night, the explosion of fire-arms was heard. It was soon discovered that a Flathead was firing at a Blackfoot, just as the latter was leaving the camp, taking with him four horses. Fortunately, the robber was not one of the band that had been received within the encampment, which, upon being proved, far from creating any suspicion, on the contrary, had the effect of their kindly offering them a grave for the unfortunate man. But whether they wished to appear to disapprove of the deed, or that they anticipated dangers from reprisals, they left the wolves to bury the body, and took their departure. Good Nicholas, the orator, joined them, in order to render the same services to the others that he had to these. He went off, promising to return soon with the evidences of his success. He has not been seen as yet, but we are informed that he and his companions have spoken so favorably of prayer and the Black-robes, that already the Sunday is religiously observed in the camp where Nicholas resides, and that a great chief, with the people of sixty lodges, intend shortly to make our acquaintance and attach themselves to the Flatheads.

[8] Probably Father Demers visiting the posts.

In the meanwhile divine justice is punishing rigorously a number of their robbers. This year the Nez Percés caught twelve of them in flagrant faults, and killed them. About the time that the Blackfoot above mentioned met his fate at the hands of a Flathead, thirty others were receiving the reward due to their crimes, from the Pend-d'Oreille tribe. A very remarkable fact in this last encounter is that of the four who commenced, and the others who finished it, not one fell; although, in order to break in on the delinquents, who were intrenched behind a kind of rampart, they were obliged to expose themselves to a brisk fire. I saw the field of combat some time afterward. Of the thirty robbers who had been slain, only five or six heads remained, and those so disfigured as to lead one to think that an age had already elapsed since their death.

Two years before, the same tribe (Pend-d'Oreilles), assisted by the Flatheads, making in all a band of seventy men, stood an attack of 1,500 Blackfeet, whom they defeated, killing in five days, during which time the battle lasted, fifty of their foes, without losing a single man on their side. They would not commence the attack until they had recited their prayers on their knees. A few days ago, the spot was pointed out to me where six Flatheads withstood 160 Blackfeet with so much resolution, that with a handful of their men who came to their aid, they gained the victory.

The most perfidious nation, after the Blackfeet, is the Bannock tribe; they also bear the Flatheads much ill will. It has happened more than once that at the very moment the Bannock tribe were receiving the greatest proofs of friendship from the Flatheads, the former were plotting their ruin. Of this you have already had one proof, but here is another. One day a detachment of 200 Bannocks visited the camp of the Flatheads, and after smoking with them returned to their encampment. The small number of the Flatheads had not, however, escaped their notice, and they determined to take advantage of their apparent weakness. Accordingly, they retraced their steps that very night to execute their base designs. But the chief, named Michael, having been advised of their intention, assembled in haste his twenty warriors, and after entreating them to confide in God, he rushed on these traitors so happily and vigorously that at the first shock they were routed. Already nine of the fugitives had fallen, and most of the others would have shared the same fate if Michael, in the very heat of the pursuit, had not recollected that it was Sunday, and on that account stopped his brave companions, saying: " My friends, it is now the time for prayer; we must retire to our camp."

It is by these and similar exploits, wherein the finger of God is visible, that the Flatheads have acquired such a reputation for valor, that notwithstanding their inferior numbers, they are feared much more than they on their side dread their bitterest enemies. These victories, however, cannot but be fatal even to the conquerors; hence we will strive to inspire all with the love of peace, which may be accomplished if each party remains at home. For this purpose we must create among them a greater taste for agriculture than for hunting. But how can we compass this unless the same measures are employed for the missions of the Rocky Mountains that were so happily adopted for Paraguay? If the true friends of religion only knew of what the Indians who surround us are capable when once converted, I cannot doubt but that they would assist us in our efforts to accomplish so beautiful, so advantageous a project. It is, moreover, through the Iroquois of the North, whose cruelty formerly exceeded that of the Blackfeet, that the knowledge of the true God came to the Flatheads, and awakened amongst them the desire of possessing the Black-gowns. We have seen to what dangers the good Flatheads exposed themselves to obtain missionaries, and what sacrifices they have made to merit the title of children of God; and now what is their actual progress? In their village, enmities, quarrels and calumnies are unknown; they are sincere and upright amongst themselves, and full of confidence in their missionaries. They carry this to such a degree that they place implicit reliance on their veracity, and cannot suppose that they have anything else in view but their happiness; they have no difficulty in believing the mysteries of our faith, or in approaching the tribunal of penance: difficulties which appear insurmountable to the pride and cowardice of many civilized Christians. The first time they were asked if they believed firmly in all that was contained in the Apostles' Creed, they answered, " Yes — very much." When they were spoken to about confession, some wished it to be public.

This will explain to you how it happened that before we resided three months amongst them we were enabled to baptize all the adults, and four months later to admit a large number to frequent communion. There are whole families who never let a Sunday go by without approaching the holy table. Often twenty confessions are heard consecutively without there being matter for absolution. This year we performed the devotion of the month of Mary, and I can flatter myself that the exercises were attended with as much piety and edification as in the most devout parishes of Europe. At the end of the month a statue was borne in triumph to the very place where our Blessed Mother deigned to honor us with the aforementioned apparition. Since that day a sort of pilgrimage has been established there, under the name of " Our Lady of Prayer." None pass the pious monument without stopping to pray on their knees; the more devout come regularly twice a day to speak to their Mother and her divine Son, and the children add to their prayers the most beautiful flowers they can cull in the prairies.

On the feast of the Sacred Heart we made use of this monument, decorated with garlands of flowers, as a repository, and our people received for the first time the benediction of the blessed sacrament; a happiness which they now enjoy every Sunday after vespers. Some of them already understand the nature of the devotion of the Sacred Heart. To propagate it we have laid the foundations of several societies, of which all the most virtuous men, women and young people have become members. Victor, the great chief, is prefect of one of these associations, and Agnes, his wife, is president of another. They were not elected through any deference for their dignity or birth, but solely on account of their great personal merits. A fact which proves that the Flatheads regard merit more than rank is, that the place of great chief becoming vacant by the death of Peter, they chose for his successor the chief of the men's society, and for no other reason did he obtain this high dignity than for the noble qualities, both of heart and head, which they all thought he possessed. Every night and morning, when all is quiet in the camp, he harangues the people; the subject of his discourse being principally a repetition of what the Black-robes have said before. This good chief walks faithfully in the footsteps of his predecessor, which is no slight praise. This last, who was baptized at the age of eighty, and admitted to communion in his eighty-second year, was the first to deserve this double favor, more on account of his virtue than his years. The day of his baptism he said to me, " If during my life I have committed faults they were those of ignorance; it appears to me that I never did anything, knowing it to be wrong." At the time of his first communion, which preceded his death but a few days, having been asked if he had not some faults with which to reproach himself since his baptism — " Faults," he replied, with surprise, " how could I ever commit any, I whose duty it is to teach others how to do good? " He was buried in the red drapery he was accustomed to hang out on Sunday to announce that it was the day of the Lord. Alphonsus in the prime of youth soon followed him. He said to me on the day of his baptism: " I dread so much offending again the Great Spirit, that I beg of him to grant me the grace to die soon." He fell sick a few days afterward and expired with the most Christian dispositions, thanking God for having granted his prayer. In the hope of their glorious resurrection, their mortal remains have been deposited at the foot of the large cross.

Of twenty persons who died within the year, we have no reason to fear for the salvation of one.

24

CHAPTER X.

*   *   *   *   *   *   *   *   *

NOT having been able this year to obtain either provisions or sufficient clothes to supply the wants of our
mission, I started (April 13th) for Fort Vancouver, the
great mart of the honorable Hudson Bay Company, and distant about a thousand miles from our establishment. The
continuation of this narrative will show you that this necessary journey was providential. I found myself during this
trip a second time amongst the Kalispel tribe.

They continue with much fervor to assemble every morning and evening to recite prayers in common, and manifest
the same attention and assiduity in listening to our instructions. The chiefs on their side are incessant in exhorting the people to the practice of every good work. The
two principal obstacles that prevent a great number from
receiving baptism are — first, the plurality of wives; many
have not the courage to separate themselves from those by
whom they have children. The second is their fondness
for gambling, in which they risk everything. I baptized
sixty adults amongst them during this last journey.

Crossing a beautiful plain near the Clark or Flathead

river, called the Horse Prairie, I heard that there were thirty lodges of the Skalzi or Kootenai tribe at about two days' journey from us.   I determined whilst awaiting the descent of the skiff, which could only start six days later, to pay them a visit, for they had never seen a priest in their lands before.   Two half-breeds served as my guides and escorts on this occasion.   We galloped and trotted all the day, traveling a distance of sixty miles.   We spent a quiet night in a deep defile, stretched near a good fire, but in the open air.

The next day (April 14th), after having traversed several mountains and valleys, where our horses were up to their knees in snow, we arrived about three o'clock in sight of the Kootenai camp.   They assembled immediately on my approach; when I was about twenty yards from them the warriors presented their arms, which they had hidden until then under their buffalo robes.   They fired a general salute, which frightened my mule and made her rear and prance, to the great amusement of the savages.   They then defiled before me, giving their hands in token of friendship and congratulation.   I observed that each one lifted his hand to his forehead after having presented it to me.   I soon convoked the council in order to inform them of the object of my visit.   They unanimously declared themselves in favor of my religion, and adopted the beautiful custom of their neighbors, the Flatheads, to meet night and morning for prayers in common.   I assembled them that very evening for this object and gave them a long instruction on the principal dogmas of our faith.   The next day I baptized all their little children and nine of their adults, previously instructed, amongst whom was the wife of an Iroquois, who had resided for thirty years with this tribe.   The Iroquois and a Canadian occupy themselves in the absence of a priest in instructing them.

My visit could not be long; I left the Kootenai village about twelve o'clock, accompanied by twelve of these warriors and some half-blood Crees, whom I had baptized in

1840. They wished to escort me to the entrance of the large Flathead lake, with the desire of giving me a farewell feast; a real banquet of all the good things their country produced. The warriors had gone on ahead and dispersed in every direction, some to hunt and others to fish. The latter only succeeded in catching a single trout. The warriors returned in the evening with a bear, goose and six swan's eggs. *"Sed quid hoc inter tantos?"* The fish and goose were roasted before a good fire, and the whole mess was soon presented to me. Most of my companions preferring to fast, I expressed my regret at it, consoling them, however, by telling them that God would certainly reward their kindness to me. A moment after we heard the last hunter returning, who we thought had gone back to the camp. Hope shone on every countenance. The warrior soon appeared laden with a large elk, and hunger that night was banished from the camp. Each one began to occupy himself; some cut up the animal, others heaped fuel on the fire and prepared sticks and spits to roast the meat. The feast which had commenced under such poor auspices continued a great part of the night. The whole animal, excepting a small piece that was reserved for my breakfast, had disappeared before they retired to sleep. This is a sample of savage life. The Indian when he has nothing to eat does not complain, but in the midst of abundance he knows no moderation. The stomach of a savage has always been a riddle to me.

The plain that commands a view of the lake is one of the most fertile in the mountainous regions. The Flathead river runs through it and extends more than 200 miles to the northeast. It is wide and deep, abounding with fish and lined with wood, principally with the cottonwood, aspen, pine and birch. There are beautiful sites for villages, but the vicinity of the Blackfeet must delay for a long while the good work, as they are only at two days' march from the great district occupied by these brigands, from whence they often issue to pay their neighbors predatory visits. A second obstacle would be the great distance from any post of the Hudson Bay Company; consequently the difficulty of procuring what is strictly necessary. The lake is highly romantic, and is from forty to fifty miles long. Mountainous and rocky islands of all sizes are scattered over its bosom, which present an enchanting prospect. These islands are filled with wild horses. Lofty mountains surround the lake and rise from its very brink.

On the 16th of April, after bidding adieu to my traveling companions, I started early in the morning, accompanied by two Canadians and two savages. That evening we encamped close to a delightful spring, which was warm and sulphurous, having traveled a distance of about fifty miles. When the savages reach this spring they generally bathe in it. They told me that after the fatigues of a long journey they find that bathing in this water greatly refreshes them. I found here ten lodges of the Kalispel tribe; the chief, who was by birth of the Nez Percé tribe, invited me to spend the night in his wigwam, where he treated me most hospitably. This was the only small Kalispel camp that I had as yet met in my journeys. I here established, as I have done wherever I stopped, the custom of morning and evening prayers.

During the evening the chief, who had looked very gloomy, made a public exposition of his whole life. " Black-robe," said he, " you find yourself in the lodge of a most wicked and unhappy man; all the evil that a man could do on earth, I believe I have been guilty of: I have even assassinated several of my near relations; since then, there is nought in my heart but trouble, bitterness and remorse. Why does not the Great Spirit annihilate me? I still possess life, but there will be neither pardon nor mercy for me after death." These words and the feeling manner with which they were addressed to me drew tears of compassion from my eyes. " Poor, unfortunate man," I replied, " you are really to be pitied, but you increase your misery by thinking that you cannot obtain pardon. The devil, man's evil spirit, is the author of this bad thought. Do not listen to him, for he would wish to precipitate you into that bad place (hell). The Great Spirit who created you is a Father infinitely good and merciful. He does not desire the death of the sinner, but rather that he should be converted and live. He receives us into his favor and forgets our crimes, notwithstanding their number and enormity, the moment we return to him contrite and repentant. He will also forgive you if you walk in the path which his only Son, Jesus Christ, came on earth to trace for us."

I then recounted the instance of the good thief and the parable of the prodigal son. I made him sensible of the proof of God's goodness in sending me to him. I added that perhaps his life was drawing to a close, and that he might be in danger of falling into the bad place on account of his sins; that I would show him the right path, which if he followed he would certainly reach heaven. These few words were as balm poured on his wounded spirit. He became calmer, and joy and hope appeared on his countenance. "Black-robe," said he, "your words reanimate me: I see, I understand better now, you have consoled me, you have relieved me from a burden that was crushing me with its weight, for I thought myself lost. I will follow your directions; I will learn how to pray. Yes, I feel convinced that the Great Spirit will have pity on me." There was fortunately in the camp a young man who knew all the prayers, and was willing to serve as his catechist. His baptism was deferred until the autumn or winter.

The results of my visit to the Cœur d'Alènes were very consoling. They form a small but interesting tribe, animated with much fervor. As soon as they were certain of my visit, they deputed couriers in every direction to inform the savages of the approach of the Black-robe; and all, without exception, assembled at the outlet of the great lake which bears their name, and which was the place I had indicated. An ingenuous joy, joined to wonder and contentment, shone on every face when they saw me arrive in the midst of them.

Every one hastened to greet me. It was the first visit of the kind they had received, and the following is the order they observed. Their chiefs and old men marched at the head; next came the young men and boys; then followed the women — mothers, young girls, and little children. I was conducted in triumph by this multitude to the lodge of the great chief. Here, as everywhere else in the Indian country, the everlasting calumet was first produced, which went round two or three times in the most profound silence. The chief then addressed me, saying: "Black-robe, you are most welcome amongst us. We thank you for your charity toward us. For a long time we have wished to see you, and hear the words which will give us understanding. Our fathers invoked the sun and earth. I recollect very well when the knowledge of the true and one God came amongst them; since which time we have offered to him our prayers and vows. We are, however, to be pitied. We do not know the word of the Great Spirit. All is darkness as yet to us, but to-day I hope we shall see the light shine. Speak, Black-robe, I have done — every one is anxious to hear you."

I spoke to them for two hours on salvation and the end of man's creation, and not one person stirred from his place the whole time of the instruction. As it was almost sunset, I recited the prayers that I had translated into their language a few days before. After which I took some refreshments, consisting of fragments of dried meat and a piece of cooked moss, tasting like soap and as black as pitch. All this, however, was as grateful to my palate as though it had been honey and sugar, not having eaten a mouthful since daybreak. At their own request I then continued instructing the chiefs and their people until the night was far advanced. About every half hour I paused, and then the pipes would pass around to refresh the listeners and give time for reflection.

It was during these intervals that the chiefs conversed on what they had heard, and instructed and advised their

followers. On awakening the next morning, I was surprised to find my lodge already filled with people. They
had entered so quietly that I had not heard them. It was
hardly daybreak when I arose, and they all, following my
example, placed themselves on their knees, and we made
together the offering of our hearts to God, with that of the
actions of the day. After this the chief said: " Black-
gown, we come here very early to observe you — we wish
to imitate what you do. Your prayer is good; we wish to
adopt it. But you will leave us after two nights more, and
we have no one to teach us in your absence." I had the
bell rung for morning prayers, promising him at the same
time that the prayers should be known before I left them.

After a long instruction on the most important truths of
religion, I collected around me all the little children, with
the young boys and girls; I chose two from among the latter, to whom I taught the Hail Mary, assigning to each one
his own particular part; then seven for the Our Father;
ten others for the Commandments, and twelve for the
Apostles' Creed. This method, which was my first trial of
it, succeeded admirably. I repeated to each one his part
until he knew it perfectly; I then made him repeat it five
or six times. These little Indians, forming a triangle, resembled a choir of angels, and recited their prayers, to
the great astonishment and satisfaction of the savages. They
continued in this manner morning and night, until one of
the chiefs learned all the prayers, which he then repeated
in public.

I spent three days in instructing them. I would have remained longer, but the savages were without provisions.
There was scarcely enough for one person in the whole
camp. My own provisions were nearly out, and I was still
four days' journey from Fort Colville. The second day
of my stay among them, I baptized all their small children,
and then twenty-four adults, who were infirm and very old.
It appeared as though God had retained these good old
people on earth to grant them the inexpressible happiness

of receiving the sacrament of baptism before their death. They seemed by their transports of joy and gratitude at this moment, to express that sentiment of the scripture: " My soul is ready, O God, my soul is ready." Never did I experience in my visits to the savages so much satisfaction as on this occasion, not even when I visited the Flatheads in 1840; nor have I elsewhere seen more convincing proofs of sincere conversion to God. May he grant them to persevere in their virtuous resolutions. Reverend Father Point intends passing the winter with them to confirm them in their faith.[1] After some advice and salutary regulations, I left this interesting colony, and, I must acknowledge, with heartfelt regret. The great chief allowed himself scarcely a moment's repose for three nights I spent amongst them; he would rise from time to time to harangue the people, and repeat to them all he was able to remember of the instructions of the day. During the whole time of my mission, he continued at my side, so anxious was he not to lose a single word. The old chief, now in his eightieth year, was baptized by the name of Jesse.

In the spring the territory of this tribe enchants the traveler who may happen to traverse it. It is so diversified with noble plains and enameled with flowers, whose various forms and colors offer to experienced botanists an interest-

---

[1] *Further history of the Cœur d'Alène Mission.*— The mission to the Cœur d'Alènes was accordingly opened by Father Point and Brother Huet, and the day of their arrival being the first Friday in November, the establishment received the name of Sacred Heart of Jesus in commemoration of the feast. " The site chosen, a beautiful spot in the fall, but mostly under water in the spring, lay on the banks of the St. Joseph river. But this location was changed in 1846 for another on the banks of Cœur d'Alène river, where the Fathers lived for a number of years. The place is known to-day as Cataldo, or Old Mission. Later on it was found convenient or necessary to locate the mission on the present site, known as De Smet, on Hangman's creek, not far from Farmington.— The Cœur d'Alènes are to-day the best and most industrious Indians in the Rocky Mountains."— *Palladino* (1891).

ing *parterre*. These plains are surrounded by magnificent forests of pine, fir and cedar. To the west their country is open, and the view extends over several days' journey. To the south, east and north, you see towering mountains, ridge rising above ridge, robed with snow, and mingling their summits with the clouds, from which, at a distance, you can hardly distinguish them. The lake forms a striking feature in this beautiful prospect, and is about thirty miles in circumference. It is deep, and abounds in fish, particularly in salmon trout, common trout, carp, and a small, oily fish, very delicious, and tasting like the smelt. The Spokan river rises in the lake, and crosses the whole plain of the Cœur d'Alènes. The valley that borders above the lake is from four to five miles wide, exceedingly fertile, and the soil from ten to fifteen feet deep. Every spring, at the melting of the snow, it is subject to inundations, which scarcely ever last longer than four or five days; at the same time augmenting, as in Egypt, the fertility of the soil. The potato grows here very well, and in great abundance.

The Spokan river is wide, swift and deep in the spring, and contains, like all the rivers of Oregon, many rapid falls and cascades. The navigation of the waters of this immense territory is generally dangerous, and few risk themselves on them without being accompanied by experienced pilots. In descending Clark's river, we passed by some truly perilous and remarkable places, where the pilots have full opportunity to exhibit their dexterity and prudence. The rapids are numerous and the roar of the waters incessant, the current sweeping on at the rate of ten or twelve miles an hour; the rugged banks and projecting rocks creating waves resembling those of the troubled sea. The skilful pilot mounts the waves, which seem ready to engulf us, the canoe speeds over the agitated waters, and with the aid of the paddle, skilfully plied, bears us unharmed through numberless dangers.

The most remarkable spot on this river is called the *Cabinets;* it consists of four apartments, which you have hardly time to examine, as you are scarcely half a minute passing by them. Represent to yourself chasms between two rocky mountains of a stupendous height, the river pent in between them in a bed of thirty or forty feet, precipitating itself down its rocky channel with irresistible fury, roaring against its jagged sides, and whitening with foam all around it. In a short space it winds in four different directions, resembling very much forked lightning. It requires very great skill, activity and presence of mind to extricate yourself from this difficult pass.[2]

The Spokan lands are sandy, gravelly and badly calculated for agriculture. The section over which I traveled consisted of immense plains of light, dry and sandy soil, and thin forests of gum pines. We saw nothing in this noiseless solitude but a buck, running quickly from us and disappearing almost immediately. From time to time the melancholy and piercing cry of the wood snipe increased the gloomy thoughts which this sad spot occasioned. Here, on a gay and smiling little plain, two ministers have settled themselves, with their wives, who had consented to share their husbands' *soi-distant* apostolical labors. During the four years they have spent here, they have baptized several of their own children. They cultivate a small farm, large enough, however, for their own maintenance and the support of their animals and fowls. It appears they are fearful that should they cultivate more they might have too frequent visits from the savages. They even try to prevent their encampment in their immediate neighborhood, and therefore they see and converse but seldom with the heathens, whom they have come so far to seek. A band of Spokans received me with every demonstration of friendship, and were enchanted to hear that the right kind of Black-robes intended soon to form an establishment in the vicinity. I baptized one of their little children who was dying.

[2] The Northern Pacific road now runs along the brink of this chasm, and affords a startling view of the river from a great height.

It was in these parts that in 1836 a modern Iconoclast, named Parker, broke down a cross erected over the grave of a child by some Catholic Iroquois, telling us emphatically, in the narrative of his journey, that he did not wish to leave in that country an emblem of idolatry.[3] Poor man! — not to know better in this enlightened age! Were he to return to these mountains, he would hear the praises of the holy name of Jesus resounding among them; he would hear the Catholics chanting the love and mercies of God from the rivers, lakes, mountains, prairies, forests and coasts of the Columbia. He would behold the cross planted from shore to shore for the space of a thousand miles — on the loftiest height of the Pointed Heart territory, on the towering chain which separates the waters of the Missouri from the Columbia rivers; in the plains of the Willamette, Cowlitz and Bitter Root — and, whilst I am writing to you, the Reverend Mr. Demers is occupied in planting this same sacred symbol amongst the different tribes of New Caledonia. The words of him who said that this holy sign *would draw all men to himself,* begin to be verified with regard to the poor destitute sheep of this vast continent. Were he who destroyed that solitary, humble cross now to return, he would find the image of Jesus Christ crucified, borne on the breast of more than 4,000 Indians; and the smallest child would say to him: " Mr. Parker, we do not adore the cross; do not break it, because it reminds us of Jesus Christ who died on the cross to save us — we adore God alone."

In the beginning of May I arrived at Fort Colville on the Columbia river. This year the snow melted away very early; the mountain torrents had overflowed, and the small rivers that usually moved quietly along in the month of April, had suddenly left their beds and assumed the appearance of large rivers and lakes, completely flooding all the lowlands. This rendered my journey to Vancouver by

[3] *Journal of an Exploring Tour Beyond the Rocky Mountains, under the Direction of the A B C F M:* by Rev. Samuel Parker, A.M., p. 281.

land impossible, and induced me to wait, *nolens volens,* at
the fort, for the construction of the barges, which were not
ready until the 30th of the same month, when I was again
able to pursue my journey on the river. On the same day
that I arrived among the Skoyelpi or Chaudière tribe, who
resided near the fort, I undertook to translate our prayers
into their language. This kept me only one day, as their
language is nearly the same as that of the Flatheads and
Kalispels, having the same origin. They were all very
attentive in attending my instructions, and the old as well
as the young tried assiduously to learn their prayers. I
baptized all the younger children who had not received
the sacrament before, for Mr. Demers had already made
two excursions amongst them, with the most gratifying
success. The great chief and his wife had long sighed for
baptism, which holy sacrament I administered to them,
naming them Martin and Mary. This chief is one of the
most intelligent and pious I have become acquainted with.

The work of God does not, however, proceed without
contradictions; it is necessary to prepare one's self for them
beforehand when undertaking any enterprise amongst
the tribes. I have had some hard trials in all my visits.
I expected them, when on the 13th of May, I started to
see the Okinagan tribe, who were desirous to meet a
priest. The interpreter, Charles, and the chief of the
Skoyelpi, wished to accompany me. In crossing the Columbia river my mule returned to the shore, and ran at
full speed into the forest; Charles pursued her, and two
hours afterward I was told that he had been found dead
in the prairie. I hastened immediately, and perceived from
a distance a great gathering of people. I soon reached
the spot where he was lying, and, to my great joy, perceived that he gave signs of life. He was, however, senseless, and in a most pitiful state. A copious bleeding and
some days of rest restored him and we resumed our journey. This time the mule had a large rope tied around her
neck, and we crossed the river without any accidents; we

took a narrow path that led us by mountains, valleys, forests and prairies, following the course of the river Skarameep. Toward evening we were on the borders of a deep impetuous torrent, having no other bridge than a tree which was rather slight and in constant motion from the rushing of the waters. It reminded me of the bridge of souls spoken of in the Potawatomi legends. These savages believe that souls must traverse this bridge before they reach their elysium in the west. The good, they say, pass over it without danger; the bad, on the contrary, are unable to hold on, but stumble, stagger and fall into the torrent below, which sweeps them off into a labyrinth of lakes and marshes; here they drag out their existence; wretched, tormented by famine and in great agony, the living prey of all sorts of venomous reptiles and ferocious animals, wandering to and fro without ever being able to escape. We were fortunate enough to cross the trembling bridge without accident. We soon pitched our camp on the other side, and in spite of the warring waves which in falls and cascades thundered all night by our side, we enjoyed a refreshing sleep. The greater part of the next day the path conducted us through a thick and hilly forest of fir trees; the country then became more undulating and open. From time to time we perceived an Indian burial-ground, remarkable only for the posts erected on the graves, and hung with kettles, wooden plates, guns, bows and arrows, left there by the nearest relatives of the deceased — humble tokens of their grief and friendship.

We encamped on the shore of a small lake called the Skarameep,[4] where was a Skoyelpi village; I gave these savages several instructions and baptized their infants. In memory of my visit, they gave the name of Leêeyou Pierre

[4] There is a small lake called Karamip on the map in this part of Washington. Father De Smet's movements would seem to point to Kettle lake and river, but the native name for the latter is given as Ne-hoi-al-pit-kwu.

(Father Peter) to an immense rocky mountain which dominates the whole region. At my departure the whole village accompanied me. The country over which we traveled is open; the soil sterile and sandy, and the different chains of mountains that traverse it seem to be nothing but sharp pointed rocks, thinly covered with cedars and pines. Toward evening we came up with the men of the first Okinagan encampment, who received us with the greatest cordiality and joy. The chief who came out to meet us was quite conspicuous, being arrayed in his court dress — a shirt made of a horse-skin, the hair of which was outside, the mane partly on his chest and back, giving him a truly fantastic and savage appearance. The camp also joined us, and the fact of my arrival having been soon noised abroad in every direction, we saw, issuing from the defiles and narrow passes of the mountains, bands of Indians who had gone forth to gather their harvest of roots. Many sick were presented to me for baptism, of which rite they already knew the importance.

Before reaching the rendezvous assigned us, on the borders of the Okinagan lake, I was surrounded by more than 200 horsemen, and more than 200 others were already in waiting. We recited together night prayers, and all listened with edifying attention to the instruction I gave them. The interpreter and Martin continued the religious conversation until the night was far advanced; they manifested the same anxiety to hear the word of God that the Cœur d'Alènes had shown. All the next day was spent in prayer, instructions and hymns — I baptized 106 children and some old people, and in conclusion named the plain where these consoling scenes occurred, the " Plain of Prayer." It would be impossible for me to give you an idea of the piety, the happiness of these men, who are thirsting for the life-living waters of the divine word. How much good a missionary could do, who would reside in the midst of a people who are so desirous of receiving instruction, and correspond so faithfully with the grace of God. After some regulations and advice, I left this interesting people, and pursuing my journey for three days over mountains and through dense forests, arrived safely at Fort Colville.

Amongst the innumerable rivers that traverse the American continent, and afford means of communication between its most distant portions, the Columbia river is one of the most remarkable, not only on account of its great importance, west of the mountains, but also from the dangers that attend its navigation. At some distance from the Pacific Ocean, crossing a territory which exhibits, in several localities, evident marks of former volcanic eruptions, its course is frequently impeded by rapids, by chains of volcanic rocks, and immense detached masses of the same substance which, in many places, obstruct the bed of the river.

I embarked on this river, on the 30th of May, in one of the barges of the Hudson Bay Company; Mr. Ogden,[5] one of the principal proprietors, offered me a place in his. I shall never forget the kindness and friendly manner with which this gentleman treated me throughout the journey, nor the many agreeable hours I spent in his company. I found his conversation instructive, his anecdotes and *bon mots* entertaining and timely; it was with great regret that I parted from him.

I will not detain you with a description of the rapids, falls and cascades, which I saw on this celebrated river; for from its source in the mountains to the cascades it is but a succession of dangers. I will endeavor, however, to give you some idea of one of its largest rapids, called by the Canadian voyageurs the Great Dalles. A dalle is a

[5] Peter Skeen Ogden, son of Chief Justice Ogden of Quebec, formerly a Tory resident of New York. Served successively with Astor, the Northwest Company and the Hudson Bay Company; discoverer of Humboldt river; died at Oregon City in 1854, at the age of sixty.

place where the current is confined to a channel between
two steep rocks, forming a prolonged narrow torrent, but
of extraordinary force and swiftness. Here the river is
divided into several channels separated from one another
by masses of rocks, which rise abruptly above its surface.
Some of these channels are navigable at certain seasons
of the year, although with very great risk, even to the
most experienced pilot. But when, after the melting of
the snow, the river rises above its usual level, the waters
in most of these channels make but one body, and the
whole mass of these united streams descends with irresistible fury. At this season the most courageous dare not
encounter such dangers, and all navigation is discon-
tinued. In this state the river flows with an imposing
grandeur and majesty, which no language can describe.
It seems at one moment to stay its progress; then leaps
forward with resistless impetuosity, and then rebounds
against the rock-girt islands of which I have already
spoken, but which present only vain obstructions to its
headlong course. If arrested for a moment, its accumu-
lated waters proudly swell and mount as though instinct
with life, and the next moment dash triumphantly on, en-
veloping the half smothered waves that preceded them as
if impatient of their sluggish course, and wild to speed
them on their way.

Along the shore, on every projecting point, the Indian
fisherman takes his stand, spreading in the eddies his in-
geniously worked net, and in a short time procures for
himself an abundant supply of fine fish. Attracted by the
shoals of fish that come up the river, the seals gambol
amid the eddying waves — now floating with their heads
above the river's breast, and anon darting in the twinkling
of an eye from side to side, in sportive joy, or in swift
pursuit of their scaly prey.

But this noble river has far other recollections associated
with it. Never shall I forget the sad and fatal **accident**

25

which occurred on the second day of our voyage, at a spot called the "Little Dalles." [6] I had gone ashore and was walking along the bank, scarcely thinking what might happen; for my breviary, papers, bed, in a word, my little all, had been left in the barge. I had proceeded about a quarter of a mile, when seeing the bargemen push off from the bank and glide down the stream with an easy, careless air, I began to repent having preferred a path along the river's side, so strewn with fragments of rocks that I was compelled at every instant to turn aside or clamber over them. I still held on my course, when all at once the barge is so abruptly stopped that the rowers can hardly keep their seats. Regaining, however, their equilibrium, they ply the oars with redoubled vigor, but without any effect upon the barge. They are already within the power of the angry vortex; the waters are crested with foam; a deep sound is heard which I distinguish as the voice of the pilot encouraging his men to hold to their oars — to row bravely. The danger increases every minute, and in a moment more all hope of safety has vanished. The barge, the sport of the vortex, spins like a top upon the whirling waters — the oars are useless — the bow rises — the stern descends, and the next instant all have disappeared. A death-like chill shot through my frame — a dimness came over my sight, as the cry "we are lost!" rang in my ears, and told but too plainly that my companions were buried beneath the waves. Overwhelmed with grief and utterly unable to afford them the slightest assistance, I stood a motionless spectator of this tragic scene. All were gone, and yet upon the river's breast there was not the faintest trace of their melancholy fate. Soon after the whirlpool threw up, in various directions,

---

[6] "When near the Okinagan Dalles, on being told by the boatman that the pass was a bad one, he requested to be put on shore. A little while after, the boat was engulfed in a whirlpool and, with the exception of the Father's interpreter and another man who escaped, all on board perished."— *Palladino.*

the oars, poles, the capsized barge, and every lighter article
it had contained. Here and there I beheld the unhappy
bargemen vainly struggling in the midst of the vortex.
Five of them sank never to rise again. My interpreter
had twice touched bottom and after a short prayer was
thrown upon the bank. An Iroquois saved himself by
means of my bed; and a third was so fortunate as to seize
the handle of an empty trunk, which helped him to sustain
himself above water until he reached land.

The rest of our journey was more fortunate. We
stopped at Forts Okinagan[7] and Walla Walla,[8] where I baptized several children.

The savages who principally frequent the borders of the
Columbia river are from the lakes; the chief of whom, with
several of the nation, have been baptized; also the Skoyelpi
or Chaudières, the Okinagans, Cinqpoils, Walla Wallas,
Pierced Noses, Cayuses, Attayes, Spokans, the Indians
from the falls and cascades, and the Chinooks and Clat-
sops.

We arrived at Fort Vancouver[9] on the morning of the
8th of June. I enjoyed the happiness and great consolation of meeting in these distant parts two respectable
Canadian priests — the Reverend Mr. Blanchet, grand
vicar of all the countries west of the mountains claimed

[7] See note page 553.

[8] A Northwest Company trading post, built in 1818 by Donald Mc-
Kenzie; first called Fort Nez Percé; burned in 1842 and rebuilt the
year following of adobe; abandoned in 1855. The later military post
and the present city, both of the same name, were located in the vicinity, though not upon the site of the old fort.

[9] " The metropolitan establishment of the Hudson Bay Company on
the Pacific between the years 1825, when it was begun, and 1847, when
the headquarters of the company were removed to Victoria."—*Ban-
croft*. The fort consisted of an inclosure 750 by 500 feet, surrounded
by a palisade over twenty feet in height, within which were some forty
buildings, including a Catholic chapel. There was a village of sixty
houses adjacent, and a farm some nine square miles in extent, 1,500
acres or over being in cultivation.

by the British crown, and the Reverend Mr. Demers.[10]
They are laboring in these regions for the same object
that we are trying to accomplish in the Rocky Mountains.
The kindness and benevolence with which these reverend
gentlemen received me are proofs of the pure zeal which
actuates them for the salvation of these savages.   They
assured me that immense good might be done in the extensive regions that border on the Pacific, if a greater
number of missionaries, with means at their command,
were stationed in these regions; and they urged me very
strongly to obtain from my superiors some of our Fathers.
I will try to give you in my next some extracts from the
letters of these missionaries, which will make the country
known to you, its extent, and the progress of their mission.

The Governor of the honorable Company of Hudson
Bay, Dr. McLoughlin, who resides at Fort Vancouver,
after having given me every possible proof of interest, as
a good Catholic, advised me to do everything in my power
to gratify the wishes of the Canadian missionaries.   His
principal reason is, that if Catholicity was rapidly planted
in these tracts where civilization begins to dawn, it would
be more quickly introduced thence into the interior.   Already a host of ministers have overrun a part of the country, and have settled wherever they may derive some advantages for the privations their philanthropy imposes on
them.   Such is the state of these regions of the new world,
as yet so little known: you perceive that our prospects are
by no means discouraging.   Permit me therefore to repeat

10 " 'A scene here ensued so affecting and so edifying,' writes Archbishop Seghers, 'that it drew tears from the eyes of the only witness
present, Father Demers, from whose lips we received the moving narrative.   No sooner had Father De Smet descried the Vicar General
than he ran to prostrate himself at his feet, imploring his blessing;
and no sooner had the Very Reverend Blanchet caught sight of the
valiant missionary than he also fell on his knees, imploring the blessing
of the saintly Jesuit.   Admirable struggle, where the last place, not the
first, was the object of the contestants.' "— *Palladino.*   Blanchet and
Demers came to Oregon from Canada in 1838.

the great principle you have so often recommended to me, and which I have not forgotten: " Courage and confidence in God! " With the mercy of God, the Church of Jesus Christ may soon have the consolation of seeing her standard planted in these distant lands on the ruins of idolatry and of the darkest superstition. Pray then that the Lord of such a rich harvest may send us numerous fellow laborers; for in so extensive a field we are but five, and beset with so many dangers, that at the dawn of day we have often reason to doubt whether we will live to see the sun go down. It is not that we have anything to fear from the climate; far from it — for, if here death came only by sickness, we might indeed count upon many years, but water, fire, and the bow, often hurry their victims off when least expected. Of 100 men who inhabit this country, there are not ten who do not die by some or other fatal accident.

The afternoon of the 30th of June I resumed my place in one of the barges of the English Company, and took my leave of the worthy and respectable Governor.[11] To my great joy I found that the Reverend Mr. Demers was one of the passengers, being about to undertake an apostolic excursion among the different tribes of New Caledonia, who, according to the accounts of several Canadian travelers, were most anxious to see a Black-gown and hear the word of God. The wind being favorable, the sails of the barge were unfurled, and the sailors plying their oars at the same time, the 11th of July saw us landed safely at Fort Walla Walla. The next day I parted, with many regrets, from my esteemed friends, Reverend Mr. Demers, and Mr. Ogden. Accompanied only by my interpreter, we continued our land route to the 19th, through woods and immense plains. The high plains which separate the

[11] Father De Smet, during his sojourn on the lower Columbia, made a journey up the Willamette to St. Paul Mission, the residence of Reverend Blanchet. This was a short distance above the Falls of the Willamette.

waters of the Snake river from those of the Spokan, offer
some natural curiosities. I fancied myself in the vicinity
of several fortified cities, surrounded by walls and small
forts, scattered in different directions. The pillars are
regular pentagons, from two to four feet in diameter, erect,
joined together, forming a wall from forty to eighty feet
high, and extending several miles in the form of squares
and triangles, detached from one another, and in different
directions.

On our road we met some Nez Percés, and a small band
of Spokans, who accosted us with many demonstrations of
friendship, and although very poor, offered us more salmon than we could carry. The Pointed Hearts (a tribe
which shall ever be dear to me) came to meet us, and
great was the joy on both sides, on beholding one another
again. They had strictly observed all the rules I had
laid down for them at my first visit. They accompanied
me for three days, to the very limits of their territory.
We then planted a cross on the summit of a high mountain, covered with snow, and after the example of the Flatheads, all the people consecrated themselves inviolably to
the service of God. We remained there that night. The
next morning, after reciting our prayers in common, and
giving them a long exhortation, we bade them farewell.

The 20th I continued my journey over terrific mountains, steep rocks, and through apparently impenetrable
forests. I could scarcely believe that any human being
had ever preceded us over such a road. At the end of
four days' journey, replete with fatigue and difficulties,
we reached the borders of the Bitter Root river, and on
the evening of July 27th I had the happiness of arriving
safely at St. Mary's, and of finding my dear brethren in
good health.

The Flatheads, accompanied by Father Point, had left
the village ten days before, to procure provisions. A few
had remained to guard the camp, and their families
awaited my return. The 29th, I started to rejoin the Flat-

heads on the Missouri river. We ascended the Bitter
Root to its source, and the 1st of August, having clam-
bered up a high mountain, we planted a cross on its very
summit, near a beautiful spring, one of the sources of the
Missouri. The next day, after a forced march, we joined
the camp, where we had such a budget of news to open,
so many interesting facts to communicate to each other,
that we sat up a greater part of the night. The Reverend
Father Point and myself accompanied our dear neophytes,
who to obtain their daily bread are obliged to hunt the
buffalo even over the lands of their most inveterate enemies, the Blackfeet. On the 15th of August, the feast of
the Assumption, (the same on which this letter is dated)
I offered up the sacrific of the mass in a noble plain,
watered by one of the three streams that form the head
waters of the Missouri, to thank God for all the blessings
he had bestowed on us during this last year. I had the
consolation of seeing fifty Flatheads approach the holy
table in so humble, modest and devout a manner, that to
my perhaps partial eye, they resembled angels more than
men. On the same day I determined, for the interest of
this mission, which seems so absolutely to require it, to
traverse for the fourth time the dangerous American desert. If heaven preserves me, (for I have to travel through
a region infested by thousands of hostile savages) I will
send you the account of this last journey.

You see then, Reverend Father, that in these deserts we
must more than ever keep our souls prepared to render
the fearful account, in consequence of the perils that surround us; and as it would be desirable that we could be
replaced immediately, in case of any accident occurring —
again I say to you, pray that the Lord may send us fellow
laborers. "*Rogate ergo Dominum messis ut mittat oper-
arios in messem suam.*" And thousands of souls, who would
otherwise be lost, will bless you one day in eternity. Reverend Father Point has expressed a desire to be sent
amongst the Blackfeet. Until they are willing to listen to

the word of God, which I think will be before long, he intends to preach the gospel to the Pointed Hearts and the neighboring tribes. I trust we shall be able to make as cheering a report of these as we have already done of our first neophytes. I have found them all in the best dispositions. The Reverend Father Mengarini remains with the Flatheads and Pend d'Oreilles.

On my first journey, in the autumn of 1841, which ended at Fort Colville, I baptized 190 persons of the Kalispel tribe. On my visit, last spring, to the various distant tribes, (of which I have just finished giving you the account) I had the consolation of baptizing 418 persons, 60 of whom were of the Pend d'Oreille tribe of the great lake; 82 of the Kootenais or Skalzi; 100 of the Pointed Hearts; 56 of the Skoyelpi; 106 of the Okinagans, and 14 in the Okinagan and Walla Walla Forts.— These, with 500 baptized last year, in different parts of the country, mostly amongst the Flatheads and Kalispels, and 196 that I baptized on Christmas day, at St. Mary's, with the 350 baptized by Reverend Fathers Mengarini and Point, make a total of 1,654 souls, wrested from the power of the devil. For what the scripture calls the " spirit of the world " has not wherewith to introduce itself amongst them. These poor people find their happiness even in this world in the constant practice of their Christian duties. We may almost say of them, that all who are baptized are saved.— Since God has inspired you with a zealous desire to second the views of the Association for the Propagation of the Faith, entreat those pious persons to whom you may communicate your designs, to redouble their prayers in our behalf. I conclude by beseeching you earnestly to remember me frequently and fervently in the holy sacrifice.

CHAPTER XI.

RETURN TO ST. LOUIS IN FALL OF 1842.[1]

Safely through Blackfoot country — Agreeable visit with the Crows — They make moral resolves — Continues journey with small escort — Through the dark and bloody ground — Routine of travel — Bill of fare — Meets a steamboat — Perils of Upper River navigation — Safe arrival at St. Louis.

IN my last letter of August, I promised to write to you from St. Louis, should I arrive safely in that city. Heaven has preserved me, and here I am about to fulfil my promise. Leaving Reverend Father Point and the Flathead camp on the river Madison, I was accompanied by twelve[2] of our Indians. We traveled in three days a distance of 150 miles, crossing two chains of mountains, in a section of country frequently visited by the Blackfeet warriors, without, however, meeting with any of these scalping savages. At the mouth of the Twenty-five Yard river, a branch of the Yellowstone, we found 250 huts, belonging to several nations, all friendly to us — the Flatheads, Kalispels, Nez Percés, Cayuses, and Snakes. I spent three days amongst them to exhort them to perseverance, and to make some preparations for my long journey. The day of my departure, ten neophytes presented themselves at my lodge to serve as my escort, and to introduce me to the Crow tribe.

On the evening of the second day we were in the midst of this large and interesting tribe. The Crows had perceived us from a distance; as we approached, some of them recog-

[1] This chapter consists of Letter XVI, *Letters and Sketches* and the last letter (XII) *Voyages aux M.-R.* It was written at the University of St. Louis and sent in English to a Father of the Society, November 1, 1842, and to Father De Smet's brother Francis two days later. The English text is here followed where practicable.

[2] Fr. six.

nized me, and at the cry of " the Black-robe! the Black-robe!" the Crows, young and old, to the number of 3,000, came out of their wigwams.

On entering the village, a comical scene occurred, of which they suddenly made me the principal personage. All the chiefs and about fifty of their warriors hastened around me, and I was literally assailed by them. Holding me by the gown, they drew me in every direction, whilst a robust savage of gigantic stature seemed resolved to carry me off by main force. All spoke at the same time, and appeared to be quarreling, whilst I, the sole object of all this contention, could not conceive what they were about. I remained passive, not knowing whether I should laugh or be serious. The interpreter soon came to my relief, and said that all this uproar was but an excess of politeness and kindness toward me, as every one wished to have the honor of lodging and entertaining the Black-gown. With his advice I selected my host, upon which the others immediately loosed their hold, and I followed the chief to his lodge, which was the largest and best in the camp. The Crows did not tarry long before they all gathered around me and loaded me with marks of kindness. The social calumet, emblem of savage brotherhood and union, went round that evening so frequently that it was scarcely ever extinguished. It was accompanied with all the antics for which the Crows are so famous, when they offer the calumet to the Great Spirit, to the four winds, to the sun, fire, earth and water.

These Indians are unquestionably the most anxious to learn; the most inquisitive, ingenious, and polished of all the savage tribes east of the mountains. They profess great friendship and admiration for the whites. They asked me innumerable questions; among others, they wished to know the number of the whites. " Count," I replied, " the blades of grass upon your immense plains, and you will know pretty nearly the number of the whites." They all smiled, saying that the thing was impossible, but they understood my meaning. And when I explained to them the vast extent of the " villages " inhabited by white men (New York, Philadelphia, London, Paris), the grand lodges (houses) built as near each other as the fingers of my hand, and four or five piled up, one above the other — (meaning the different stories of our dwellings) ; when I told them that some of these lodges (speaking of churches and towers) were as high as mountains, and large enough to contain all the Crows together; that in the grand lodge of the national council (the Capitol at Washington) all the great chiefs of the whole world could smoke the calumet at their ease; that the roads in these great villages were always filled with passengers, who came and went more thickly than the vast herds of buffaloes that sometimes cover their beautiful plains; when I explained to them the extraordinary celerity of those moving lodges (the cars on the railroad) that leave far behind them the swiftest horse, and which are drawn along by frightful machines, whose repeated groanings re-echo far and wide, as they belch forth immense volumes of fire and smoke; and next, those fire canoes (steamboats), which transport whole villages, with provisions, arms and baggage, in a few days, from one country to another, crossing large lakes, (the seas) ascending and descending the great rivers and streams; when I told them that I had seen white men mounting up into the air (in balloons) and flying with as much agility as the warrior eagle of their mountains, then their astonishment was at its height; and all placing their hands upon their mouths, sent forth at the same time, one general cry of wonder. " The Master of Life is great," said the chief, " and the white men are his favorites."

But what appeared to interest them more than aught else, was prayer (religion) ; to this subject they listened with the strictest undivided attention. They told me that they had already heard of it, and they knew that this prayer made men good and wise on earth, and insured their happiness in the future life. They begged me to permit the whole camp to assemble, that they might hear for themselves the words of the Great Spirit, of whom they had been told such wonders. Immediately three United States flags were erected on the field, in the midst of the camp, and 3,000 savages, including the sick, who were carried in skins, gathered around me. I knelt beneath the banner of our country, my ten Flathead neophytes by my side, and surrounded by this multitude, eager to hear the glad tidings of the gospel of peace. We began by intoning two canticles, after which I recited all the prayers, which we interpreted to them: then again we sang canticles, and I finished by explaining to them the Apostles' Creed and the Ten Commandments. They all appeared to be filled with joy, and declared it was the happiest day of their lives. They begged me to have pity on them — to remain among them and instruct them and their little children in the knowledge, love and service of the Great Spirit. I promised that a Blackgown should visit them, but on condition that the chiefs would engage themselves to put a stop to the thievish practices so common amongst them, and to oppose vigorously the corrupt morals of their tribe. Believing me to be endowed with supernatural powers, they had entreated me from the very commencement of our conversation to free them from the sickness that then desolated the camp, and to supply them with plenty. I repeated to them on this occasion that the Great Spirit alone could remove these evils — God, I said, listens to the supplications of the good and pure of heart; of those who detest their sins, and wish to devote themselves to his service — but he shuts his ear to the prayers of those who violate his holy law. In his anger, God had destroyed by fire five infamous " villages " (Sodom, Gomorrah, etc.) in consequence of their horrid abominations — that the Crows walked in the ways of these wicked men, consequently they could not complain if the Great Spirit seemed to punish them by sickness, war and famine. They were themselves the authors of all their calamities — and if they did not change their mode of life very soon, they might expect to see their misfortunes increase from day to day — while the most awful torments awaited them and all wicked men after their death. I assured them in fine that heaven would be the reward of those who would repent of their evil deeds and practice the religion of the Great Spirit.

The grand orator of the camp was the first to reply: " Black-gown," said he, " I understand you. You have said what is true. Your words have passed from my ears into my heart — I wish all could comprehend them." Whereon, addressing himself to the Crows, he repeated forcibly, " Yes, Crows, the Black-gown has said what is true. We are dogs, for we live like dogs. Let us change our lives and our children will live." I then held long conferences with all the chiefs assembled in council. I proposed to them the example of the Flatheads and Pend d'Oreilles, whose chiefs made it their duty to exhort their people to the practice of virtue, and who knew how to punish as they deserved all the prevarications against God's holy law. They promised to follow my advice, and assured me that I would find them in better dispositions on my return. I flatter myself with the hope that this visit, the good example of my neophytes, but principally the prayers of the Flatheads, will gradually produce a favorable change among the Crows. A good point in their character, and one that inspires me with almost the certainty of their amendment, is that they have hitherto resisted courageously all attempts to introduce spirituous liquors among them. " For what is this fire-water good? " said the chief to a white man who tried to bring it into their country, " it burns the throat and stomach; it makes a man like a bear who has lost his senses. He bites, he growls, he scratches and he howls, he falls down as if he were dead. Your fire-water does nothing but harm — take it to our enemies, and they will kill each other, and their wives and children will be worthy of pity. As for us we do not want it, we are fools enough without it."

A very touching scene occurred during the council. Sev-

eral of the savages wished to examine my missionary cross;
I thence took occasion to explain to them the sufferings of
our Savior, Jesus Christ, and the cause of his death on the
cross — I then placed my cross in the hands of the great
chief; he kissed it in the most respectful manner; raising his
eyes to heaven, and pressing the cross with both his hands
to his heart, he exclaimed, " O Great Spirit, take pity on
me and be merciful to thy poor children." And his people
followed his example.[3]

I was in the village of the Crows when news was brought
that two of their most distinguished warriors had fallen
victims to the rage and cruelty of the Blackfeet. The her-
alds or orators went round the camp, proclaiming in a loud
voice the circumstances of the combat and the tragic end of
the two brave men. A gloomy silence prevailed everywhere, only interrupted by a band of mourners, whose appearance alone was enough to make the most insensible
heart bleed, and rouse to vengeance the entire nation. This
band was composed of the mothers of the two unfortunate
warriors who had fallen, their wives carrying their new-
born infants in their arms, their sisters, and all their little
children. The unhappy creatures had their heads shaven
and cut in every direction; they were gashed with numerous
wounds, whence the blood constantly trickled. In this
pitiable state they rent the air with their lamentations and
cries, imploring the warriors of their nation to have compassion on them — to have compassion on their desolate
children — to grant them one last favor, the only cure for
their affliction, and that was, to go at once and inflict signal
vengeance on the murderers. They led by the bridle all
the horses that belonged to the deceased. A Crow chief
mounting immediately the best of these steeds, brandished
his tomahawk in the air, proclaiming that he was ready to
avenge the deed. Several young men rallied about him.

[3] This, and Father De Smet's previous visit to the Crows in 1840
(see p. 239) appear to have been the only advances made to them by
Catholic priests until the year 1880.

They sang together the war-song, and started the same day, declaring that they would not return empty-handed (viz: without scalps).

On these occasions the near relations of the one who has fallen distribute everything that they possess, retaining nothing but some old rags wherewith to clothe themselves. The mourning ceases as soon as the deed is avenged. The warriors cast at the feet of the widows and orphans the trophies torn away from the enemies. Then passing from extreme grief to exultation, they cast aside their tattered garments, wash their bodies, besmear themselves with all sorts of colors, deck themselves off in their best robes, and with the scalps affixed to the end of poles, march in triumph round the camp, shouting and dancing, accompanied at the same time by the whole village.

On the 25th I bade adieu to my faithful companions, the Flatheads, and the Crows. Accompanied by the Iroquois Ignatius, a Cree half-breed named Gabriel, and by two brave Americans, who, although Protestants, wished to serve as guides to a Catholic missionary, I once more plunged into the arid plains of the Yellowstone. Having already described this region, I have nothing new to add concerning it. This desert is undoubtedly dangerous, and has been the scene of more tragic deeds, combats, stratagems and savage cruelties, than any other region. At each step, the Crow interpreter, Mr. V. C., who had sojourned eleven years in the country, recounted different transactions; pointing, meanwhile, to the spots where they had occurred, which, in our situation, made our blood run cold, and our hair stand erect. It is the battle-ground where the Crows, the Blackfeet, Sioux, Cheyennes, Assiniboins, Aricaras, and Minnetarees, fight out their interminable quarrels, avenging and revenging, without respite, their mutual wrongs.

After six days' march, we found ourselves upon the very spot where a combat had recently taken place. The bloody remains of ten Assiniboins who had been slain were scattered here and there — almost all the flesh eaten off by the

wolves and carnivorous birds. At the sight of these man-
gled limbs — of the vultures that soared above our heads,
after having satiated themselves with the unclean repast,
and the region round me, which had so lately resounded
with the savage cries of more savage men, engaged in mutual carnage — I own that the little courage I thought I
possessed seemed to fail me entirely, and give place to a
secret terror, which I sought in vain to stifle or conceal from
my companions. We observed in several places the fresh
tracks of men and horses, leaving no doubt in our minds as
to the proximity of hostile parties; our guide even assured
me that he thought we were already discovered, but by continuing our precautions he hoped we might perhaps elude
their craftiness and malicious designs, for the savages very
seldom make their attacks in open day.

The following is the description of our regular march
until the 10th of September. At daybreak we saddled our
horses and pursued our journey; at 10 o'clock we break-
fasted in a suitable place, that would offer some advantage
in case of an attack. After an hour and a half or two hours'
rest, we resumed our march a second time, always trotting
our horses, until sunset, when we unsaddled them to dine
and sup; we then lighted a good fire, hastily raised a little
cabin of branches, to induce our ever watchful foes, in case
they pursued us, to suppose that we had encamped for the
night; for as soon as the inimical videttes discover anything of the kind, they make it known by a signal to the
whole party. They then immediately assemble and concert
the plan of attack. In the meantime, favored by the darkness, we pursued our journey quietly until ten or twelve
o'clock at night, and then, without fire or even shelter, each
one disposed himself as well as he might, for sleep. It appears to me that I hear you ask: But what did you eat for
your breakfast and supper? Examine the notes of my
journal, and you will acknowledge that our fare was such
as would excite the envy of the most fastidious gastronome.
From the 25th of August to the 10th of September, 1842,

we killed, to supply our wants, as we journeyed on, three fine buffalo cows and two large bulls (only to obtain the tongue and marrow bones) ; two large deer, as fat as we could have wished; three goats, two black-tail deer, a big-horn or mountain sheep, two fine grey bears, and a swan — to say nothing of the pheasants, fowls, snipe, ducks and geese. In the midst of so much game, we scarcely felt the want of bread, sugar or coffee. Humps, tongues and ribs replaced these. And the bed? It is soon arranged. We were in a country where you waste no time in taking off your shoes; you wrap your buffalo robe around you, the saddle serves as a pillow, and thanks to the fatigues of a long journey of about forty miles under a burning sun, you have scarcely laid your head upon it before you are asleep.

The American gentlemen who carry on the Assiniboin fur trade at Fort Union, at the mouth of the Yellowstone, received me with great politeness and kindness. I rested there during three days. A journey so long and continuous, through regions where the drought had been so great that every sign of vegetation had disappeared, had very much exhausted our poor horses. The 1,800 miles that we had yet to travel were not to be undertaken lightly. After hav-ing well considered everything, I resolved to leave my horses at the fort, and to trust myself to the impetuous waters of the Missouri in a skiff, accompanied by Ignatius and Gabriel. The result was most fortunate, for on the third day of our descent, to our great surprise and joy, we heard the puffing of a steamboat. It was a real God-send to us; accordingly, our first thought was to thank God, in all the sincerity of our hearts. We soon beheld her ma-jestically ascending the stream. It was the first boat that had ever attempted to ascend the river in that season of the year, laden with merchandise for the Fur Company. Four gentlemen from New York, proprietors of the boat, invited me to enter and remain on board. I accepted with unfeigned gratitude their kind offer of hospitality; the more so, as they assured me that several war-parties were lying in am-

26

bush along the river. On entering the boat I was an object of great curiosity — my black gown, my missionary cross, my long hair, attracted attention. I had thousands of questions to answer and many long stories to relate about my journey.

I have but a few words to add. I baptized some fifty little ones, principally in the forts. The waters were low, the sand-banks and snags everywhere numerous; the boat consequently encountered many obstacles in her passage. We were frequently in great danger of perishing. Her keel was pierced by pointed rocks, her sides rent by the snags. Twenty times the wheels had been broken to pieces. The pilot's house had been carried away in the tempest; the whole cabin would have followed if it had not been made fast by a large cable. Our boat appeared to be little more than a mere wreck, and in this wreck, after forty-six days' navigation from the Yellowstone, we arrived safely at St. Louis.

On the last Sunday of October, at twelve o'clock, I was kneeling at the foot of St. Mary's Altar, in the Cathedral, offering up my thanksgiving to God for the signal protection he had extended to his poor, unworthy servant. From the beginning of April I had traveled 5,000 miles. I had descended and ascended the dangerous Columbia river. I had seen five of my companions perish in one of those life-destroying whirlpools, so justly dreaded by those who navigate that stream. I had traversed the Willamette, crossed the Rocky Mountains, passed through the country of the Blackfeet, the desert of the Yellowstone, and descended the Missouri; and in all these journeys I had not received the slightest injury. " *Dominus memor fuit nostri et benedixit nobis.*"